2017 YEARBOOK

OF THE GENERAL ASSEMBLY

CUMBERLAND PRESBYTERIAN CHURCH

Office of the General Assembly

Cumberland Presbyterian Church

May 2017

8207 Traditional Place

Cordova (Memphis), Tennessee 38016

Compiled and edited by Elizabeth A. Vaughn for the Office of the General Assembly of the Cumberland Presbyterian Church.

Published and distributed exclusively by The Discipleship Ministry Team, CPC, Memphis, Tennessee, for the Office of the General Assembly. Additional copies may be acquired through Cumberland Presbyterian Resources.

The Discipleship Ministry Team of the Ministry Council of the Cumberland Presbyterian Church is the successor organization to the Board of Christian Education of the Cumberland Presbyterian Church.

Funded, in part, by your contributions to Our United Outreach.

First Edition 2017 (First Printing)

ISBN-13: 978-1-945929-11-3
ISBN-10: 1945929111

OUR UNITED OUTREACH
Made Possible In Part By Your Tithe To Our United Outreach

CUMBERLAND PRESBYTERIAN CENTER OFFICES
8207 TRADITIONAL PLACE
CORDOVA, TENNESSEE 38016
www.cumberland.org

Central Telephone for Center Offices: (901)276-4572, Historical Foundation Telephone: (901)276-8602

BOARD OF STEWARDSHIP, FOUNDATION AND BENEFITS
www.cumberland.org/bos

Phone (901)276-4572	FAX (901)272-3913
Robert Heflin, Executive Secretary	
rah@cumberland.org	Ext-207
Mark Duck, Coordinator of Benefits	
rmd@cumberland.org	Ext-204
Kathryn Gilbert Craig, Administrative Assistant	
kgc@cumberland.org	Ext-206

CENTRAL ACCOUNTING
Phone (901)276-4572	FAX (901)272-3913
Dan Scherf, Accounting Supervisor	
dscherf@cumberland.org	Ext-233

CP RESOURCES
resources@cumberland.org	(901)276-4581

GENERAL ASSEMBLY OFFICE
www.cumberland.org/gao

Phone (901)276-4572	FAX (901)272-3913
Michael Sharpe, Stated Clerk	
msharpe@cumberland.org	Ext-225
Elizabeth Vaughn, Assistant to the Stated Clerk	
eav@cumberland.org	Ext-226

HISTORICAL FOUNDATION OF THE CPC & CPCA
www.cumberland.org/hfcpc

Phone (901)276-8602	FAX (901)272-3913
Susan Knight Gore, Archivist	skg@cumberland.org
Missy Rose, Archival Assistant	jmr@cumberland.org

OUR UNITED OUTREACH
www.cumberland.org/ouo
4782 Waverly Court, Ooltewah, TN 37363

Cliff Hudson, Development Director   Phone (901)276-4572 Ext-210
gchudson3@gmail.com

REGIONAL DIRECTORS

Calotta Edsell   cedsell@hotmail.com
  Arkansas & West Tennessee Presbyteries (864)915-6105

Carolyn Harmon   richardharmon09@comcast.net
  Presbytery of East Tennessee (423)639-3037

Jeff McMichael   revmcmichael@outlook.com
  Covenant, Cumberland & North Central Presbyteries (270)617-4016

Susan Parker   (256)247-3877
  Grace & Hope Presbyteries park9301@bellsouth.net

MINISTRY COUNCIL
www.cpcmc.org

Phone (901)276-4572	FAX (901)276-4578
Edith Old, Director of Ministries	
eold@cumberland.org	Ext-228
Executive Assistant to the Director of Ministries	Ext-217

PASTORAL DEVELOPMENT MINISTRY TEAM
Phone (901)276-4572	FAX (901)276-4578
Team Leader	
	Ext-235

COMMUNICATIONS MINISTRY TEAM
Phone (901)276-4572	FAX (901)276-4578
Mark J. Davis, Team Leader/Editor	
mdavis@cumberland.org	Ext-216
Sowgand Sheikholeslami, Senior Art Director	
sowgand@cumberland.org	Ext-211

DISCIPLESHIP MINISTRY TEAM
Phone (901)276-4572	FAX (901)276-4578
Elinor Brown, Team Leader	
esb@cumberland.org	Ext-205
Matthew Gore, Resources Development & Distribution	
mhg@cumberland.org	Ext-252
Nathan Wheeler, Youth & Young Adult Ministry	
nwheeler@cumberland.org	Ext-218
Cindy Martin, Adult & Third Age Ministry	
chm@cumberland.org	Ext-219
Jodi Rush, Children & Family Ministry	
jhr@cumberland.org	Ext-223
Greg Miller, Part-time Shipping Clerk	Ext-256

MISSIONS MINISTRY TEAM
Phone (901)276-4572	FAX (901)276-4578
Milton Ortiz, Team Leader	
mortiz@cumberland.org	Ext-234
Jinger Ellis, Manager, Finance and Administration	
jellis@cumberland.org	Ext-230
Pam Phillips-Burk, Congregational/Women's Ministry	
pam@cumberland.org	Ext-203
Johan Daza, Cross-Culture Immigrant Ministries USA	
jdaza@cumberland.org	Ext-202
T.J. Malinoski, Evangelism & New Church Development	
tmalinoski@cumberland.org	Ext-232
Lynn Thomas, Global Cross-Culture Missions	
4833 Caldwell Mill Lane, Birmingham, AL 35242	Ext-261
lynndont@gmail.com	(205)601-5770
Julie Min, Bilingual English/Korean Administrative Assistant	Ext-224

OTHER CHURCH OFFICES

BETHEL UNIVERSITY
www.bethelu.edu

325 Cherry Avenue, McKenzie, TN 38201
Phone (731)352-4000	FAX (731)352-6387

Walter Butler, President
Dale Henry, Vice President for Development
David Huss, Vice President for Finance
Cindy Mallard, Vice President for College of Arts & Sciences
Phyllis Campbell, Chief Academic Officer
Joe Hames, Vice President for College of Health Sciences
Kelly Kelley, Vice President for College of Professional Studies

CHILDREN'S HOME
cpch@cpch.org   www.cpch.org

909 Greenlee Street, Denton, TX 76201
  Mail Address: Drawer G, Denton, TX 76202
Phone (940)382-5112	FAX (940)387-0821
Richard Brown, President, CEO & General Counsel	(817)360-6874
rbrown@cpch.org	
Jennifer Livings, Vice President of Programs	(469)235-5921
jlivings@cpch.org	
Debbie Garrett, Asst Vice President of Development	(731)446-6241
dgarrett@cpch.org	
Mary Dickerman, Develoopment Operations	(972)765-1180
mdickerman@cpch.org	

MEMPHIS THEOLOGICAL SEMINARY
www.MemphisSeminary.edu

168 East Parkway South, Memphis, TN 38104-4395
Phone (901)458-8232	FAX (901)452-4051

Daniel J. Earheart-Brown, President
Cassandra Price-Perry, Vice-President of Operations/CFO
Peter Gathje, Interim Vice-President of Academic Affairs/Dean
Keith Gaskin, Vice President of Advancement
Laurie Sharpe, Executive Assistant to the President

PROGRAM OF ALTERNATE STUDIES
www.MemphisSeminary.edu/program-of-alternate-studies

168 East Parkway South, Memphis, TN 38104-4395
Phone (901)334-5853	FAX (901)452-4051

Michael Qualls, Director
  mqualls@MemphisSeminary.edu
Karen Patten, Administrative Assistant
  kpatten@MemphisSeminary.edu

2017 YEARBOOK

General Assembly
Cumberland Presbyterian Church

Vision of Ministry

Biblically-based and Christ-centered
 born out of a specific sense of mission,
 the Cumberland Presbyterian Church strives to be true to its heritage:
 to be open to God's reforming spirit,
 to work cooperatively with the larger Body of Christ,
 and to nurture the connectional bonds that make us one.
The Cumberland Presbyterian Church seeks—to be the hands and feet of Christ in
witness and service to the world and, above all, the Cumberland Presbyterian Church
lives out the love of God to the glory of Jesus Christ.

Containing Statistics for the Year 2016

Changes Made to Other Data Through Print Time

(The Yearbook is updated periodically on our website www.cumberland.org/gao)

Edited by Elizabeth Vaughn

TABLE OF CONTENTS

GENERAL ASSEMBLY OFFICERS

MODERATOR
THE REVEREND DWAYNE TYUS
426 W Old Hickory Boulevard
Madison, TN 37115
dwayne.tyus@gmail.com
(615)720-2564

VICE MODERATOR
THE REVEREND NOBUKO SEKI
2-14-16 Higashi-cho
Koganei-Shi Tokyo
184-0011 JAPAN
nobukoseki866@gmail.com
(042)231-1279

STATED CLERK AND TREASURER
THE REVEREND MICHAEL SHARPE
8207 Traditional Place
Cordova, TN 38016
(901)276-4572
FAX (901)272-3913
msharpe@cumberland.org

ENGROSSING CLERK
THE REVEREND VERNON SANSOM
7810 Shiloh Road
Midlothian, TX 76065
(972)825-6887
vernon@sansom.us

THE BOARD OF DIRECTORS OF THE GENERAL ASSEMBLY CORPORATION

(Members whose terms expire in 2017)
(1)REV. JOHN BUTLER, 501 Cherokee Drive, Campbellsville, KY 42718
    jbutler@iccable.com
(1)MS. BETTY JACOB, PO Box 158, Broken Bow, OK 74728
    chocpres@pine-net.com
(Members whose terms expire in 2018)
(1)MS. CALOTTA EDSELL, 7044 Woodsong Cove, Germantown, TN 38138
    cedsell@hotmail.com
(1)REV. NORLAN SCRUDDER, 29688 S 534 Road, Park Hill, OK 74451
    ndscrudder@gmail.com
(Members whose terms expire in 2019)
(2)MR. TIM GARRETT, 150 Third Avenue South, Suite 2800, Nashville, TN 37201
    tgarrett@bassberry.com
(2)REV. BOBBY COLEMAN, 704 E Webb Street, Mountain View, AR 72560
    bobby.coleman@gmail.com

*Ecumenical Partners
+Cumberland Presbyterians in America
Numbers in parenthesis denote number of terms.

MINISTRY COUNCIL

(Members whose terms expire in 2017)
(2)REV. DONNY ACTON, 1413 Oakridge Drive, Birmingham, AL 35242
(3)REV. MICHELE GENTRY DE CORREAL, Urb San Jorge casa 28, Km 8 via a La Tebaida
    Armenia, Quinido, COLOMBIA, SOUTH AMERICA
(2)REV. LANNY JOHNSON, 120 S Mill Street, Morrison, TN 37357
(1)MR. ADAM MCREYNOLDS, PO Box 162, Bethany, IL 61914
(2)REV. TOM SANDERS, 4201 W Kent Street, Broken Arrow, OK 74012
(Members whose terms expire in 2018)
(2)MR. KENNETH BEAN, 1035 Stonewall Street N, McKenzie, TN 38201
(1)REV. PHILLIP LAYNE, 10699 Griffith Highway, Whitwell, TN 37397
(1)REV. PAULA LOUDER, 98 Gallant Court, Clarksville, TN 37043 (resigned)
(2)REV. RON MCMILLAN, 675 Kimberly Drive, Atoka, TN 38004
(1)MS. VICTORY MOORE, 17388 Chandlerville Road, Virginia, IL 62691
(Members whose terms expire in 2019)
(1)MS. KAREN AVERY, 9420 Layton Court NE, Albuquerque, NM 87111
(1)MS. CARLA BELLIS, 19264 Law 2170, Aurora, MO 65605
(3)REV. TROY GREEN, 105 Cobb Hollow Lane, Petersburg, TN 37144
(1)MS. TSURUKO SATOH, 8710 Hickory Falls Lane, Pewee Valley, KY 40056
(1)REV. MIKE WILKINSON, 1504 Clear Brook Drive, Knoxville, TN 37922

YOUTH ADVISORY MEMBERS
(1)MR. CAMERON ALDERSON, 122 E Cherry Street, Chandler, IN 47610
(2)MR. CALEB DAVIS, 502 S Alley Street, Jefferson, TX 75657
(1)MS. CHARLI UHLRICH, 250 County Road 1950 N, Bethany, IL 61914

ADVISORY MEMBERS
REV. MICHAEL SHARPE, 8207 Traditional Place, Cordova, TN 38016
REV. DWAYNE TYUS, 901 W Old Hickory Boulevard, Madison, TN 37115

COMMUNICATIONS MINISTRY TEAM

(Members whose terms expire in 2017)
(3)MS. B. DENISE ADAMS, 126 Ray, Monticello, AR 71655
(2)MS. DUSTY LUTHY, 2026 Washington Street, Paducah, KY 42003
(Members whose terms expire in 2018)
(3)REV. MICHAEL CLARK, 80 Bryan Drive, Winchester, TN 37398
(3)REV. JAMES D. MCGUIRE, 220-2 Southwind Circle, Greeneville, TN 37743
(Members whose terms expire in 2019)
(2)REV. NICHOLAS CHAMBERS, 11300 Road 101, Union, MS 39365
(2)REV. STEVEN SHELTON, 7886 Farmhill Cove, Bartlett, TN 38135

*Ecumenical Partners
+Cumberland Presbyterians in America
Numbers in parenthesis denote number of terms.

DISCIPLESHIP MINISTRY TEAM

(Members whose terms expire in 2017)
(2)MS. LE ILA DIXON, 4406 John Reagan Street, Marshall, TX 75672
(2)REV. DREW GRAY, 8220 Timberland Drive, West Paducah, KY 42086
(3)MS. SAMANTHA HASSELL, 510 N Main Street, Sturgis, KY 42459
(Members whose terms expire in 2018)
(3)MS. JOANNA WILKINSON, 1174 Tanglewood Street, Memphis, TN 38114
(2)MS. RACHEL COOK, 210 Bynum Street, Scottsboro, AL 35768
(2)REV. CHRISTIAN SMITH, 475 State Street, Cookeville, TN 38501
(Members whose terms expire in 2019)
(2)REV. NANCY MCSPADDEN, 120 Roberta Drive, Memphis, TN 38112
(2)REV. JOSEFINA SANCHEZ, 7 Hancock Street, Melrose, MA 02176
(1)REV. JESSE THORNTON, 122 E Cherry Street, Chandler, IN 47610

MISSIONS MINISTRY TEAM

(Members whose terms expire in 2017)
(3)REV. JIMMY BYRD, 176 E Valley Road, Whitwell, TN 37397
(1)MS. DONNA CHRISTIE, 3221 Whitehall Road, Birmingham, AL 35209
(3)REV. RICARDO FRANCO, 7 Hancock Street, Melrose, MA 02176
(1)MRS. KAREN TOLEN, 6859 A East County Road 000N, Trilla, IL 62469
(Members whose terms expire in 2018)
(2)MR. TIM CRAIG, 8958 Carriage Creek Road, Arlington, TN 38002
(2)REV. CARDELIA HOWELL-DIAMOND, 1580 Jeff Road NW, Huntsville, AL 35806
(3)MS. SHERRY POTEET, P.O. Box 313, Gilmer, TX 75644
(2)MS. MELINDA REAMS, 10 W Azalea Lane, Russellville, AR 72802
(Members whose terms expire in 2019)
(2)REV. VICTOR HASSELL, 510 N Main Street, Sturgis, KY 42459
(2)MR. DOMINIC LAU, 3820 Anza Street, San Francisco, CA
(2)MS. BRITTANY MEEKS, 710 N Avalon Street, Memphis, TN 38107
(2)REV. CHRIS WARREN, 906 Prince Lane, Murfreesboro, TN 37129

PASTORAL DEVELOPMENT MINISTRY TEAM

(Members whose terms expire in 2017)
(2)REV. AMBER CLARK, 80 Bryan Drive, Winchester, TN 37398
(2)REV. DREW HAYES, 6322 Labor Lane, Louisville, KY 40291
(Members whose terms expire in 2018)
(2)REV. DUAWN MEARNS, 107 Westoak Place, Hot Springs, AR 71913
(3)REV. LINDA SNELLING, 15791 State Highway W, Ada, OK 74820
(Members whose terms expire in 2019)
(2)REV. SANDRA SHEPHERD, 525 Summit Oaks Court, Nashville, TN 37221

*Ecumenical Partners
+Cumberland Presbyterians in America
Numbers in parenthesis denote number of terms.

GENERAL ASSEMBLY BOARD OF:

I. TRUSTEES OF BETHEL UNIVERSITY

(Members whose terms expire in 2017)
(2)*MS. LISA COLE, PO Box 198615, Nashville, TN 37219
(2)MR. CHESTER (CHET) DICKSON, 24 W Rivercrest Drive, Houston, TX 77042
(1)REV. NANCY MCSPADDEN, 120 Roberta Drive, Memphis, TN 38112
(3)MR. BOBBY OWEN, 1625 Cabot Drive, Franklin, TN 37064
(2)DR. ED PERKINS, 721 Paris Street, McKenzie, TN 38201
(1)MR. KENNETH (KEN) D. QUINTON, 2912 Waller Omer Road, Sturgis, KY 42459
(3)REV. ROBERT (ROB) TRUITT, 1238 Old East Side Road, Burns, TN 37029
(1)REV. ROBERT (BOB) WATKINS, 10950 West Union Hills Drive #1356, Sun City, AZ 85373
(Members whose terms expire in 2018)
(3)MR. CHARLIE GARRETT, 107 Willow Green Drive, Jackson, TN 38305
(2)+REV. ELTON C. HALL, SR., 305 Tiffton Circle, Hewitt, TX 76643
(2)MS. DEWANNA LATIMER, 1077 Jr. Jones Road, Humboldt, TN 38343
(1)MR. LYNDLE MCCURLEY, 198 Rock Creek Drive, Mountain Home, AR 72653
(1)*DR. E. RAY MORRIS, PO Box 924528, Norcross, GA 30010
(1)MR. STEVE PERRYMAN, 535 Ranch Road, Rogersville, MO 65742
(Members whose terms expire in 2019)
(2)MR. JEFF AMREIN, 11711 Paramont Way, Prospect, KY 40059
(3)*JUDGE BEN CANTRELL, 415 Church Street #2513, Nashville, TN 37219
(1)*MR. SCOTT CONGER, 551 Westmoreland Place, Jackson, TN 38301
(3)+DR. ARMY DANIEL, 3125 Searcy Drive, Huntsville, AL 35810
(2)MR. BILL DOBBINS 5716 Quest Ridge Road, Franklin, TN 37064
(3)DR. ROBERT LOW, c/o New Prime, Inc., 2740 W Mayfair Avenue, Springfield, MO 65803
(1)*DR. BROCK MARTIN, 419 Browning Avenue, Huntingdon, TN 38344

Trustee Emeritus – Dr. Vera Low, 3653 Prestwick Court, Springfield, MO 65809 (deceased)

II. TRUSTEES OF CUMBERLAND PRESBYTERIAN CHILDREN'S HOME

(Members whose terms expire in 2016)
(2)MR. RICHARD DEAN, 2140 Cove Circle North, Gadsden, AL 35903
(1)MRS. KAY GOODMAN, 1042 Bobcat Road, Sanger, TX 76266
(2)REV. MELISSA KNIGHT, 9799 Savoy Way, Live Oak, CA 95953
(2)MS. PATRICIA LONG, 525 E Oak Street, Aledo, TX 76008
(Members whose terms expire in 2017)
(1)MS. CAROLINE BOOTH, 2200 Westview Trail, Denton, TX 76207
(3)MS. MAMIE HALL, 305 Tiffton Circle, Hewitt, TX 76643
(1)MR. CHARLES HARRIS, 3293 Birch Avenue, Grapevine, TX 76051
(1)MR. KNIGHT MILLER, 1035 Garden Creek Circle, Louisville, KY 40223
(1)MR. JOHN O'CARROLL, 1701 Live Oak Lane, Southlake, TX 76092
(3)REV. DON TABOR, 9611 Mitchell Place, Brentwood, TN 37027
(Members whose terms expire in 2018)
(1)REV. DUANE DOUGHERTY, 212 County Road 4705, Troup, TX 75789
(1)MRS. CAROLYN HARMON, 4435 Newport Highway, Greeneville, TN 37743
(1)DR. ROBIN HENSON, 8220 Westwind Lane, North Richland Hills, TX 76182
(1)REV. JOYCE MERRITT, 3929 Snail Shell Cove, Rockvale, TN 37153

*Ecumenical Partners
+Cumberland Presbyterians in America
Numbers in parenthesis denote number of terms.

III. TRUSTEES OF HISTORICAL FOUNDATION

(Members whose terms expire in 2017)
(3)+MS. EDNA BARNETT, 7 Breezewood Cove, Jackson, TN 38305
(2)MR. MICHAEL FARE, 401 E Deanna Lane, Nixa, MO 65714
(2)+MS. DOROTHY M. HAYDEN, 3103 Carolina Avenue, Bessemer, AL 35020
(1)+MS. PAT WARD, 2620 Rabbit Lane, Madison, AL 35756
(3)+REV. RICK WHITE, 124 Towne West, Lorena, TX 76655
(Members whose terms expire in 2018)
(1)REV. LISA OLIVER, 110 Allen Drive, Hendersonville, TN 37075
(3)DR. SIDNEY L. SWINDLE, 4407 Swann Avenue, Tampa, FL 33609
(Members whose terms expire in 2019)
(1)MS. ROBIN MCCASKEY HUGHES, 1205 Olde Bridge Road, Edmond, OK 73034
(3)REV. MARY KATHRYN KIRKPATRICK, 401 1/2 Henley-Perry Drive, Marshall, TX 75670
(1)MS. ASHLEY LINDSEY, 2090 Claypool Boyce Road, Alvaton, KY 42122

IV. TRUSTEES OF MEMPHIS THEOLOGICAL SEMINARY OF THE CUMBERLAND PRESBYTERIAN CHURCH

(Members whose terms expire in 2017)
(1)*REV. NANCY COLE, 3346 Arcadia Drive, Tuscaloosa, AL 35404
(1)REV. ANNE HAMES, 118 Paris Street, McKenzie, TN 38201
(2)*REV. ROBERT MARBLE, 515 Shamrock Drive, Little Rock, AR 72205 (resigned)
(2)REV. JENNIFER NEWELL, 2322 Marco Circle, Chattanooga, TN 37421
(1)REV. SUSAN PARKER, 655 York Drive, Rogersville, AR 35652
(1)REV. STEWART SALYER, 2211 Foxfire Road, Clarksville, TN 37043
(3)+DR. JOE WARD, 2620 Rabbit Lane, Madison, AL 35758
(3)*MS. RUBY WHARTON, 1183 E Parkway South, Memphis, TN 38114
(Members whose terms expire in 2018)
(3)REV. KEVIN BRANTLEY, 308 A Chestnut Street, Sacramento, KY 42372
(1)REV. KEVIN HENSON, 1101 Bear Creek Parkway, Ste 3210, Keller, TX 76248
(1)REV. LINDA HOWELL, PO Box 80050, Keller, TX 76244
(3)MR. MARK MADDOX, 225 Oak Drive, Dresden, TN 38225
(2)MS. SONDRA RODDY, 2583 Hedgerow Lane, Clarksville, TN 37043
(3)MR. TAKAYOSHI SHIRAI, 25 Minami Kibogaoka Asahi-ku, Yokohama, Kanagawa-ken 241-0824 JAPAN
(2)*REV. MELVIN CHARLES SMITH, 1263 Haynes Street, Memphis, TN 38114
(2)*MS. LATISHA TOWNS, The Med, 877 Jefferson Avenue, Memphis, TN 38103
(Members whose terms expire in 2019)
(3)MR. MICHAEL R. ALLEN, 149 Windwood Circle, Alabaster, AL 35007
(2)*MR. JOHNNIE COOMBS, PO Box 127, Blue Mountain, MS 38610 (resigned)
(3)MS. DIANE DICKSON, 24 West Rivercrest, Houston, TX 77042
(1)*MS. JANE ASHLEY FOLK, 4405 Dunwick Lane, Fort Worth, TX 76109
(2)*DR. RICK KIRCHOFF, 2044 Thorncroft Drive, Germantown, TN 38138
(3)*DR. INETTA RODGERS, 1824 S Parkway E, Memphis, TN 38114
(1)*DR. DEBORAH SMITH, 584 E McLemore Avenue, Memphis, TN 38106
(1)MS. MARIANNA (MOLLY) WILLIAMS, 947 Troy Avenue, Dyersburg, TN 28024

V. STEWARDSHIP, FOUNDATION AND BENEFITS

(Members whose terms expire in 2017)
(1)MR. RANDY DAVIDSON, PO Box 880, Ada, OK 74821
(3)MR. CHARLES DAY, 9312 Owensboro Road, Falls of Rough, KY 40119
(3)MS. SYLVIA HALL, 930 Sherry Circle, Hixson, TN 37343
(3)MR. JACKIE SATTERFIELD, 2303 County Road 730, Cullman, AL 35055

*Ecumenical Partners
+Cumberland Presbyterians in America
Numbers in parenthesis denote number of terms.

(Members whose terms expire in 2018)
(3)MR. ANDREW B. FRAZIER, JR., 107 Doris Street, Camden, TN 38320
(1)MR. JAMES SHANNON, 2307 Littlemore Drive, Cordova, TN 38016
(2)MR. MICHAEL ST. JOHN, 324 Carriage Place, Lebanon, MO 65536
(Members whose terms expire in 2019)
(2)REV. CHARLES (BUDDY) POPE, 2391 Fairfield Pike, Shelbyville, TN 37160
(3)MS. SUE RICE, 1301 Brooker Road, Brandon, FL 33511
(3)MS. DEBBIE SHELTON, 1255 MG England Road, Manchester, TN 37355
(1)MS. ANDREA SMITH, 1715 Water Cure Road, Winchester, TN 37398

GENERAL ASSEMBLY COMMISSIONS:

I. MILITARY CHAPLAINS AND PERSONNEL

(2) Term Expires in 2017–REV. MARY MCCASKEY BENEDICT, 892 Pen Oak Drive, Cookeville, TN 38501
(1) Term Expires in 2018–REV. TONY JANNER, 104 Northwood Drive, McKenzie TN 38201
(2) Term Expires in 2019–REV. CASSANDRA THOMAS, 1920 Dancy Street, Fayetteville, NC 28301

These three persons and the Stated Clerk represent the denomination as members of the Presbyterian Council for Chaplains and Military Personnel, 4125 Nebraska Avenue NW, Washington, DC 20016

GENERAL ASSEMBLY COMMITTEES

I. JUDICIARY

(Members whose terms expire in 2017)
(1)REV. HARRY CHAPMAN, 4908 El Picador Court SE, Rio Rancho, NM 87124
    wrightrev2gmail.com
(2)REV. ROBERT D. RUSH, 12935 Quail Park Drive, Cypress, TX 77429
    robertrush832@gmail.com
(3)MR. WENDELL THOMAS, JR., 1200 Paradise Drive, Powell, TN 37849
    volbaby@comcast.net
(Members whose terms expire in 2018)
(2)REV. ANNETTA CAMP, 2263 Mill Creek Road, Halls, TN 38040
    anetta@cumberlandchurch.com
(3)MS. KIMBERLY SILVUS, 1128 Madison Street, Clarksville, TN 37040
    kgsilvus@gmail.com
(1)MR. BILL TALLY, 907 Tipperary Drive, Scottsboro, AL 35768
    wtally@scottsboro.org
(Members whose terms expire in 2019)
(3)REV. ANDY MCCLUNG, 919 Dickinson Street, Memphis, TN 38107
    scubarev@att.net
(1)MS. RACHEL MOSES, 1138 Blaine Avenue, Cookeville, TN 38501
    coachrach@aol.com
(1)REV. JAN OVERTON, 3320 Pipe Line Road, Birmingham, AL 35243
    jan@crestlinechurch.org

II. JOINT COMMITTEE ON AMENDMENTS

The committee consists of five members of the Judiciary Committee of the Cumberland Presbyterian Church in America and the Cumberland Presbyterian Church.

III. NOMINATING

(Members whose terms expire in 2017)
(1)REV. TOBY DAVIS, 1211 AR 223 Highway, Pineville, AR 72566 (resigned)
    pastortobydavis@gmail.com
(1)MRS. FRANCES DAWSON, PO Box 904, Scottsboro, AL 35768
    rdpfcd@scottsboro.org
(1)MS. ELLIE SCRUDDER, 29688 S 535 Road, Park Hill, OK 74451
    escrudder@gmail.com
(1)REV. KEVIN SMALL, 6492 E 400th Road, Martinsville, IL 62442
    revkev61@gmail.com
(Members whose terms expire in 2018)
(1)REV. THOMAS CAMPBELL, PO Box 343, Calico Rock, AR 72519
    tdcampbellar@gmail.com
(1)MS. HEATHER MORGAN, 1468 Williams Cove Road, Winchester, TN 37398
    htmorgan87@gmail.com
(Members whose terms expire in 2019)
(1)MS. FAYE DELASHMIT, 2705 Garrett Drive, Bowling Green, KY 42104
    steve.delashmit@twc.com
(1)REV. DEREK JACKS, 341 Shadeswood Drive, Hoover, AL 35226
    pastorderek@homewoodcpc.com
(1)REV. STEPHEN LOUDER, 98 Gallant Court, Clarksville, TN 37043
    pastorsteve@clarksvillecpc.com
(1)MS. JANIE STAMPS, 4008 Logan Lane, Fort Smith, AR 72903
    bjstamps@msn.com

IV. OUR UNITED OUTREACH COMMITTEE

(Members whose terms expire in 2017)
(3)MS. SHARON RESCH, PO Box 383, Dongola, IL 62926
(3)REV. WILLIAM RUSTENHAVEN III, PO Box 1303, Marshall, TX 75671
(Members whose terms expire in 2018)
(2)MR. RANDY WEATHERSBY, 6130 US Highway 278 E, Cullman, AL 35055
(2)MS. ROBIN WILLS, 4607 E Richmond Shop Road, Lebanon, TN 37090
(Members whose terms expire in 2019)
(1)REV. BRUCE HAMILTON, 1037 Binns Drive, Monticello, AR 71655

V. PLACE OF MEETING

THE STATED CLERK OF THE GENERAL ASSEMBLY
THE MODERATOR OF THE GENERAL ASSEMBLY
A REPRESENTATIVE OF WOMEN'S MINISTRIES OF THE MISSIONS MINISTRY TEAM

*Ecumenical Partners
+Cumberland Presbyterians in America
Numbers in parenthesis denote number of terms.

VI. UNIFIED COMMITTEE ON THEOLOGY AND SOCIAL CONCERNS

(Members whose terms expire in 2017)

(1)+MS. SHARON COMBS, PO Box 122, Sturgis, KY 42459
   (270)860-4175
(1)+REV. EDMOND COX, 249 Mimosa Circle, Maryville, TN 37801
   (865)789-6161
(2)+DR. NANCY FUQUA, 1963 County Road 406, Towncreek, AL 35672
   fuq23@bellsouth.net; (256)566-1226
(2)REV. RANDY JACOB, PO Box 158, Broken Bow, OK 74728 (deceased)
   chocpres@pine-net.com; (580)584-3770; (580)236-2469 cell
(1)+REV. LARUTH JEFFERSON, 25757 Primose Lane, Southfield, MI 48033
   (248)945-0349
(1)+DR. PHILLIP REDRICK, 228 Church Street NW, Huntsville, AL 35801 (deceased)
   (256)882-6333
(1)+REV. ROBERT E THOMAS, 1017 N Englewood, Tyler, TX 75702
   (903)592-0238

(Members whose terms expire in 2018)

(2)REV. GEORGE ESTES, 7910 Cloverbrook Lane, Germantown, TN 38138
   geoestes@gmail.com; (901)755-6673
(2)REV. SHELIA O'MARA, PO Box 170, Gadsden, TN 38337
   chaplainshelia@aol.com; (443)699-2321; (443)370-7218 cell
(2)MR. DAVID PHILLIPS-BURK, 3325 Bailey Creek Cove N, Collierville, TN 38017
   dlphillipsburk@aol.com; (256)520-1380

(Members whose terms expire in 2019)

(3)+MRS. JIMMIE DODD, c/o Hopewell CPCA, 4100 Millsfield Highway, Dyersburg, TN 38024
   dodd125@gmail.com
(3)REV. BYRON FORESTER, 2376 Eastwood Place, Memphis, TN 38112
   bforester@bellsouth.net; (901)246-1242
(1)REV. MARCUS HAYES, 2901 Sandage Avenue, Apt 304, Fort Worth, TX 76109
   marcus.hayes@att.net
(2)REV. JOHN A. SMITH, 916 Allen Road, Nashville, TN 37214
   john.a.smith.81@gmail.com; (615)545-6486
(3)+ELDER JOY WALLACE, 6940 Marvin D Love Freeway, Dallas, TX 75237
   jwallace@wlgllc.net

President of Memphis Theological Seminary - Ex-officio Member
   REV. JAY EARHEART-BROWN, 866 N McLean Boulevard, Memphis, TN 38107
   jebrown@memphisseminary.edu; (901)278-0367

OTHER DENOMINATIONAL PERSONNEL

REPRESENTATIVES TO:
American Bible Society: REV. MICHAEL SHARPE, 8207 Traditional Place, Cordova, TN 38016

Caribbean and North American Area Council, World Communion of Reformed Churches:
STATED CLERK MICHAEL SHARPE, 8207 Traditional Place, Cordova, TN 38016

(Member whose terms expire in 2017)

(3)MS. LAURIE SHARPE, 3423 Summerdale Drive, Bartlett, TN 38133

*Ecumenical Partners
+Cumberland Presbyterians in America
Numbers in parenthesis denote number of terms.

LIVING GENERAL ASSEMBLY MODERATORS

2016—REV. DWAYNE TYUS, 426 Old Hickory Boulevard, Madison, TN 37115

2015—REV. MICHELE GENTRY, Urb San Jorge casa 28, Km 8 via a La Tebaida
      Armenia, Quindio, COLOMBIA, SA

2014—REV. LISA HALL ANDERSON, 1790 Faxon Avenue, Memphis, TN 38112

2013—REV. FOREST PROSSER, 1157 Mountain Creek Road, Chattanooga, TN 37405

2012—REV. ROBERT D. RUSH, 12935 Quail Park Drive, Cypress, TX 77429

2011—REV. DON M. TABOR, 9611 Mitchell Place, Brentwood, TN 37027

2009—ELDER SAM SUDDARTH, 206 Ha Le Koa Court, Smyrna, TN 37167

2008—REV. JONATHAN CLARK, 88 Woodcrest Drive, Winchester, TN 37398

2007—REV. FRANK WARD, 8207 Traditional Place, Cordova, TN 38016

2006—REV. DONALD HUBBARD, 2128 Campbell Station Road, Knoxville, TN 37932

2005—REV. LINDA H. GLENN, 49 Mason Road, Threeway, TN 38343

2004—REV. EDWARD G. SIMS, 2161 N. Meadows Drive, Clarksville, TN 37043

2003—REV. CHARLES MCCASKEY, 679 Canter Lane, Cookeville, TN 38501

1999—ELDER GWENDOLYN G. RODDYE, 3728 Wittenham Drive, Knoxville, TN 37921

1998—REV. MASAHARU ASAYAMA, 3-15-9 Higashi, Kunitachi-shi, Tokyo, JAPAN

1996—REV. MERLYN A. ALEXANDER, 80 N. Hampton Lane, Jackson, TN 38305

1995—REV. CLINTON O. BUCK, PO Box 770068, Memphis, TN 38117

1993—REV. ROBERT M. SHELTON, 7128 Lakehurst Avenue, Dallas, TX 75230

1992—REV. JOHN DAVID HALL, 109 Oddo Lane SE, Huntsville, AL 35802

1990—REV. THOMAS D. CAMPBELL, PO Box 315, Calico Rock, AR 72519

1989—REV. WILLIAM RUSTENHAVEN, Jr., 703 W. Burleson, Marshall, TX 75670

1988—ELDER BEVERLY ST. JOHN, 5436 Edmondson Pike Apt 75A, Nashville, TN 37211

1981—REV. W. JEAN RICHARDSON, 7533 Lancashire, Powell, TN 37849

IN MEMORY OF:

Moderator of the180th General Assembly
REV. BOYCE WALLACE
Died January 4, 2017

Moderator of the171st General Assembly
REV. RANDY JACOB
Died January 29, 2017

---

*Ecumenical Partners
+Cumberland Presbyterians in America
Numbers in parenthesis denote number of terms.

SYNOD AND PRESBYTERY CLERKS

SYNOD OF GREAT RIVERS

The Reverend Andy McClung
919 Dickinson Street
Memphis, TN 38107
(901)606-6615
scubarev@att.net

Arkansas Presbytery (GRAR)

Janie Stamps
4008 Logan Lane
Fort Smith, AR 72903
(479)478-0161 (Home)
(479)883-5633 (Cell)
(479)782-0454 FAX
bjstamps@msn.com (Home)

Missouri Presbytery (GRMI)

Larry Nottingham
PO Box 281
Stockton, MO 65785
(417)276-3792
mopresbyterycpc2@yahoo.com

West Tennessee Presbytery (GRWT)

The Reverend Andy McClung
919 Dickinson Street
Memphis, TN 38107
(901)606-6615
scubarev@att.net

**SYNOD OF MIDWEST
(MI)**

Debra Shanks
3997 N 100th Street
Casey, IL 62420
(217)932-2995
royndebbie@hotmail.com

Covenant Presbytery (MICO)

Reese Baker
1175 Rowland Cemetery Road
Fredonia, KY 42411
(270)545-3483
rbaker@kynet.biz

Cumberland Presbytery (MICU)

The Reverend Darrell Pickett
113 Woods Drive
Glasgow, KY 42141
(270)834-6102
dpickett@glasgow-ky.com

North Central Presbytery (MINC)

The Reverend Ralph Blevins
1623 County Road 2375 E
Geff, IL 62842
(618)854-2494
statedclerk@ncpwebsite.com

SYNOD AND PRESBYTERY CLERKS

MISSION SYNOD
(MS)

Mary Kathryn Kirkpatrick
501 Indian Springs Road
Marshall, TX 75672
(903)935-3787
marykathryn@cumberlandofmarshall.org

Andes Presbytery (MSAN)

The Reverend Diana Valdez
Calle 65 #98-45, interior 174
Altos de la Macarena
(Robledo-LaCampina)
Medellin, Antioquia
Colombia, South America
(57)313-826-3153
dianamariavaldezduque@gmail.com

Cauca Valley Presbytery (MSCA)

Jairo Lopez
Paraiso la Morada
5ta Etapa, Casa 36, Jamundi
Colombia, South America
011-5726-615410

Choctaw Presbytery (MSCH)

The Reverend Virginia Espinoza
PO Box 132
Boswell, OK 74727
(580)434-7971
vespinoza@choctawnation.com

Presbytery del Cristo (MSDC)

Karen Avery
9420 Layton Court NE
Albuquerque, NM 87111
(505)821-7668
kavery5@comcast.net

Emaus Presbytery (MSEM)

Cecilia Tarborda
Calle 20D #42C-56
Bello, Colombia
(57)300-783-5638
chilalu1147@hotmail.com

Hong Kong Presbytery (MSHK)

The Reverend Ella Hung
2/F Welland Plaza
188 Nam Chong Street
Sham Shui Po, Hong Kong
(011)852-2783-8923
(011)852-2771-2726 FAX
siukee@taohsien.org.hk

Japan Presbytery (MSJA)

Takoyoshi Shirai
25 Minami Kobogaoka
Asahi-ku Yokohama
Kanagawa-ken
241-0824 JAPAN
(011)81-45-361-0059
cpc_japan@ybb.ne.jp

Red River Presbytery (MSRR)

The Reverend Vernon Sansom
7810 Shiloh Road
Midlothian, TX 76065
(972)825-6887
vernon@sansom.us

SYNOD AND PRESBYTERY CLERKS

Trinity Presbytery (MSTR)

Paula Hayes
PO Box 5449
Longview, TX 75608
(903)759-1896 (Home)
(903)759-0092 (Work)
phayes7442@aol.com

SYNOD OF SOUTHEAST
(SE)

The Reverend Forest Prosser
1157 Mountain Creek Road
Chattanooga, TN 37405
(423)877-4114
forestprosser@comcast.net

Cumberland East Coast Presbytery (SEEC)

The Reverend Douglas Park
316 Prospect Avenue Apt 6D
Hackensack, NJ 07601
(201)694-3005
jiwoos@gmail.com

Presbytery of East Tennessee (SEET)

The Reverend Ronald L. Longmire
2041 Eckles Drive
Maryville, TN 37804
(865)984-1647
ronaldlongmire@charter.net

Grace Presbytery (SEGR)

Jessie Dunnaway
New Hope CP Church
5521 Double Oak Lane
Birmingham, AL 35242
(205)991-5252
jessie@newhopecpc.org

Hope Presbytery (SEHO)

Dianne Vandiver
4500 County Road 50
Lexington, AL 35648
(256)247-3827 (Home)
(256)222-8434 (Cell)
diannevandiver08@gmail.com

Robert Donnell Presbytery (SERD)

Frances Dawson
PO Box 904, 221 S Market St.
Scottsboro, AL 35768
(256)244-0554 (Cell)
(256)259-0904 (Business)(FAX)
rdpfcd@scottsboro.org

Tennessee-Georgia Presbytery (SETG)

The Reverend Kriss McGowan
(interim)
885 Mount Calvary Road
Whitwell, TN 37397
(423)432-0037 (Cell)
(423)463-8609 (Home)
tngastatedclerk@gmail.com

SYNOD AND PRESBYTERY CLERKS

TENNESSEE SYNOD
(TN)

The Reverend Charles McCaskey
565 East Tenth Street
Cookeville, TN 38501
(931)526-6585 (Office)
(931)372-2620 FAX
charles@cookevillecpchurch.org

Columbia Presbytery (TNCO)

The Reverend Charles (Buddy) Pope
2391 Fiarfield Pike
Shelbyville, TN 37160
(931)205-6897
pope6897@yahoo.com

Murfreesboro Presbytery (TNMU)

The Reverend Charles McCaskey
565 East Tenth Street
Cookeville, TN 38501
(931)526-6585 (Office)
(931)528-2273 FAX
charles@cookevillecpchurch.org

Nashville Presbytery (TNNA)

The Reverend Fred Polacek
907 Graham Drive
Old Hickory, TN 37138
(615)754-5328 (Home)
revfredp@gmail.com

MINISTERS GAINED AND LOST IN 2016

MINISTERS RECEIVED BY ORDINATION

NAME	PRESBYTERY	DATE
Brockman, Anna Sweet	East Tennessee	11/26/16
Broyles, Lon Byrd	East Tennessee	10/30/16
Choi, Eun Sang (Sean)	East Tennessee	10/01/16
Dewhirst, Timothy	Red River	07/10/16
Fowler, Emily	Red River	11/13/16
Hardin, Kenny	Cumberland	09/10/16
Jones, Steve	Nashville	07/24/16
Price, William	West Tennessee	08/02/16
Reno, Michael	Missouri	06/12/16
Young, Brandon Taylor	Nashville	05/22/16

MINISTERS REINSTATED OR RECEIVED FROM OTHER DENOMINATIONS

NAME	PRESBYTERY	CHURCH	DATE
DeBerry, Jacqueline	West Tennessee	Evangelical PC	10/01/16
Krueger, Courtney	Tennessee-Georgia	Baptist	11/06/16
Potter, Bruce	Tennessee-Georgia	ordination restored	10/01/16
Scott, Adrian	Red River	Baptist	04/22/17
Webb, Lonnie G, Sr	Red River	Assemblies of God	04/22/17

MINISTERS WHO HAVE MOVED TO OTHER DENOMINATIONS

NAME	DENOMINATION	DATE
Rose, Missy	PCUSA	10/01/2016
McMillan, Lloyd Aaron	EPC	08/11/2016
Moore, Angela	United Church of Christ	03/11/2016
Paleak, Jock	PCUSA	03/26/2016
Richards, Kenneth	ECO	03/30/2016

MINISTERS DROPPED FROM MINISTRY BY PRESBYTERY

NAME	PRESBYTERY	DATE
Axton, Durant (Peck)	North Central	04/09/2016

MILITARY CHAPLAINS

Acuff, David (M8)
4969 Quail Lane
Columbia, SC 29206
david.acuff@us.army.mil
(803)790-9151   TNNA#7300

Baranoski, Timothy (M8)
1205 Tomahawk Drive B
Jber, AK 99505
(615)440-3499
timothy.i.baranoski.mil@mail.mil

Headrick, Anthony (M8)
3327 N Eagle Road Ste 110-132
Meridian, ID 83646
chaps2a@yahoo.com
(619)435-0825   SEGR#0100

LeFavor, David E (M8)
4100 W 3rd Street
Dayton, OH 45428
david.lefavor@med.va.gov
(813)613-4133   SEGR#0100

Logan, Jason B (M8)
212 Saddlebag Court
Rineyville, KY 40162
jason.b.logan.mil@mail.mil
(410)305-8494   TNMU#7200

Nash, Zachary (M8)
(on file in General Assembly Office)
zachary.nash@us.af.mil
( )   GRWT#9100

O'Mara, Shelia (M8)
PO Box 170
Gadsden, TN 38337
chaplainshelia@aol.com
(443)699-2321   MSDC#8700

Santillano, Ray Paul (M8)
1270 Polo Road Apt 618
Columbia, SC 29223
ramon.santillano@us.army.mil
(915)500-4928   MSTR#8100

Turner, Glyn (M8)
5005 Eagle Drive
Gulfport, MS 39501
(585)307-7715
glynturner@outlook.com

NON-MILITARY CHAPLAINS

Aden, Marty (M9)
202 Bennington Place
Wilmington, NC 28412
maden@ec.rr.com
(910)274-8465   MSRR#8400

Anderson, Lisa (M9)
1790 Faxon Avenue
Memphis, TN 38112
anderli60@gmail.com
(901)246-8052   GRWT#9305

Bone, Leslie (M9)
16504 George Franklyn Drive
Independence, MO 64055
lesliebone@comcast.net
(816)373-6625   GRMI#4100

Bowers, Sharon G (M9)
201 Wild Buffalo Drive
Kyle, TX 78640
sharon.bowers@gmail.com
(512)230-7078   MSTR#8100

Brown, Mark (M9)
752 Hawthorne Street
Memphis, TN 38107
dmbrown@utmem.edu
(901)274-1474   GRWT#9100

Carter, Patricia (M9)
2509 Decatur Stratton Road
Decatur, MS 39327
revtree@yahoo.com
(601)635-4120   SEGR#0100

Cook, Lisa (M9)
4101 Dalemere Court
Nashville, TN 37207
tgoose@comcast.net
(615)868-4118   TNNA#7300

Diamond, James (M9)
214 Falmouth Drive
Georgetown, KY 40324
jamesdiamond007@twc.com
(502)642-5020   TNMU#7200

Ferrol, Ruben (M9)
13018 E 28th Street
Tulsa, OK 74134
rubeferrol@msn.com
(610)966-7289   MSRR#8400

Fowler, Emily (M9)
5225 Maple Avenue Apt 5304
Dallas, TX 75235
emilykaye.fowler@gmail.com
(817)983-3559   MSRR#8400

Gentry, Michele (M9)
Urb San Jorge casa 28
Km 8 via a La Tebaida
Armenia, Quindio, Colombia
South America
gentry.andes@yahoo.com
(318)285-1161   MSAN#8900

Hames, Anne (M9)
118 Paris Street
Mc Kenzie, TN 38201
FAX: (731)352-4069
hamesa@bethel-college.edu
(731)352-4066   GRWT#9100

Hartung, J Thomas (M9)
2291 Americus Boulevard W Apt 1
Clearwater, FL 33763
revtom6@aol.com
(727)797-2882   SEGR#0100

Hayes, Jennifer (M9)
2901 Sandage Avenue Apt 304
Fort Worth, TX 76109
hayesj712@gmail.com
(205)533-1018

Jackson, Terry (M9)
1461 Mt Pleasant Road
Hernando, MS 38632
tjackson48@comcast.net
(662)429-9741   GRWT#9100

Kelly, Patrick L (M9)
1449 Rainbow Road
Mountain City, TN 37683-2110
(423)727-4067   SEET#2200

Kennemer, Darren (M9)
8828 Highway 119
Alabaster, AL 35007
(205)663-3152
darren.kennemer@va.gov   SERD#0107

Knight, Melissa (M9)
5730 Haley Road
Meridian, MS 39305
(530)632-6472
revlissa@gmail.com   MSDC#8700

Lombard, Kristi (M9)
902 Clearview
Krum, TX 76249
pastorkristi@yahoo.com
(940)435-5077   MSRR#8400

McCarty, John (M9)
305 W Martindale Drive
Marshall, TX 75672
mtsjohn@gmail.com
(423)650-8788   SETG#2100

McClung, Tiffany (M9)
919 Dickinson Street
Memphis, TN 38107
tmcclung@memphisseminary.edu
(901)606-6604   GRWT#9100

McSpadden, Nancy (M9)
120 Roberta Drive
Memphis, TN 38112

revnancy77@gmail.com
(870)612-0067   GRAR#1100

Melson, Glenda (M9)
331 Tickle Weed Road
Swansea, SC 29160
glendamelson@fidnet.com
(417)588-2758   SEET#2200

Messer, James C (M9)
3653 Old Madisonville Road
Henderson, KY 42420
jcmess@hotmail.com
(270)827-0711   MINC#5304

Mills, David M (M9)
60 Huge Oak Street
Bertram, TX 78605
(512)355-3511   MSTR#8100

Oliver, Lisa (M9)
110 Allen Drive
Hendersonville, TN 37075
( )   TNMU#7200

Pickett, Patricia (M9)
1460 Cheatham Dam Road
Ashland City, TN 37015
tovahtoo@aol.com
(615)792-4973   TNNA#7300

Richards, Carroll (M9)
210 Allison Drive
Lincoln, IL 62656
FAX: (217)732-7894
dr_cr@comcast.net
(217)732-7894   MINC#5200

Ruggia, Mario (Bud) (M9)
603 Rumsey Street
Kiowa, KS 67070
ruggia@aol.com
(620)825-4076   MSRR#8400

Scott, Lisa (M9)
lascott1979@att.net
(816)332-0604   GRMI#4100

Scott, Jerry (M9)
2310 Sentell Drive
Maryville, TN 37803
dmjlscott@yahoo.com
(865)809-2621   SEET#2200

Smith, James A (M9)
309 Lutes Road
Paducah, KY 42001
james1493@att.net
(901)574-2345   MICO#3400

Smith, John Adam (M9)
916 Allen Road
Nashville, TN 37214
john.a.smith.81@gmail.com
(615)545-6486

Sumrall, Phil (M9)
107 Barnhardt Circle
Fort Oglethorpe, GA 30742
phil.sumrall@gmail.com
(423)903-1938   SETG#2100

Travis, Kermit (M9)
3220 Sharon Highway
Dresden, TN 38225
(731)364-2315   GRWT#9415

Truax, Robert Lee, Jr (M9)
2989 Champions Drive Apt 204
Lakeland, TN 38002
revtruax@yahoo.com
(901)266-5927   GRWT#9100

Varner, Susan (M9)
14709 Glisten Lane
Little Rock, AR 72223
smvarner76@yahoo.com
(901)371-1249   GRAR#1100

West, David (M9)
2027 Lucille Street
Lebanon, TN 37087
(217)732-7568   MINC#5405

Wilson, Don   <M1 M9>
7300 Calle Montana NE
Albuquerque, NM 87113
(505)823-2594
don-wilson07@comcast.net

MEMORIAL ROLL OF MINISTERS

IN MEMORY OF
MINISTERS LOST BY DEATH

NAME	PRESBYTERY	AGE	DATE
Benson, William	Grace	69	11/06/16
Blakeburn, Roy E	East Tennessee	87	04/14/16
Fleming, Patrick T	Arkansas	53	08/07/16
Gross, Ronald	North Central	86	01/15/17
Hatcher, Carlton	Cumberland	87	01/01/16
Hom, Paul	del Cristo	85	03/14/17
Jacob, Randy	Choctaw	80	01/29/17
Malone, Michael	Murfreesboro	49	05/28/16
Maynard, Terrell	Grace	72	03/14/17
Murrie, Willard	Covenant	97	04/20/17
Neafus, Kenneth	Cumberland	71	08/08/16
Ortiz, Jaime	Andes	83	03/29/16
Phelps, Earl	West Tennessee	87	04/20/16
Reid, Richard	East Tennessee	52	07/13/16
Shelton, Robert E	Red River	75	11/01/16
Smith, Albert J	North Central	87	02/10/17
Smith, Billy T	Nashville	86	06/16/16
Talley, James E	Cumberland	89	03/15/16
Vasseur, Terry	Covenant	78	02/05/17
Wallace, Andrew	North Central	56	08/14/16
Wallace, Boyce	Cauca Valley	87	01/04/17
Westfall, Charles	Covenant	89	03/12/17
Wooten, Wallace	Arkansas	88	12/28/16
Yaple, George	Hope	90	04/24/17

SURVIVING SPOUSES OF MINISTERS BY PRESBYTERY
(Deceased spouse in parenthesis.)

ANDES

Myriam de Ortiz
(Jaime Ortiz)
     Cra 50D #62-69 Barrio Prado Centro
     Medellin, Antioquia
     Colombia, South America
     (574)551-6267

ARKANSAS

Batholomew, Maudline
(Harold Bartholomew)
     13395 Highway 265
     Prairie Grove, AR 72753
     (479)846-2850

DuBose, Sandra
(Paul DuBose)
     207 7th Street
     Cotter, AR 72626
     (870) 373-1021

Elkins, Patsy
(Robert Harold Elkins)
     525 Elkins Road
     Magazine, AR 72943
     (479)637-3723
     robtelkins@cej.net

Faith, Jeannine
(Charles Faith)
     4710 Mount Olive Road
     Melbourne, AR 72556
     (870)368-4069

Fleming, Angela
(Patrick Fleming)
     616 N Border Street
     Benton, AR 72015
     (501)994-4678
     ptfleming@live.com

Hollenbeck, Linda
(Edward B. Hollenbeck)
     409 Carson Drive
     Benton, AR 72015
     (501)315-9737

Kinslow, Jean
(Alfred Kinslow)
     29209 Perdido Beach Blvd
     Vista Bella #701
     Orange Beach, AL 36561
     (251)981-8385

Wynne, Glenna
(W. J. Wynne)
     1501 W Block
     El Dorado, AR 71730
     (870)863-9444

CAUCA VALLEY

Munoz, Aliria Correal de
(Gerardo Munoz)
     5405 Robelene Drive
     Metaire, LA 70003
     gwilson54@cox.net

Wallace, Beth
(Boyce Wallace)
     Cra 101 No 15-93
     Cali, COLOMBIA, SA
     (352)339-1579
     hbwcali@yahoo.com

Yepez, Mrs. (??)
(Juan Yepez)
     Colombia, South America

CHOCTAW

Jacob, Betty
(Randy Jacob)
     PO Box 158
     Broken Bow, OK 74728
     (580)584-2099
     chocpres@pine-net.com

COLUMBIA

Barker, Nicky
(Jack Barker)
     40 Watson Street
     Savannah, TN 38372
     (731)926-1577

Bates, Betty Ruth
(Harold Bates)
     204 Apache Trail
     Columbia, TN 38401
     (931)381-6737

Burns, Angela C.
(Bobby G. Burns)
     328 Dunnaway Road
     Shelbyville, TN 37160
     (931)294-5105

Denton, Virgie
(Clyde Denton)
     2538 County Club Lane
     Columbia, TN 38401
     (931)388-7154

Gibson, Ernestine
(Charles Gibson)
     33 Hilldale Church Road
     Fayetteville, TN 37334
     (931)433-2666

Green, Marie
(Odis Green)
     18 Oakwood Street NW
     Rome, GA 30165
     (706)291-1738

Sain, Sally
(Edwin Sain)
     27 Hilltop Road
     Fayetteville, TN 37334
     (931)433-8708
     ssain@fpunet.com

Seaton, Whitney
(Charlie Seaton)
     111 W Hardin Drive
     Columbia, TN 38401
     (931)388-0319

Wilkins, Dianne S
(Marvin Edward Wilkins)
     209 Mackey Street
     Rogersville, AL 35652
     (256)247-5557
     marvinwilkins@msn.com

COVENANT

Atchison, Cheryl
(Dean Atchison)
     206 Marsha Drive
     Ledbetter, KY 42058

Cannon, Joyce
(Chester Cannon)
     1026 W Center Street
     Madisonville, KY 42431

Clark, Eileen
(Morris Clark)
     8720 State Route 132 W
     Clay, KY 42404

Dixon, Sonja
(Robert Dixon)
     8550 Lafayette Road
     Hopkinsville, KY 42240
     (270)886-7647
     sonjadixon@earthlink.net

Gerard, Vanda
(Eugene "Stan" Gerard
     615 N 42nd Street
     Paducah, KY 42001
     (270)443-2889

Lively, Louella
(James Lively)
     c/o Owensboro Care Center
     1205 Leitchfield Road
     Owensboro, KY 42303
     (270)527-3776

Marsiglio, June
(Roger Marsiglio)
     505 Logan
     Providence, KY 42450)

Moss, Lou
(Larry Moss)
     167 Bluegrass Drive
     LaCenter, KY 42056
     (270)292-2000

Murphy, Robbie
(Vernon Murphy)
     128 New Liberty Church Road
     Kevil, KY 42053
     (270)522-3398

Owen, Pat
(Bert Owen)
     7906 Manner Pointe Drive
     Louisville, KY 40220
     (502)749-1940
     bertorpatowen@insightbb.com

SURVIVING SPOUSES OF MINISTERS BY PRESBYTERY CONTINUED
(Deceased spouse in parenthesis.)

Pettit, Jennie
(William H. Pettit)
    248 Skyline Drive
    Princeton, KY 42245
    (270)365-9076

Vasseur, Loretta
(Terry Vasseur)
    121 Crossland Road
    Murray, KY 42071
    (270)876-8083

CULLMAN

Kimbrell, Glenda
(Bobby Kimbrell)
    9479 Cumberland Oaks Drive
    Pinson, AL 35126
    (205)680-1743

Weathersby, Dorothy
(E.W. Weathersby)
    1203 2nd Avenue NE
    Cullman, AL 35055
    (256)734-2886

CUMBERLAND

Ferree, Carole
(Ronald Ferree)
    2475 Fallen Timber Road
    Campbellsville, KY 42718
    (270)465-1150

Graham, Mary
(Harold Graham)
    103 Freeman Green Drive
    Elizabethtown, KY 42701
    (270)360-1191

Hatcher, Cherry Lee
(Carlton Hatcher)
    2111 Robin Road
    Bowling Green, KY 42101
    (270)842-8488

Johnson, Genevie
(Robert Johnson)
    351 Bacon Court
    Harrodsburg, KY 40330
    (859)734-3789

Milam, Dona
(Robert Milam)
    9294 Owensboro Road
    Falls of Rough, KY 40119
    (270)879-8985

Mouser, Wynemia Despain
(Calvin Mouser)
    16305 Highland Drive
    McKenzie, TN 38201
    (270)932-7377

Phelps, Diann
(John Phelps)
    4743 Happy Hollow Road
    Hawesville, KY 42348
    (270)927-9835
    haor@juno.com

Renner, Wallace
(Patricia Renner)
    1648 Griffith Avenue
    Owensboro, KY 42301
    (270)685-4359
    pwrenner@adelphia.com

Sprague, Rose
(George Sprague)
    101 Clyde Morris Hall #242
    Ormond Beach, FL 32174

DEL CRISTO

Appleby, Judy
(Bob Appleby)
    3265 16th Street
    San Francisco, CA 94103
    (415)703-6090
    gfcc@gum.org

Chang, Grace
(John Chang)
    1753 Castro Drive
    San Jose, CA 95130
    (408)370-0643

Ellis, Ernestine
(John Ellis)
    1432 Cape Verde Place
    Tucson, AZ 85748
    (520)296-9027

Freeman, ??
(Jack Freeman)
    3559 Cody Way
    Sacramento, CA 95864
    (916)489-2567

Hom, Christian
(Paul Hom)
    722 24th Avenue
    San Francisco., CA
    (415751-9766

Kennedy, Louise
(John F Kennedy)
    4916 44th Street
    Lubbock, TX 79414
    (806)796-0738

Matlock, Bettye
(Joe Matlock)
    5905 Hickory Grove Lane
    Bartlett, TN 38134
    (901)937-8457

EAST TENNESSEE

Alexander, Carolyn Roberts
(Don Charles Alexander)
    220 107 Cutoff
    Greeneville, TN 37743
    (423)638-8453
    alexandercda@msn.com

Blakeburn, Wiletta
(Roy E Blakeburn)
    111 Park Place
    Greeneville, TN 37743
    (423)787-9609
    blakeburnr@aol.com

Broyles, Elizabeth
(Lon Broyles)
    753 Snapp Bridge Road
    Limestone, TN 37681
    (865)483-8433

Broyles, Minnie
(Raymond Broyles)
    4944 Kilaminajaro
    Old Hickory, TN 37138-4102
    (615)428-8640

Dobson, Valdean
(Howard Dobson)
    150 Liberty Way
    Greeneville, TN 37645
    (423)798-8947

Johnson, Rebecca
(Scott Johnson)
    512 Rolling Creek Circle
    Knoxville, TN 37922
    (865)966-3699

Reid, Donna
(Richard Reid)
    104 Gregg Street
    Jackson, TN 38301
    (731)453-5302

Scott, Betty
(Lee Scott)
    319 Lavista Drive
    Maryville, TN 37804
    (731)415-2936

GRACE

Baker, Ola
(L. G. Baker)
    7208 12th Street
    Tampa, FL 33604
    (813)5239-3356

Benson, Annette
(William Benson)
    137 W Lowndes Drive
    Columbus, MS 39701
    (662)386-3433
    willardb715@gmail.com

Brown, Marye
(Richard C Brown)
    2100 NE 140th Street Apt 510E
    Edmond, OK 73013
    (205)663-5486

Buerhaus, Charity
(Chuck Buerhaus)
    313 S Main Street
    Piedmont, AL 36272
    (256)447-6195

SURVIVING SPOUSES OF MINISTERS BY PRESBYTERY CONTINUED
(Deceased spouse in parenthesis.)

Hegwood, Clara
(James "Pete" Hegwood)
125 Pinewood Lane
Montevallo, AL 35115
(205)665-2134

Maynard, Jackie
(Terrell Maynard)
3 Nelson Cove
Milan, TN 38358
(731)437-0026

Mims, Martha Jo
(Howell "Gay" Mims)
3011 Wolfe Road
Columbus, MS 39705
(662)328-3778
mjmims@muw.edu

Phillips, Edna
(Troy Phillips)
2024 Hilltop Road
Rock Hill, SC 29732
(803)325-1416

Tant, Becky
(Robert H Tant)
516 Davis Drive
Glencoe, AL 35905
(256)494-9450
rtant82091@aol.com

HOPE

Bright, Mildred
(J. P. Bright)
1716 Broadway Boulevard
Florence, AL 35630
(256)766-8361

Copeland, Frances S.
(Bill Copeland)
142 Thornton Terrace Drive
Rogersville, AL 35652
(256)247-1688

Hyden, Mae
(Lee Hyden)
2195 Allsboro Road
Cherokee, AL 35616
(256)360-2896

Yaple, Audrey
(George Yaple)
2051 Lost Creek Road
Carbon Hill, AL 35549
(205)924-9921

MISSOURI

Bornert, Paughnee
(Robert D. Bornert)
932 E Snider Street
Springfield, MO 65803
(417)833-2627

Cantrell, Mary
(Ernest Cantrell)
7047 N Garnet Lane
Strafford, MO 65757
(417)736-9017

Cravens, Doris
(Marvin L Cravens)
604 N Hovis Street
Mountain Grove, MO 65711
(417)926-5778

Cravens, Hallie
(Ellis Cravens)
9566 Highway Z
Hartville, MO 65667
(417)668-5954

Dailey, Sarah
(Larry Dailey)
656 Grand Point Boulevard
Sunrise Beach, MO 65079
(573)374-9537

Gardner, Dossie
(Don Gardner)
26 W Pearl
Aurora, MO 65605
(417)678-3278

Gould, Marjorie
(Robert Gould)
204 W Pleasant
Aurora, MO 65605
(417)678-5422

Hensley, Jean Ann
(Howard Hensley)
537 Piperpoint
Rogersville, MO 65742
(414)753-1108

McCloud, Johnnie
(Theron McCloud)
419 Magnolia Court
Lebanon, MO 65536
(417)532-3388
jmccloud@advertisenet.com

Scobey, Darlis
(James Scobey)
105 Oak Hill Downs Street
Farmington, MO 63640
(573)756-1683

MURFREESBORO

Basham, Earline
(Willard Basham)
335 Myers Road
Winchester, TN 37398

Breeding, Karen
(Gordon Breeding)
1907 Susan Drive
Murfreesboro, TN 37129
(615)867-3660
zanylady1000@yahoo.com

Denman, Susie
(E. H. Denman)
525 Golf Club Drive
Smithville, TN 37166
(615)597-7122

Dickerson, Helen
(Andrew Mizel Dickerson, Jr.)
914 Dogwood Drive
Murfreesboro, TN 37129

Martin, Peggy
(James W Martin)
1922 Battleground Drive
Murfreesboro, TN 37129
(615)896-4442

Martindale, Dana
(J. Craig Martindale)
2913 Pellas Place
Murfreesboro, TN 37127
(615)653-0858
w5bu@hotmail.com

Salisbury, Helen Margaret
(A.D. Salisbury)
1927 Memorial Boulevard
Murfreesboro, TN 37129

Salisbury, Rebecca
(Loyce Estes)
1033 Twin Oaks Drive
Murfreesboro, TN 37130
(615)410-7801
rebsalisbury@yahoo.com

Watson, Mary Leota
(David E Watson)
804 W Main Street
McMinnville, TN 37110
(931)473-7561
leotaw@blomand.net

NASHVILLE

Allen, Hester
(Paul Allen)
300 Bantam Court
LaVerne, TN 37086

Andrews, Jane
(Leonard Andrews)
7390 Cabot Drive
Nashville, TN 37209
(615)352-0145

Burnett, Mary Lee
(Cecil Burnett)
321 Raindrop Lane
Hendersonville, TN 37075

Maxedon, Chris
(Julian Maxedon)
2260 Highway 31
White House, TN 37188

Smith, Dolores
(Billy T Smith)
c/o Brookdale of Clarksville
2183 Memorial Drive
Clarksville, TN 37043
(931)358-3765

Stiles, Peggy
(John Stiles)
300 Bantam Court
Clarksville, TN 37043

SURVIVING SPOUSES OF MINISTERS BY PRESBYTERY CONTINUED

(Deceased spouse in parenthesis.)

NORTH CENTRAL

Gross, June
(Ronald Gross)
  2436 N 420th Street
  Oblong, IL 62449
  (217)932-2788

McCain, Violet
(Terence McCain)
  15804 Camden Avenue
  Eastpointe, MI 48021
  (586)774-4861

Smith, Evelyn
(Albert J. Smith)
  407 W Main Street Apt 131
  Wilkesboro, NC 28697
  (217)725-6870

Springer, Eileen
(Robert Springer)
  403 Prairie Ridge Court
  Eureka, IL 61530
  (309)467-5030

RED RIVER

Brown, Beth
(LaRoyce Brown)
  311 S 8th Street
  Marlow, OK 73055
  (580)658-3989

Morgan, Sharon
(Jerome Morgan)
  8420 Baumgarten Drive
  Dallas, TX 75228

Shelton, Barbara Ann
(Robert E Shelton)
  10508 Royalwood Drive
  Dallas, TX 75238
  (214)349-7162
  bshelton67@yahoo.com

Turpen, Mary Lou
(Brent Turpen)
  PO Box 577
  Locust Grove, OK 74352
  (918)803-2281
  mlturpen@hotmail.com

ROBERT DONNELL

Hunter, Jean
(James E. Hunter)
  1905 Delynn
  Hazel Green, AL 35750
  (256)838-3902

TENNESSEE-GEORGIA

Galloway, Katherine
(Cliff Galloway)
  7127 White Oak Valley Road
  McDonald, TN 37353

Kapperman, Linda
(Glenn Kapperman)
  2719 Rio Grande Road
  Chattanooga, TN 37421
  (423)894-7924

Naugher, Catherine
(Doyce Naugher)
  985 Mt Pleasant Road
  Rydal, GA 30171
  (770)382-1982

TRINITY

Allen, Ann M
(Paul Allen)
  311 E Hawkins Parkway Apt 115
  Longview, TX 75605
  (903)759-5508

Johnson, Clyde
(Dave Johnson)
  2801 E Travis Apt 108
  Marshall, TX 75672
  (903)938-9953

Leslie, Jenann
(Marvin E. Leslie)
  300 Henley Perry Drive
  Marshall, TX 75670
  (903)938-6642
  jenann.leslie@gmail.com

Ward, Suzie
(Kevin Ward)
  216 E Caroline
  Marshall, TX 75672

WEST TENNESSEE

Brown, Beverly
(Paul B. Brown)
  406 N McNeil Street
  Memphis, TN 38112
  (901)278-6909

Brown, Phyllis
(David Brown)
  1930 Mignon
  Memphis, TN 38107
  (901)274-1513

Butler, Shirley
(George A Butler)
  306 Flora Circle
  Newbern, TN 38059

Cook, Marcine
(Paul V. Cook)
  144 Big John Drive
  Martin, TN 38237
  (731)587-0787
  marcine175@aol.com

Davis, Willene
(Harold Davis)
  7820 Walking Horse Circle #311
  Germantown, TN 38138
  (901)757-1394

Drylie, Linda
(James Drylie)
  512 JE Blaydes Parkway
  Atoka, TN 38004
  (901)837-1627

Forester, Willie Mae
(J. C. Forester)
  833 Main Street
  McKenzie, TN 38201
  (731)352-3107

Hall, Patsy
(Charles R. Hall)
  4341 Pebble Garden Court
  Birmingham, AL 35235
  (205)538-7993

Hicks, Ruby
(Willam D. Hicks)
  3938 Cardinal Drive
  Union City, TN 38261
  (731)885-5887

Knight, Helen
(James Knight)
  8081 Jills Creek Drive
  Bartlett, TN 38133
  (901)387-0675

Laurence, Brenda
(G. Larry Laurence)
  2823 Nine Mile Road
  Enville, TN 38332
  (731)687-2022
  southernmoma@hotmail.com

Leslie, Cheryl
(Randall Leslie)
  3374 Walnut Grove Road
  Memphis, TN 38111
  (901)458-4413

Leslie, Marilyn
(Eugene Leslie)
  13155 Center Hill Road
  Olive Branch, MS 38654
  (731)613-0425
  eleslie1@bellsouth.net

McMahen, Sandra
(Rowe Gene McMahen)
  92 Stonewall Circle
  McKenzie, TN 38201
  (731)352-3067

Phelps, Doris
(Earl Phelps)
  172 Michie-Pebble Hill Road
  Stantonville, TN 38379
  (731)632-5107

Stott, Beverly
(Melvin Buddy Stott)
  911 Low Gap Road
  Princeton, WV 24740
  (731)364-5863
  bevstott@frontiernet.net

CUMBERLAND PRESBYTERIANS
SERVING OUTSIDE THE UNITED STATES

Please e-mail missionaries before mailing anything to them to determine the best way to send them letters or packages. If you want to communicate with missionaries in closed countries, first e-mail the Missions Ministry Team (Lthomas@cumberland.org) and we will forward your e-mail to the missionary.

Lee & Leslie Attema—Belize
email: leslieattema@icloud.com

Beth Wallace (Missionary Emeritus)—Colombia
e-mail: hbwcali@yahoo.com
oovoo and facetime: Boyce Wallace

Anay Ortega—Guatemala
e-mail: anayortegamonroy@hotmail.com
skype: Anay Ortega Monroy
oovoo: Anay Ortega

Fhanor & Socorro Pejendino—Guatemala
email: pastorfhanor@gmail.com
skype: Fhanor Pejendino Arcos
oovoo: pastorestulua

T T G—Kyrgyzstan
email: Lthomas@cumberland.org

D S L—Laos and Cambodia
email: Lthomas@cumberland.org

Carlos & Luz Dary Rivera—Mexico
email: caralrifra@une.lnet.co
oovoo: Carlos Rivera

Daniel & Kay Jang—Philippines
Ilollo Cumberland Mission Church
email: goingup129@hanmail.net

John & Joy Park—Iloilo, Philippines
email: barkmoksa@hanmail.net

Kenneth & Delight Hopson—Uganda
e-mail: ken.hopson@wgm.org
skype: Delight Hopson
oovoo: Kenneth Hopson

Jacob & Lindsey Sims—Brazil
e-mail: jacobdsims@gmail.com
Facebook - Sims Family Mission

Patrick & Jessica Wilkerson—deputation
e-mail: patrickwilkerson3@gmail.com

The Cumberland Presbyterian Church
has five families working in closed countries as
humanitarian workers.

NEW CHURCH DEVELOPMENTS & MISSION PROBES

ANDES

Aguadas
Cra 3 #7-14
Aguadas, Caldas
Colombia, SA
(576)851-4773
jeob40@hotmail.com
Pastor: Joaquin Orozco   (M1)
Began: 1996 (as re-development)

Chinchina
Mz 2 Casa 21, Urb. Milan
Dosquebradas, Ris
Colombia, SA
(476)322-2177
oikoninonia@gmail.com
Pastor: Rodrigo Martinez   (M1)

CAUCA VALLEY

Bugalagrande
Cra 8 No 7A-12
Bugalagrande, Colombia, SA

Carmelo
Veredo Carmelo
Limones, Cauca, Colombia, SA
Pastor: Juan Ventura   (M3)

Casa de Oracion

Dia de Salvacion
Pastor: Luis Cantor
(   )256-2835

Golondrinas
Corregimiento Golondrinas
Montebello, Colombia, SA
vallejo903@hotmail.com
Pastor: Ariel Vallejo

Guachucal
Centro
Guachucal, Colombia, SA
Iflesianuevavida15@gmail.com
Pastor: Martin Termal   (M3)

Ipiales
Cra 2A No 12-54
Ipiales, Colombia, SA
pastoscarealpe@hotmail.com
Pastor: Oscar Realpe   (M1)

Juanico
Vereda Juanico
Guapi, Colombia, SA
Pastor: Bernabe Angulo   (M3)

Limones
Corregimiento Limones
Guapi, Colombia, SA
Pastor: Henry Angulo   (M3)

Los Monos
Vereda Los Monos
Sapuyes, Colombia, SA
Pastor: Mario Paredes   (LS)

Manantial de Vida
Vereda de Brazo Seco
El Charco, Colombia, SA
Pastor: Sofinias Velazco   (M3)

Morales
Morales, Colombia, SA
johnydiana7@hotmail.com
Pastor: John Agredo   (M3)

Rios de Agua Viva
Trav 87 No 2-24
Buenatura, Colombia, SA
euripidesmoreno1@hotmail.com
Pastor: Euripides Moreno   (M1)

Sapuyes
Iglesia Presbiteriana C
Sapyues, Colombia, SA
walterviteri@gmail.com
Pastor: Oscar Rosero   (M3)

Villa Gorgona
Manzana C Casa 5 Santa Ana
Villa Gorgona, Colombia, SA
daniel_blanco04@hotmail.com
Pastor: Daniel Blanco   (M3)

Villavicencio
Villavicencio, Colombia, SA
german_millanco12@yahoo.com.mx
Pastor: German Millan

COVENANT

Cadiz
Cadiz, KY
Pastor: Danny York   (M1)
Began: 2008

DEL CRISTO

316 Christian Fellowship
2200 E Dartmouth Circle
Englewood, CO 80113
(720)253-3425
jeanhess@316denver.com
Pastor: Rick & Jean Hess   (M1)
Began: 08/10

Agape (formerly Marantha East)
12008 Fred Carter
El Paso, TX 79936
(915)592-6138
yaanaivitaly@yahoo.com
Pastor: Alfredo Rincon   (M1)
Began: 2007

Bethesda Korean Fellowship
139 Silverado Drive
Santa Teresa, NM 88008
(915)329-3451
pyongsanyu@hotmail.com
Pastor: Pyong San Yu   (M1)
Began: 03/10

EMAUS

Amaga
Cra 49 #49-18
Amaga, Antioquia
Colombia, South America
(574)847-3250
rebcaldas@une.net.co
Pastor: Jhon Jairo Arias   (M1)
Began: 1997

Envigado
Calle 38 Sur #40-45
Envigado, Antioquia
Colombia, South America
Pastor: Juan Fernando Maarales
          (M3)
Juanm@unisbc.edu.co

Istmina
San Barrio San Francisco
Istmina, Choco
Colombia, South America
Pastor: Yeison David Lopez

La America
Carrera 99 #41a-21
Medellin
Colombia, South America
adanvarilla@hotmail.com
Pastor: Lida Patricia Vargas (M3)
Adan Manuel Varilla   (M3)

GRACE

(0312)
Comunidad Biblica of Miami
6375 W Flagler Street
Miami, FL 33144
(305)801-6424
tonymardo@comcast.net
Pastor: Mardoqueo Munoz
Began: 01/16
(0309)
Naples Fellowship
842 Bent Creek Way
Naples, FL 34114
(931)273-0768
revga@hotmail.com
Pastor: Ramon Garcia   (M1

JAPAN

(8314)
Ichikawa Grace Mission Point
3-19-5 Sugano
Ichikawa-shi, Chiba-ken
272-0824 JAPAN
(047)326-8675
(047)326-8675 FAX
fwgc6854@mb.infoweb.ne.jp
Pastor: Yasuo Masuda   (M2)

RED RIVER

Church of St. Giles
3500 S Peoria Avenue
Tulsa, OK 74105
(918)760-6145
Pastor: William G. Webb, Jr. (M1)
(8426)
Marantha
2801 Biway Street
Fort Worth, TX 76114
(817)210-5571
sledadmartinez164@gmail.com
Pastor: Soledad Martinez   (M1)
Began: 2015

TENNESSEE-GEORGIA

Pikeville Mission
530 Sequatchie Road
Pikeville, TN 37367
(423)447-6897
Pastor: Rhonda McGowan   (M1)

WEST TENNESSEE

(9437)
Comunidad Cristiana Amor Y Fe
3097 Knight Road
Memphis, TN 38118
(830)872-6090
paul-tuba@hotmail.com
Pastor: Lugwin Paul Puloc Munoz
Began: 3/2016
(9196)
Cristo Salva Fellowship
3442 Tutwiler
Memphis, TN 38122
diannwhite12@yahoo.com
Pastor: Carlos Solito   (M1)
(9323)
Grace Fellowship
9160 Tchulahoma Road
Southaven, MS 38671
(662)393-2552
tthompson393@aol.com
Pastor: Tommy Thompson   (M1)

Iona Community of Faith
1790 Faxon Avenue
Memphis, TN 38112
website: www.iona.gutensite.com
(901)283-8062
wa4mff@aol.com
Pastor: Barry Anderson   (M1)

PROVISIONAL CHURCHES

"A provisional fellowship is a pre-existing non-English congregation that is being received into the Cumberland Presbyterian Church through an authorized assimilation process.

ARKANSAS

_____ (2135)
Arkansas Korean Loving Church
8201 Frenchmans Lane
Little Rock, AR 72209
(501)247-9527
Pastor: Jinook Jung

COVENANT

_____ (3420)
Zion CP Fellowship
1347 S 6th Street
Paducah, KY 42003
(270)442-6414
zioncpcinfo@gmail.com
Pastor: Steve/Teresa Shauf (M1)
Began: 10/2012

CUMBERLAND EAST COAST

_____ (2445)
Immanuel Presbyterian Church
67-17 215th
Oakland Gardens, NY 11364
Pastor: Soo Yeol Park
(646)599-4941
shwbpark@naver.com
_____ (2138)
Our Good Presbyterian Church
32132 Huntly Circle
Salisbury, MD 21804
(443)783-3809 (cell)
Pastor: Hyoung Sik Choi (M1)
Began: 2001

TENNESSEE GEORGIA

Baek Seok Church
3075 Landington Way
Duluth, GA 30096
(404)398-8469
mnb0924@yahoo.co.kr
Pastor: Seung Chon Han (M1)
_____ (2150)
Divinity Church
3480 Summit Ridge Parkway
Duluth, GA 30096
Pastor: Rev. Frederick Nah
Began: 2013

GJHS Ministries
3327 Duluth Highway
Duluth, GA 30096
(770)940-2365
gjhministryatl@gmail.com
Pastor: Jung Hee Jung (M1)
_____ (2130)
Korean Livingstone Presbyterian Church
3340 Bentbill xing
Cumming, GA 30041
(770)912-8477
barkmoksa@hanmail.net
Pastor: Rev Young Rae Park
(M1)

New York Chowon Mission Church
254-18 Northern Boulevard
Little Neck, NY 11362
(917)992-5200
lovedasol@gmail.com
Pastor: Si Hoon Park (M1)

Phillipians Church
2310 His Way
Lawrenceville, GA 30044
(678)462-7526
agatopia@hanmail.net
Pastor: Jin Koo Kang (M1)

Trinity Church
1050 Grace Drive
Lawrenceville, GA 30043
(678)622-2717
samil2110@yahoo.com
Pastor: Rev. Min Soo Kim (M1)
_____ (2103)
The Cross Mission
5260 Coacoochee Ter
Alpharetta, GA 30022
(404)421-4262
Pastor: Jea Kwang Lee (M1)
_____ (2125)
Walking with God Presbyterian Church
3299 Highway 120
Duluth, GA 30096
(678)600-2787
jaeyu117@yahoo.com
Pastor: Jae Hyung Yu (M1)

We Community Church
302 Satellite Boulevard
Suwanee, GA 30024
(678)908-9191
powerment@hotmail.com
Pastor: Hyang Koo Lee

TRINITY

_____
Ye Rang Korean Church (8602)
12320 Alameda Trail Circle #1309
Austin, TX 78727
(512)474-2646
preacherofgod@gmail.com
Pastor: Sung In Park (M1)

WEST TENNESSEE

_____
Redeemer Evangelical Church
7011 Poplar Avenue
Germantown, TN 38138
(901)737-3370
jimmylatimer@redeemerevangelical.com
Pastor: James M. Latimer

MISSION CHURCHES AND PASTORS
UNDER CARE OF MISSIONS MINISTRY TEAM
(General Assembly Ministry Council)

AUSTRALIA
"Australia CP Council of Churches"

Citinse Mission
(Provisional)
  2142 Swan Avenue
  Strathfield, NSW
  rsk2002@empal.com
  Pastor: Suk Kyn Ryu   (M1)

Darwin Dasom Korean
(Provisional)
  44 Dripstone Road
  Causurina, NT 0820
  hansongwee2@gmail.com
  Pastor: Sun Hee (Sunny) Hwang(M1)

Disciples
(Provisional)
  237 Botany Road
  Waterloo, NSW
  oldrooney@hotmail.com
  Pastor: Sung Yong Cho   (M1)

Hansaesun
(Provisional)
  21 James Street Lidcomb
  Lidcomb
  hansaesunchurch@gmail.com
  Pastor: Young Kwang Kim   (M3)

Melbourne Bang Joo
(Provisional)
  117 Murrumbeena Road
  Murrumbeena, VIC 3163
  min0430446647@gmail.com
  Pastor: Min Huh   (M1)

Sydney Korean
(Provisional)
  458 Burwood Road
  Belmore NSW 2192
  sydneykoreanchurch@gmail.com
  Pastor: Jong One Choi   (M1)

PROVISIONAL PASTORS:

Cho, Sung Yong
  6/58-62 Carnarvon Street
  Silverwater, NSW
  oldrooney@hotmail.com
Choi, Jong One
  458 Burwood Road
  Belmore 2192, NSW
  Phone: 61-414-641-200
  johnillcho@hanmail.net
Huh, Min
  2112 Eunka Street
  Chadstone, VIC 3148
  min0430446647@gmail.com
Hwang, Sun Hee
  1512 Lindsay Street
  Darwin, NT 0800
  hangsongwee@hanmail.net
Ryu, Suk Kyu
  9155 Manson Road
  Strathfield, NSW 2131
  rsk2002@empal.com

LICENTIATES:

Kim, Jiho
  31 Olga Street
  Chatswood NSW 2067
  lovepresage@naver.com
Kim, Young Kwang
  25 Clemsford Avenue
  Epping, NSW 2121
  basskk77@naver.com

CANDIDATES:

Lee, Donghyung
  7/1-3 Mary Street
  Lidcombe NWS 2141
  ldh8940@gmail.com
Lee, Joung Me (Sharon)
  2 Belmore Street
  Ryde NSW 2112
  jmlee153@naver.com
Lee, Seok Yun
  18 Queen Street
  NT0820
  lee7315465@naver.com
Nam, Mee Yae
  10 Blain Street
  Toongabbie NSW 2146
  ehddid2@daum.net
Park, Myung Soon
  237 Botany Road
  Waterloo NSW
Park, Yong Chul (John)
  2 Belmore Street
  Ryde NSW 2112
  morning0588@gmail.com

BRAZIL
Hosted by Missions Ministry Team

_____ (8313)
Mata De Sao Joao Church
  Nucleo Colonial JK
  Lote 56 Mata De Sao Joao
  48280-000, Bahia, BRAZIL
  (5571)9641-1307
  Pastor: Keishi Ishitsuka   (M1)
  (5571)9641-1307
  kishitsuka@hotmail.com

ORDAINED:

Santos, Carlos Nucleo
  Colonial JK
  Lote 56 Mata De Sao Joao
  48280-000, Bahia, BRAZIL
  (5571)3482-3484
  san_coc@hotmail.com

MISSIONARIES:

Jacob and Lindsey Sims
  Condomino Paarque Stella Maris
  Rua Italo Gaudensi, QD O, Casa 2
  BRAZIL
  (5571)8115-6481
  jacobdsims@gmail.com

GUATEMALA
"Guatemala CP Council of Churches"
24 Avenida 0-97 Zona 7
Colonia Altamira II Ciudad De
Guaremala, Guatermala

_____
Casa de Fe y Oracion
  31 calle 9-75 Colonia Miralvally
  Zona 6 de Mixco
  Guatemala

_____
Comunidad de Fe
  13 Avenida 20-58
  Colonia La Reformita Zona 12
  Ciudad de Fuatemala
  Guatemala

MISSIONS

_____
Nueva Esperanza
  17 Avenida 50-51 Zona 12
  Colonia La Colina Cuidad de
  Guatemala
  Guatemala

MISSIONARIES:

Reverend Fhanor Pejendino
  ph_apear@hotmail.com
Reverend Socorro Pejendino
  pastorasocorrod@hotmail.com
Ms Anay Ortega

HAITI
"Haiti CP Council of Churches"
<u>Hosted by Hope Presbytery</u>

<u>PROVISIONAL CHURCHES:</u>

Eglise Evangelique de Dufour
  Pastor: Jean Joab St Rouis   (M3)

Eglise E U-Chunen Gris de Gris-Gris
  Pastor: Kemson Lundy   (M3)

Eglise Evangelique de Lexi
  Pastor: Smith Fauvelt   (M3)

Eglise Evangelique de Mache Kabrit
  Pastor: Evetuel Theissaint   (M3)

Eglise Evangelique de Nan Akou
  Pastor: Sheslaire Georges   (M3)

Eglise Evangelique de Saint-Jules
  Pastor: Eddy Edouard   (M3)

MEXICO
"Mexico CP Council of Churches"
<u>Hosted by Red River Presbytery</u>

<u>PROVISIONAL CHURCHES:</u>

Casa del Alfarero
  C Norte 12 A Esq OTE 53
  Chalco Edo
  Mexico
  54-4-627-5570
  alaprep28@hotmail.com
  Pastor: Alejandro Alejo   (M1)

Iglesia Marantha
  Arroyo de Miumbre #1749
  Col Felipe Augeles
  Ciudad Juarez
  Mexico
  54-53-67-9103
  jessevega69@gmail.com
  Pastor: Jedidiah Vega   (M1)

Restauration de Vida
  Calle Benito Juarez #35
  Colonia Guadalupe Victoria
  Delegacion Gustavo A Madero
  Mexico
  54-5-318-7622
  castro_dan@hotmail.com
  Pastor: Jose Dan Castro   (M1)

MISSIONS

Fuente de Vida - Ajusco
  Calle Primera Cerrada de Hombres
  Ilustres 2B Colonia Santa Ceilia
  Tepetlapa Delebacion
  Xochimilco CP
  Ciudad Mexico

MISSIONARIES:

Reverend Carlos Rivera
Reverend Luz Dary Rivera

PROVISIONAL PASTORS:

Alejo, Alejandro (Robledo)
  Casa del Alfarero CP Church
  C Norte 12 Esq Ote 53 Col Union
  de GPE
  Chalco Mexico
  Phone: 46-27-5570
  aleprep28@hotmail.com
Castro, Jose Dan (Solis)
  Restauracion de Vida CP Church
  Calle C Col San Marcos
  Azcapotzalco C P 02020 Mexico
  Phone: 55-53-18-7622
  castro_dan@hotmail.com
Gallardo, Gabriel (Uzziel)
  NCD Mission Ajusco 1a Cda
  Hombres Ilustres 20B Sta Cecilia
  Tepetiapa Xochimilco Mexico
  DF CP 16880
  Phone: 55-48-1563
  pastoruzziel@hotmail.com
Mata, Jorge Fernando
  Marantha CP Church Towi 8127 Sta
  Fe Cd C Jaurez
  Chihuahua Mexico
  Phone: 656-62-59-975
  pastormata@hotmail.com

CANDIDATES:

Hernandez, Octavio
  c/o Iglesia Marantha
  Phone: 65-61-939157

PHILIPPINES
"Philippine CP Council of Churches"

God is our Hiding Place
(Provisional)
 Brgy Tabuc Suba Jaro Tall
 Iloilo, Philippines

Gracious Jesus Cumberland
Presbyterian
(Church)
 Cabang
 Oton, Iloilo
 Pastor: Alexander Duyac, Jr.   (M1)
_____(2321)
Iloilo Cumberland Presbyterian
(Church)
 PO Box 5
 Aduana Street
 Iloilo City 5000, Philippines
 Pastor: J Sean Saim   (M1)

Mostro Cumberland Presbyterian
(Mission)
 Brgy Mostro Anilao
 Iloilo, Philippines
 Pastor: Romeo Agana   (M2)

Pavia Cumberland Presbyterian
(Mission)
 Brgy Anilao Pavio
 Iloilo, Philippines
 Pastor: Manual Job Baldevia   (M1)

Sohoton Cumberland Presbyterian
(Mission)
 Brgy Sohoton Barotac Nuevo
 Iloilo, Philippines
 Pastor: Harold Henry Bonete   (M2)

MISSIONARIES:

Mr Daniel and Kay Jang
Reverend John and Joy Park

PASTORS:

Baldevia, Manuel Job
Duyac, Alexander, Jr.
 Brgy, Cabang, Oton, Iloilo
Saim, J Sean Espanueva
 c/o Iloilo CP Church
Saquilon, Ruperto Atlin (provisional)

LICENTIATES:

Agana, Romeo G, Jr.
 c/o Iloilo CP Church
Bonete, Harold Henry
 c/o Iloilo CP Church
Tagurigan, Alpha Faith Singcuenco
 c/o Iloilo CP Church

CANDIDATES:

Dyuac, Aldrandreb D
 c/o Gracious Jesus CP Church
Garnica, Darrel Von
 c/o Gracious Jesus CP Church
Yutig, Lucelle E
 c/o Gracious Jesus CP Church

SOUTH KOREA
"Korean CP Council of Churches"

_____(2221)
First Cumberland Presbyterian Church
of Korea
(Church)
 Hyundai I-park B-02
 Burim-dong 113
 Dongan-gu, Anyang-si
 Gyeonggi-do, Korea 431-787
 Phone: 82-70-8872-8033
 Pastor: Heungsoo Kang   (M1)
 Clerk: Yoon JinSub
 303-101 Raenian Ever heim Apt
 Naeson 2-dong, Uiwangsi
 Gyeonggi-do, Korea 437-761
 jinsyoon@gmail.com

Glory Church
(Mission)
 302 Si-Bum Building
 1342 Seocho 2-dong, Seocho-gu
 Seoul, Korea 137-861
 Phone: 82-2-3474-8405
 Pastor: Geumtaek Lim   (M1)
_____(2323)
New Life Church
(Mission)
 325-1 Donghyeon-dong
 Jecheon-si
 Chungcheongbud-do, Korea 390-190
 Phone: 82-10-6655-9188
 Pastor: Woonyong Yu   (M1)

Seum Church
(Mission)
 Seobu-ro 2105 beongil 26-6 101 ho
 Jang-gu, Suwan City, South Korea
_____(2324)
Ye-Il Church
(Mission)
 15 Seogyeong-ro, 28beong-gil
 Heungdeok-gu, Cheongiu-si
 Chungcheongbuk-do, Korea 361-803
 Phone: 82-42-232-6000
 Pastor: Dawie Ahn(M1)

PASTORS:

Ahn, Dawit (David)
 606-304 Gapyeong Jugong Apt
 Jungnim-dong, Heungdeck-gu
 Cheongju-si
 Chungcheongbuk-do
 Korea 361-850
 Phone: 82-10-2421-0219
 ankim91@hanmail.net
Kang, Huengsoo
 Hyundai I-park B-02, Burim-dong 113
 Dongan-gu, Anyang-si
 Gyeonggi-do, Korea 431-787
 Phone: 82-10-8428-0084
 halieus@hanmail.net
Kim, YoungHo (Steve)
 B02 Hyundai I-Space 1608-2
 Burim Dong, Dong An Gu
 AnYang City, Kyunggi Do S Korea
 Phone: 231-348-8033
 paidion4377@naver.com
Lee, Sangdo
 507-1501 Samik Green Apt
 Myeongil 1-dong, Gngdong-gu
 Seoul, Korea 134-782
 Phone: 82-10-3353-2907
 humanolsd@hanmail.net

Lee, Yongrae
 507 Je-Il Officetel, 99-20
 Yulgeon-dong, Jangan-gu
 Suwon-si, gyeonggi-do, Korea
 Phone: 82-10-9928-9012
 path0316@naver.com
Lim, Geumtaek
 302-si-Bum Building
 1342 Seocho 2dong, Seccho-gu
 Seoul, Korea 137-861
 Phone: 82-11-9044-5250
 limkt114@hanmail.net
Park, Bo-Seong
 304-28 Sinlim-Dong, Kwanak-Gu
 Seoul, Korea
 Phone: 002-884-3474
Yu, Woonyong
 325-1 Donghyeon-dong, Jecheon-si
 Chungcheongbuk-do, Korea 390-190
 Phone: 82-10-6655-9188
 lifeyu@hanmail.net

LICENTIATES:

Choi, Justin
 823-4 Naeson 1-dong, Uiwang-si
 Gyeonggi-do, Korea 437-838
 Phone: 82-10-2668-8795
 rev.choi@hotmail.com
Lee, Il-Do (Derek)
 151-2 Ongnyeon-dong
 Yeonsu-gu, Incheon, Korea
 Phone: 82-10-2627-2152
 monya215@naver.com

CAMP GROUNDS

ARKANSAS PRESBYTERY

Camp Peniel
Monte Williams
83 Camp Peniel Drive
Solgohachia, AR 72156
(501)354-5282

CHOCTAW PRESBYTERY

Camp Israel Folsom
Box 158
Broken Bow, OK 74728
(580)584-2099

COLUMBIA PRESBYTERY

Crystal Springs Camp, Inc.
21 Crystal Springs Camp Road
Kelso, TN 37348
(931)937-8621
Medley@cafes.net
Camp Manager: Carol Medley

PRESBYTERY OF EAST TENNESSEE

Camp Chilhowee
c/o Bill & Traci Pressley
1920 Old Chilhowee Loop Road
Maryville, TN 37865
(865)983-7084

Camp John Speer
c/o Dennis Elwell
2154 Viking Mountain Road
Greeneville, TN 37743
(423)636-1366
dpelwell@gmail.com
www.campjohnspeer.com

GRACE PRESBYTERY

Camp Bailey
Route 1 Box 386
Union, MS 39365

Caretaker: Mr. Lynn Frederick
P. O. Box 574
Carthage, MS 39051

MISSOURI PRESBYTERY

Camp Cumberland
South Greenfield, Missouri
(417)637-2059
Renee Rogers, Business Manager

MURFREESBORO PRESBYTERY

Crystal Springs
21 Crystal Springs Camp Road
Kelso, TN 37348
(931)937-8621

NASHVILLE PRESBYTERY

Camp Crystal Springs
21 Crystal Springs Camp Road
Kelso, TN 37348
(931)937-8621
Carol Medley, Director

TENNESSEE-GEORGIA PRESBYTERY

Camp Glancy
1370 Coppinger Cove Road
Sequatchie, TN 37374

TRINITY PRESBYTERY

Camp Gilmont
Rt. 6, Box 254
Gilmer, TX 75644
(903)797-6400

WEST TENNESSEE PRESBYTERY

Camp Clark Williamson
390 Mason Road
Humboldt, TN 38343
(800)655-8204
(731)784-3221
Mike Hannaford, Administrator
www.campclarkwilliamson.com

Explanation of Symbols

MC= Abbreviation for name of county or state if more than one church in the presbytery has the same name.

4= The number of Sundays each month the church engages in worship
M= Manse
E= Every Home Plan for The Cumberland Presbyterian
W= Organized women's ministry

P = Provisional Church
C = Church
F = Fellowship
U = Union Church

Synod/Presbytery Abbreviations

Church Name

Church Number

Telephone Number

Little Brown Church (MC) (4MEWC) GRWT9450

County

2307 Country Lane
Pleasant Valley, TN 37001
(901)654-0058 <Kingdom>

PA: John Doe   <M1>
1 Church St.
Pleasant Valley, TN 37001
(901)654-3210

AP: Mary Smith   <M1>
20 Serenity Lane
Pleasant Valley, TN 37001
(901)654-0123

CL: Jane Doe
30 Charity Rd.
Pleasant Valley, TN 37001
(901)654-2345

DE = Denominational Employee
ED = Editor
FM = Former Moderator
IT = In Transit to another Presbytery
M1 = Ordained Minister
M2 = Licentiate
M3 = Candidate
M4 = Minister of another denomination enrolled as a member through reciprocal agreement (Constitution 5.3)
M5 = Member of another denomination
M6 = Layperson serving church
M7 = Associate or Assistant Pastor
M8 = Military Chaplain
M9 = Non-Military Chaplain
M0 = Mentored Minister
MY = Missionary
OM = Other approved ministry
OP = Member of another presbytery
PR = Professor, Teacher
RT = Retired **or HR (honorably retired)**
ST = Student

CL= Clerk of Session
CO= Chair of commission appointed to govern church

AP = Associate/AssistantPastor
IP = Interim Pastor
LS = Layperson serving church
OD= Member of another denomination
PA = Installed Pastor
SS = Stated Supply

SUMMARY OF STATISTICS OF PRESBYTERIES BY SYNODS

GENERAL	1.Church Number	2.Active	3.Total	4.Church School	5.Prof. of Faith	6.Gains	7.Losses	8.Children Baptized	9. OUR UNITED OUT-REACH	10. Total Out-Reach Giving	11. All Other Expenses	12. Total Income Received	13. Value Church Prop. 1=1000
	1	2	3	4	5	6	7	8	9	10	11	12	13

GR: SYNOD OF GREAT RIVERS

Arkansas	(53)	54 1,985	2,883	1,135	53	163	257	16	134,302	423,787	1,966,667	2,385,401	22,324
Missouri	(20)	20 647	1,064	402	30	65	52	19	55,678	319,442	673,897	715,329	7,769
West Tennessee	(105)	93 5,554	8,948	3,288	83	205	516	35	298,909	837,986	5,450,303	6,174,899	56,919
SYNOD	(178)	167	12,895		166		825		488,889		8,090,867		87,012
TOTALS		8,186		4,825		433		70		1,581,215		9,275,629	

MI:SYNOD OF THE MIDWEST

Covenant	(43)	44 2,740	5,265	1,745	20	167	30	9	129,962	305,021	1,360,838	1,585,001	25,163
Cumberland	(52)	66 2,544	4,176	1,576	20	152	312	14	104,290	314,093	2,426,513	2,646,300	23,565
North Central	(30)	31 1,110	1,963	897	15	18	46	16	85,105	215,441	731,012	1,083,007	10,910
SYNOD	(125)	141	11,404		55		388		319,357		4,518,363		59,638
TOTALS		6,394		4,218		337		39		834,555		5,314,308	

MS:MISSION SYNOD

Andes	(16)	9 1,635	1,787	666	106	132	148	0	16,136	78,278	215,591	298,603	1,487
Cauca Valley	(16)	23 3,162	3,404	2,901	0	659	949	0	11,500	73,180	491,833	566,030	60,861
Choctaw	(3)	7 82	139	71	3	8	2	3	2,840	1,405	14,032	14,376	215
del Cristo	(53)	11 1,476	3,187	577	19	74	81	8	76,127	411,190	3,355,257	3,604,602	11,515
Emaus	(7)	4 331	363	140	16	44	35	0	0	14,625	56,658	80,171	269
Hong Kong	(10)	10 1,526	2,251	517	52	90	29	14	13,867	285,560	2,401,522	2,793,464	4,366
Japan	(18)	13 1,150	2,211	659	24	46	48	4	36,260	231,444	1,205,955	1,409,739	3,129
Red River	(58)	24 2,405	3,877	1,484	84	261	319	17	120,839	675,545	2,309,899	2,873,417	34,580
Trinity	(46)	22 1,511	2,191	756	7	135	184	25	107,355	526,225	2,756,087	3,163,241	26,328
SYNOD	(225)	123	19,410		311		1,795		384,924		12,806,834		142,750
TOTALS		13,278		7,771		1,449		71		2,297,452		14,803,643	

SE:SYNOD OF THE SOUTHEAST

Cum East Coast	(1)	7 137	167	52	0	5	5	0	1,300	23,058	109,096	133,057	280
East Tennessee	(64)	38 2,699	4,584	1,571	50	120	175	24	278,030	620,422	3,786,528	4,337,201	36,788
Grace	(104)	35 2,513	3,774	1,405	27	119	146	13	153,835	369,187	2,077,547	2,466,169	30,799
Hope	(10)	16 840	1,336	482	17	35	98	8	50,103	183,309	1,002,362	1,055,555	9,404
Robert Donnell	(27)	15 831	1,543	346	14	31	25	4	59,780	202,392	1,020,793	1,163,568	13,270
Tennessee-Georgia	(39)	25 1,778	2,205	687	14	54	90	7	71,177	229,968	1,886,037	2,025,788	21,081
SYNOD	(245)	136	13,609		122		539		614,225		9,882,363		111,622
TOTALS		8,798		4,543		364		56		1,628,336		11,181,338	

TN:TENNESSEE SYNOD

Columbia	(30)	38 1,280	2,156	771	26	51	160	11	81,976	259,277	1,618,109	1,972,228	20,778
Murfreesboro	(52)	45 3,028	4,517	2,033	34	90	153	8	284,876	508,522	2,719,385	3,394,543	34,168
Nashville	(62)	38 2,754	4,505	1,872	77	145	437	17	202,727	564,950	4,302,845	4,627,183	51,082
SYNOD	(144)	121	11,178		137		750		569,579		8,640,339		106,028
TOTALS		7,062		4,676		286		36		1,332,749		9,993,954	

GRAND	(917)	688	68,496		791		4,297		2,376,974		43,938,766		507,050
TOTALS		43,718		26,033		2,869		272		7,674,307		50,568,872	

Andes Presbytery
MISSION SYNOD

GENERAL		MEMBERSHIP			CHANGES			FINANCES				
1.Church Number	2.Active	3.Total	4.Church School	5.Prof. of Faith	6.Gains	7.Losses	8.Children Baptized	9. OUR UNITED OUT-REACH	10. Total Out-Reach Giving	11. All Other Expenses	12. Total Income Received	13. Value Church Prop. |1=1000
1	2	3	4	5	6	7	8	9	10	11	12	13
Armenia* 8903	546	546	100	40	29	29	0		17,982	36,164	44,633	450
Cartago 8906	89	143	70	9	2	49	0		3,181	14,363	19,310	100
Dosquebradas 8907	236	240	120	0	17	16	0		3,133	29,079	32,423	112
El Rebano* 8905	294	308	75	15	39	0	0		14,614	23,223	44,439	161
La Virginia Mis* 8913	32	34	51	4	7	7	0		1,419	3,991	5,212	21
Manizales 8914	110	114	60	10	2	4	0		7,818	14,643	22,809	13
Pereira 8916	230	298	135	25	28	30	0		30,131	70,017	108,618	500
Quimbaya 8920												
Presbytery 8900								16,136				
TOTALS 9	1,635	1,787	666	106	132	148	0	16,136	78,278	215,591	298,603	1,487

*Math error corrected. **Purged roll..

CHURCHES, PASTORS, AND CLERKS:

Armenia (4MWC)MSAN8903
Cra 15 #16-39
Armenia, Quindio
Colombia, South America
(574)745-4860 <S America>
FAX: (574)745-4895
ipc-armenia@hotmail.com
PA: John Jairo Correa <M1>
Calle 2 Norte #16-39
Armenia, Quindio
Colombia, South America
(574)745-0496
jjcedp07@hotmail.com
AP: Esperanza Diaz <M1>
Calle 2 Norte #16-19
Armenia, Quindio
Colombia, South America
(576)745-0496
CL: Jose Leobardo Castro
Calle 16 #14-43
Armenia, Quindio
Colombia, South America
57(310)-389-2361

Cartago (4MW C)MSAN8906
Cra 12 #8-47
Cartago, Valle
Colombia, South America
(572)214-5060 <S America>
FAX: (572)214-5060
presbicartago@gmail.com
PA: Juan Alexander Castano <M1>
Cra 9 norte #18-09 Barrio Villa Elena
Colombia, South America
(314)539-6086
juanalexandercastanovelez@yahoo.es
CL: Anciana Claudia Milena Munoz
Cra 4 #16-54
Colombia, South America

(311)753-5212
clamile74@hotmail.com

Dosquebradas (4MWC)MSAN8907
Calle 51 #15-32 (mailing)
Cra 15 A #50-31 (physical)
barrio Los Naranjos
Dosquebradas, Risaralda
Colombia, South America
(574)322-2938 <S America>
PA: Juan Esteban Blandon <M1>
Calle 51 #15-32
barrio Los Naranjos
Dosquebradas, Risaralda
Colombia, South America
(574)322-2938
juanestebanblandon@yahoo.com
CL: Anciana Diana Carolina Pineda
Cra 15 #56-33 Barrio Santa Teresita
Colombia, South America
(321)253-5887
dicapina18@gmail.com

El Rebano-Caldas (4WMCF)MSAN8905
Calle 128 Sur #48-13
barrio Central
Caldas, Antioquia
Colombia, South America
(574)278-0787 <S America>
FAX: (574)278-0787
rebcaldas@une.net.co
PA: Juan Alexander Castano <M1>
Calle 127 sur #42-38 Apto 301
Caldas, Antioquia
Colombia, South America
(574)306-4435
FAX: (574)278-0787
juanalexandercastanovelez@yahoo.com
CL: Consuelo Pena
Calle 130 Sur #57-09, Int 301
Caldas, Antioquia
Colombia, South America

(574)338-6190
FAX: (574)278-0787
chelitopeco@hotmail.com

La Virginia (4WMF)MSAN8913
Cra 4 bis #10-35
La Virginia, Risalda
Colombia, South America
(576)368-3589 <S America>
CL: Nora Patricia Diaz
Cra 4 bis #10-35
LaVirginia, Risalda
Colombia, South America
(311)312-2349
noris_1985@hotmail.com

Manizales (4WMC)MSAN8914
Calle 22 #25-33
Manizales, Caldas
Colombia, South America
(576)883-0383 <S America>
FAX: (576)833-0383
manizales50ipc@hotmail.com
PA: William Diaz <M1>
Calle 42 #26B-68
Manizales, Caldas
Colombia, South America
(574)890-2972
manizales50ipc@hotmail.com
CL: Luz Dary Herrera
Calle 5 #22-56
Manizales, Caldas
Colombia, South America
(576)889-0994

Pereira (4MWC)MSAN8916
Cra 12 bis #11-69
Pereira, Risaralda
Colombia, South America
(574)333-9295 <S America>
FAX: (574)324-4110

ANDES PRESBYTERY CONTINUED

cumberlandpres@une.net.co
PA: David Montoya   <M1>
  Cra 12 bis #11-69
  Pereira, Risaralda
  Colombia, South America
  (574)324-4109
  FAX: (574)324-4110
  adamonva@gmail.com
AP: Luz Maria Heilbron   <M1>
  Cra 12 bis #11-51
  Pereira, Risaralda
  Colombia, South America
  (576)333-9295
  pastorapresbi@hotmail.com
AP: Ricardo Castaneda
  Urbanizacion Casas de Milan
  Manzana 2 Casa 21
  (305)337-5131
  rijcha@gmail.com
AP: Diana Maria Valdez   <M1>
  Urbanizacion Casas de Milan
  Manzana 2 Casa 21
  (305)240-3165
  dianamariavaldezduque@gmail.com
AP: Geovanny Lopez   <M2>
  Jardin Etapa 1 Manzana 11 Casa 9
  Colombia, South America
  (314)347-5132
  carlogyo@hotmail.com
CL: Shirley Murillo
  Cra 12 bis #11-69
  Pereira, Risaralda
  Colombia, South America

Quimbaya   (C)MSAN89220
  Cra 6 #25-54
  Quimbaya, Quindio
  Colombia, SA
  (576)752-3570
SS: Jorge Enrique Jimenez   <M2>
  Urb Manantiales MzC Casa 6
  Armenia, Quindio
  Colombia, South America
  (321)643-0693
  joenjimu@yahoo.es
CL: Session Clerk
  Cra 6 #25-54
  Quimbaya, Quindio
  Colombia, SA

OTHERS ON MINISTERIAL ROLL:

Arias, John Jairo   <M1 WC>
  Calle 144 sur #196-08 / Apto 202
  Caldas, Antioquia
  Colombia, South America
  (57)317-693-1162
  sajoarias@hotmail.com
Gentry, Michele   <M1 M9>
  Urb San Jorge casa 28
  Km 8 via a La Tebaida
  Armenia, Quindio
  Colombia, South America
  (318)285-1161
  gentry.andes@yahoo.com
Guerrero, Luz Dary   <M1 MY>
  Calle 22 #25-33
  Manizales, Caldas
  Colombia, South America
  (576)888-4203
  clementinajacobo7@hotmail.com
Munoz, Gerardo   <M1 WC>

Orozco, Joaquin   <M1 OM>
  Cra 3 #7-14
  Aguadas, Caldas
  Colombia, South America
  (576)851-4773
  jeob40@hotmail.com
Martinez, Rodrigo   <M1 WC>
  Mz2 Casa 21 Urb Casas De Milan
  Dosquebradas, Risaralda
  COLOMBIA, SA
  oikoinonia@gmail.com
  (576)322-2177
Valencia, Nulbel   <M1 RT>
  Diag 11D Casa 11 urbGemelas
  Dosquebradas, Risaralda
  Colombia, South America
  (576)330-7704
  nava1928@hotmail.com
Velez, Gabriel   <M1 RT>
  Calle 8A #16A-26, Villa Fanny
  Dosquebradas, Risaralda
  Colombia, South America
  (576)330-1168

OTHER LICENTIATES ON ROLL:

Cardona, Nancy   <M2 ST>
  Calle 51 #15-32
  Dosquebradas, Risaralda
  Colombia, South America
  (576)322-2938
  nancycardona10@yahoo.com
Giraldo, Juan Pablo   <M2>
  Calle 51 #15-32
  barrio Los Naranjos
  Dosquebradas, Risaralda
  Colombia, South America
  (576)322-2938
Sarmiento, Liliana Patricia   <M2>
  Calle 50 #15-24 Barrio
  Los Naranjos Dosquebradas
  Colombia, South America
  (312)622-2797
  lilianasarmi23@gmail.com

OTHER CANDIDATES ON ROLL:

Castaneda, Liliana   <M3>
  Cra 4 #21-39 Barrio La Paz Quimbaya
  Colombia, South America
  (317)290-0110
  licabo2008@hotmail.com
Correa, Juan David   <M3>
  Calle 78 #87014 Robledo Palenque
  Medellin
  Colombia, South America
  (312)769-7711
  juanda_519@hotmail.com
Giraldo, Marcela   <M3>
  Calle 68 D #40-15
  Manizales, Caldas
  Colombia, South America
  (576)878-5412
Llanos, Victor Hugo   <M3>
  Calle 22 #25-33 Manizales
  Colombia, South America
  (316)285-4359
  victorllanos40@hotmail.com
Lopez, Martin Emilio   <M3>
  Calle 15 #10-22
  La Virginia, Risaralda
  Colombia, South America
  (310)820-6216
  lopezrestrepomartinemilio@yahoo.es

Osorio, Jorge   <M3>
  Cra 16 #11-07
  Colombia, South America
  (320)757-1888
  jopingo@hotmail.es
Rodriquez, Luz Adriana   <M3>
  Calle 15 #10-22 La Virginia
  (314)612-9702
  annasantilo2@hotmail.com

Arkansas Presbytery
GREAT RIVERS SYNOD

GENERAL		MEMBERSHIP		CHANGES				FINANCES				
1.Church Number	2.Active	3.Total	4.Church School	5.Prof. of Faith	6.Gains	7.Losses	8.Children Baptized	9. OUR UNITED OUT-REACH	10. Total Out-Reach Giving	11. All Other Expenses	12. Total Income Received	13. Value Church Prop. 1=1000
1	2	3	4	5	6	7	8	9	10	11	12	13
Appleton* 1202	11	11	20	0	0	19	0	500	2,127	15,103	17,230	40
Arkansas Loving* 2135	27	28	21	0	1	28	0	500	7,150	91.715	98,865	700
Barren Fork 1501	99	112	57	1	2	1	0	7,460	13,146	70,114	86,944	400
Ben Lomond 1301	5	7	10	0	0	0	0	0	2,898	11,945	20,463	80
Bethesda 1302	53	73	42	8	13	2	0	0	9,533	78,333	77,528	957
Booneville 1401	43	49	6	2	5	1	0	6,113	13,530	48,092	61,130	395
Byron 1508	11	11	12	No Report Received			0	300	0	0	0	287
Calico Rock 1503	98	115	53	0	3	4	0	14,225	49,081	90,972	140,053	1,524
Camden 1303	47	47	43	3	5	7	3	2,429	8,500	52,936	65,000	330
Camp Ground 1101	39	88	15	0	0	2	0	6,407	12,992	50,068	63,175	650
Caulksville 1402	193	230	60	1	1	5	1	4,931	45,514	90,880	110,212	695
Crossroads 1102	33	33	16	0	33	0	0	495	4,686	59,023	30,130	0
Dilworth 1304	6	12	14	0	0	0	0	0	4,728	22,389	38,384	125
Dover 1203	21	21	15	No Report Received			0	3,221	0	0	0	275
E. T. Allen 1307	17	17	12	No Report Received			0	0	0	0	0	225
Faith-Hopewell 1502	92	117	57	2	3	7	0	11,672	20,423	104,896	116,721	1,400
Falls Chapel 1308	45	45	32	2	10	2	0	0	6,241	51,643	72,392	n/a
Fellowship (BC) 1505	96	189	35	2	4	2	0	13,200	25,520	106,411	131,991	1,465
Fellowship (OC) 1309	38	55	38	2	0	1	0	4,174	7,497	37,197	41,800	117
Fomby 1310	7	21	8	0	1	1	0	0	3,669	12,147	16,361	138
Fort Smith 1406	35	170	15	0	0	2	0	1,984	3,755	50,864	21,742	800
Grace 1405	33	33	14	6	6	1	0	4,588	9,742	32,481	45,810	272
Gum Springs (WC) 1205	7	8	11	0	0	1	0	0	1,106	7,605	9,684	n/a
Hector 1207	13	48	12	0	0	1	0	0	5,686	20,114	30,258	93
Lake Hamilton 1221	68	68	23	No Report Received			0	0	0	0	0	400
Lockesburg 1311	3	3	0	No Report Received			0	0	0	0	0	162
Marietta* 1408	46	46	24	1	5	6	1	0	735	26,084	37,828	350
Mars Hill 1211	28	41	28	0	2	1	0	500	500	23,745	24,920	225
Mt. Carmel* 1212	38	39	20	2	0	1	0	6,810	8,697	39,978	63,337	200
Mt. Olive 1517	16	26	10	0	0	5	0	1,115	21,646	11,401	35,254	230
New Hope 1510	10	10	8	0	1	1	0	2,638	3,164	15,662	26,432	375
Old Union 1409	31	42	28	4	4	12	0	5,336	7,230	22,933	57,025	123
Oxford 1511	26	26	35	0	0	0	0	350	6,715	7,963	20,809	175
Palestine* 1103	80	80	55	0	0	38	3	3,850	14,101	118,208	131,251	1,575
Pilot Prairie 1411	8	14	6	No Report Received			0	0	0	0	0	50
Pine Bluff, 1st 1104	13	103	0	No Report Received			0	0	0	0	0	766
Pine Ridge* 1105	14	23	10	0	1	3	0	0	2,676	38,166	51,263	402
Pineville 1512	68	86	35	7	14	1	2	9,425	26,077	130,586	119,544	750
Pleasant Grove 1214	5	9	5	No Report Received			0	0	0	0	0	70
Provo 1314	11	38	25	No Report Received			0	0	0	0	0	125
Rodney 1513	19	19	15	3	4	0	0	123	1,042	18,611	21,663	65
Rose Hill 1106	65	65	40	0	4	1	0	8,250	13,595	67,782	82,503	1,000
Russellville 1216	121	228	40	0	3	3	0	3,390	6,287	170,467	169,199	1,700
Salem (FC)* 1514	23	23	10	0	0	6	0	1,764	2,750	16,980	16,540	250
Searcy 1218	29	53	20	0	0	1	0	1,200	3,335	20,119	26,949	400
Shaver 1413	1	1	0	No Report Received			0	0	0	0	0	10
Shell Chapel 1108	6	28	0	0	0	0	0	637	2,976	9,936	10,301	500
Sherwood** 1220	17	27	5	0	0	153	0	120	1,045	42,055	45,975	777
Sidney 1515	9	18	9	No Report Received			0	0	0	0	0	200
Sulphur Springs 1315	48	48	4	1	1	1	0	0	0	27,455	27,513	27
Trimble Camp G* 1504	42	49	24	0	30	1	0	4,297	10,960	44,519	36,316	365
Trinity 1219	14	35	0	1	2	2	2	0	803	20,499	21,479	220
Walkerville 1317	12	12	12	0	0	0	0	2,298	3,815	27,893	24,403	150
Walnut Grove 1414	35	65	15	5	5	0	0	0	2,758	29,256	30,221	175
TOTALS 54	1,985	2,883	1,135	53	163	257	16	134,302	423,787	1,966,667	2,385,401	22,324

*Math error corrected. **Purged roll.

ARKANSAS PRESBYTERY CONTINUED

CHURCHES, PASTORS, AND CLERKS:

Appleton   (W4C)GRAR1202
608 McGowan Road (mailing)
320 Tate Street (physical)
Atkins, AR 72823
( )   <Pope>
CL: Pam Simpson
3 Highway 124
Jerusalem, AR 72080
(501)669-2999

Arkansas Loving   (P)GRAR2135
1603 Coolhurst Avenue
Sherwood, AR 72120
(501)247-5953   <Pulaski>
swcho100491@gmail.com
PA: Jinook Jung   <M1>
1603 Coolhurst Avenue
Sherwood, AR 72120
(501)247-5953
swcho100491@gmail.com
CL: Sun Cha Stamp
121 Gravel Lane
Sherwood, AR 72120

Barren Fork   (4MWC)GRAR1501
782 Barren Fork Road
Mount Pleasant, AR 72561
(870)346-5121   <Izard>
PA: Alan Meinzer   <M1>
780 Barren Fork Road
Mount Pleasant, AR 72561
(870)612-3936
brotheralan@centurylink.net
CL: Brandon Love
PO Box 262
Mount Pleasant, AR 72561
(870)291-0772

Ben Lomond   (4C)GRAR1301
180 LR 39 (mailing)
Ogden, AR 71853
495 N Main Street (physical)
Ben Lomond, AR 71823
( )   <Sevier>
kmillz13@hotmail.com
OD: Herman R Welch   <M5>
180 LR 39
Ogden, AR 71853
(903)748-2126
herawe@yahoo.com
CL: Kimberly Hatridge
PO Box 53
Ben Lomond, AR 71823
(870)287-4215

Bethesda   (4MW C)GRAR1302
395 Ouachita 47
Camden, AR 71701
(870)231-4909   <Ouachita>
PA: Ron Fell   <M1>
PO Box 285
Fairfield, IL 62837
(618)638-3744
r.fell80@gmail.com
CL: Ben Fields
451 Ouachita 47
Camden, AR 71701
(870)231-5080

bfields2011@hotmail.com

Booneville   (4MEW C)GRAR1401
PO Box 163 (mailing)
355 Sharp Street (physical)
Booneville, AR 72927
( )   <Logan>
church@boonevillecpc.com
PA: Henry Jenkins   <M1>
PO Box 148 (mailing)
90 W Grove (physical)
Magazine, AR 72943
(479)969-8351
henryj@magtel.com
CL: Janet Bedene
PO Box 7 (mailing)
113 Pine Street(physical)
Ratcliff, AR 72951
(479)847-6746
phaparis@magtel.com

Byron   (4WC)GRAR1508
PO Box 524 (mailing)
Byron Road, Viola, AR (physical)
Calico Rock, AR 72519
(870)291-8542   <Fulton>
calicowild@hotmail.com
CL: Jeanne Perry
PO Box 524
Calico Rock, AR 72519
(870)291-8542
calicowild@hotmail.com

Calico Rock   (4MEWC)GRAR1503
PO Box 315 (mailing)
692 AR 56 Highway E (physical)
Calico Rock, AR 72519
(870)297-3931   <Izard>
FAX: (870)297-3151
crcpc01@gmail.com
PA: Thomas D Campbell   <M1>
PO Box 343
Calico Rock, AR 72519
(870)297-3931
FAX: (870)297-3151
tdcampbellar@gmail.com
CL: Carolyn Jeffery
PO Box 183
Calico Rock, AR 72519
(870)297-8530
cjeffery6@gmail.com

Camden   (4MEWC)GRAR1303
1545 California Avenue
Camden, AR 71701
(870)836-8712   <Ouachita>
CL: Jimmy Vaughan
1607 W 3rd Street
Fordyce, AR 71742
(870)818-1512
jvaughan103@hotmail.com

Camp Ground   (4WMC)GRAR1101
1548 E AR 274 Highway
Hampton, AR 71744
(870)798-4302   <Calhoun>
PA: Garland Skidmore   <M1>
2083 US Highway 278 E
Hampton, AR 71744
(870)798-4634
CL: Shirley Strickland

1783 E AR 274 Highway
Hampton, AR 71744
(870)918-2344
strick6@sat-co.net

Caulksville   (4MWC)GRAR1402
PO Box 2 (mailing)
23 W Main, Caulksville, AR (physical)
Ratcliff, AR 72951
(479)635-4301   <Logan>
PA: Bill Van Meter   <M1>
10626 Highway 41
Charleston, AR 72933
(479)965-2998
revbill46@gmail.com
CL: Cherre Nietert
10201 Nietert Lane
Branch, AR 72928
(479)438-0673

Crossroads   (4C)GRAR1102
16904 Old Mill Road
Little Rock, AR 72206
(501)888-4190
PA: Jack Ryan   <M1>
8806 Kennesaw Mountain Drive
Mabelvale, AR 72103
(501)749-8572
PA: Dwight Shanley   <M1>
16904 Old Mill Road
Little Rock, AR 72206
(501)888-4190
dwightshanley@att.net
CL: Betty Kettles
16904 Old Mill Road
Little Rock, AR 72206
(501)888-4190
r.kettles@yahoo.com

Dilworth   (4C)GRAR1304
305 N 6th Street (mailing)
De Queen, AR 71832
2517 N Red Bridge Road (physical)
Horatio, AR 71842
(870)642-8051   <Sevier>
mtcarmel2@windstream.net
OD: Byron G Sullivan   <M5>
305 N 6th Street
De Queen, AR 71832
(870)642-8051
mtcarmel2@windstream.net
CL: Nita Sue Sullivan
305 N 6th Street
De Queen, AR 71832
(870)642-8051
mtcarmel2@windstream.net

Dover   (4MWC)GRAR1203
29 Maple Street (mailing)
Hector, AR 72843
96 Waters Street (physical)
Dover, AR 72837
(479)331-3130   <Pope>
markoe@centurytel.net
OD: Mike Galloway   <M5>
2821 Linker Mount Road
Dover, AR 72837
(479)331-0254
markoe@centurytel.net
CL: Beth McAlister
29 Maple Street

ARKANSAS PRESBYTERY CONTINUED

Hector, AR 72843
beth.ann56@hotmail.com

E T Allen   (4WC)GRAR1307
PO Box 822 (mailing)
153 Highway 71 N
Ashdown, AR 71822
( )   <Little Rive>
CL: Glen Ray Bowman
1050 Oak Place
Ashdown, AR 71822
(903)824-5000
botech64@aol.com

Faith-Hopewell   (4WC)GRAR1502
3895 Harrison Street
Batesville, AR 72501
(870)612-5949   <Independence>
PA: Rian Puckett   <M1>
55 Ham Street
Batesville, AR 72501
(731)288-7742
bro.rianpuckett@gmail.com
CL: Ionna Hess
3075 O'Neal Road
Batesville, AR 72501
(870)793-5530
ionnahess@yahoo.com

Falls Chapel   (4MC)GRAR1308
182 Hunter Falls Loop (mailing)
127 LW Davis Road (physical)
Lockesburg, AR 71846
( )   <Sevier>
CL: Ann Keith
182 Hunter Falls Loop
Lockesburg, AR 71846
(870)289-6834
memaplayground@windstream.net

Fellowship (BC)   (4EWC)GRAR1505
PO Box 866 (mailing)
1206 E 9th Street (physical)
Mountain Home, AR 72653
(870)425-5419   <Baxter>
info@fellowshipcumberland.org
PA: Gary Robert Tubb   <M1>
103 Forest Drive
Mountain Home, AR 72653
grtubb@yahoo.com
(870)424-0603
CL: Andy Marts
393 County Road 1085
Mountain Home, AR 72653
(870)481-6092
amarts@centurytel.net

Fellowship (OC)   (4WC)GRAR1309
478 Ouachita 54 (mailing)
2855 Ouachita 3 (physical)
Camden, AR 71701
( )   <Ouachita>
PA: Roberta Smith Johnson   <M1>
397 Ouachita 54
Camden, AR 71701
(870)231-5827
CL: Charles T Jeffus
478 Ouachita 54
Camden, AR 71701
(870)231-9994
charlesjeffus@yahoo.com

Fomby   (4C)GRAR1310
704 Highway 317 (mailing)
1215 Highway 32 E (physical)
Ashdown, AR 71822
(870)898-2856   <Little Rive>
carole4485@att.net
CL: Carole C Booth
704 Highway 317
Ashdown, AR 71822
(870)898-2856
carole4485@att.net

Fort Smith   (4MEWC)GRAR1406
605 N 47th Street
Fort Smith, AR 72903
(479)782-0454   <Sebastian>
FAX: (479)782-0454
ksstamps@msn.com
CL: Janie Stamps
4008 Logan Lane
Fort Smith, AR 72903
(479)478-0161
bjstamps@msn.com

Grace   (4C)GRAR1405
2451 Wedington Drive
Fayetteville, AR 72701
(479)442-6772   <Washington>
PA: Tom Merchant   <M1>
18784 Shoreline Way
Fayetteville, AR 72703
(231)557-5435
merchantt48@gmail.com
CL: Robin Thomas
1195 N White Rock Lane
Fayetteville, AR 72704
(479)521-0371
rthomas@mman.com

Gum Springs(WC)   (4C)GRAR1205
1717 W Arch Avenue (mailing)
Gum Springs Road (physical)
Searcy, AR 72143
(501)268-2615   <White>
SS: Jim Bradberry   <M3>
120 Hummingbird Lane
Searcy, AR 72143
(501)278-9750
CL: J C Holleman
1717 W Arch Avenue
Searcy, AR 72143
(501)268-2615

Hector   (4MWC)GRAR1207
PO Box 53 (mailing)
29 Maple (physical)
Hector, AR 72843
(479)747-7561   <Pope>
CL: Beth McAlister
PO Box 53
Hector, AR 72843
(479)747-7561
beth.ann56@hotmail.com

Lake Hamilton   (4 C)GRAR1221
2891 Airport Road
Hot Springs, AR 71913
(501)760-3800   <Garland>
lakehamiltoncpc@yahoo.com
CL: Tamara Stroope

2891 Airport Road
Hot Springs, AR 71913

Lockesburg   (1C)GRAR1311
279 N Park Avenue (mailing)
114 W Walnut (physical)
Lockesburg, AR 71846
( )   <Sevier>
CL: Joe E Bush
279 N Park Avenue
Lockesburg, AR 71846
(870)289-2433

Marietta   (4C)GRAR1408
623 Church Street (mailing)
2604 West Main (physical)
Charleston, AR 72933
(479)965-0224   <Franklin>
CL: Tim Aldridge
623 Church Street
Charleston, AR 72933
(479)965-7639
dcotim58@live.com

Mars Hill   (4WC)GRAR1211
172 Thompson Lane (mailing)
1224 State Route 363 (physical)
Pottsville, AR 72858
( )   <Pope>
PA: Jo Warren   <M1>
811 Wall Street
Morrilton, AR 72110
(501)354-4139
pastorjo47@ymail.com
CL: Gary Thompson
172 Thompson Lane
Pottsville, AR 72858
(479)970-4652
thompgary@gmail.com

Mt Carmel   (4C)GRAR1212
1470 Mt Carmel Road W
London, AR 72847
(479)293-4447   <Pope>
mtcarmel@centurylink.net
CL: Jennifer Metz
276 Metz Lane
London, AR 72847
(479)293-4229
jmetz54@hotmail.com

Mt Olive   (4EC)GRAR1517
214 Bear Trail Hollow (mailing)
5539 Mt Olive Road (physical)
Melbourne, AR 72556
(870)368-4923   <Izard>
bobeth@centurytel.net
PA: Christopher Anderson   <M1>
14 Indian Springs Road
Batesville, AR 72501
(870)805-0886
csanderson@memphisseminary.edu
CL: Mary Beth Jeffery
214 Bear Trail Hollow
Melbourne, AR 72556
(870)368-4923
bobeth@centurytel.net

New Hope   (2C)GRAR1510
25 Pine Hill Road (mailing)
3655 Bethesda Road (physical)

ARKANSAS PRESBYTERY CONTINUED

Batesville, AR 72501
( )   <Independence>
verenaherrin@yahoo.com
PA: Rian Puckett   <M1>
55 Ham Street
Batesville, AR 72501
(731)288-7742
bro.rianpuckett@gmail.com
CL: Verena Herrin
25 Pine Hill Road
Batesville, AR 72501
(870)793-6145
verenaherrin@yahoo.com
_____

Old Union   (4C)GRAR1409
PO Box 477 (mailing)
Old Union Road (physical)
Magazine, AR 72943
( )   <Logan>
PA: Henry Jenkins   <M1>
PO Box 148
Magazine, AR 72943
(479)969-8352
henryj@magtel.com
CL: Lee Strickland
PO Box 477
Magazine, AR 72943
(479)849-0198
eljws1@live.com
_____

Oxford   (4U)GRAR1511
618 Camp Ground Road (mailing)
211 Main Street (physical)
Oxford, AR 72565
( )   <Izard>
SS: Bobby D Coleman   <M1>
704 E Webb Street
Mountain View, AR 72560
(870)213-5410
bobbycoleman@gmail.com
CL: Willetta Everett
618 Camp Ground Road
Oxford, AR 72565
(870)258-7798
weverett@centurytel.net
_____

Palestine   (4MEWC)GRAR1103
PO Box 98 (mailing)
223 South Main Street (physical)
Palestine, AR 72372
(870)581-2600   <St. Francis>
FAX: (870)581-2600
PA: Jason Chambers   <M1>
131 E Woods Street
Palestine, AR 72372
(870)807-1930
jmchambers@memphisseminary.edu
CL: Lisa Alldredge
PO Box 803
Palestine, AR 72372
(870)581-2913
lsatmall@yahoo.com
_____

Pilot Prairie   (4MC)GRAR1411
PO Box 1873
Waldron, AR 72958
(479)637-3938   <Scott>
CL: Lee Ann Forest
PO Box 1873
Waldron, AR 72958
_____

Pine Bluff 1st   (4W C)GRAR1104
2401 Camden Road
Pine Bluff, AR 71603
( )   <Jefferson>
PA: Barbara Brewer   <M1>
1360 White Oak Bluff Road
Rison, AR 71665
(870)325-6449
CL: Catherine Currington
205 Moss Road
White Hall, AR 71602
(870)247-3839
_____

Pine Ridge   (4C)GRAR1105
4890 Grant 14
Grapevine, AR 72057
(870)942-1827   <Grant>
PA: James (Jim) Bradshaw   <M1>
415 S Red Street
Sheridan, AR 72150
(870)942-2525
CL: Buren Walker
336 Grant 748
Sheridan, AR 72150
(870)942-4790
_____

Pineville   (4MWC)GRAR1512
PO Box 256 (mailing)
1229 AR 223 Highway (physical)
Pineville, AR 72566
(870)297-4104   <Izard>
PA: Robert (Toby) Davis   <M1>
1211 AR 223 Highway
Pineville, AR 72566
(901)826-5755
pastortobydavis@gmail.com
CL: Janie Jenkins
PO Box 504
Calico Rock, AR 72519
(870)297-3991
djjenkins@centurytel.net
_____

Pleasant Grove   (2C)GRAR1214
1083 Highway 305 S
Searcy, AR 72143
(501)796-3466   <White>
CL: Robbie Stroud
1922 Highway 31 N
Beebe, AR 72012
(501)882-3262
_____

Provo   (4C)GRAR1314
131 LR 47 (mailing)
Ashdown, AR 71822
125 Dooley Road (physical)
Lockesburg, AR 71846
( )   <Sevier>
CL: Betty Crow Ward
180 B McHorse Road
Lockesburg, AR 71846
_____

Rodney   (2EC)GRAR1513
117 Flint Rock Trail (mailing)
1333 Rodney Road (physical)
Jordan, AR 72519
( )   <Baxter>
PA: Dave Williamson   <M1>
PO Box 67
Dolph, AR 72528
(870)499-7448
CL: Carol Lee

1364 Rodney Road
Jordan, AR 72519
(870)499-3238
txgrany69@yahoo.com
_____

Rose Hill   (4MWC)GRAR1106
1031 Binns Drive (mailing)
2133 Highway 83 N (physical)
Monticello, AR 71655
(870)367-5114   <Drew>
gsaray@att.net
PA: Bruce Hamilton   <M1>
1037 Binns Drive
Monticello, AR 71655
(870)224-5007
bruce@hamiltonnet.org
CL: Stephanie Ray
122 E Shelton Avenue
Monticello, AR 71655
(870)723-3785
gsaray@att.net
_____

Russellville   (4WC)GRAR1216
1200 N Arkansas Avenue
Russellville, AR 72801
(479)968-1061   <Pope>
FAX: (479)880-0071
fcpcrussellville@yahoo.com
PA: Steve Mosley   <M1>
320 N Sherman Circle
Russellville, AR 72801
(479)968-1061
FAX: (479)880-0071
stevemosley@hotmail.com
CL: Deanna Boston
721 Kovel Court
Russellville, AR 72801
(479)890-3880
fcpcrussellville@yahoo.com
_____

Salem (FC)   (4MWC)GRAR1514
1003 Flint Springs Road (mailing)
Viola, AR 72583
Highway 5 S, Salem, AR (physical)
( )   <Fulton>
salemcumberlandchurch@gmail.com
SS: Bobby D Coleman   <M1>
704 E Webb Street
Mountain View, AR 72560
(870)269-6010
bobby.coleman@gmail.com
CL: Bonnie Brown
1003 Flint Springs Road
Viola, AR 72583
(870)458-2657
bbrown325@centurytel.net
_____

Searcy   (4MWC)GRAR1218
100 E Race Street
Searcy, AR 72143
(501)268-8278   <White>
SS: Jim Bradberry   <M3>
120 Hummingbird Lane
Searcy, AR 72143
(501)278-9750
CL:Howard Johnson
2180 Holmes Road
Searcy, AR 72143
(501)268-3071
howardwjohnson@gmail.com
_____

ARKANSAS PRESBYTERY CONTINUED

Shaver   (1C)GRAR1413
(no longer has services 10/30/13)
   401 Shaver Road (mailing)
   1448 Shaver Road (physical)
   Paris, AR 72855
   ( )   <Logan>

Shell Chapel   (4WC)GRAR1108
   2143 Grider Field Road (mailing)
   3110 Highway 425 (physical)
   Pine Bluff, AR 71601
   (870)535-5408   <Jefferson>
CL: Joyce Shell
   2143 Grider Field Road
   Pine Bluff, AR 71601
   (870)535-5408
   mkshell@earthlink.net

Sherwood   (4WC)GRAR1220
   1402 E Kiehl Avenue
   Sherwood, AR 72120
   (501)835-8889   <Pulaski>
PA: William Guthrie   <M1>
   11130 Frenchmen Loop Apt B
   Maumelle, AR 72113
   (501)584-0019
   billybarloe@yahoo.com
CL: Tawanna Rhodes
   PO Box 1648
   North Little Rock, AR 72115
   (501)658-2920
   scifimom58@comcast.net

Sidney   (2U)GRAR1515
   Batesville, AR 72501
   ( )   <Sharp>
PA: Alan Meinzer   <M1>
   780 Barren Fork Road
   Mount Pleasant, AR 72561
   (870)612-3936
   brotheralan@centurylink.net
CL: Jodi Moody
   127 Arkansas Highway 58
   Sidney, AR 72577
   (870)283-6766

Sulphur Springs   (4C)GRAR1315
   3225 Ouachita 2 (mailing)
   3086 Ouachita 2 (physical)
   Louann, AR 71751
   (870)689-3598   <Ouachita>
   mdarden@oeccwildblue.com
CL:Peggy Muckelrath
   128 Ouachita 55
   Louann, AR 71752
   (870)689-3409
   pmukelrath@oecc.com

Trimble Camp G   (4WC)GRAR1504
   PO Box 150 (mailing)
   Trimble Camp Ground Road (physical)
   Dolph, AR 72528
   (870)297-8088   <Izard>
PA: Joel Snyder   <M1>
   224 Lord Lane
   Mountain View, AR 72560
   (870)269-9743
   synyder.joel@ymail.com
CL: Jana Cowgill
   1037 Chriswood Drive
   Clarkridge, AR 72623

   (870)421-2106

Trinity   (4MEWC)GRAR1219
   809 W Wall Street
   Morrilton, AR 72110
   (501)354-4139   <Conway>
PA: Gordon Warren   <M1>
   811 Wall Street
   Morrilton, AR 72110
   (501)208-1120
   jogordonwarren@suddenlink.net
CL: Jammie Bonds
   809 Wall Street
   Morrilton, AR 72110
   (501)354-4139

Walkerville   (4MEWC)GRAR1317
   10160 Highway 19 S
   Magnolia, AR 71753
   ( )   <Columbia>
CL: Stella Edwards
   10570 S Highway 19
   Emerson, AR 71740
   (870)696-3973
   jse10570@gmail.com

Walnut Grove   (4WC)GRAR1414
   4724 N State Highway 23 (mailing)
   1294 Six Mile Road (physical)
   Magazine, AR 72943
   ( )   <Logan>
   danekas@centurytel.net
SS: Don Kennedy   <M3>
   5335 Dizzy Dean Road
   Booneville, AR 72927
   (479)675-4418
   donkennedy@centurytel.net
CL: Debbie Danekas
   4724 N State Highway 23
   Booneville, AR 72927
   (479)675-5004
   danekas@centurytel.net

OTHERS ON MINISTERIAL ROLL:

Blackburn, Samuel N   <M1 WC>
   6706 S 6th Street
   Fort Smith, AR 72908
   (479)649-9436
Blanton, D B   <M1 RT>
   ADDRESS UNKNOWN
Bowling, Andrew   <M1 WC>
   20945 Highway 16 E
   Siloam Springs, AR 72761
   (479)524-6576
Brown, Amy   <M1 WC>
   679 Freeze Bend Road
   Newport, AR 72112
Cadenbach, Mark   <M1 OM>
   91 Elzadah Lane
   Salem, AR 72576
   (890)955-9250
   cadenbm@nctc.net
Chang, Leo   <M1 WC>
   819 W Division SE
   Springfield, MO 65803
   (901)287-9901
Cook, Carl   <M1 WC>
   475 Western Hills Loop
   Mountain Home, AR 72653
   (870)425-2570

   carlc@suddenlink.net
Davenport, Vondal   <M1 WC>
   57 Main Street
   Ratcliff, AR 7951
   (479)965-2036
Deere, Thomas (Tom)   <M1 WC>
   460 Yukon Drive
   Russellville, AR 72811
   (479)498-0318
   tdeere@suddenlinkmail.com
Fisk, James R   <M1 WC>
   1 Webb Lane
   Bella Vista, AR 72714
   jimfisk95@yahoo.com
   (479)886-1216
Hamelink, Ronald L   <M1 WC>
   5045 Starlite Court
   Las Cruces, NM 88012
   (575)640-4341
   hamronelink@yahoo.com
Holley, Ann   <M1 WC>
   PO Box 345
   Lockesburg, AR 71846
   (870)289-3421
   ladyrev1115@yahoo.com
Jeffrey, Sarah Ann   <M1 WC>
   5271 Highway 202 E
   Yellville, AR 72687
   (870)453-7076
   FAX: (870)715-9229
   annjeffrey2001@yahoo.com
Jones, Michael   <M1 WC>
   120 Jennifer Lane
   Branson, MO 65616
   (417)334-2058
Jones, Victor   <M1 WC>
   7017 Highway 177 S
   Jordan, AR 72519
   (870)499-5882
   pam.jones@centurytel.net
Mars, Stan   <M1 WC>
   PO Box 274
   Mt Pleasant, AR 72561
   (217)254-5120
   smars2@liberty.edu
Martin, William E, Jr   <M1 WC>
   PO Box 98
   131 E Wood Avenue
   Palestine, AR 72372
   (870)581-2530
   juniormartin@yahoo.com
McSpadden, Nancy   <M1 M9>
   120 Roberta Drive
   Memphis, TN 38112
   (870)612-0067
   revnancy77@gmail.com
Niswonger, Richard   <M1 WC>
   20941 Highway 16 E
   Siloam Springs, AR 72761
   (479)524-4081
   rniswonger@cox.net
O'Neal Danhof, Clair   <M1 WC>
   301 Whispering Hills Street
   Hot Springs, AR 71901
   acglenn@aol.com
Ostrander, Shirley   <M1 WC>
   210 Glen Park Drive #3
   Cordova, TN 38018
   (901)827-4830
Pedigo, Russell   <M1 WC>
   1002 Haney Avenue

ARKANSAS PRESBYTERY CONTINUED

El Dorado, AR 71730
(870)862-4689
russell_pedigo@hotmail.com

Shanley, Dwight   <M1 WC>
16904 Old Mill Road
Little Rock, AR 72206
(501)888-4190
dwightshanley@att.net

Suttle, Michael   <M1 WC>
159 Ouachita 593
Camden, AR 71701
(870)836-0008
m_s_suttle@msn.com

Sweigart, John M   <M1 WC>
PO Box 876
Dover, AL 72837
(479)229-4041

Terrell, Elizabeth   <M1 WC>
2073 Vinton Avenue
Memphis, TN 38104
(901)647-2788

Treadaway, Kenneth A   <M1 WC>
172 Miller County 494
Texarkana, AR 71854
treadaways@ark.net
(870)574-1609

Varner, Susan   <M1 M9>
14709 Glisten Lane
Little Rock, AR 72223
(901)371-1249
smvarner76@yahoo.com

Wood, Wayne   <M1 WC>
HC 61 Box 600
Calico Rock, AR 72519
(870)297-2205
FAX: (870)297-3151
bexarwood@centurytel.net

Woodliff, George   <M1 HR>
4405 W Persimmon Street #316A
Fayetteville, AR 72704
(479)410-1933
mwoodliff@kih.net

OTHER LICENTIATES ON ROLL:

Harbour, Ethan   <M2>
77 Burton Road
Booneville, AR 72927
(479)849-6329
ethanharbour@gmail.com

Washburn, Gloria   <M2>
PO Box 2484
Jordan, AR 72519
(870)321-3539
grwashburn07@gmail.com

OTHER CANDIDATES ON ROLL:

Anderson, Kyle   <M3>
828 E Main Street
Batesville, AR 72501
(870)834-5799
kanderson@memphisseminary.edu

Vaughan, Jimmy   <M3>
1607 W 3rd Street
Fordyce, AR 71742
(870)818-1512
jvaughan103@hotmail.com

Walsh, Devin   <M3>
801 East "M" Street
Russellville, AR 72801
(479)890-6716

Warren, Elizabeth
811 W Wall Street
Morrilton, AR 72110
(501)354-4139

Cauca Valley Presbytery
MISSION SYNOD

	GENERAL		MEMBERSHIP			CHANGES				FINANCES			
	1.Church Number	2.Active	3.Total 4.Church School		5.Prof. of Faith	6.Gains 7.Losses 8.Children Baptized			9. OUR UNITED OUT-REACH	10. Total Out-Reach Giving	11. All Other Expenses	12. Total Income Received	13. Value Church Prop. 1=1000
	1	2	3	4	5	6	7	8	9	10	11	12	13
Betania	8204	35	41	15	0	3	0	0		300	6,757	5,272	77
Bethel*	8205	172	172	250	0	52	0	0		2,059	13,951	15,990	40
Caleb*	8223	75	90	60	0	10	38	0		1,860	13,089	13,549	49
Cali Central*	8208	207	207	39	0	8	39	0		6,683	53,675	48,428	324
Divino Redentor	8206	181	181	130	0	10	39	0		6,578	58,378	47,746	77
Emaus*	8219	77	83	50	0	18	0	0		576	4,855	6,519	18
Filipos*	8211	98	83	0	0	0	4	0		900	4,863	9,664	64
Getsemani*	8210	50	50	62	0	19	3	0		1,064	10,937	10,639	78
Guabas		85	85	45	0	27	0	0		760	1,200	6,336	4
Ipiales		43	57	25	0	8	81	0		200	4,708	5,655	13
Maranatha*	8220	80	139	150	0	24	15	0		512	23,108	14,487	12
Nueva Esperanza*	8221	80	87	22	0	18	51	0		3,560	20,212	24,290	0
Nueva Jerusalen*	8222	120	145	47	0	74	4	0		1,288	9,795	10,866	72
Popayan*	8227	797	800	875	0	150	450	0		4,409	85,313	122,996	46
Principe De Paz*	8201	16	18	15	0	4	41	0		600	3,032	6,199	148
Renacer*	8225	531	583	595	0	156	63	0		22,831	101,303	124,134	312
Rey de Reyes*		92	98	100	0	16	39	0		1,078	10,792	12,091	14
Samaria*	8217	41	86	55	0	15	0	0		1,460	8,113	9,573	59
San Juan B*		49	49	94	0	9	20	0		860	7,357	8,596	3
San Lucas*	8215	63	69	46	0	25	0	0		5,282	10,797	11,762	82
San Marcos*	8218	68	68	26	0	0	7	0		1,762	11,257	14,668	106
San Pablo*	8212	132	143	200	0	6	28	0		6,430	15,564	22,381	90
Tulua Central*	8226	70	70	0	0	7	27	0		2,128	12,782	14,189	41
Presbytery	8200								11,500				
TOTALS	23	3,162	3,404	2,901	0	659	949	0	11,500	73,180	491,833	566,030	60,861

*Math error corrected. **Purged roll.

CHURCHES, PASTORS, AND CLERKS:

Betania   (4WF)MSCA8204
Av 5 No 29-12
Cali, Colombia, South America
(   )894-0624   <S America>
PA: Mario Gaviria   <M1>
Cra 27 No 7-48
Cali, Colombia, South America
(   )372-3869
mariogaviria50@hotmail.com
CL: Ana Bechara de Montoya
Aereo 851
Cali, Colombia, South America

Bethel   (4MWC)MSCA8205
Calle 14 Oeste No 48-17
Cali, Colombia, South America
(   )554-7514   <S America>
SS:Rodrigo Torres   <M2>
Calle 14 Oeste No 48-17
Cali, Colombia, South America
(011)882-8372
rojoana@hotmail.com
CL: Ana Leyda Meneses
Aereo 10701
Cali, Colombia, South America

Caleb   (4F)MSCA8223

Av 47 Oeste No 9 A-24
Montebello, Colombia, South America
(   )323-8070   <S America>
PA: Gildardo Agudelo   <M1>
Cra 73C No 1A-54
Cali, Colombia, South America
pastorgildardoaguedelo@outlook.ar
CL: Carmen Rosa
Ave 47 Oe 9-51
Montebello, Colombia, South America

Cali Central   (4MWC)MSCA8208
Av De Las Americas 19N-18
Cali, Colombia, South America
(   )668-7109   <S America>
PA: Sergio Betancur   <M1>
Av De Las Americas 19N-18
Cali, Colombia, South America
(   )334-2904
sergiobetancurposada@hotmail.com
CL: Nancy Trejos
Av De Las Americas 19N-18
Cali, Colombia, South America
nantre6@hotmail.com

Divino Redentor   (4MWC)MSCA8206
Cra 3 No 36-29
Juan XXIII
Buenaventura, Colombia, South America
(   )242-8399   <S America>

PA: Wilfrido Quinonez   <M1>
Cra 3 No 36-29
Juan XXIII
Buenaventura, Colombia, South America
(310)412-1711
wilqui07@hotmail.com
CL: Marlen Palacios
Cra 3 No 36-29
Juan XXIII
Buenaventura, Colombia, South America

Emaus   (4WC)MSCA8219
Diag 1 sur Cra 49-1
Buenaventura, Colombia, South America
(   )244-2624   <S America>
SS: Manuel Medina   <M2>
Diag 1 sur Cra 49-1
Buenaventura, Colombia, South America
(   )244-2624
emauspres@hotmail.com
CL: Omairo Valasco Cosme
Aereo 969
Buenaventura, Colombia, South America

Filipos   (4WF)MSCA8211
Calle 34 No 24A-36
Cali, Colombia, South America
(   )438-2563   <S America>
PA: Roberto Fonseca   <M1>
Cra D1 No 46C-22

CAUCA VALLEY PRESBYTERY CONTINUED

Cali, Colombia, South America
( )446-7370
robertoaltafuya@yahoo.com.ar
CL: Nancy Cortez
Calle 34 No 24A-36
Cali, Colombia, South America

Getsemani   (ARC)MSCA8210
Cra 15 No 8-43
El Cerrito, Colombia, South America
( )256-4261   <S America>
SS: Luis Cantor   <M3>
Cra 15 No 8-43
El Cerrito, Colombia, South America
(000)256-4261
pastoralberto7328@hotmail.com
CL: Amparo Renjifo
Cra 15 No 8-43
El Cerrito, Colombia, South America

Guabas
Corregimiento Guabas
Guacari, Colombia, South America

Maranatha   (4WF)MSCA8220
Calle 12 No 4-69
Guapi, Colombia, South America
(092)840-0940
FAX (092)840-0120   <S America>
CL: John Fredy Zamora
Calle 12 No 4-69
Guapi, Colombia, South America

Nueva Esperanza   (F)MSCA8221
Cra 89 4C-35
Cali, Colombia, South America
( )332-5849   <South America>
nuevaesperanza1983@hotmail.com
PA: Jorge Valencia   <M1>
Cra 89 4C-35
Cali, Colombia, South America
( )332-5840
CL: Janeth Zuniga
Cra 89 4C-35
Cali, Colombia, South America
tinta_y_papel@hotmail.com

Nueva Jerusalen   (4F)MSCA8222
Cra 73 CN No 1A-54 (Lourdes)
Cali, Colombia, South America
( )323-3009   <S America>
SS: Fabian Florez   <M3>
Cra 73 CN No 29-36
Cali, Colombia, South America
( )323-4447
fabianflorezpastor@yahoo.es
CL: Adriana Montenegro
Aereo 6365
Cali, Colombia, South America

Popayan   (ARC)MSCA8227
Cra 9 No 6N-87
Popayan, Colombia, South America
(092)823-8988   <S America>
PA: Johnny Montano   <M1>
Cra 9 No 6 6N-87
Popayan, Colombia, South America
(092)823-8988
jmonsolis@bmail.com
CL:Diego Orlando Golu
Cra 9 No 6 6N-87

Popayan, Colombia, South America

Principe De Paz   (4WC)MSCA8201
Cra 27 No 7-48
Cali, Colombia, South America
( )556-6527   <S America>
CL: Mismery Garcia
Cra 27 No 7-48
Cali, Colombia, South America

Renacer   (4WF)MSCA8225
Diag 26M Trv 73A-69
Cali, Colombia, South America
( )422-3940   <S America>
PA: Wilson Lopez   <M1>
Cra 100 No 34-65
Cali, Colombia, South America
( )327-2543
wilsonig7@gmail.com
CL: Sucelly Zamora
Diag 26M Trv 73A-69
Cali, Colombia, South America

Rey de Reyes
Calle 6A No 17-03
Tulua, Colombia, South America
presbyreydereyes@hotmail.com
PA: Bertulio Torres
Calle 5A No 22-03
Tulua, Colombia, South America
bertulioevangelista@hotmail.com
CL: Jeymi Jimenez
Calle 6A No 17-03
Tulua, Colombia, South America

Samaria   (4MWC)MSCA8217
Trans 30 No 17F-122
Cali, Colombia, South America
( )448-5880   <S America>
PA: Juan Bautista Reina   <M1>
Trans 30 No 17F-122
Cali, Colombia, South America
( )442-4562
juanbahu@hotmail.com
CL: Maria Josefa Martinez
Aereo 4290
Cali, Colombia, South America

San Juan Bautista
Corrigimiento Cucurrupi
Cucurrupi, Colombia, South America
SS: Andres Felipa Lerma   <M3>
Cucurrupi, Colombia, South America
CL: Session Clerk
Cucurrupi, Colombia, South America

San Lucas   (4WC)MSCA8215
Calle 26 No 29-53
Palmira, Colombia, South America
( )272-7584   <S America>
sanlucaspalmira@hotmail.com
SS: Alexander Quintero   <M2>
Calle 26 No 29-53
Palmira, Colombia, South America
( )272-7584
maalgo75@hotmail.com
CL: Leydi Marcela Quintero
Calle 26 No 29-53
Palmira, Colombia, South America

San Marcos   (4MWC)MSCA8218

Calle 46 A No 4N-25
Cali, Colombia, South America
( )446-3311   <S America>
SS: Diego Palomino
Calle 46 A No 4N-25
Cali, Colombia, South America
diegofer323@gmail.com
CL: Luz Dazy Ceballos
Calle 46 A No 4N-25
Cali, Colombia, South America

San Pablo   (4MWC)MSCA8212
Cra 8 No 5-27
Guacari, Colombia, South America
( )253-2751   <S America>
PA: Aldrin Calero   <M1>
Cra 8 No 5-27
Guacari, Colombia, South America
( )253-0453
aldrin_calero@hotmail.com
CL: Liliana Soto
Cra 8 No 5-27
Guacari, Colombia, South America

Tulua Central   (4WF)MSCA8226
Calle 41A No 26-26
Tulua, Colombia, South America
( )224-5004   <S America>
iglesiacentral@hotmail.com
PA: Orlando Mendez   <M3>
Calle 41A No 26-26
Tulua, Colombia, South America
orlandomendezf@hotmail.com
CL: Luz Miria Montoya
Calle 41A No 26-26
Tulua, Colombia, South America

OTHERS ON MINISTERIAL ROLL:

Aguirre, Luciria   <M1 WC>
Calle 3B No 97-05
Cali, Colombia, South America
(300)686-9161
pastorluciana50@yahoo.com.co
Ariza, Fabiola   <M1 WC>
Calle 1A No 62A-130 Apto 124
Cali, Colombia, South America
fatvioleta@hotmail.com
(316)419-8414
Caicedo, Efrain   <M1 WC>
Calle 29 No 29A-03
Cali, Colombia, South America
Camacho, Blanca   <M9>
Calle 4D 89-26 Apto 205
Cali, Colombia, South America
blancanidiacamacho@yahoo.com
Fonseca, Roberto   <M1 WC>
Cll 46 A No 4N 25
Cali, Colombia, South America
( )446-7370
Gaviria, Mario   <M1 WC>
Cra 27 No 7-48
Cali, Colombia, South America
( )372-3869
pastormariogaviria@hotmail.com
Giraldo, William   <M1 WC>
Calle 62 No 1B-15
Cali, Colombia, South America
( )439-5436
giraldo_william@yahoo.co
Gonzalez, Rito   <M1 MY>

CAUCA VALLEY PRESBYTERY CONTINUED

Cali, Colombia, South America

Jimenez, Raul   <M9>
  Calle 3B No 97A-05 Apto 102C
  Cali, Colombia, South America

Madrid, Alejandro   <M1 WC>
  Calle 12 No 4-69
  Guapi, Colombia, South America

Pejendino, Fhanor   <M1 MY>
  Cll 41 A No 26-26
  Tulua, Colombia, South America
  (317)654-5750
  ph_apear@hotmail.com

Pejendino, Socorro   <M1 MY>
  Cll 41 A No 26-26
  Tulua, Colombia, South America
  (317)654-5750
  pastorasocorrod@hotmail.com

Racines, Jairo   <M1 WC>
  Calle 39 No 13-40
  Cali, Colombia, South America
  (311)385-6546
  senicartheos@live.com

Rodriguez, Jairo   <M1 WC>
  Cra 1D 2 53 41
  Cali, Colombia, South America
  jairo.hrodriguez@hotmail.com
  (572)377-8741

Sanchez, Sol Maria   <M9>
  Av Americas 19N - 18
  Cali, Colombia, South America
  sol.marias@hotmail.com

Solis, Arcadio   <M1 WC>
  Cra 42 D1 No 55-69
  Cali, Colombia, South America
  (   )328-5486

Torres, Mariano
  Cra 34 No 4-34A 34
  Buenaventura, Colombia, South America

OTHER LICENTIATES ON ROLL:

Paredes, Flavio   <M2>
  Cra 7 No 1-76
  Ipiales, Colombia, South America
  fepa5308@hotmail.com

OTHER CANDIDATES ON ROLL:

Artega, Jose Felix   <M3>
  Ipiales, Colombia, South America

Caicedo, Jose Urier   <M3>
  Cra 4 sur 9C-15
  Jamundi, Colombia, South America
  joseurier@hotmail.com

Gonzalez, Patricia   <M3>
  Tulua, Colombia, South America
  adriapatriciag@gmail.com

Guanaquillo, Samuel   <M3>
  Aereo 10701
  Cali, Colombia, South America
  FAX: (408)255-5938
  samijg@hotmail.com

Gutierrez, Consuelo   <M3>
  Calle 18N No 4N-49
  Cali, Colombia, South America
  consuelogutierrezrico@hotmail.com

Gutierrez, Diana   <M3>
  Cra 100 No 34-65
  Cali, Colombia, South America
  gutierrezdp21@hotmail.com

Gutierrez, Gloria   <M3>
  Valle 18N No 4rN-49
  Cali, Colombia, South America
  gloritabondadosa@hotmail.com

Guyara, Elizabeth   <M3>
  Ave 3 No 19-18
  Cali, Colombia, South America
  bethgu00@hotmail.com

Hoyos, Javier   <M3>
  Calle 34 24A-36
  Cali, Colombia, South America

Madrid, Alejandro   <M3>
  Popayan
  Cali, Colombia South America
  ale.madrid@yahool.com

Madrid, Jorge Alexis   <M3>
  Popayan
  Cali, Colombia South America
  sacrydea@hotmail.com

Micolta, Ruby Mabely   <M3>
  Calle 51N No 11-85
  Popayan, Colombia, South America
  rumami@gmail.com

Munoz, Arlex   <M3>
  Ave 3N No 19-18
  Cali, Colombia, South America
  armisport2@gmail.com

Paz, Ivan   <M3>
  Pasto, Colombia, South America
  ivanpaz1234@hotmail.com

Ponce, Dennis Adrian   <M3>
  Buenaventura, Colombia, South America

Restrepo, Johanna   <M3>
  Calle 14 Oe No 48-17
  Cali, Colombia, South America
  rojo_nana@hotmail.es

Rizo, Yency   <M3>
  Diag 26 H 2 83-35
  Cali, Colombia, South America

Valencia, Ana Dolly   <M3>
  Cra 27 No 7 48
  Cali, Colombia, South America
  anadollycuartas@hotmail.com

Vargas, Guido   <M3>
  Calle 73N 7B-07
  Popayan, Colombia, South America
  g_var9@yahoo.com

Choctaw Presbytery
MISSION SYNOD

GENERAL		MEMBERSHIP			CHANGES				FINANCES				
1.Church Number	2.Active	3.Total	4.Church School	5.Prof. of Faith	6.Gains	7.Losses	8.Children Baptized	9. OUR UNITED OUT-REACH	10. Total Out-Reach Giving	11. All Other Expenses	12. Total Income Received	13. Value Church Prop. 1=1000	
	1	2	3	4	5	6	7	8	9	10	11	12	13
Coal Creek	6102	8	29	11	3	3	0	0	79	350	3,327	2,716	11
Lone Star	6105	9	20	9	0	0	2	0	121	418	2,345	3,122	68
McGee Chapel	6106	35	35	10	No Report Received			0	484	0	0	0	100
Panki Bok	6108	2	4	2	No Report Received			0	26	0	0	0	6
Pigeon Roost	6109	5	21	5	0	0	0	0	91	418	2,596	3,500	3
Rock Creek	6111	14	21	14	0	5	0	3	39	219	5,764	5,038	24
Round Lake	6112	9	9	20	No Report Received			0	0	0	0	0	3
Presbytery									2,000				
TOTALS	7	82	139	71	3	8	2	3	2,840	1,405	14,032	14,376	215

CHURCHES, PASTORS, AND CLERKS:

Coal Creek   (4WC)MSCH6102
Route 1 Box 1215
Coalgate, OK 74538
( )   \<Atoka\>
PA: Nathan Scott   \<M1\>
960 S Katy Road
Atoka, OK 74525
(580)364-6155
CL: Lola John
Route 1 Box 1215
Coalgate, OK 74538
(580)258-8244

Lone Star   (2WC)MSCH6105
PO Box 44 (mailing)
206 S Newell Street (physical)
Coalgate, OK 74538
( )   \<Atoka\>
SS: Hannah Bryan   \<M1\>
32 Trenton Lane
Mead, OK 73449
(580)775-4955
hbryan@choctawnation.com
CL: Evangeline Robinson
PO Box 44
Boswell, OK 74727
(580)513-0170
erobinson@choctawarchiving.com

McGee Chapel   (2EW C)MSCH6106
PO Box 158 (mailing)
99 Chapel Circle (physical)
Broken Bow, OK 74728
(580)584-2099   \<McCurtain\>
FAX: (580)584-2099
chocpres@pine-net.com
CL: Betty Jacob
PO Box 158
Broken Bow, OK 74728
(580)584-2099
FAX: (580)584-2099
chocpres@pine-net.com

Panki Bok   (2C)MSCH6108

PO Box 158 (mailing)
Broken Bow, OK 74728
Eagletown, OK 74734 (physical)
( )   \<McCurtain\>
CL: Session Clerk
PO Box 158
Broken Bow, OK 74728

Pigeon Roost   (2C)MSCH6109
960 S Katy Road
Atoka, OK 74525
(580)889-2292   \<Choctaw\>
PA: Virginia Espinoza   \<M1\>
PO Box 132
Boswell, OK 74727
(580)775-4138
vespinoza@choctawnation.com
CL: Virginia Espinoza
960 S Katy Road
Atoka, OK 74525
(580)889-2292

Rock Creek   (2WC)MSCH6111
c/o Betty Walton (mailing)
PO Box 126
Talihina, OK 74571
Honobia, OK (physical)
(918)567-2370   \<LeFlore\>
PA: Nathan Scott   \<M1\>
960 S Katy Road
Atoka, OK 74525
(580)364-6155
CL: Betty Walton
PO Box 126
Talihina, OK 74571
(918)567-2370

Round Lake   (1WC)MSCH6112
Box 127
Tupelo, OK 74572
(580)317-7427   \<Coal\>
PA: Hannah Bryan   \<M1\>
32 Trenton Lane
Mead, OK 73449
(580)775-4955
hbryan@choctawnation.com
CL: Vickie McClure

Box 127
Tupelo, OK 74572
(580)317-7427

OTHERS ON MINISTERIAL ROLL:

OTHER CANDIDATES ON ROLL:

Crosby, Ronald   \<M3\>
407 N "A" Street
Calera, OK 74730
Scott, Linda   \<M3\>
960 S Katy Road
Atoka, OK 74525
(580)889-2292

Columbia Presbytery
TENNESSEE SYNOD

	1.Church Number	2.Active	3.Total	4.Church School	5.Prof. of Faith	6.Gains	7.Losses	8.Children Baptized	9. OUR UNITED OUT-REACH	10. Total Out-Reach Giving	11. All Other Expenses	12. Total Income Received	13. Value Church Prop. 1=1000
	1	2	3	4	5	6	7	8	9	10	11	12	13
Ash Hill	7101	37	66	26	0	0	0	0	2,874	7,251	20,006	28,787	300
Belleview*	7104	13	23	0	0	0	2	0	0	4,958	17,330	19,896	600
Boonshill	7106	24	64	24	0	0	0	0	800	2,950	21,804	28,378	321
Champ	7108	9	9	5	0	0	0	0	0	1,750	16,541	15,692	40
Chapel Hill	7109	34	32	19	2	0	1	2	1,000	4,517	46,460	46,547	410
Columbia*	7110	40	40	15	0	1	49	0	0	0	0	0	1,500
Elora	7111	5	5	6	0	0	0	0	0	300	9,576	11,556	168
Fayetteville	7112	117	276	65	5	9	6	0	14,400	26,442	189,698	220,034	2,400
Fiducia	7113	11	11	8	0	0	0	0	0	600	13,445	14,835	80
Flintville	7115	7	7	11	0	0	0	0	0	2,372	14,974	13,404	25
Franklin*	7116	20	20	10	0	0	8	1	0	545	40,358	36,968	800
Green Hill	7118	16	16	15	0	0	0	0	2,460	11,804	13,857	42,332	86
Harpeth Lick	7119	34	43	7	4	8	3	0	1,500	5,963	31,098	42,296	200
Hohenwald*	7120	12	21	0	0	8	0	0	0	0	31,090	50,445	250
Howell	7121	53	121	65	2	5	5	1	3,000	28,199	59,786	82,031	750
Jenkins	7144	83	156	35	1	2	31	0	16,514	47,103	189,004	244,096	3,623
Kelso	7122	29	87	22	1	1	0	1	4,000	5,841	55,439	77,007	200
Kingdom	7123	10	10	4	0	1	1	0	520	2,275	10,636	13,183	175
Lawrenceburg*	7124	20	20	12	0	1	0	0	0	900	30,050	36,205	1,230
Lewisburg, 1st	7125	67	174	68	0	0	2	0	250	6,553	118,991	108,696	500
McCains	7126	46	46	22	1	0	3	0	4,500	8,751	52,182	64,152	464
Mt. Carmel	7127	69	96	18	1	4	6	0	1,000	2,100	69,474	92,716	1,000
Mt. Hebron*	7128	4	4	4	0	0	1	0	0	100	8,389	6,487	141
Mt. Joy	7129	50	106	20	2	2	1	0	1,164	1,164	58,383	84,806	300
Mt. Lebanon	7130	41	41	25	0	1	4	0	1,311	6,397	36,376	42,966	125
Mt. Moriah	7131	53	118	20	0	2	0	1	0	14,898	39,845	49,955	250
Mt. Nebo	7132	7	7	7	0	0	0	0	0	1,040	18,446	19,486	90
Mt. Pleasant	7133	47	97	21	2	2	2	0	3,204	8,181	54,719	61,386	1,000
New Bethel	7134	10	10	10	0	0	0	3	316	316	2,614	5,460	100
Petersburg	7135	42	52	43	1	1	0	1	8,750	20,356	42,545	62,901	232
Pleasant Mount*	7136	35	82	29	0	3	1	0	2,200	4,198	52,217	59,732	500
Richland	7137	60	122	52	1	1	4	0	1,500	7,710	64,540	67,909	150
Santa Fe	7138	22	22	18	0	0	0	0	0	4,577	19,042	22,568	0
Swan	7140	13	13	10	0	0	0	0	50	1,068	23,277	25,084	300
Union Grove	7141	10	10	0	0	0	0	0	0	2,640	12,973	15,484	100
Waynesboro	7142	45	45	15	1	1	19	1	7,013	11,568	71,088	77,544	618
West Point*	7143	62	62	30	1	1	6	1	3,650	3,889	61,856	81,205	1,000
TOTALS	38	1,280	2,156	771	26	51	160	11	81,976	259,277	1,618,109	1,972,228	20,778

*Math error corrected. **Purged roll.

CHURCHES, PASTORS, AND CLERKS:
_____

Ash Hill   (4WC)TNCO7101
  4930 Ash Hill Road
  Spring Hill, TN 37174
  (931)381-3367   <Williamson>
PA: James R Miller   <M1>
  1214 Whitney Drive
  Columbia, TN 38401
  (931)215-2108
  rev.james.miller@charter.net
CL: Helen Logue
  1603 Emerald Court
  Franklin, 37064
  (615)599-6764

Belleview   (4WC)TNCO7104
  1752 Burke Hollow Road (mailing)
  Nolensville, TN 37135
  4724 Murfreesboro Road (physical)
  Franklin, TN 37064
  (   )   <Williamson>
PA: James R Miller   <M1>
  1214 Whitney Drive
  Columbia, TN 38401
  (931)381-3367
  rev.james.miller@charter.net
CL: John Koelz
  4498 South Caruthers Road
  Franklin, TN 37074
  (615)595-7394
  koel3358@bellsouth.net

Boonshill   (4C)TNCO7106
  91 Red Oak Road (mailing)
  Petersburg, TN 37144
  Rt 2 (physical)
  Boonshill, TN
  (   )   <Lincoln>
OD: Thomas Smith   <M5>
  467 Gunter Hollow Drive
  Fayetteville, TN 37334
  (931)607-6008
  tomandbobbi6764@gmail.com
CL: Sammy Luna
  91 Red Oak Road
  Petersburg, TN 37144
  (931)703-0536
  srluna@ardmore.net

COLUMBIA PRESBYTERY CONTINUED

Champ   (2C)TNCO7108
290 Sullenger Bend Road (mailing)
Belvidere, TN 37306
61 Tucker Creek Road (physical)
Mulberry, TN
( )   <Lincoln>
PA: Elmer L Alverson   <M1 HR OP>
354 Roy Davis Road
New Market, AL 35761
(256)828-4503
1941buddy@att.net
CL: Diann Adams
2800 Hillsboro Road
Huntsville, AL 35805
(256)534-6076

Chapel Hill   (4MWC)TNCO7109
4801 Eagleville Pike (mailing)
302 N Horton Parkway (physical)
Chapel Hill, TN 37034
(931)364-7819   <Marshall>
PA: Joe Wiggins   <M1>
2734 US Highway 41A S
Eagleville, TN 37060
(615)274-2011
jwigginz@aol.com
CL: Spence Walls
4521 Polaris Drive
Chapel Hill, TN 37034
(931)364-2573
walls.family95@yahoo.com

Columbia   (4MWC)TNCO7110
1106 Nashville Highway
Columbia, TN 38401
(931)388-9177   <Maury>
pastor@fcpccolumbia.com
CL: Session Clerk
1106 Nashville Highway
Columbia, TN 38401
(931)388-9177   <Maury>
pastor@fcpccolumbia.com

Elora   (2C)TNCO7111
69 Bear Wallow Road (mailing)
Flintville, TN 37335
Elora, TN 37328 (physical)
( )   <Lincoln>
SS: John Blair   <M1>
108 Cliff Drive
Lawrenceburg, TN 38464
(931)762-2480
jnbblair@charter.net
CL: Jim Ramsey
69 Bear Wallow Road
Flintville, TN 37335
(931)937-8765
jim.brenda.ramsey710@gmail.com

Fayetteville   (4WC)TNCO7112
1015 Lewisburg Highway
Fayetteville, TN 37334
(931)433-5441   <Lincoln>
FAX: (931)433-0056
cpc@fpunet.com
PA: Timothy Smith   <M1>
214 Jeffrey Drive
Fayetteville, TN 37334
(931)438-2820
FAX: (931)433-0056
tims38@hotmail.com
CL: Larry Ventress

1003 First Avenue
Fayetteville, TN 37334
(931)433-5053
FAX: (931)433-0056
dooda49@fpunet.com

Fiducia   (2EW C)TNCO7113
108 Cliff Drive (mailing)
Lawrenceburg, TN 38478
1695 Fiducia Road (physical)
Prospect, TN 38477
( )   <Giles>
PA: John Blair   <M1>
108 W Cliff Drive
Lawrenceburg, TN 38464
(931)766-2480
jnbblair@charter.net
CL: Ewing Brooks
1429 Crooked Hill Road
Pulaski, TN 38478
(931)363-5985

Flintville   (2C)TNCO7115
35 Well Lee Road (mailing)
9 Flintville School Road (physical)
Flintville, TN 37335
( )   <Lincoln>
PA: John Blair   <M1>
108 W Cliff Drive
Lawrenceburg, TN 38464
(931)766-2480
jnbblair@charter.net
CL: Jimmie D Wicks
35 Wells Lee Road
Flintville, TN 37335
(931)937-8562
bfwicks@bellsouth.net

Franklin   (4MC)TNCO7116
PO Box 1134 (mailing)
615 West Main Street (physical)
Franklin, TN 37065
(615)599-0029   <Williamson>
FAX: (615)807-2959
cp1876@hotmail.com
PA: John Hyden   <M1>
6525 Peytonsville Arno Road
College Grove, TN 37046
(615)975-9584
cp1876@hotmail.com
CL: Dorris Douglass
724 Fair Street
Franklin, TN 37064
(615)790-7914
FAX: (615)595-1247
ansercher@aol.com

Grace   (4C)TNCO7145
1153 Lewisburg Pike
Franklin, TN 37068
CLOSED 4/2016

Green Hill   (3WC)TNCO7118
1900 Unionville-Deason Road
Bell Buckle, TN 37020
(931)294-2040   <Bedford>
CL: Angela Burns
328 Dunnaway Road
Shelbyville, TN 37160
(931)294-5105

Harpeth Lick   (4C)TNCO7119
6981 Arno Allisona Road

College Grove, TN 37046
( )   <Williamson>
SS: Larry Guin   <M1>
125 Glider Loop
Eagleville, TN 37060
(615)668-5236
lguin43@hotmail.com
CL: Virginia Lou Rogers
8876 Horton Highway
College Grove, TN 37046
(615)368-2202
mudpuddle42@gmail.com

Hohenwald   (4MWC)TNCO7120
PO Box 456 (mailing)
201 Park Avenue S (physical)
Hohenwald, TN 38462
(931)796-3657   <Lewis>
CL: Sandra Burgdorf
750 Long Branch Road
Hohenwald, TN 38412
(931)796-5729
outdoor111@hughes.net

Howell   (4MWC)TNCO7121
43 Brown Teal Road
Fayetteville, TN 37334
(931)433-0818   <Lincoln>
PA: Todd Gaskill   <M1>
430 Haysland Road
Petersburg, TN 37144
(931)580-2708
tgaskill@pens.com
CL: Tim Porter
85 Icy Bank Road
Fayetteville, TN 37334
(931)433-8306

Jenkins   (4MWC)TNCO7144
PO Box 518 (mailing)
2501 York Road (physical)
Nolensville, TN 37135
(615)776-2339   <Williamson>
FAX: (615)776-3520
jenkinspastor@gmail.com
PA: Jason Mikel   <M1>
4630 Mt Sharon Road
Greenbrier, TN 37073
(615)243-8938
jasonemikel@gmail.com
CL: Joyce A Allemore
2442 Fly Road
Nolensville, TN 37135
(615)776-2985
jallemore@yahoo.com

Kelso   (4MWC)TNCO7122
PO Box 28 (mailing)
16 Teal Hollow Road (physical)
Kelso, TN 37348
( )   <Lincoln>
SS: Tony Gaskin   <M1>
1414 Saint Joseph Street NW
Cullman, AL 35055
(256)338-7893
tgaskin46@hotmail.com
CL: Bill Dickey
1501 Swanson Boulevard
Fayetteville, TN 37334
(931)433-2462

Kingdom   (4C)TNCO7123
4532 Barfield Crescent Road (mailing)

COLUMBIA PRESBYTERY CONTINUED

Murfreesboro, TN 37128
800 Kingdom Road (physical)
Unionville, TN 37180
( )   <Bedford>
SS: Larry Guin   <M1>
125 Glider Loop
Eagleville, TN 37060
(615)668-5236
lguin43@hotmail.com
CL: Thelma Shockey
4532 Barfield Crescent Road
Murfreesboro, TN 37128
(615)896-1890

Lawrenceburg   (4MWC)TNCO7124
228 S Military Avenue
Lawrenceburg, TN 38464
(931)762-4343   <Lawrence>
cumberlandpresby@bellsouth.net
CL: Kaye Luffman
5 Powell Circle
Five Points, TN 38457
(931)556-2252
kluffman@hotmail.com

Lewisburg 1st   (4MWC)TNCO7125
210 Haynes Street (mailing)
402 2nd Avenue N (physical)
Lewisburg, TN 37091
(931)359-3857   <Marshall>
FAX: (931)270-8624
fcpclewisburg@bellsouth.net
PA: Roger Reid   <M1>
1505 Experiment Farm Road
Lewisburg, TN 37091
(931)422-5257
drrtr@yahoo.com
CL: Tammy Caneer-Carter
1400 Green Valley Road
Pulaski, TN 38478
(931)637-7374
FAX: (931)270-8624
cantam@bellsouth.net

McCains   (4MWC)TNCO7126
PO Box 29 (mailing)
3532 McCains Lane (physical)
Columbia, TN 38401
(931)540-0160   <Maury>
PA: Tommy Clark   <M1>
124 Roberta Drive
Memphis, TN 38112
(615)430-9158
fattire77@gmail.com
CL: Gary Weatherford
3926 Campbellsville Pike
Columbia, TN 38401
(931)388-0599
gmweatherford@cs.com

Mt Carmel   (4C)TNCO7127
4810 Ash Hill Road (mailing)
Spring Hill, TN 37174
2300 Lewisburg Pike (physical)
Franklin, TN 37064
(615)591-3930   <Williamson>
CL: Peggy S Fisher
4810 Ash Hill Road
Spring Hill, TN 37174
(615)944-9300
fishpest@ymail.com

Mt Hebron   (4C)TNCO7128

59 Giles Hollow Road (mailing)
927 Shelbyville Highway (physical)
Fayetteville, TN 37334
( )   <Lincoln>
PA: Todd Gaskill   <M1>
430 Haysland Road
Petersburg, TN 37144
(931)580-2708
tgaskill@pens.com
CL: Jimmy Buchanan
59 Giles Hollow Road
Fayetteville, TN 37334
(931)433-6446

Mt Joy   (4MWC)TNCO7129
8364 Mt Joy Road
Mount Pleasant, TN 38474
( )   <Maury>
CL: Connie Deason
PO Box 391
Columbia, TN 38402
(931)381-4719
deasonconnie_1@att.net

Mt Lebanon   (4EC)TNCO7130
4497 Kedron Road
Spring Hill, TN 37174
( )   <Maury>
mortonco@bellsouth.net
PA: Patric Fife   <M1>
73 Jordan Road
Lawrenceburg, TN 38464
(931)629-8146
pnlfifernak@gmail.com
CL: Judy L Morton
1272 John Sharp Road
Columbia, TN 38401
(931)381-1140
mortonco@bellsouth.net

Mt Moriah   (4C)TNCO7131
485 Agnew Road (mailing)
463 Big Dry Creek Road (physical)
Pulaski, TN 38478
( )   <Giles>
PA: Steve Nave   <M1>
5172 Fall River Road
Leoma, TN 38468
(931)424-0020
thenaves@wildblue.net
CL: Dickson Marks
485 Agnew Road
Pulaski, TN 38478
(931)363-2432
jmarks0912@mindspring.com

Mt Nebo   (4C)TNCO7132
84 S Old Military Road (mailing)
Saint Joseph, TN 38481
473 Mt Nebo Road (physical)
Iron City, TN 38463
( )   <Lawrence>
LS: Sean Richardson   <M6>
4227 Highway 43 N
Ethridge, TN 38456
(931)829-2094
sean@misterrichardson.com
CL: William B Gabel
104 Spring Street
Saint Joseph, TN 38481
(931)845-4203
stjoemerry@gmail.com

Mt Pleasant   (4EWC)TNCO7133
PO Box 689 (mailing)
504 Florida Avenue (physical)
Mount Pleasant, TN 38474
(931)379-3662   <Maury>
PA: Robert Mullenix   <M1>
1408 Azalee Lane
Chapel Hill, TN 37034
(931)364-4611
glonix@live.com
CL: Rickey Massey
609 Circle Drive
Mount Pleasant, TN 38474
(931)379-3617
rickeymassey@bellsouth.net

New Bethel   (2C)TNCO7134
5060 Reynolds Road
Columbia, TN 38401
(931)364-2378   <Marshall>
SS: John Eatherly   <M1>
1377 Moss Road
Chapel Hill, TN 37034
(931)364-2087
jrev@united.net
CL: James W Hood
1532 Lewisburg Pike
Franklin, TN 37064
(615)591-8689

Petersburg   (4MWC)TNCO7135
PO Box 82 (mailing)
303 Russell Street (physical)
Petersburg, TN 37144
(931)607-1859   <Lincoln>
petersburgpreacher@att.net
PA: Troy Green   <M1>
105 Cobb Hollow Lane
Petersburg, TN 37144
(931)659-6627
thegreens101@att.net
CL: Ann Hemphill
803 Washington Street W Apt B
Fayetteville, TN 37334
(931)433-8380
ahemphill@fpunet.com

Pleasant Mount   (4WC)TNCO7136
609 Woods Drive (mailing)
1620 Fountain Heights Road (physical)
Columbia, TN 38401
( )   <Maury>
CL: Ryan Pilkinton
1676 Vaughn Road
Columbia, TN 38401
(931)374-2767
rpilkinton@maurycoop.com

Richland   (4C)TNCO7137
304 S Monte Murrey Road (mailing)
3452 Spring Place Road (physical)
Lewisburg, TN 37091
(931)270-6135   <Marshall>
PA: Charles (Buddy) Pope   <M1>
2391 Fairfield Pike
Shelbyville, TN 37160
(931)205-6897
pope6897@yahoo.com
CL: Douglas A Looney
3045 Monte Murrey Road
Lewisburg, TN 37091
(931)359-3781
ld.looney@yahoo.com

COLUMBIA PRESBYTERY CONTINUED

Santa Fe   (4WC)TNCO7138
  PO Box 58 (mailing)
  2630 Santa Fe Pike (physical)
  Santa Fe, TN 38482
  (931)682-3555   <Maury>
SS: Sherry Ladd   <M1>
  4521 Turkey Creek Road
  Williamsport, TN 38487
  (931)682-2263
  revsherryladd@gmail.com
CL: Whitney Seaton
  111 W Hardin Drive
  Columbia, TN 38401
  (931)388-9319

Swan   (4C)TNCO7140
  4521 Turkey Creek Road (mailing)
  Williamsport, TN 38487
  2250 Swan Creek Road (physical)
  Centerville, TN 37033
  (931)682-2263   <Hickman>
  revsherryladd@gmail.com
PA: Sherry Ladd   <M1>
  4521 Turkey Creek Road
  Williamsport, TN 38487
  (931)682-2263
  revsherryladd@gmail.com
CL: George C Ladd
  4521 Turkey Creek Road
  Williamsport, TN 38487
  (931)682-2263
  gladd@hughes.net

Union Grove   (4C)TNCO7141
  2409 Green Mills Road Lot 30 (mailing)
  1452 Cliff White Road (physical)
  Columbia, TN 38401
  (931)486-2799   <Maury>
  patricia.cates@att.net
PA: Scott Yates   <M1>
  8818 New Town Road
  Rockvale, TN 37153
  (615)274-3000
  scott@scottyates.net
CL: Patricia Cates
  2409 Green Mills Road Lot 30
  Columbia, TN 38401
  (931)486-2799
  patricia.cates@att.net

Waynesboro   (4MEWC)TNCO7142
  PO Box 234 (mailing)
  110 North High Street (physical)
  Waynesboro, TN 38485
  (931)722-5621   <Wayne>
CL: Susan Myers
  PO Box 234
  Waynesboro, TN 38485
  (931)722-5621
  warden02@tds.net

West Point   (4MC)TNCO7143
  1431 Spainwood Street (mailing)
  1533 Theta Pike (physical)
  Columbia, TN 38401
  (931)388-7268   <Maury>
PA: Terry Peery   <M1>
  1431 Spainwood Street
  Columbia, TN 38401
  (931)381-6871
  coppreacher@gmail.com
CL: Mike McCord

  4543 Snow Creek Road
  Santa Fe, TN 38482
  (931)682-2500
  mmccord59@bellsouth.net

OTHERS ON MINISTERIAL ROLL:

Blair, Fonda   <M1 WC>
  PO Box 11093
  Murfreesboro, TN 37129
  (615)605-9755
  fblair4334@gmail.com
Cole, Dwayne   <M1 HR>
  6460 Village Parkway
  Anchorage, AK 99504
  (907)854-5793
  tadpolejr@aol.com
Heflin, Robert   <M1 DE>
  4144 Meadow Court Drive
  Bartlett, TN 38135
  (901)382-8198
  rdheflin@bellsouth.net
Kelly, Lawrence (Larry)   <M1 HR>
  77 Stonewall Court
  Mount Juliet, TN 37122
  (615)934-1517
Kinnaman, Richard Terry   <M1 WC>
  2018 Spring Meadow Circle
  Spring Hill, TN 37174
  (615)302-3321
  kinnaman91@att.net
Liles, Dwight   <M1 WC>
  8467 Joy Road
  Mount Pleasant, TN 38474
  (931)379-0326
  dwightliles@att.net
Lunn, Calvin   <M1 WC>
  859 Cranford Hollow Road
  Columbia, TN 38401
  (931)381-2397
  thelunns@bellsouth.net
Rolman, William L Jr   <M1 WC>
  602 Canyon Drive
  Columbia, TN 38401
  (931)388-2611
  wlrolman@charter.net
Smith, Kirk   <M1 RT>
  813 1st Avenue
  Fayetteville, TN 37334
  (931)438-8649
  kirks37334@att.net
Trotter, Wendell   <M1 HR>
  1516 Fell Avenue NE
  Huntsville, AL 35811
  (256)519-6571
  wendelltrotter@knology.net

OTHER LICENTIATES ON ROLL:

King, Mark   <M2>
  717 Big Swan Creek Road
  Hampshire, TN 38461
  (931)626-6915

OTHER CANDIDATES ON ROLL:

Rochelle, Jimmy
  809 Woods Drive
  Columbia, TN 38401
  (931)388-1947
  tnpappy53@yahoo.com

Covenant Presbytery
MIDWEST SYNOD

GENERAL		MEMBERSHIP			CHANGES				FINANCES				
1.Church Number	2.Active	3.Total	4.Church School	5.Prof. of Faith	6.Gains	7.Losses	8.Children Baptized	9. OUR UNITED OUTREACH	10. Total Out-Reach Giving	11. All Other Expenses	12. Total Income Received	13. Value Church Prop. 1=1000	
1	2	3	4	5	6	7	8	9	10	11	12	13	
Bayou de Chien 3401	40	77	28	No Report Received			0	0	0	0	0	516
Benton 3403	15	40	15	No Report Received			0	165	0	0	0	215
Bethel 3404	182	363	101	No Report Received			0	18,808	0	0	0	2,500
Calvary 3405	23	52	25	No Report Received			0	0	0	0	0	0332
Camp Ground 5103	15	50	22	0	0	1	0	1,812	6,323	25,133	26,021	782
Chandler 5302	110	387	78	2	2	2	0	13,126	41,743	154,340	185,554	1,399
Ebenezer 5105	20	25	15	No Report Received			0	0	0	0	0	50
Ebenezer Hall 5106	1	11	5	No Report Received			0	831	0	0	0	57
Flat Lick 3606	45	96	30	No Report Received			0	2,446	0	0	0	350
Fredonia 3608	95	239	70	0	2	3	0	15,722	41,072	133,466	186,529	1,015
Gilead 5110	50	155	31	No Report Received			0	2,139	0	0	0	375
Good Spring 3609	20	50	14	1	1	1	0	2,200	29,560	18,934	47,900	140
Highland 3414	100	212	76	2	17	5	1	6,600	34,659	163,056	209,700	1,000
Hopewell 3610	104	104	30	0	1	0	0	720	1,171	47,449	53,369	120
Hopkinsville 3611	49	72	43	0	3	4	2	1,100	5,631	103,201	43,031	850
Liberty 3406	97	107	55	No Report Received			0	0	0	0	0	720
Lisman* 3613	28	47	20	1	2	0	0	1,331	7,866	48,622	44,179	225
Macedonia 3614	22	22	15	No Report Received			0	0	0	0	0	300
Madisonville 3615	40	150	25	No Report Received			0	616	0	0	0	356
Margaret Hank 3415	83	113	20	1	9	3	1	3,600	3,600	0	100,775	750
Marion First 3616	44	137	20	No Report Received			0	2,280	0	0	0	698
Milburn Chapel** 3416	86	244	56	1	113	0	0	0	20,065	163,180	173,162	1,800
Mt. Carmel 3617	75	135	10	1	1	1	1	0	3,393	52,574	31,897	600
Mt. Pleasant 3618	21	25	22	0	0	2	0	0	3,594	16,423	23,036	35
Mt. Sterling 5117	180	270	80	No Report Received			0	0	0	0	0	340
Mt. Zion 5118	12	12	0	0	0	0	0	2,525	7,325	13,343	22,636	35
New Hope 3410	165	236	159	No Report Received			0	11,245	0	0	0	1,550
No. Pleasant Gr 3411	23	53	31	No Report Received			0	0	0	0	0	200
Oak Grove 3412	60	98	40	No Report Received			0	0	0	0	0	400
Oak Grove Union 3619	29	29	29	0	0	1	0	5,261	12,583	23,504	52,341	200
Oakland 3413	45	132	32	No Report Received			0	0	0	0	0	1,250
Piney Fork 3620	39	80	28	0	3	0	0	777	8,583	45,339	51,901	320
Pleasant Valley 3418	5	7	5	No Report Received			0	0	0	0	0	150
Providence 1st 3621	8	51	0	No Report Received			0	0	0	0	0	80
Rose Creek 3622	27	58	10	0	0	2	0	2,995	9,819	46,225	52,624	900
Rozzell Chapel 3419	63	103	58	2	2	1	0	3,500	22,721	59,033	100,926	380
Sturgis 3625	108	220	64	9	11	4	3	17,295	45,313	247,016	179,420	2,100
Sugar Grove 3626	71	145	39	No Report Received			0	3,000	0	0	0	700
Union Chapel 5123	33	54	19	No Report Received			0	0	0	0	0	150
Unity 3422	115	193	65	No Report Received			0	2,400	0	0	0	350
Vaughn's Chapel 3423	48	63	12	No Report Received			0	3,506	0	0	0	400
Village 5125	10	10	11	No Report Received			0	1,000	0	0	0	10
Wheatcroft 3627	32	57	10	No Report Received			0	2,962	0	0	0	110
Woodlawn 3417	72	303	47	No Report Received			0	0	0	0	0	1,744
TOTALS	44	2,740	5,265	1,745	20	167	30	9	129,962	305,021	1,360,838	1,585,001	25,163

*Math error corrected. **Purged roll.

COVENANT PRESBYTERY CONTINUED

CHURCHES, PASTORS, AND CLERKS:

Bayou de Chine   (4MWC)MICO3401
2 Kingston Road
Water Valley, KY 42085
(270)355-2089   <Graves>
PA: Robert Goodman   <M1>
2 Kingston Road
Water Valley, KY 42085
(580)756-4726
rgoodman4gvn@hotmail.com
CL: Mark Crass
1990 Kingston Road
Water Valley, KY 42085
(270)355-2381
jimcrassauto10@bellsouth.net

Benton   (4WC)MICO3403
2968 Aurora Highway (mailing)
Hardin, KY 40248
Kentucky Highway 58 (physical)
Benton, KY 42025
( )   <Marshall>
CL: Michele Shearer
2969 Aurora Highway
Hardin, KY 42048
(270)354-8656
mshearer92858@hotmail.com

Bethel   (4WC)MICO3404
12304 Wickliffe Road
Kevil, KY 42053
(270)876-7239   <Ballard>
FAX: (270)876-7513
bethelcpchurch@gmail.com
PA: Drew Gray   <M1>
8220 Timberland Drive
West Paducah, KY 42086
(270)331-5569
drewgray01@gmail.com
CL: Teresa Higdon
230 Lake Point Drive
Paducah, KY 42003
(270)554-5003
teresa@qservicesco.com

Calvary   (4MC)MICO3405
98 Calvary Church Road
Mayfield, KY 42066
(270)376-5525   <Graves>
CL: Darla Jo Tucker
665 McNutt Road
Wingo, KY 42088
(270)376-2065

Camp Ground   (4C)MICO5103
2645 Lick Creek Road (mailing)
70 Tunnel Lane (physical)
Anna, IL 62906
(618)833-9000   <Union>
IP: Joe Vance   <M3>
1740 N Friendship Road
Paducah, KY 42001
CL: Sandra Boaz
2645 Lick Creek Road
Anna, IL 62906
(618)833-8216
skboaz@yahoo.com

Chandler   (4MWC)MICO5302

338 S State Street
Chandler, IN 47610
(812)925-6175   <Warrick>
FAX: (812)925-3628
chandlercpc2@hotmail.com
PA: Jesse Thornton   <M1 MY>
1016 S Fly Avenue
Goreville, IL 62939
(812)925-6475
FAX: (812)925-3628
jessthornton@msn.com
CL: Robert Hooper
PO Box 351
Chandler, IN 47610
(812)925-6965
rwhooper@yahoo.com

Ebenezer   (C)MICO5105
Thompsonville, IL 62890
( )   <Saline>
CL: Pat Fletcher
24535 Kaskaskia Road
Thompsonville, IL 62890
(618)627-2288

Ebenezer Hall   (4WC)MICO5106
9850 Lick Creek Road (mailing)
750 Grand View (physical)
Buncombe, IL 62912
(618)833-8280   <Union>
CL: Carolyn Hammon
9850 Lick Creek Road
Buncombe, IL 62912
(618)833-8280

Flat Lick   (4WC)MICO3606
415 Bennetttown Street (mailing)
Herndon, KY 42236
9355 Lafayette Road (physical))
Herndon, KY 42236
(270)885-1350   <Christian>
pastorsteve88@yahoo.com
CL: Mike Barbee
415 Bennetttown Street
Herndon, KY 42236
(270)498-3664

Fredonia   (4MEWC)MICO3608
204 West Pierson Street (mailing)
303 Cassidy Avenue (physical)
Fredonia, KY 42411
(270)545-3481   <Caldwell>
SS: Larry Buchanan   <M1>
730 Shelby Road
Salem, KY 42078
(270)988-1880
lbuchanan.tse@gmail.com
CL: Cindy Cruce
46 Penn Drive
Marion, KY 42064
(270)965-4520
ccruce@fredoniavalleybank.com

Gilead   (4EC)MICO5110
3470 Gilead Church Road (mailing)
4385 Gilead Church Road (physical)
Simpson, IL 62985
(618)695-2653   <Johnson>
tim-arm@live.com
CL: Tim Armstrong
745 Webb Town Road

Tunnel Hill, IL 62972
(618)559-7021
tim-arm@live.com

Good Spring   (2WC)MICO3609
1800 Old Fredonia Road (mailing)
Princeton, KY 42445
4142 Good Spring Road (physical)
Fredonia, KY 42411
( )   <Caldwell>
CL: Mike Stephens
1800 Old Fredonia Road
Princeton, KY 42445
(270)559-6032
mwstephens1800@gmail.com

Highland   (4MWC)MICO3414
3950 Lovelaceville Road
Paducah, KY 42001
(270)554-3572   <McCracken>
hcpsec@highlandcpc.comcastbiz.net
PA: Olen (Bud) Russell   <M1>
9595 Wickliffe Road
Wickliffe, KY 42087
olen552@aol.com
(270)562-1096
CL: Elaine S Overton
3915 Lovelaceville Road
Paducah, KY 42001
(270)554-1259
jred3915@bellsouth.net

Hopewell   (4C)MICO3610
768 Lola Road (mailing)
1235 Lola Road (physical)
Salem, KY 42078
(270)988-3859   <Livingston>
SS: Troy Newcomb   <M2>
PO Box 858
Salem, KY 42078
(270)210-4902
newcomb.troy@yahoo.com
SS: Larry Buchanan   <M1>
730 Shelby Road
Salem, KY 42078
(270)988-1880
lbuchanan.tse@gmail.com
CL: Michael Heneisen
1162 Hampton Road
Salem, KY 42078
(270)988-4856
heneisen@tds.net

Hopkinsville   (4MWC)MICO3611
2701 Faircourt
Hopkinsville, KY 42240
(270)886-1464   <Christian>
FAX: (270)885-1531
cumberland1@bellsouth.net
PA: Robert T Spurling Jr   <M1>
305 Wayne Drive
Hopkinsville, KY 42240
(865)803-8582
CL: Marcia Ballard
306 Lucky Debonair
Hopkinsville, KY 42240
(270)839-5482

Liberty   (4C)MICO3406
510 Richardson Street (mailing)
150 Liberty Road (physical)

COVENANT PRESBYTERY CONTINUED

Murray, KY 42071
( )   <Calloway>
PA: Gary Vacca   <M1>
2203 Creekwood Drive
Murray, KY 42071
(270)978-0818
garyvacca@spirualliving.com
CL: Brenda Lawson
441 Old Shiloh Road
Murray, KY 42071
(270)227-5872
bsnip10@hotmail.com
_____
Lisman   (4EC)MICO3613
153 Woodland Acres (mailing)
Dixon, KY 42409
2085 State Route 270 W (physical)
Clay, KY 42404
( )   <Webster>
PA: John R Shoulta   <M1>
1154 Mt Carmel Road
White Plains, KY 42464
(270)676-3563
johnshoulta@bellsouth.net
CL: Nancy Burnett
451 Jim Villines Road
Dixon, KY 42409
(270)639-6204
_____
Macedonia   (4WC)MICO3614
18030 Beulah Road (mailing)
Princeton, KY 42445
Highway 291 (physical)
Dalton, KY
( )   <Hopkins>
CL: Narvin Darnall
18030 Beulah Road
Princeton, KY 42445
(279)836-7089
narvin-d@yahoo.com
_____
Madisonville   (4MWC)MICO3615
PO Box 392 (mailing)
1540 Anton Road (physical)
Madisonville, KY 42431
(270)821-5970   <Hopkins>
SS: Shelley Hunt   <M2 ST>
6035 State Route 506
Marion, KY 42064
sheljean@kynet.biz
(270)704-2189
CL: Jean Duncan
330 S Daves Street
Madisonville, KY 42431
(270)821-5138
jduncan42431@att.net
_____
Margaret Hank   (4WC)MICO3415
1526 Park Avenue
Paducah, KY 42001
(270)443-3689   <McCracken>
holyday@vci.net
PA: Christopher Fleming   <M1>
133 Minerva Place
Paducah, KY 42001
(615)424-8561
holyday@vci.net
CL: Amy Fleming
133 Minerva Place
Paducah, KY 42001
(270)443-3689

holyday@vci.net
_____
Marion First   (4MEWC)MICO3616
PO Box 323 (mailing)
224 W Bellville Street (physical)
Marion, KY 42064
(270)965-4746   <Crittenden>
firstcpchurch@mchsi.com
PA: Dee Ann Thompson   <M1>
226 W Bellville Street
Marion, KY 42064
(270)445-0310
deethomp5@hotmail.com
CL: Jo Ann McClure
PO Box 92
Marion, KY 42064
(270)965-3323
_____
Milburn Chapel   (4EC)MICO3416
3760 Metropolis Lake Road
West Paducah, KY 42086
(270)488-2588   <McCracken>
milburnchapel@gmail.com
PA: Glenn Warren   <M1>
9735 Crotzer Road
West Paducah, KY 42086
(931)209-5431
gwarren224@gmail.com
CL: Joe Neal Neftzger
903 E 6th Street
Metropolis, IL 62960
(618)524-5349
milburnchapel@gmail.com
_____
Mt Carmel   (4MW C)MICO3617
11504 Mt Carmel Road (mailing)
11410 Mt Carmel Road (physical)
White Plains, KY 42464
(270)676-3563   <Hopkins>
bshoulta@bellsouth.net
PA: John R Shoulta   <M1>
11504 Mt Carmel Road
White Plains, KY 42464
(270)676-3563
johnshoulta@bellsouth.net
CL: Larry Putman
1319 Mt Carmel Pond River Road
White Plains, KY 42464
(270)676-3628
_____
Mt Pleasant   (4 C)MICO3618
16647 State Route 109
Sullivan, KY 42460
( )   <Union>
PA: Dale Williams   <M1>
3156 State Route 2837
Clay, KY 42404
(270)664-2044
CL: Richard White
2465 State Route 270 E
Sturgis, KY 42459
(270)333-6109
whitefarms1@att.net
_____
Mt Sterling   (4MWC)MICO5117
1780 Mt Sterling Road
Brookport, IL 62910
(618)564-2616   <Massac>
FAX: (618)564-2616
mscpchurch@yahoo.com
PA: David LeNeave   <M1>

8725 Hamletsburg Road
Brookport, IL 62910
(618)564-2437
mscpchurch_bd@yahoo.com
CL: Gary N Angelly
8646 Independence Road
Brookport, IL 62910
(618)564-2874
FAX: (618)564-2874
angelly@djklink.net
_____
Mt Zion   (4WC)MICO5118
PO Box 383 (mailing)
1159 Mt Zion Road (physical)
Dongola, IL 62926
(618)827-4463   <Union>
jsr487@frontier.com
SS: Donna Davenport   <M1>
PO Box 234
Wingo, KY 42088
chamberdonna@yahoo.com
(270)376-5488
SS: Philip Brown   <M1>
540 Mt Pisgah Road
Dongola, IL 62926
(618)697-0972
brownlp75@yahoo.com
CL: Sharon R. Resch
PO Box 383
Dongola, IL 62926
(618)827-4463
jsr487@frontier.com
_____
New Hope   (4MWC)MICO3410
7620 Cross Mill Road
Paducah, KY 42001
(270)554-0473   <McCracken>
newhopecpchurch@hotmail.com
PA: Curtis Franklin   <M1>
7620 Cross Mill Road
Paducah, KY 42001
(270)625-1898
brocurtis@fredonia.biz
CL: Leslie Wright
6575 New Hope Church Road
Paducah, KY 42001
(270)534-1699
leslie.wright@mccracken.kyschools.us
_____
North Pleasant Grove (4WC)MICO3411
Murray, KY 42071
( )   <Calloway>
PA: April Watson   <M1>
529 W Bellville
Marion, KY 42064
(270)965-2850
aprilwatson@hotmail.com
CL: Fred Kemp
276 Airport Road
Murray, KY 42071
_____
Oak Grove   (4MWC)MICO3412
2465 Magness Road
Benton, KY 42025
(270)437-4606   <Calloway>
PA: Randy Lowe   <M1>
222 McDougal Drive
Murray, KY 42071
(270)753-8255
loweshodle@aol.com
CL: Jeff Gordon

COVENANT PRESBYTERY CONTINUED

2465 Magness Road
Benton, KY 42025
(270)437-4613
jgordon@wk.net
_____

Oak Grove Union   (4C)MICO3619
  Highway 132
  Clay, KY 42404
  (270)664-0008   <Webster>
  jvfulton@wk.net
CL: Daniel M Heady
  2564 State Route 132 W
  Dixon, KY 42409
  (270)748-6848
  danielheady@kycourts.net
_____

Oakland   (4MWC)MICO3413
  9104 US Highway 68 W
  Calvert City, KY 42029
  (270)898-2630   <Marshall>
PA: Danny York   <M1>
  5420 State Routh 902 W
  Fredonia, KY 42411
  (270)350-7262
  nonnieyork@yahoo.com
CL: John Jenkins
  1265 Elva Loop Road
  Symsonia, KY 42082
  (270)705-3229
_____

Piney Fork   (4WC)MICO3620
  4294 Coppers Spring Road
  Marion, KY 42064
  ( )   <Crittenden>
PA: William E Martin, Jr   <M1>
  741 Chapel Hill Road
  Marion, KY 42064
  (870)270-3344
  juniormartin@yahoo.com
CL: Sarah Ford
  220 S Weldon Street
  Marion, KY 42064
  (270)965-3833
_____

Pleasant Valley   (4C)MICO3418
  111 College Drive
  Kevil, KY 42053
  (270)224-2497   <Ballard>
SS: April Watson   <M1>
  529 W Bellville
  Marion, KY 42064
  (270)965-2850
  aprilwatson@hotmail.com
CL: William E Kilby
  PO Box 413
  La Center, KY 42056
  (270)665-5405
_____

Providence 1st   (4MEWC)MICO3621
  305 Locust Street (mailing)
  119 Locust Street (physical)
  Providence, KY 42450
  (270)667-2485   <Webster>
  chalit@apex.net
SS: Paul Stone   <M1>
  3490 State Route 2837
  Clay, Kentucky 42404
  (270)664-6244
  stonepstc@aol.com
CL: Paul Northern
  317 N Broadway

Providence, KY 42450
(270)667-2636
_____

Rose Creek   (4WC)MICO3622
  7650 Island Ford Road (mailing)
  Hanson, KY 42413
  7220 Rose Creek Road (physical)
  Nebo, KY 42441
  ( )   <Hopkins>
PA: Paul Stone   <M1>
  3490 State Route 2837
  Clay, KY 42404
  (270)664-6244
CL: Joseph E Peyton
  7650 Island Ford Road
  Hanson, KY 42413
  (270)619-0636
  jepeyton@madisonville.com
_____

Rozzell Chapel   (4C)MICO3419
  1258 Rozzell Church Road
  Mayfield, KY 42066
  (270)623-6866   <Graves>
PA: D Frederick (Fred) Fahl   <M1>
  500 3rd Street
  Fulton, KY 42041
  (270)472-1476
  dffahl@gmail.com
CL: Donna Davenport   <M1>
  PO Box 234
  Wingo, KY 42088
  (270)804-3526
  chamberdonna@yahoo.com
_____

Sturgis   (4MWC)MICO3625
  504 N Main Street
  Sturgis, KY 42459
  (270)333-2851   <Union>
  FAX: (270)333-3118
  sturgiscpc@att.net
PA: Victor Hassell   <M1>
  510 N Main Street
  Sturgis, KY 42459
  (270)333-9170
  FAX: (270)333-3118
  hassellvictor@hotmail.com
CL: Barbara B Sutton
  849 State Route 950
  Morganfield, KY 42437
  (270)333-4385
_____

Sugar Grove   (4MWC)MICO3626
  585 Sugar Grove Church Road
  Marion, KY 42064
  (270)965-4435   <Crittenden>
PA: Dennis Weaver   <M1>
  1750 Government Road
  Princeton, KY 42245
  (731)592-9054
  dsweaver@memphisseminary.edu
CL: Gladys Brown
  6781 State Route 120
  Marion, KY 42064
  (270)965-2969
  gbrown6781@live.com
_____

Union Chapel   (4C)MICO5123
  313 E Illinois Street (mailing)
  2210 Droit Road (physical)
  Galatia, IL 62935
  ( )   <Saline>

CL: Session Clerk
  313 E Illinois Street
  Galatia, IL 62935
_____

Unity   (4MWC)MICO3422
  1503 Story Avenue (mailing)
  Murray, KY 42071
  1929 E Unity Church Road (physical)
  Hardin, KY 42048
  (270)354-8216   <Marshall>
  cprevbhayes@gmail.com
PA: Brian Hayes   <M1>
  69 Cactus Drive
  Benton, KY 42025
  (270)210-8165
  cprevbhayes@gmail.com
CL: Jonathan Whisman
  5352 Murray Highway
  Hardin, KY 42048
  (270)437-3949
  jwhisman@wk.net
_____

Vaughn's Chapel   (4MWC)MICO3423
  4775 Calvert City Road
  Calvert City, KY 42029
  (270)395-7318   <Marshall>
PA: Wendell Ordway   <M1>
  4775 Calvert City Road
  Calvert City, KY 42029
  (270)395-7318
CL: John P Case
  93 W Second Avenue
  Calvert City, KY 42029
  (270)395-4203
_____

Village   (4C)MICO5125
  319 County Road 450 N
  Norris City, IL 62869
  (618)962-3256   <White>
CL: Charles F Edwards
  324 County Road 250 N
  Norris City, IL 62869
  (618)962-3256
  (618)962-3256
_____

Wheatcroft   (4WC)MICO3627
  PO Box 7 (mailing)
  47 Hammock Street E (physical)
  Wheatcroft, KY 42463
  ( )   <Webster>
PA: Dale Williams   <M1>
  3156 State Route 2837
  Clay, KY 42404
  (270)664-2802
  dalewilliams@roadrunner.com
CL: Jackie Gass
  3394 State Route 147
  Sebree, KY 42455
  (270)664-9310
_____

Woodlawn   (4MWC)MICO3417
  3402 Old Benton Road
  Paducah, KY 42002
  (270)442-7713   <McCracken>
  woodlawnchurch@live.com
CL: Todd Belt
  3402 Old Benton Road
  Paducah, KY 42002
  (270)442-7713
  woodlawnyouth@msn.com

COVENANT PRESBYTERY CONTINUED

OTHERS ON MINISTERIAL ROLL:

Aden, Dare   <M1 WC>
  1280 Kimber Road
  Dongola, IL 62926
  (618)827-3625
  FAX: (618)827-4612
  dare_aden@hotmail.com

Ballow, Brent   <M1 WC>
  715 Highland Church Road
  Paducah, KY 42001
  (270)564-8891
  hcppastor@bellsouth.net

Barnett, Rudolph   <M1 WC>
  RR 5 Box 267
  McLeansboro, IL 62859
  (618)643-3253

Board, N Ray   <M1 WC>
  267 State Route 293 N
  Princeton, KY 42445
  (270)365-3850
  rayboard@att.net

Facker, David   <M1 WC>
  3409 Benton Road
  Paducah, KY 42003
  (270)442-7713
  woodlawnpastor@live.com

French, Jeff   <M1 WC>
  5 Rose Petal Lane
  Dawson Springs, KY 42408
  (270)993-0855
  brojeff7@bellsouth.net

Fulton, James V   <M1 WC>
  1520 Oak Grove Road
  Benton, KY 42025
  (270)437-4320

Gerard, Eugene S   <M1 OM>
  615 N 42nd Street
  Paducah, KY 42001
  (270)443-2889

Guarneros, Stephen H   <M1 WC>
  506 Clifton Court
  Hopkinsville, KY 42240
  (270)869-7544
  pastorsteve88@yahoo.com

Heidel, Jason   <M1 WC>
  218 Morningside Drive
  Hopkinsville, KY 42240
  (270)498-7380
  heidelj@hotmail.com

Hughes, Douglas   <M1 WC>
  5545 Hocker Road
  Paducah, KY 42001
  (270)488-2588
  milburnchapel@gmail.com

Lawson, James   <M1 OM>
  1003 West 3rd Street
  Fulton, KY 42041
  (270)472-5272
  ridgepointefarm@bellsouth.net

Lively, Louella   <M1 WC>
  c/o Owensboro Care Center
  1205 Leitchfield Road
  Owensboro, KY 42303
  (270)527-3776

Mays, Ronald B   <M1 PR>
  1100 Cindy Lane
  Mayfield, KY 42066
  (270)247-0070
  rbmays@wk.net

Moore, Hillman C   <M1 RT>
  300 Medical Parkway Ste 2320
  Lakeway, TX 78738
  (731)437-9561
  hillmancm@att.net

Potts, Danny   <M1 WC>
  418 Eddings Street Apt 2
  Fulton, KY 42041
  (270)376-2901

Rudolph, Allie D   <M1 WC>
  855 Old Rosebower Church Road
  Paducah, KY 42003
  (270)898-4903
  rallie307@aol.com

Shauf, Steve   <M1 OM>
  719 Bellevue Drive
  Paducah, KY 42001
  (270)331-5247
  theshaufs@hotmail.com

Shauf, Teresa   <M1 OM>
  719 Bellevue Drive
  Paducah, KY 42001
  (270)331-5217
  theshaufs@hotmail.com

Shirey, John   <M1 RT>
  10181 State Route 56 W
  Sturgis, KY 42459
  (270)389-3562
  amshirey7@ips.com

Smith, James A   <M1 M9 WC>
  309 Lutes Road
  Paducah, KY 42001
  (901)574-2345
  james1493@att.net

Williams, David J   <M1 WC>
  20 Acorn Drive
  Harrisburg, IL 62946
  (618)252-1851

OTHER LICENTIATES ON ROLL:

Ashley, Jack (Nick)   <M2 ST>
  2625A Raleigh Drive
  Evansville, IN 47715
  (812)204-1422
  edencarteringusa@aol.com

Hassell, Samantha   <M2 ST>
  510 N Main Street
  Sturgis, KY 42459
  (270)333-9170
  hassell_samantha@hotmail.com

Hopkins, Daniel   <M2 ST>
  1608 Oak Park Boulevard
  Calvert City, KY 42029
  (270)205-1847
  danielhopkins2469@yahoo.com

Hopkins, Wayne   <M2 ST>
  1413 E Unity Church Road
  Hardin, KY 42048
  (270)437-4481

Rogers, John   <M2>
  308 Rushing Road
  Paducah, KY 42001
  (270)534-1195
  johnr308@comcast.net

OTHER CANDIDATES ON ROLL:

Alderson, Cameron   <M3 ST>
  122 E Cherry Street
  Chandler, IN 47610
  (812)925-6475

Impastato, Paulino   <M3>
  1547 Mt Zion Church Road
  Marion, KY 42064
  (270)965-9528

Kibler, Taylor   <M3>
  1070 W Main Street Apt 1720
  Hendersonville, TN 37075
  (615)509-7114
  taylorkibler@gmail.com

Luthy, Dusty   <M3>
  400 S Friendship Road Apt G
  Paducah, KY 42003
  (270)933-2722
  dustyluthy@gmail.com

Turner, Andrew   <M3>
  3295 Mount Moriah Road
  Galatia, IL 62935
  (618)294-0838
  turner87029@gmail.com

Cumberland Presbytery
MIDWEST SYNOD

	GENERAL	MEMBERSHIP			CHANGES				FINANCES			
	1.Church Number	2.Active	3.Total	4.Church School	5.Prof. of Faith	6.Gains	7.Losses	8.Children Baptized	9. OUR UNITED OUT-REACH	10. Total Out-Reach Giving	11. All Other Expenses	12. Total Income Received	13. Value Church Prop. 1=1000
	1	2	3	4	5	6	7	8	9	10	11	12	13
Antioch	3101	30	30	16	No Report Received			0	0	0	0	0	300
Auburn	3301	57	100	30	No Report Received			0	0	0	0	0	405
Bald Knob**	3302	4	6	4	0	0	137	0		680	13,067	14,317	250
Bethel	3102	61	61	28	0	0	1	0	2,000	4,076	29,871	38,758	0
Bethel #1	3103	13	71	11	0	0	0	0	1,000	1,820	19,591	15,426	200
Beulah*	3501	24	26	35	0	0	0	0	2,454	2,454	26,434	22,209	123
Boiling Springs	3303	16	19	14	No Report Received			0	0	0	0	0	27
Bowling Green	3304	150	230	75	1	3	3	1	15,069	28,408	243,419	261,827	1,110
Bridgeport 1st**	3131	87	87	9	0	6	27	0	0	16,306	141,911	104,063	651
Brier Creek	3503	85	164	60	2	6	1	0	8,240	14,261	68,079	82,340	300
Campbellsville	3104	86	94	56	1	4	2	0	0	6,874	148,917	148,254	1,844
Caneyville	3201	3	5	27	No Report Received			0	0	0	0	0	157
Casey's Fork	3105	14	19	14	No Report Received			0	1,468	0	0	0	37
Cedar Flat	3106	14	53	20	0	1	6	0	0	1,346	23,110	21,917	90
Clear Point*	3107	30	30	17	1	0	18	1	1,882	3,412	23,147	18,864	100
Clifton Mills	3202	12	35	46	0	0	0	0	0	2,113	12,606	28,009	275
Coyle	3203	33	33	24	1	4	2	1	0	1,868	33,547	36,169	200
Dukes	3204	12	44	5	0	0	5	0	0	1,780	12,421	14,828	300
Ephesus	3205	12	14	0	0	0	10	0	0	1,194	10,220	7,335	150
Fairview*	3504	11	29	0	0	1	0	0	1,581	2,977	9,477	16,294	20
Freedom	3207	62	88	52	1	1	2	1	1,677	11,086	80,638	91,724	450
Garfield	3208	62	116	50	1	5	1	0	0	3,449	121,741	120,158	495
Gasper River	3306	36	49	20	No Report Received			0	0	0	0	0	105
Gill's Chapel	3307	7	23	0	No Report Received			0	0	0	0	0	34
Glasgow	3108	185	231	125	4	10	8	0	0	3,906	200,694	188,573	2,600
Good Hope	3109	25	25	25	No Report Received			0	0	0	0	0	50
Green Ridge	3308	36	59	17	0	2	1	0	3,820	5,703	44,345	54,628	440
Greensburg*	3110	143	184	55	1	55	4	1	12,231	19,076	118,023	122,309	1,000
Greenville	3505	17	48	0	0	0	1	0	600	7,059	54,805	54,553	535
Harrodsburg	3111	15	136	12	1	1	1	0	2,648	2,823	0	19,900	383
Heartsong*	3222	48	48	20	0	25	2	0	0	1,000	52,000	55,000	1,650
High Point	3314	18	18	12	1	1	3	0	0	1,500	15,702	16,763	500
Hopewell	3112	14	25	14	No Report Received			0	0	0	0	0	60
Irvington	3210	20	26	5	0	0	0	0	0	1,485	23,936	55,417	80
Leitchfield	3211	50	77	25	No Report Received			0	1,250	0	0	0	550
Lewisburg	3309	26	68	27	0	1	3	0	500	7,660	57,554	72,679	300
Liberty	3116	27	58	12	0	2	2	0	0	2,088	59,799	55,617	750
Lick Branch	3117	64	191	38	No Report Received			0	0	0	0	0	90
Little Muddy	3310	19	19	14	0	0	0	0	2,800	19,500	10,839	33,267	119
Louisville Japanese	3223								1,500				
Louisville 1st	3212	64	126	38	No Report Received			0	0	0	0	0	1,000
Magnolia	3214	70	70	50	0	0	3	0	0	24,200	56,000	81,500	550
Monroe Chapel	3119	34	56	24	1	1	1	1	2,138	3,624	17,203	24,590	150
Morgantown	3311	21	21	6	No Report Received			0	0	0	0	0	80
Mt. Moriah	3120	16	32	10	0	0	0	1	0	1,878	22,339	21,975	75
Mt. Olive	3216	15	15	9	0	0	2	0	0	1,465	9,715	12,424	70
Mt. Olivet	3312	43	42	20	0	0	1	1	0	919	41,992	32,744	1,121
Mt. Pleasant	3217	50	68	40	0	0	0	0	3,969	7,480	43,795	40,786	230
Mt. Vernon	3218	24	32	14	0	0	0	0	0	1,291	22,972	24,051	70
Mt. Zion (AC)	3121	5	18	8	No Report Received			0	0	0	0	0	0
Mt. Zion (DC)	3507	30	64	21	2	2	0	0	3,172	7,097	39,534	43,308	255
Neal's Chapel	3122	20	41	6	0	0	2	0	0	1,960	17,914	19,238	150
Needham*	3219	17	17	7	0	4	3	0	0	1,092	6,680	17,325	6
New Cypress	3508	11	25	0	0	0	2	1	1,212	1,760	9,202	12,480	122
Oak Forest	3123	95	211	89	0	6	11	0	4,282	12,800	52,200	74,550	115
Owensboro	3509	121	121	56	0	5	7	4	7,644	19,365	180,773	191,722	1,646
Pleasant Hill	3510	4	5	4	No Report Received			0	0	0	0	0	230
Point Pleasant	3313	4	4	0	0	0	1	0	0	250	2,111	2,920	0

Cumberland Presbytery   (Continued)
MIDWEST SYNOD

GENERAL	MEMBERSHIP			CHANGES				FINANCES				
1.Church Number	2.Active	3.Total	4.Church School	5.Prof. of Faith	6.Gains	7.Losses	8.Children Baptized	9. OUR UNITED OUT-REACH	10. Total Out-Reach Giving	11. All Other Expenses	12. Total Income Received	13. Value Church Prop. 1=1000
1	2	3	4	5	6	7	8	9	10	11	12	13
Poplar Grove* 3511	6	15	6	0	0	26	0	1,601	2,117	21,575	16,004	90
Radcliff* 3220	27	27	12	0	2	3	1	0	2,615	42,278	44,893	237
Sacramento 3512	105	206	60	0	2	6	0	11,582	24,220	88,173	115,807	89
Salem 3127	9	32	0	No Report Received			0	0	0	0	0	35
Seven Springs 3128	16	35	18	No Report Received			0	0	0	0	0	267
Shiloh 3129	40	86	26	2	2	1	0	5,101	14,028	67,010	60,190	400
Short Creek 3221	21	53	16	0	0	1	0	2,869	8,930	20,309	29,239	95
Wisdom 3130	20	30	10	0	0	0	0	0	1,098	8,845	9,356	75
TOTALS 66	2,544	4,176	1,576	20	152	312	14	104,290	314,093	2,426,513	2,646,300	23,565

*Math error corrected. **Purged roll.

CHURCHES, PASTORS, AND CLERKS:
_____

Antioch   (4C)MICU3101
  103 Clarksdale Circle (mailing)
  Glasgow, KY 42141
  68 Antioch Church Road (physical)
  Knob Lick, KY 42154
  ( )   <Metcalfe>
SS: Michael E Fancher   <M3>
  356 Breeding Road
  Edmonton, KY 42129
  (270)432-3138
  princo1975@live.com
CL: Kathy B Nason
  103 Clarksdale Circle
  Glasgow, KY 42141
  (270)670-4796

_____

Auburn   (4MWC)MICU3301
  Box 6
  Auburn, KY 42206
  (270)542-4304   <Logan>
PA: Grant Minton   <M1>
  PO Box 270
  Auburn, KY 42206
  (270)542-7991
  FAX: (270)271-4603
  gminton@logantele.com
CL: Ashley Engler
  695 Howlett Road
  Auburn, KY 42206
  (270)542-6730

_____

Bald Knob   (4C)MICU3302
  102 Bald Knob Church Road
  Russellville, KY 42276
  ( )   <Logan>
PA: Byron Dumas   <M1 OP>
  1775 Theresa Drive
  , TN 37043
  (931)358-3348
  lodumas7346@aol.com

CL: Kathleen Tynes
  3175 Caney Fork Road
  Lewisburg, KY 42256
  (270)755-4218

_____

Bethel   (2WC)MICU3102
  454 Iron Mountain Road (mailing)
  Center, KY 42214
  ( )   <Metcalfe>
SS: Keith G Atwell   <M1>
  7688 Hardyville Road
  Hardyville, KY 42746
  (270)528-3667
CL: Steven McMullen
  454 Iron Mountain Road
  Center, KY 42214
  (270)565-5440
  mcmfarm@yahoo.com

_____

Bethel #1   (4MWC)MICU3103
  1259 Perryville Road (mailing)
  2586 Perryville Road (physical)
  Harrodsburg, KY 40330
  ( )   <Mercer>
PA: John Contini   <M1>
  4344 Poor Ridge Pike
  Lancaster, KY 40444
  (859)339-0747
  john@hillsideheritagefarm.com
CL: James L Wheeler
  1259 Perryville Road
  Harrodsburg, KY 40330
  (859)734-2045
  jlwheeler@roadrunner.com

_____

Beulah   (4WC)MICU3501
  2856 Beda Road (mailing)
  320 Beulah Church Road (physical)
  Hartford, KY 42347
  (270)298-3352   <Ohio>
  FAX: (270)298-7007
  cmwsaw2@bellsouth.net
PA: Michael Justice   <M1>

  250 W 5th Street #B
  Russellville, KY 42276
  (270)726-6673
CL: Chuck Westerfield
  2856 Beda Road
  Hartford, KY 42347
  (270)298-3352
  FAX: (270)298-7007
  smwsaw@connectgradd.net

_____

Boiling Springs   (4C)MICU3303
  3360 Highway 259 (mailing)
  2412 Highway 259 (physical)
  Portland, TN 37148
  (615)325-2618   <Sumner>
PA: Chris Darland   <M1>
  582 Ada Drive
  Harrodsburg, KY 40330
  (859)734-2254
CL: Pearl Kepley
  3380 Highway 259
  Portland, TN 37148
  (615)325-3645

_____

Bowling Green   (4MWC)MICU3304
  807 Campbell Lane
  Bowling Green, KY 42104
  (270)781-3295   <Warren>
  FAX: (270)781-2368
  bgcpc@insightbb.com
PA: Steve Delashmit   <M1>
  2705 Garrett Drive
  Bowling Green, KY 42104
  (270)796-8822
  FAX: (270)781-2368
CL: Hoy Hodges
  295 Carver Lane
  Alvaton, KY 42122
  (270)843-4008
  hhlaw319@aol.com

_____

Bridgeport 1st   (4C)MICU3131
  515 DeKalb Street

CUMBERLAND PRESBYTERY CONTINUED

Bridgeport, PA 19405
(610)275-6942   <Philadelphi>
PA: Donald Grey Barnhouse, Jr   <M1>
51 Harristown Road
Paradise, PA 17562
(717)768-0048
donaldbarnhouse@gmail.com
CL: William McLay
9 E Brown Street
Norristown, PA 19401
(610)277-8295

Brier Creek   (4MWC)MICU3503
3467 State Route 175 N
Bremen, KY 42325
(270)525-3611   <Muhlenberg>
PA: Marc Bell   <M1>
3467 State Route 175 N
Bremen, KY 42325
(270)846-4203
marc.bell1@att.net
CL: Sherry Skimehorn
59 Whitmer Street
Central City, KY 42330
(270)525-3472
skimehor@bellsouth.net

Campbellsville   (4MWC)MICU3104
500 Cumberland Way
Campbellsville, KY 42718
(270)465-4091   <Taylor>
FAX: (270)469-9651
firstcpchurch@windstream.net
PA: John Butler   <M1>
501 Cherokee Drive
Campbellsville, KY 42718
(270)403-7602
rev.butlerj8134@gmail.com
PA: Wayne E Brooks   <M1>
1505 Parkview Drive
Campbellsville, KY 42718
(270)465-9235
webrooks@windstream.net
CL: Faye Adams
902 Rosecrest Avenue
Campbellsville, KY 42718
(270)789-1791
newlifeblessed@yahoo.com

Caneyville   (4EWC)MICU3201
PO Box 334 (mailing)
203 River Park Drive (physical)
Caneyville, KY 42721
(   )   <Grayson>
PS: Steven Smith   <M3 ST>
100 Valleyview Drive
Leitchfield, KY 42754
CL: Mary Alice Woosley-Logsdon
PO Box 334
Leitchfield, KY 42721
(270)230-2818
FAX: (270)879-9211
alicewoosley71@yahoo.com

Casey's Fork   (1C)MICU3105
PO Box 186 (mailing)
Highway 90 (physical)
Marrowbone, KY 42759
(502)864-3129   <Cumberland>
CL: Jimmy Mosby
210 Bombshell Creek Road

Burkesville, KY 42717
_____

Cedar Flat   (C)MICU3106
1444 Milam Clark Road (mailing)
Summer Shade, KY 42166
Cedar Flat - Curtis Road (physical)
Edmonton, KY 42129
(   )   <Metcalfe>
CL: Janet A Proffitt
1444 Milam Clark Road
Summer Shade, KY 42166
(270)428-4379

Clear Point   (4MWEC)MICU3107
113 Woods Drive (mailing)
Glasgow, KY 42141
Bowling Green, KY 42104
(   )   <Hart>
PA: Darrell Pickett   <M1>
113 Woods Drive
Glasgow, KY 42141
(270)834-6102
dpickett@glasgow-ky.com
CL: Connie Pickett
113 Woods Drive
Glasgow, KY 42141
dpickett@glasgow-ky.com

Clifton Mills   (4WC)MICU3202
521 Butler Hobbs Road (mailing)
Hardinsburg, KY 40143
6406 W Highway 86 (physical)
Irvington, KY 40146
(270)547-5717   <Breckinridge>
CL: Edna M Hobbs
521 Butler Hobbs Road
Hardinsburg, KY 40143
(270)756-2592
tejthbs@att.net

Coyle   (4C)MICU3203
1285 Centerview Rough River Lane
Hudson, KY 40145
(270)257-0851   <Breckinridge>
tucker_rd@bellsouth.net
PA: Billy Ray Carter   <M1>
33 Mockingbird Drive
Leitchfield, KY 42754
(270)259-3897
cartercbc@windstream.net
CL: Ralph D Tucker
1285 Centerview Rough River Lane
Hudson, KY 40145
(270)257-0851
tucker_rd@bellsouth.net

Dukes   (4C)MICU3204
4743 Happy Hollow Road (mailing)
7814 State Route 144 E (physical)
Hawesville, KY 42348
(270)927-9577   <Hancock>
CL: Joe Wilborn
4743 Happy Hollow Road
Hawesville, KY 42348
(270)927-9577
joeandkimwilborn@bellsouth.net

Ephesus   (4EC)MICU3205
2300 Ephesus Church Road (mailing)
30 Ephesus Church Loop (physical)
Harned, KY 40144

(   )   <Breckinridge>
bridget.keesee@ky.gov
CL: Bridget Keesee
2300 Ephesus Church Road
Harned, KY 40144
(270)756-9278
bridget.keesee@ky.gov

Fairview   (4C)MICU3504
PO Box 195 (mailing)
Sacramento, KY 42372
Fairview Road (physical)
Bremen, KY
(270)736-5189   <Muhlenberg>
PA: Terry Fortner   <M1>
1079 Luzerne Depoy Road
Greenville, KY 42345
(270)836-3635
terryfortner@att.net
CL: Ottis E Markwell
PO Box 195
Sacramento, KY 42372
(270)736-5189

Freedom   (4MWC)MICU3207
224 John Drane Lane (mailing)
394 John Drane Lane (physical)
Harned, KY 40144
(270)617-4016   <Breckinridge>
PA: Jeff McMichael   <M1>
224 John Drane Lane
Harned, KY 40144
(270)617-4016
revmcmichael@outlook.com
CL: Larry Collard
4634 Highway 261 N
Hardinsburg, KY 40143
(270)617-0609

Garfield   (4MWC)MICU3208
PO Box 39 (mailing)
90 W Highway 86 (physical)
Garfield, KY 40140
(270)580-4796   <Breckinridge>
mccallum@bbtel.com
PA: Frank McCallum   <M1>
PO Box 56
Garfield, KY 40140
(270)580-4796
mccallum@bbtel.com
CL: Stephen J Tabor
PO Box 39
Garfield, KY 40140
(270)536-3297
btabor@bbtel.com

Gasper River   (4C)MICU3306
3201 Bucksville Road (mailing)
3005 Bucksville Road (physical)
Auburn, KY 42206
(270)542-8998   <Logan>
SS: Byron Dumas   <M1 OP>
1775 Theresa Drive
Clarksville, TN 37043
(931)358-3348
CL: Sandy Tinsley
3201 Bucksville Road
Auburn, KY 42206
(270)542-7900
tinsley@logantele.com

CUMBERLAND PRESBYTERY CONTINUED

Gill's Chapel   (4EC)MICU3307
  PO Box 127 (mailing)
  Lewisburg, KY 42256
  955 Hermon Road (physical)
  Guthrie, KY 42234
  (270)755-4282   <Todd>
  sam60romines@hotmail.com
PA: Sam Romines   <M1>
  PO Box 127
  Lewisburg, KY 42256
  (270)755-4282
  sam60romines@hotmail.com
CL: Sam Romines
  PO Box 127
  Lewisburg, KY 42256
  (270)755-4282
  sam60romines@hotmail.com

Glasgow   (4MWC)MICU3108
  101 Cumberland Street
  Glasgow, KY 42141
  (270)651-3308   <Barren>
  gcpc@glasgow-ky.com
PA: Kenny Hardin   <M1>
  606 Lexington Drive
  Glasgow, KY 42141
CL: Buelon R (Pete) Moss
  101 Cumberland Street
  Glasgow, KY 42141
  (270)646-0305
  mossbue@auburn.edu

Good Hope   (2C)MICU3109
  700 Dutton Creek Road (mailing)
  Lemon Bend Road (physical)
  Campbellsville, KY 42718
  (270)789-1482   <Taylor>
  glwgaw@windstream.net
PA: Earl West   <M1>
  246 Maple Avenue
  Greensburg, KY 42743
  (207)932-5010
  west5010@windstream.net
CL: Gayle Whitley
  700 Dutton Creek Road
  Campbellsville, KY 42718
  (270)789-1482
  glwgaw@windstream.net

Green Ridge   (4MWC)MICU3308
  7424 Highland Lick Road
  Lewisburg, KY 42256
  (270)726-8497   <Logan>
  brojoe2@logantele.com
CL: Shannon Wells
  1720 Crawford Road
  Lewisburg, KY 42256
  (270)277-9977
  chps@bellsouth.net

Greensburg   (4MEWC)MICU3110
  699 Old Hodgenville Road
  Greensburg, KY 42743
  (270)932-4864   <Green>
  greensburgcpc@windstream.net
CL: John David Pickett
  1956 Greensburg Road
  Campbellsville, KY 42718
  (270)405-0201
  johnpickett77@gmail.com

Greenville   (4WC)MICU3505
  234 Sunset Park (mailing)
  108 S Cherry Street (physical)
  Greenville, KY 42345
  (270)338-0882   <Muhlenberg>
PA: Arthur L Burrows, Jr   <M1>
  PO Box 511
  Hopkinsville, KY 42241
  (270)886-1301
CL: Joseph Harris
  234 Sunset Park
  Greenville, KY 42345
  (270)338-6555
  josephharris234@yahoo.com

Harrodsburg   (4MWC)MICU3111
  1113 Louisville Road
  Harrodsburg, KY 40330
  (   )   <Mercer>
PA: Chris Darland   <M1>
  582 Ada Drive
  Harrodsburg, KY 40330
  (859)734-2254
CL: Nancy R Tatum
  4955 Louisville Road
  Salvisa, KY 40372
  (859)865-4482

Heartsong   (4C)MICU3222
  6322 Labor Lane (mailing)
  6104 Bardstown Road (physical)
  Louisville, KY 40291
  (502)635-8587   <Jefferson>
PA: Drew Hayes   <M1>
  8220 Timberland Drive
  West Paducah, KY 42086
  (270)331-5569
  drewgray01@gmail.com
CL: Susan Lawson
  6322 Labor Lane
  Louisville, KY 40291
  (502)968-0006

High Point Community   (C)MICU3314
  203 S Main Street Apt 312 (mailing)
  Somerset, KY 42501
  190 Longview Drive (physical)
  West Somerset, KY 42503
  (606)271-0842   <Pulaski>
  highpointcpc@gmail.com
PA: Fred Michael (Mike) Adams   <M1>
  42 Julies Way
  Somerset, KY 42503
  (606)451-9155
  fma46@twc.com
CL: Betty Huffman
  203 S Main Street Apt 312
  Somerset, KY 42501
  (606)561-3645
  betty.huffman@hotmail.com

Hopewell   (4C)MICU3112
  1012 N Jackson Highway (mailing)
  Hardyville, KY 42746
  Hopewell Church Road (physical)
  Canmer, KY 42722
  (   )   <Hart>
CL: Kaye Atwell
  1012 N Jackson Highway
  Hardyville, KY 42746
  (270)528-5341

  mkatwell@yahoo.com

Irvington   (4MWC)MICU3210
  4108 Highway 477 (mailing)
  Webster, KY 40176
  111 W Walnut Street (physical)
  Irvington, KY 40146
  (   )   <Breckinridge>
PA: Charles Meredith   <M1>
  144 Barbara Circle
  Elizabethtown, KY 42701
  (270)307-0607
CL: Ruby Bell
  4108 Highway 477
  Webster, KY 40176
  (270)547-7455
  rrbells@bbtel.com

Leitchfield   (4MC)MICU3211
  501 W Chestnut Street
  Leitchfield, KY 42754
  (270)259-3835   <Grayson>
PA: Jim Butler   <M1>
  507 W Chestnut Street
  Leitchfield, KY 42754
  (502)635-8587
  jbutler54@insightbb.com
CL: Arita French
  245 Embry Road
  Leitchfield, KY 42754
  (270)259-4457
  kenarita@windstream.net

Lewisburg   (4MWC)MICU3309
  PO Box 127 (mailing)
  101 Church Street (physical)
  Lewisburg, KY 42256
  (270)755-4282   <Logan>
PA: Sam Romines   <M1>
  PO Box 127
  Lewisburg, KY 42256
  (270)755-4282
  sam60romines@hotmail.com
CL: Ralph Cropper
  178 Cardinal Street
  Lewisburg, KY 42256
  (270)755-2357
  ralph.cropper@novelis.com

Liberty   (4WC)MICU3116
  PO Box 4105 (mailing)
  4139 Old Columbia Road (physical)
  Campbellsville, KY 42718
  (270)849-7377   <Taylor>
PA: Earl West   <M1>
  246 Maple Avenue
  Greensburg, KY 42743
  (207)932-5010
  west5010@windstream.net
CL: Barbara Davenport
  216 Happy Hill Drive
  Campbellsville, KY 42718
  (270)465-3633
  teebdee@windstream.net

Lick Branch   (4C)MICU3117
  50 B Jones Road (mailing)
  7318 Lecta Kino Road (physical)
  Glasgow, KY 42141
  (270)670-6698   <Barren>
  doncynem@gmail.com

CUMBERLAND PRESBYTERY CONTINUED

OD: Jerry D Martin <M5>
292 Bristletown Road
Glasgow, KY 42141
(270)678-2476
doncynem@glasgow-ky.com
CL: Nancy Jolly
2979 Kino Road
Glasgow, KY 42141
(270)428-5722
jollyfarms@scrtc.com

_____

Little Muddy (4MC)MICU3310
1061 Sugar Grove Road (mailing)
170 Little Muddy Church Road (physical)
Morgantown, KY 42261
( ) <Butler>
CL: William Gabe Keen
822 Sugar Grove Road
Morgantown, KY 42261
(270)526-5895

_____

Louisville 1st (4MWC)MICU3212
4610 Manslick Road
Louisville, KY 40216
(502)368-4709 <Jefferson>
FAX: (502)368-4709
firstcumberland@att.net
PA: Rodney E Harris <M1>
7420 Conjar Court
Louisville, KY 40214
(502)368-5501
rodneypat@insightbb.com
CL: Carrie Roth
4610 Manslick Road
Louisville, KY 40216
(502)368-4709
firstcumberland@att.net

_____

Louisville Japanese (4C)MICU3223
8710 Hickory Falls Lane
Pewee Valley, KY 40056
(502)657-9643
PA: Iwao Satoh
8710 Hickory Falls Lane
Pewee Valley, KY 40056
(502)657-9643
iwaosatoh@gmail.com
CL: Session Clerk
8710 Hickory Falls Lane
Pewee Valley, KY 40056
(502)657-9643

_____

Magnolia (4MWC)MICU3214
PO Box 1 (mailing)
235 Old L and N Turkpike (physical)
Magnolia, KY 42757
(270)324-3472 <LaRue>
magnoliacpchurch@gmail.com
SS: Anthony Harris <M2>
1604 Parkview Drive
Campbellsville, KY 42718
(270)403-1126
aharris044@gmail.com
CL: Charlotte Tucker
1080 Greensburg Road
Hodgenville, KY 42748
(270)358-3090
charlotte.tucker@larue.kyschools.ust

_____

Monroe Chapel (4C)MICU3119
7688 Hardyville Road (mailing)

Rt 2 Highway 88 (physical)
Hardyville, KY 42746
(270)528-3667 <Hart>
jbuggforbis@hotmail.com
SS: Richard Harrison <M3>
93 Earl Jones Road
Hodgenville, KY 42748
CL: Janie B Forbis
2465 Possum Trot Road
Hardyville, KY 42746
(270)528-3873
jbuggforbis@hotmail.com

_____

Morgantown (4MWC)MICU3311
308 Helm Lane (mailing)
118 W Ohio Street (physical)
Morgantown, KY 42261
( ) <Butler>
SS: David Hocker <M3>
309 N Taylor Street
Morgantown, KY 42261
(270)526-6027
dhocker@hocker.com
CL: Carolyn Henderson
308 Helm Lane
Morgantown, KY 42261
(270)526-3439

_____

Mt Moriah (2C)MICU3120
107 James Street (mailing)
Edmonton, KY 42129
2038 Mt Moriah Road (physical)
Summer Shade, KY 42166
( ) <Metcalfe>
CL: Sandy England
107 James Street
Edmonton, KY 42129
(270)432-3778
englandsim@scrtc.com

_____

Mt Olive (4WC)MICU3216
1295 Solway Meeting Road (mailing)
Mt Olive Church Road (physical)
Big Clifty, KY 42712
( ) <Hardin>
CL: Gayle Johnson
1295 Solway Meeting Road
Big Clifty, KY 42712
(270)862-4313
vonnie.g0000@yahoo.com

_____

Mt Olivet (4MEWC)MICU3312
2640 Mt Olivet Road
Bowling Green, KY 42101
(270)843-0223 <Warren>
SS: Robert (Bob) Bunnell <M1>
329 Lexington Drive
Glasgow, KY 42141
(270)629-6209
bob_bunnell@yahoo.com
CL: Betty Grammer
180 Sir Wilburn Way
Alvaton, KY 42122
(270)781-4435
thememaw02@walmartconnect.com

_____

Mt Pleasant (4C)MICU3217
364 E Big Reedy Road (mailing)
E Big Reedy Road (physical)
Caneyville, KY 42721
( ) <Edmonson>

PS: Greg Bowen <M3 ST>
3241 South Fork Road
Glasgow, KY 42141
CL: Gloria Slaughter
364 E Big Reedy Road
Caneyville, KY 42721
(270)286-9372
gslaughter@mtownbank.com

_____

Mt Vernon (4WC)MICU3218
1358 Ephesus Church Road (mailing)
Harned, KY 40144
2373 Brandenburg Road (physical)
Leitchfield, KY 42754
( ) <Grayson>
PA: William M Macy <M1>
1358 Ephesus Church Road
Harned, KY 40144
(270)756-2775
CL: Shirley Macy
1358 Ephesus Church Road
Harned, KY 40144
(270)756-2775
slmacy@bbtel.com

_____

Mt. Zion (AC) (1C)MICU3121
c/o Lena Bryson
1925 Loren Collins Road
Glens Fork, KY 42741
( ) <Adair>
CL: Lena Bryson
214 Buell Collins Road
Glens Fork, KY 42741
(502)378-6172

_____

Mt Zion (DC) (4MWC)MICU3507
7447 Knottsville Mt Zion Rd (mailing)
8001 Knottsville Mt Zion Rd (physical)
Philpot, KY 42366
( ) <Daviess>
PA: Dennis J Preston <M1>
7447 Knottsville Mount Zion Road
Philpot, KY 42366
(270)925-8144
dennis.preston@daviess.kyschools.us
CL: Shirley L Bratcher
3815 Locust Hill Drive
Owensboro, KY 42303
(270)993-4056
slbratcher24@yahoo.com

_____

Neal's Chapel (4C)MICU3122
62 Oscar Gilpin Road (mailing)
860 Lecta Kino Road (physical)
Glasgow, KY 42141
( ) <Barren>
CL: Pam H Browning
62 Oscar Gilpin Road
Glasgow, KY 42141
(270)670-1047
pshbrowning@hotmail.com

_____

Needham (4WC)MICU3219
3179 Meeting Creek Road (mailing)
State Route 84 (physical)
Eastview, KY 42732
( ) <Hardin>
PA: Shelby O Haire <M1>
3179 Meeting Creek Road
Eastview, KY 42732
(270)862-3887

CUMBERLAND PRESBYTERY CONTINUED

CL: Odelia Dewall
2548 Meeting Creek Road
Eastview, KY 42732
(270)862-4362

New Cypress   (4C)MICU3508
127 W 23rd Street (mailing)
Owensboro, KY 42303
4814 Highway 81 S (physical)
Rumsey, KY 42371
( )   <McLean>
PA: Terry Fortner   <M1>
1079 Luzerne Depoy Road
Greenville, KY 42345
(270)836-3635
terryfortner@att.net
CL: Phyllis Davis
127 W 23rd Street
Owensboro, KY 42303
(270)926-6033
phyllisdavis966@hotmail.com

Oak Forest   (4MWC)MICU3123
170 Milby Rattliff Road
Summersville, KY 42782
(270)932-4685   <Green>
OD: Robert Knight   <M5>
1360 Free Union Road
Columbia, KY 42728
(270)384-0677
CL: Mike Durrett
170 Milby Rattliff Road
Summersville, KY 42782
(270)932-4685
thedurretts@windstream.net

Owensboro   (4C)MICU3509
910 Booth Avenue
Owensboro, KY 42301
(270)683-4479   <Daviess>
brotim.cpc@gmail.net
PA: Timothy McGuire   <M1>
PO Box 42
Mt Sherman, KY 42764
(270)766-9027
brotim.cpc@gmail.com
CL: Becky Pedigo
2508 Duke Drive Apt 10
Owensboro, KY 42301
(270)999-8301
becky_pdg@yahoo.com

Pleasant Hill   (4MEC)MICU3510
10851 Highway 593
Owensboro, KY 42301
(386)689-9340   <Daviess>
CL: Carole Robertson
4709 Forrest Drive
Owensboro, KY 42303
(270)315-5288

Point Pleasant   (1C)MICU3313
7030 State Route 269
Beaver Dam, KY 42320
( )   <Butler>
SS: David Hocker   <M3>
309 N Taylor Street
Morgantown, KY 42261
(270)526-6027
CL: Kathy Pharris
7030 State Route 269

Beaver Dam, KY 42320
(270)274-7418
kathyspharris@yahoo.com

Poplar Grove   (4WC)MICU3511
2929 Kentucky 254 W (mailing)
5112 State Highway 1155 (physical)
Sacramento, KY 42372
( )   <McLean>
PA: James E Talley   <M1>
203 Browning Place
Hopkinsville, KY 42240
(270)886-4184
CL: Gibson H Riggs
PO Box 224
Calhoun, KY 42327
(270)273-3280
FAX: (270)273-3280
riggsg@bellsouth.net

Radcliff   (4U)MICU3220
1751 S Logsdon Parkway
Radcliff, KY 40159
(270)351-6199   <Hardin>
radpres@bbtel.com
OD: John Lentz   <M5>
1876 Highway 44 E
Shepherdsville, KY 40165
(502)543-2659
lentzhome@aol.com
CL: Patricia T. Crosby
851 S Archer Street
Radcliff, KY 40160
(270)351-8548
ptcrosby@bbtel.com

Sacramento   (4MWC)MICU3512
PO Box 257 (mailing)
40 Lyons Lane (physical)
Sacramento, KY 42372
(270)736-5176   <McLean>
rev.butlerj8134@gmail.com
CL: Brenda Lee
386 Dillahay Dame Loop
Island, KY 42350
(270)736-5160

Salem   (2C)MICU3127
1570 Old Salem Church Road (mailing)
291 Clay Wright Road (physical)
Greensburg, KY 42743
( )   <Green>
CL: Joan Cook
1570 Old Salem Church Road
Greensburg, KY 42743
(502)932-5717

Seven Springs   (2C)MICU3128
1607 Seven Springs Church Road
Center, KY 42214
(270)565-4865   <Metcalfe>
PA: Randall Gray   <M1>
1230 New Liberty Big Meadow Road
Knob Lick, KY 42154
(270)432-5322
CL: Louise London
2466 Highway 1048
Center, KY 42214
(270)565-3015

Shiloh   (4MEWC)MICU3129

252 Tabernacle Road (mailing)
1186 Shiloh Road (physical)
Campbellsville, KY 42718
(270)789-2346   <Taylor>
CL: Sue Campbell
333 Campbell Road
Campbellsville, KY 42718
(270)465-5492

Short Creek   (4WC)MICU3221
9312 Owensboro Road (mailing)
Hollow Church Road (physical)
Falls of Rough, KY 40119
( )   <Grayson>
PS: Steven Smith   <M3 ST>
100 Valleyview Drive
Leitchfield, KY 42754
CL: George Fentress
11680 Owensboro Road
Falls of Rough, KY 40119
(270)879-8883

Wisdom   (2C)MICU3130
254 Echo Road (mailing)
State Route 640 (physical)
Knob Lick, KY 42129
( )   <Metcalfe>
CL: Frances Royse
491 Cave Ridge Road
Knob Lick, KY 42154
(270)432-0112
froyse@scrtc.com

OTHERS ON MINISTERIAL ROLL:

Akai, Anum   <M1 WC>
458 Dean Taylor Court
Simpsonville, KY 40067
(502)405-3120
Barrett, Geoff   <M1 RT>
155 Maude Lane
Harrodsburg, KY 40330
(859)748-0450
glbarrett@live.com
Barton, Robert   <M1 RT>
22460 Klines Resort Road #290
Three Rivers, MI 49093
(859)613-2686
csm2ndinfbde2002@yahoo.com
Blevins, Tom   <M1 WC>
50 Blevins Road
Center, KY 42214
(270)565-1792
Boggs, Robert   <M1 WC>
89 Maple Leaf Lane
Leitchfield, KY 42754
(270)259-5546
Brantley, Kevin T   <M1 WC>
308 A A Chestnut Street
Greensburg, KY 42372
(270)405-2222
ktbrantley1971@gmail.com
Bruington, Don   <M1 WC>
PO Box 105
Falls of Rough, KY 40119
(270)257-2228
Byrd, James F   <M1 WC>
1158 Cornishville Road
Harrodsburg, KY 40330
(859)734-0534
jfbyrd@bluezoomwifi.com

CUMBERLAND PRESBYTERY CONTINUED

Cottingim, Tom   `<M1 WC>`
353 Atwood Drive
Lexington, KY 40515
(859)273-3800
FAX: (859)272-4315
t.cottingim@insightbb.com

Diamond, James   `<M1 M9>`
214 Falmouth Drive
Georgetown, KY 40324
(502)642-5020
jamesdiamond007@twc.com

Ferree, Carole   `<M1 WC>`
2475 Fallen Timber Road
Campbellsville, KY 42718
(270)465-1150
ferree047@wildblue.net

Gary, Brian   `<M1 WC>`
105 Wilma Avenue
Radcliff, KY 40160
(502)351-6938

Jones, Joseph M   `<M1 RT>`
405 Lakeview Drive
Campbellsville, KY 42718
joepegjones@windstream.net

Love, James R   `<M1 WC>`
14382 Sonora Hardin Springs Road
Eastview, KY 42732
(502)862-4119

Milby, Elizabeth L   `<M1 WC>`
207 Summersville Road
Greensburg, KY 42743
(270)932-5659

Norris, Freddie   `<M1 WC>`
330 Lexington Drive
Glasgow, KY 42141
(270)651-7932

Perkins, William H   `<M1 WC>`
PO Box 632
Central City, KY 42330
(270)754-5333

Ranson, Doris   `<M1 WC>`
9440 Fenwick Road
Owensboro, KY 42301
(270)229-2875
dorisranson@bellsouth.net

Renner, Wallace   `<M1 WC>`
1648 Griffith Avenue
Owensboro, KY 42303
(270)685-4359
pwrenner@adelphia.net

Ricketts, Roger   `<M1 WC>`
205 Contantz Drive
Canton, MO 63435

Thompson, Eugene   `<M1 WC>`
2825 Albatross Road
Del Ray Beach, FL 33444

Thompson, W Fay   `<M1 RT>`
210 Macbeth Lane
Glasgow, KY 42141
(270)646-2218

Tucker, James D   `<M1 WC>`
PO Box 34
Mc Daniels, KY 40152
(270)257-8971

Underwood, Jerrell M   `<M1 RT>`
PO Box 9
Garfield, KY 40140
(270)536-3706

Vaught, Joseph R   `<M1WC>`
7424 Highland Lick Road
Lewisburg, KY 42256
(270)726-8497
brojoe2@logantele.com

Wilson, Brenda   `<M1 WC>`
35 Collins Drive
Elizabethtown, KY 42701
(270)249-3835
susieq2007@windstream.net

___

OTHER LICENTIATES ON ROLL:

Smith, Nicholas   `<M2>`
101 Cumberland Street
Glasgow, KY 42141
(270)651-3308
pastornic@gcpchurch.tv

Watts, Glenn David   `<M2 ST>`
7400 Willowbend Drive
Crestwood, KY 40014
(502)241-0436
hongkongbrother@hotmail.com

___

OTHER CANDIDATES ON ROLL:

Craddock, Barry   `<M3>`
147 Moss Way
Glasgow, KY 42141

Cumberland East Coast Presbytery
SOUTHEAST SYNOD

GENERAL		MEMBERSHIP			CHANGES				FINANCES				
	1.Church Number	2.Active	3.Total	4.Church School	5.Prof. of Faith	6.Gains	7.Losses	8.Children Baptized	9. OUR UNITED OUT- REACH	10. Total Out- Reach Giving	11. All Other Expenses	12. Total Income Received	13. Value Church Prop. 1=1000
	1	2	3	4	5	6	7	8	9	10	11	12	13
Comeback	2446	10	10	0	0	0	5	0	100	1,200	48,121	50,224	0
Gil	2444	4	4	0	No Report Received			0	100	0	0	0	0
Hope Korean	2131	15	19	0	0	5	0	0	500	21,858	60,975	82,833	0
One Way	2137	75	101	48	No Report Received			0	300	0	0	0	255
Outreach	2143								0				
Sharing	2141	20	20	4	No Report Received			0	300	0	0	0	0
Sunnyside			2										
True Love	2443	13	13	0	No Report Received			0	0	0	0	0	25
TOTALS	7	137	167	52	0	5	5	0	1,300	23,058	109,096	133,057	280

*Math error corrected. **Purged roll.

CHURCHES, PASTORS, AND CLERKS:

___

Comeback   (C)SECE2446
316 Prospect Avenue Apt 6D (mailing)
Hackensack, NJ 07601
15 Wallington Avenue (physical)
Wallington, NJ 07057
PA: Ji Woo Park
316 Prospect Avenue Apt 6D
Hackensack, NJ 07601
(201)694-3005
jiwoos@gmail.com
CL: Session Clerk
316 Prospect Avenue Apt 6D
Hackensack, NJ 07601

___

Gil   (C)SECE2444
139 A Grove Street
Tenafly, NJ 07670

PA: Si Chun Ryu
139 A Grove Street
Tenafly, NJ 07670
(201)410-3445
isaac9191@hotmail.com
CL: Session Clerk
139 A Grove Street
Tenafly, NJ 07670

___

Hope Korean   (C)SECE2131

Presbytery del Cristo
MISSION SYNOD

	GENERAL		MEMBERSHIP			CHANGES			FINANCES			
	1.Church Number	2.Active	3.Total	4.Church School	5.Prof. of Faith	6.Gains	7.Losses	8.Children Baptized	9. OUR UNITED OUT-REACH	10. Total Out-Reach Giving	11. All Other Expenses	12. Total Income Received	13. Value Church Prop. 1=1000
	1	2	3	4	5	6	7	8	9	10	11	12	13
316 Fellowship	8710	22	27	0	1	28	1	1	0	3,670	41,104	31,528	0
Chinese	8501	582	582	205	0	37	42	0	30,936	70,012	950,560	1,024,209	3,600
Desert Gardens	8705	19	25	10	0	2	0	1	2,000	7,403	41,272	57,663	180
Grace Fellowship	8510	145	145	76	1	0	1	2	26,667	124,177	652,428	688,121	2,000
Heights	8701	308	2,473	75	0	0	10	0	0	102,129	700,516	852,659	1,852
Lubbock First	8702	82	82	33	1	8	6	0	3,375	15,460	383,496	246,076	433
Maranatha	8706	100	100	60	0	0	0	0	675	3,705	59,000	49,000	0
Redeemer	8512	51	55	62	6	7	0	1	4,000	24,033	218,614	230,017	0
St. Andrew	8703	105	201	35	2	8	10	0	7,350	40,988	324,002	311,502	1,625
Trona	8503	11	40	8	5	6	0	0	574	1,283	14,369	12,355	125
Westside*	8709	61	59	38	4	6	12	4	550	22,000	111,000	133,000	700
TOTALS	11	1,476	3,187	577	19	74	81	8	76,127	411,190	3,355,257	3,604,602	11,515

*Math error corrected. **Purged roll.

CHURCHES, PASTORS, AND CLERKS:

316 Fellowship　　(4C)MSDC8710
2200 E Dartmouth Circle
Englewood, CO 80113
PA: Jean Hess　　　　　　　　<M1>
2200 E Dartmouth Circle
Englewood, CO 80113
(303)504-0275
jeanhess@316denver.com
AP: Rick Hess　　　　　　　　<M1>
2200 E Dartmouth Circle
Englewood, CO 80113
(303)504-0275
rick@densem.edu
CL: Session Clerk
2200 E Dartmouth Circle
Englewood, CO 80113

Chinese　　　　　(4C)MSDC8501
865 Jackson Street
San Francisco, CA 94133
(415)421-1624　　　<San Francisco>
FAX: (415)421-1874
church@cumberlandsf.org
PA: Walter Lau　　　　　　　　<M1>
865 Jackson Street
San Francisco, CA 94133
(415)421-1624
FAX: (415)421-1874
walter@cumberlandsf.org
AP: Steven Chen　　　　　　　<M1>
865 Jackson Street
San Francisco, CA 94133
(415)421-1624
psalm1305@yahoo.com
AP: Sonny Wan　　　　　　　　<M1>
13 Wexford Place
Aladema, CA 94502
(415)421-1624
sonny@cumberlandsf.org
AP: Alexis Yu　　　　　　　　<M1>

1761 Willow Way
San Bruno, CA 94066
(415)421-1624
alexis.yu.k@gmail.com
CL: Jerry Young
400 Quintara Street
San Francisco, CA 94116
(415)661-2247
jjta4evrcpcc@pacbell.net

Desert Gardens　　(4C)MSDC8705
10851 E Old Spanish Trail
Tucson, AZ 85748
(520)296-0703　　　　　<Pima>
PA: Gerald (Jerry) Hagelin　　<M1>
10851 E Old Spanish Trail
Tucson, AZ 85712
(520)275-8110
azcef@cs.com
CL: Bonnie Kopke
10851 E Old Spanish Trail
Tucson, AZ 85748
(520)647-4700
bkopke@cox.net

Grace Fellowship　　(4C)MSDC8510
3265 16th Street
San Francisco, CA 94103
(415)703-6090　　　<San Francisco>
PA: Sharon Huey　　　　　　　<M1>
3265 16th Street
San Francisco, CA 94103
(415)703-6090
sharon_huey@yahoo.com
AP: Douglas Lee　　　　　　　<M1>
3265 16th Street
San Francisco, CA 94103
(415)703-6090
dlee@gfccsf.org
CL: David Williams
3265 16th Street
San Francisco, CA 94103

(415)558-8719
david.evan.williams@gmail.com

Heights　　　　(4WC)MSDC8701
8600 Academy Road NE
Albuquerque, NM 87111
(505)821-1993　　　　<Bernalillo>
FAX: (505)797-8599
PA: Lyle Reece　　　　　　　　<M1>
8600 Academy Road NE
Albuquerque, NM 87111
(505)884-2952
lreece@heightscpc.org
AP: Jerry Smyrl　　　　　　　<M1>
10617 Hagen NE
Albuquerque, NM 87111
(505)999-8852
jwsmyrl@hotmail.com
AP: Marty Goehring　　　　　<M1>
8600 Academy NE
Albuquerque, NM 87111
(505)821-3628
FAX: (505)797-8599
mgoehring@heightscpc.org
AP: Justin Richter　　　　　　<M1>
8600 Academy Road NE
Albuquerque, NM 87111
(505)363-8738
jrichter@heightscpc.org
CL: Barbara J Cok
8600 Academy Road NE
Albuquerque, NM 87112
(505)275-0108
FAX: (866)280-0731
barbara@lobo.net

Lubbock First　　(4WC)MSDC8702
7702 Indiana Avenue
Lubbock, TX 79423
(806)792-3553　　　　　<Lubbock>
joy@cpclubbock.com
PA: Steve Doles　　　　　　　<M1>
7702 Indiana Avenue

PRESBYTERY DEL CRISTO CONTINUED

Lubbock, TX 79423
(806)787-7551
steve@cpclubbock.com
CL: Diana K Akins
4712 63rd Street
Lubbock, TX 79414
(806)797-5246
FAX: (806)744-0640
akinsarms@sbcglobal.net

Maranatha   (4C)MSDC8706
PO Box 1040 (mailing)
San Elizario, TX 79849
11497 Socorro Road (physical)
Socorro, TX 79927
(915)851-8349   <El Paso>
hectoryliz@att.net
PA: Hector Mata   <M1>
PO Box 1040
San Elizario, TX 79849
(915)851-5354
hectoryliz@att.net
AP: Elizabeth Mata   <M1>
PO Box 1040
San Elizaro, TX 79849
(915)851-5354
hectoryliz@att.net
AP: Isaac Mata   <M1>
PO Box 1040
San Elizaro, TX 79849
(915)851-5354
isaacmata96@yahoo.com
AP: Lyvia Rincon   <M1>
12008 Fred Carter
El Paso, TX 79936
(915)857-1343
yaanaivitaly@yahoo.com
AP: Manuel (Alex) Saldana <M1>
536 Telop
El Paso, TX 79927
(915)317-9349
campe13@yahoo.com
CL: Miguel Flores
PO Box 1040
San Elizario, TX 79849
(915)346-2071
mr_titof@yahoo.com

Redeemer   (4C)MSDC8512
1224 Fairfax Avenue
San Francisco, CA 94124
(415)671-2194   <San Francisco>
info@redeemersf.org
PA: Danny Fong   <M1>
1224 Fairfax Avenue
San Francisco, CA 94124
(415)671-2194
dfong@redeemersf.org
CL: Daniel Kim
1224 Fairfax Avenue
San Francisco, CA 94124
(415)596-6400
dannydhkim@gmail.com

St Andrew   (4MEWC)MSDC8703
1415 N Grandview
Odessa, TX 79761
(432)367-8603   <Ector>
FAX: (432)367-8605
standrewcp@sbcglobal.net
PA: Jimmy Braswell   <M1>
1514 E 10th Street

Odessa, TX 79761
(432)335-9346
jjcgbraz@cableone.net
AP: Sharon Notley   <M1>
16500 S Grey Wolf Apt 5
Odessa, TX 79766
(432)210-9059
sharon_standrewcp@sbcglobal.net
CL: Jamie Halsell
7243 Barksdale Lane
Odessa, TX 79765
(432)530-6852

Trona   (4C)MSDC8503
83456 Argus Avenue
Trona, CA 93592
(760)382-8636   <San Bernardino>
PA: Dennis Benadom   <M1>
13314 Sage Street
Trona, CA 93562
(760)372-4536
galerose91@msn.com
CL: Cindy Barton
83426 Argus Avenue
Trona, CA 93562
(760)372-4033
cbarton53@hotmail.com

Westside   (4C)MSDC8709
PO Box 15209 (mailing)
4110 Sabana Grande Avenue (physical)
Rio Rancho, NM 87174
(505)620-2427   <Sandoval>
nancye320@aol.com
PA: Harry W Chapman   <M1>
4908 El Picador Court
Rio Rancho, NM 87124
(505)620-2427
wrightrow@gmail.com
CL: Sherry Meier
7113 Hartford Hills Drive NE
Rio Rancho, NM 87144
(505)771-0418
sjmeier53@aol.com

OTHERS ON MINISTERIAL ROLL:

Bondurant, Lee   <M1 WC>
1453 Paseo Del Sur Court
El Paso, TX 79928
(915)309-7269
lee_b5217@yahoo.com
Bower, Clay   <M1 WC>
221 Waterlemon Way
Monroe, NC 28110
(704)575-9497
cbrev.9497@gmail.com
Collins, Paul   <M1 RT>
915 Warm Sands Drive SE
Albuquerque, NM 87123
(505)294-3842
FAX: (505)254-7707
chapp3@comcast.net
Estes, George R   <M1 RT>
7910 Cloverbrook Lane
Germantown, TN 38138
(901)755-6673
geoestes@gmail.com
Estes, Sam R, Jr   <M1 RT>
4601 71st Street Apt 234
Lubbock, TX 79424

(806)407-3242
Freund, Henry O   <M1 RT>
913 Sam Houston Drive
Dyersburg, TN 38024
(731)285-1744
freundly@att.net
Fung, David   <M1 WC>
(address unknown)
Fung, Lawrence   <M1 WC>
367 Eldorado Drive
Daly City, CA 94015
(415)535-8754
revfung@gmail.com
Giron, Francisco   <M1 OM>
(address unknown)
Gonzales, Homer   <M1 WC>
8924 Armistice NE
Albuquerque, NM 87109
(505)821-4376
FAX: (505)841-4267
hgabq1985@gmail.com
Green, Paul   <M1 RT>
5228 Anchorage Avenue
El Paso, TX 79924
(915)751-7960
Kim, Byong Sam   <M1 RT>
6290 Dawnridge Court
Paradise, CA 95969
(530)877-4651
Knight, Melissa   <M1 M9>
5730 Haley Road
Meridian, MS 39305
(530)632-6472
revlissa@gmail.com
Lui, Stephen   <M1 RT>
512 16th Avenue
San Francisco, CA 94118
(415)386-2302
FAX: (415)386-2302
Luo, Tian-en   <M1 WC>
87 Berta Circle
Daly City, CA 94015
(650)754-9885
FAX: (650)754-9885
tianenyang555@gmail.comt
Maddux, Cynthia   <M1 WC>
5735 Timber Creek Place Drive Apt 212
Houston, TX 77084
(832)343-8867
cmaddux1962@gmail.com
Mata, Pablo   <M1 WC>
230 Flor Blanca
El Paso, TX 79927
(915)319-8407
pablomata@yahoo.com
McNeese, Michael C   <M1 RT>
16410 Wesley Evans Road
Prairieville, LA 70769
(520)722-1350
mcneesemc@cox.net
O'Mara, Shelia   <M1 M8>
PO Box 170
Gadsden, TN 38337
(443)699-2321
chaplainshelia@aol.com
Patterson, Jerry   <M1 WC>
7007 Whitaker Avenue
Van Nuys, CA 91406
(818)994-5828
Shin, Kyung I   <M1 WC>
1805 Gallinas Road NE
Rio Rancho, NM 87144

PRESBYTERY DEL CRISTO CONTINUED

(505)453-5461
pastorkshin@gmail.com
Sze, Joseph   \<M1 WC\>
   Rau Sao Joaquim, 382
   Liberdale, Sao Paulo, SP
   CEP 015068-000 Brazil
   pastorsze@yahoo.com
Tan, Pek Hua   \<M1 WC\>
   7 Belhaven Avenue
   Daly City, CA 94015
   (415)515-0076
   ptan27@yahoo.com
Tsujimoto, Mark   \<M1 WC\>
   88 S Broadway Unit 3210
   Millbrae, CA 94030
   (650)697-6901
   mltsujimoto@gmail.com
Wilson, Don   \<M1 M9 RT\>
   7300 Calle Montana NE
   Albuquerque, NM 87113
   (505)823-2594
   don-wilson07@comcast.net
Wong, Bruce   \<M1 WC\>
   716 Duncanville Court
   Campbell, CA 95008
   (408)628-1723
   revbwong@gmail.com
Yu, Pyong San (Sonny)   \<M1 WC\>
   139 Silverado Drive
   Santa Teresa, NM 88008
   (915)329-3451
   pyongsanyu@hotmail.com

OTHER LICENTIATES ON ROLL:

Barton, Cindy   \<M2\>
   83426 Argus Avenue
   Trona, CA 93562
   (760)372-4033
   cbarton53@hotmail.com
Bell, Michelle   \<M2\>
   8643 Dry Creek Road Unit 1226
   Centennial, CO 80112
   (303)956-3784
   mabbell@comcast.net
George, Thomas   \<M2\>
   908 N Brown Avenue
   Casa Grande, AZ 85222
   (640)447-2676
   tgeorge@aerogram.net
Okala, Achile   \<M2\>
   5887 Newcombe Court
   Arvada, CO 80004
   (720)880-8511
   achileok@me.com
Ralph, Brian   \<M2\>
   6202 Roxbury Drive #1306
   San Antonio, TX 78238
   (312)315-6915
   ralphbr1970@gmail.com
Wang, Huiling   \<M2\>
   5562 S Yank Court
   Littleton, CO 80127
   (303)330-3929
   whuiling88@yahoo.com

OTHER CANDIDATES ON ROLL:

Barricklow, Gary   \<M3\>
   3012 Winston Meadows
   Rio Rancho, NM 87144
   (505)417-0331
   garysr@barricklow.com
Cho, Kun Ho   \<M3\>
   605-H S Palm
   La Habra, CA 90631
   (949)241-6167
   pkhch3@gmail.com
Fong, Cindi   \<M3\>
   1835 Alemany Boulevard
   San Francisco, CA 94112
   (415)335-8067
   cfong@redeemersf.org
Headley, Daniel   \<M3\>
   9332 Admiral Lowell Place NE
   Albuquerque, NM 87111
   (720)724-0961
   dheadley7@yahoo.com
Hom, Patti   \<M3\>
   811 Faxon Avenue
   San Francisco, CA 94112
   (415)586-5998
   phom@gfccsf.org
Jimenez, Jacqueline   \<M3\>
   11161 San Ysidro
   Socorro, TX 79927
   (915)234-0887
   jjimenez2228@gmail.com
Little, Lee   \<M3\>
   10011 Alexandria NE
   Albuquerque, NM 87122
   (405)618-7371
   dekal31@hotmail.com
Terpstra, Tami   \<M3\>
   10 Rainbow Crest Drive
   Evergreen, CO 80439
   (303)396-3604
   tami.terpstra@yahoo.com
Young, Timothy   \<M3\>
   8064 Hummingbird Lane
   San Diego, CA 92123
   (415)350-8201
   tdy223@gmail.com

Presbytery of East Tennessee
SOUTHEAST SYNOD

	1.Church Number	2.Active	3.Total	4.Church School	5.Prof. of Faith	6.Gains	7.Losses	8.Children Baptized	9. OUR UNITED OUT-REACH	10. Total Out-Reach Giving	11. All Other Expenses	12. Total Income Received	13. Value Church Prop. 1=1000
	1	2	3	4	5	6	7	8	9	10	11	12	13
Beaver Creek	2301	500	791	275	3	14	13	5	53,405	87,033	457,015	534,048	3,600
Bethesda*	2201	33	46	42	0	0	3	0	4,087	21,832	54,670	83,505	170
Casa De Fe	2220	36	36	15	5	5	10	8	500	4,167	63,537	52,181	0
Cedar Hill	2202	54	170	38	0	0	3	1	9,381	19,247	88,866	95,645	850
Clark's Grove	2302	42	113	22	1	0	3	1	4,934	8,131	30,521	49,344	500
Corntassel	2304	15	37	24	2	3	2	0	3,129	4,457	29,106	34,557	200
Dover*	2203	36	41	15	0	6	5	0	2,627	7,553	46,275	67,844	1,834
Fairview	2204	53	103	62	18	3	1	0	5,129	17,406	95,878	164,532	603
FaithFellowship*	2319	60	132	35	0	5	14	0	0	6,200	234,721	240,262	2,786
Gass Memorial	2205	4	8	4	0	1	0	0	937	2,315	7,718	9,372	180
Greeneville	2206	397	561	96	0	4	8	1	47,168	98,894	419,706	515,552	4,200
Heartland	2306	50	130	33	8	8	1	0	3,846	7,283	77,773	105,854	550
Knoxville	2305	110	274	68	0	1	9	0	2,400	15,316	247,590	261,001	2,500
Lebanon	2207	15	19	8	0	1	3	0	1,879	8,483	37,695	34,847	300
Loudon	2307	203	203	120	1	1	8	0	0	2,582	237,419	184,913	3,744
Marietta*	2308	70	198	60	0	0	3	2	30,812	29,657	269,465	265,496	600
Maryville 1st	2309	75	227	54	0	3	4	0	2,400	9,640	119,828	110,941	1,561
Mercy	2320	14	16	13	2	0	10	1	0	650	12,000	7,485	5
Mohawk	2208	22	49	15	0	0	0	0	848	2,865	17,371	18,014	300
Mt. Carmel*	2310	46	93	25	0	0	3	0	4,250	14,748	30,835	42,441	475
Mt. Pleasant	2209	33	71	33	0	7	0	0	2,801	5,564	27,657	30,652	100
New Bethel	2210	13	29	23	0	0	0	0	1,194	1,846	20,603	15,788	333
New Hope	2311	27	36	11	0	0	0	0	3,253	15,827	19,746	32,514	800
Oak Ridge	2313	113	128	31	0	7	3	0	18,645	39,052	164,847	203,899	1,650
Oakland*	2211	23	55	0	0	26	0	3	0	6,531	0	48,799	100
Oliver Springs	2314	7	9	6	No Report Received			0	0	0	0	0	180
Philadelphia	2212	24	24	24	0	0	1	0	650	600	16,360	15,246	300
Pilot Knob	2213	9	9	27	No Report Received			0	921	0	0	0	100
Pleasant Hill	2214	22	26	17	0	0	2	0	3,203	13,084	20,538	33,622	400
Pleasant Vale	2215	11	11	26	No Report Received			0	229	0	0	0	250
Salem*	2216	23	30	33	1	0	6	0	1,276	11,321	10,082	26,033	100
Shiloh	2217	106	205	77	0	4	2	0	10,269	17,893	103,447	113,143	1,150
Talbott	2218	54	89	32	0	0	2	0	9,595	20,955	48,924	114,359	1,125
Union	2315	238	402	93	2	13	10	1	20,144	67,749	429,264	489,449	2,351
Virtue	2316	52	82	25	2	5	3	1	12,127	16,918	155,108	133,603	1,616
Walkertown	2222	21	24	26	3	3	0	0	0	2,800	27,073	26,737	0
Willoughby	2219	11	11	13	0	0	0	0	1,023	1,023	12,515	10,230	250
Young's Chapel	2317	77	97	52	0	0	43	0	14,968	30,800	152,375	168,293	1,000
TOTALS	38	2,699	4,584	1,571	50	120	175	24	278,030	620,422	3,786,528	4,337,201	36,788

*Math error corrected. **Purged roll.

PRESBYTERY OF EAST TENNESSEE CONTINUED

CHURCHES, PASTORS, AND CLERKS:

Beaver Creek (4WC)SEET2301
7225 Old Clinton Pike
Knoxville, TN 37921
(865)938-7245 <Knox>
FAX: (865)938-1465
tsweet1@comcast.net
PA: Thomas Sweet <M1>
7225 Old Clinton Pike
Powell, TN 37849
(865)938-7245
tsweet1@comcast.net
AP: Billy Price <M1>
196 S McLean Boulevard
Memphis, TN 38104
(901)494-4851
wmprice@memphisseminary.edu
AP: Fran Vickers <M1>
7225 Old Clinton Pike
Knoxville, TN 37921
(865)859-0805
franv3@comcast.net
AP: Patrick Wilkerson <M1>
903 Park Crest Court
Mount Juliet, TN 37122
(865)236-7737
patrickwilkerson3@gmail.com
CL: John Todd
4912 Montmorency Drive
Powell, TN 37849
(865)938-7211
jtodd4912@comcast.net

Bethesda (4C)SEET2201
155 Old Shiloh Road (mailing)
Greeneville, TN 37745
16340 Kingsport Highway (physical)
Fall Branch, TN 37656
(423)620-7753 <Greene>
FAX: (423)798-2042
kcor_98@yahoo.com
OD: Wade McAmis <M5>
3010 Whitehouse Road
Greeneville, TN 37745
(423)639-7711
CL: Jeff H Hayes
155 Old Shiloh Road
Greeneville, TN 37745
(423)639-8404
mdlpilot@yahoo.com

Casa De Fe (PRESC)SEET2220
493 Main Street, 2nd Floor
Malden, MA 02148
(781)322-2685 <Middlesex>
casadefepastores@verizon.net
PA: Josefina Sanchez <M1>
7 Hancock Street
Melrose, MA 02176
(479)970-8654
fsfamily64@gmail.com
CL: Myriam Santizo
125 Pennsylvania Avenue
Somerville, MA 02145
(617)666-6763

Cedar Hill (4EWC)SEET2202
4170 Newport Highway
Greeneville, TN 37743
(423)639-0268 <Greene>
cedarhill@centurylink.net
CL: Carolyn Harmon
4435 Newport Highway
Greeneville, TN 37743
(423)639-3037
richardharmon09@comcast.net

Clark's Grove (4WC)SEET2302
1662 Peppertree Drive (mailing)
Alcoa, TN 37701
3137 Old Knoxville Highway (physical)
Maryville, TN 37802
(865)982-5280 <Blount>
FAX: (865)273-8726
lwaters111@aol.com
CL: Lynn Waters
1662 Peppertree Drive
Alcoa, TN 37701
(865)982-9083
FAX: (865)379-0654
lwaters111@aol.com

Corntassel (4C)SEET2304
933 Kahite Trail (mailing)
Vonore, TN 37885
2100 Povo Road (physical)
Madisonville, TN 37354
(423)884-3909 <Monroe>
miriamf23@tds.net
PA: Bill S Middleton <M1 RT>
12826 Union Road
Knoxville, TN 37922
(865)966-1706
revbill@charter.net
CL: Carolyn Swabe
2203 Povo Road
Madisonville, TN 37354
(423)442-4377
swabec@aol.com

Dover (4MEWC)SEET2203
1550 Dover Road
Morristown, TN 37813
(423)581-4719 <Hamblen>
dovercp@comcast.net
CL: John Ayers
4371 Danbury Drive
Morristown, TN 37813
(423)586-6883
bigorange@charter.net

Fairview (4MWC)SEET2204
4720 Snapps Ferry Road
Afton, TN 37616
(423)639-9011 <Greene>
PA: Ronnie Duncan <M1>
146 Deseree Broyles Road
Chuckey, TN 37641
(423)552-0321
ronkduncan@icloud.com
CL: Rick Taylor
175 Stone Dam Road
Chuckey, TN 37641
(423)470-0216

Faith Fellowship (4EWC)SEET2319
PO Box 24162 (mailing)
Knoxville, TN 37934
14025 Highway 70 E (physical)
Lenoir City, TN 37772
(865)988-8522 <Knox>
info@faithfellowshipcp.org
PA: Greg Tucker <M1>
612A Idlewood Lane
Knoxville, TN 37923
(865)242-4086
greg.tucker311@outlook.com
CL: Regina Stinnett
508 Windham Hill Road
Knoxville, TN 37934
(865)898-3001
reginastinnett@tds.net

Gass Memorial (4C)SEET2205
PO Box 1767 (mailing)
815 Gass Memorial Road (physical)
Greeneville, TN 37744
(423)278-7610 <Greene>
FAX: (423)638-3452
gassch@comcast.net
PA: Rex Brown <M1>
134 Everhart Drive
Greeneville, TN 37745
(423)639-4298
CL: George C Mays
PO Box 1767
Greeneville, TN 37744
(423)638-8624
FAX: (423)638-3452
g.mays@comcast.net

Greeneville (4MEWC)SEET2206
201 N Main Street
Greeneville, TN 37745
(423)638-4119 <Greene>
FAX: (423)636-1017
office@gcpchurch.org
PA: James W Lively <M1>
906 Lyle Circle
Greeneville, TN 37745
(423)798-1959
FAX: (423)636-1017
jlively@gcpchurch.org
AP: Abby Cole Keller <M1>
162 Owen Lane
Greeneville, TN 37745
(423)863-6565
abbycolekeller@gmail.com
CL: Dick Parrack
201 N Main Street
Greeneville, TN 37745
(423)638-4119
FAX: (423)636-1017
parrackd@embarqmail.com

Heartland (4MWC)SEET2306
160 Harrison Road
Lenoir City, TN 37772
(865)986-3018 <Loudon>
lccpc@icx.net
PA: Kenneth P Phillips <M1>
6419 Town Creek Road East
Lenoir City, TN 37772
(865)986-7344
CL: Jennifer L Smith
1085 Crestview Circle
Lenoir City, TN 37772
(865)986-5099
jlleslie@chartertn.net

Knoxville (4WC)SEET2305
6900 Nubbin Ridge Drive

PRESBYTERY OF EAST TENNESSEE CONTINUED

Knoxville, TN 37919
(865)588-8581   <Knox>
FAX: (865)588-8581
firstcpc@earthlink.net
PA: Michael Wilkinson   <M1>
1174 Tanglewood Street
Memphis, TN 38114
(334)517-6568
pastormike@kfcpc.comcastbiz.net
CL: Dianne Pipkin
1725 Covey Rise Trail
Knoxville, TN 37922
(865)675-2872
pndpip@aol.com

Lebanon   (4MEC)SEET2207
2117 Murray Street (mailing)
Morristown, TN 37814
714 Lebanon Road (physical)
Jefferson City, TN 37760
( )   <Jefferson>
PA: Howard E Shipley   <M1>
3800 Dan Drive
Morristown, TN 37814
(423)581-1092
hshipley@charter.net
CL: Mary McCarter
804 W Jefferson Street
Jefferson City, TN 37760
(865)475-6572
mccrtrmary@aol.com

Loudon   (4MWC)SEET2307
PO Box 373 (mailing)
503 College Avenue (physical)
Loudon, TN 37774
(865)458-2270   <Loudon>
FAX: (865)458-5360
loudoncpc@bellsouth.net
CL: Russ Newman
623 Mulberry Street
Loudon, TN 37773
(865)282-1977
mulberry623@yahoo.com

Marietta   (4MC)SEET2308
11402 Hardin Valley Road (mailing)
1922 Marietta Church Road (physical)
Knoxville, TN 37932
(865)693-0080   <Knox>
mariettacpc@comcast.net
PA: Randall Mayfield   <M1>
12470 Daisywood Drive
Knoxville, TN 37932
(865)769-4756
FAX: (865)769-4756
mayfield07@comcast.net
CL: Virgil R Hubbard
2122 Campbell Station Road
Knoxville, TN 37932
(865)740-4863
vrhubbard@comcast.net

Maryville First   (4MWC)SEET2309
1301 E Broadway
Maryville, TN 37804
(865)982-7860   <Blount>
firstcumberland@gmail.com
PA: Ronald L Longmire   <M1>
2041 Eckles Drive
Maryville, TN 37804

(865)984-1647
ronaldlongmire@charter.net
CL: Tom Longmire
630 Garfield Street
Alcoa, TN 37701
(865)983-3604

Mercy   (4C)SEET2320
634 Martel Road
Lenoir City, TN 37772
(865)660-7579   <Knox>
iglesiapcmisericordia@gmail.com
PA: Alfonso Oscar Marquez   <M1>
389 Bethel Drive
Lenoir City, TN 37772
(865)660-7579
amarquez61@bellsouth.net
AP: Martha Marquez   <M1>
389 Bethel Drive
Lenoir City, TN 37772
(865)660-7579
amarquez61@bellsouth.net
AP: Miguel Gonzales   <M1>
200 Bethel Drive
Lenoir City, TN 37772
(865)988-4238
CL: Miguel Angel Gonzalez
200 Bethel Drive
Lenor City, TN 37772
(865)227-2710
mgonzalez865@bellsouth.net

Mohawk   (4MWC)SEET2208
PO Box 7 (mailing)
50 Soville Loop (physical)
Mohawk, TN 37810
( )   <Greene>
SS: Chris Franklin   <M2>
310 Yellow Springs Road
Midway, TN 37809
(423)972-3609
chrisfranklin104@comcast.net
CL: Velta Rhea Riley
2149 Phillipe Road
Mohawk, TN 37810
(423)235-6179

Mt Carmel   (4EC)SEET2310
PO Box 4 (mailing)
Coalfield, TN 37719
5515 Knoxville Highway (physical)
Oliver Springs, TN 37840
(865)435-9247   <Morgan>
PA: Donald W Acton   <M1>
1186 Jenkins Lane
Knoxville, TN 37922
(865)966-5132
CL: Lisa Layne
714 Back Valley Road
Oliver Springs, TN 37840
(865)382-8817
lalayne64@yahoo.com

Mt Pleasant   (4MWC)SEET2209
3945 Babbs Mill Road
Afton, TN 37616
( )   <Greene>
PA: James L Carter   <M1>
6155 Hummingbird Lane
Whitesburg, TN 37891
(423)587-8423

jandjmt@comcast.net
CL: Louise Gass
701 Franklin Street
Greeneville, TN 37745
(423)639-3731

New Bethel   (3WC)SEET2210
2820 Blue Springs Parkway (mailing)
90 Cox Road (physical)
Greeneville, TN 37743
( )   <Greene>
PA: Rex Brown   <M1>
134 Everhart Drive
Greeneville, TN 37745
(423)639-4298
firstcumberland@gmail.com
CL: Coriece Baxter
2820 Blue Springs Parkway
Greeneville, TN 37743
(423)638-4089

New Hope   (4C)SEET2311
904 Acorn Gap Road
Madisonville, TN 37354
( )   <Monroe>
PA: David L Koopman   <M1>
5606 Brandon Park Drive
Maryville, TN 37804
(865)660-2440
racewthrev@aol.com
CL: Yvonne Wolfe
139 Old Loudon Road
Sweetwater, TN 37874
(423)442-3045

Oak Ridge   (4EWC)SEET2313
PO Box 4836 (mailing)
127 Lafayette (physical)
Oak Ridge, TN 37831
(865)483-8433   <Anderson>
FAX: (865)483-8445
1stcpc@comcast.net
PA: Larry A Blakeburn   <M1>
790 Emory Valley Road Apt 714
Oak Ridge, TN 37830
(731)676-2978
larry@1stcpc.org
CL: Linda Diggs
315 Laurel Hollow Road
Clinton, TN 37716
(865)457-5355
ldiggs06@comcast.net

Oakland   (4C)SEET2211
694 Oakland Road
Telford, TN 37690
(423)257-2258   <Washington>
OD: Sam Smith   <M5>
114 College View Drive
Greeneville, TN 37743
(423)639-8551
CL: Freda Graham
959 Bowmantown Road
Limestone, TN 37681
(423)257-5050

Oliver Springs   (4C)SEET2314
PO Box 175 (mailing)
400 Spring Street (physical)
Oliver Springs, TN 37840
firstcumberland@gmail.com

PRESBYTERY OF EAST TENNESSEE CONTINUED

( )   <Roane>
PA: Ken Johnson   <M1>
  122 Ridge Lane
  Clinton, TN 37716
  (865)463-7090
  kenjoxav122@bellsouth.net
CL: Sid Thurmer
  PO Box 175
  Oliver Springs, TN 37840
  (865)435-5438

Philadelphia   (4MWC)SEET2212
  509 Snapp Bridge Road (mailing)
  757 Snapp Bridge Road (physical)
  Limestone, TN 37681
  ( )   <Washington>
SS: Byrd Broyles   <M1>
  295 Davy Crockett Road
  Limestone, TN 37681
  (423)257-4578
  b3broyles@outlook.com
CL: Greg Stafford
  509 Snapp Bridge Road
  Limestone, TN 37681
  (423)257-3796
  gregandlesa509@comcast.net

Pilot Knob   (2C)SEET2213
  515 Marvin Mountain Road (mailing)
  445 Gap Creek Road (physical)
  Bulls Gap, TN 37711
  ( )   <Greene>
LS: Richard Snowden   <M6>
  PO Box 6004
  Morristown, TN 37815
  (423)235-5914
  FAX: (423)254-3206
  richard.snowden@wallacehardware.com
CL: Joyce Lamb
  4185 Gap Creek Road
  Bulls Gap, TN 37711
  (423)235-6858

Pleasant Hill   (4WC)SEET2214
  13385 Kingsport Highway
  Chuckey, TN 37641
  ( )   <Greene>
PA: Rex Brown   <M1>
  134 Everhart Drive
  Greeneville, TN 37745
  (423)639-4298
  firstcumberland@gmail.com
CL: Genevieve M Bolton
  15440 Kingsport Highway
  Chuckey, TN 37641
  (423)234-7942

Pleasant Vale   (4C)SEET2215
  525 Pleasant Vale Road
  Chuckey, TN 37641
  ( )   <Greene>
OD: Chris Bains   <M5>
  155 Pelican Lane
  Greeneville, TN 37743
  (423)525-7497
CL: Howard Collins
  3750 Rheatown Road
  Chuckey, TN 37641
  (423)278-6072

Salem   (4C)SEET2216

695 West Pines Road (mailing)
  Afton, TN 37616
  1927 Lost Mountain Pike (physical)
  Greeneville, TN 37745
  ( )   <Greene>
OD: Billy Moore   <M5>
  880 Black Bear Road
  Greeneville, TN 37745
  (423)552-1594
CL: Helen Starnes
  695 West Pines Road
  Afton, TN 37616
  (423)234-0281
  cehwstarnes@comcast.net

Shiloh   (4WC)SEET2217
  1121 Shiloh Road
  Greeneville, TN 37745
  (423)639-3763   <Greene>
  shilohcpc@embarqmail.com
PA: Tammy L Greene   <M1>
  109 Armitage Drive
  Greeneville, TN 37745
  (423)972-5525
  tg6386@aol.com
CL: Marcy Brooks
  1121 Shiloh Road
  Greeneville, TN 37745
  (423)747-4500
  shilohcpc@embarqmail.com

Talbott   (4C)SEET2218
  PO Box 116 (mailing)
  7410 W Andrew Johnson Hwy (physical)
  Talbott, TN 37877
  (865)475-1221   <Hamblen>
  FAX: (865)475-1221
  talbottchurch@bellsouth.net
LS: Richard Snowden   <M6>
  PO Box 6004
  Morristown, TN 37815
  (423)235-5914
  FAX: (423)254-3206
  richard.snowden@wallacehardware.com
CL: Lon Barry Knight
  950 Rocktown Road
  Jefferson City, TN 37760
  (865)548-8449
  lonknight1@hughes.net

Union   (4WC)SEET2315
  400 Everett Road
  Knoxville, TN 37934
  (865)966-9040   <Knox>
  FAX: (865)675-3787
  union@unioncpchurch.com
PA: Leonard E Turner, Jr   <M1>
  12651 Wagon Wheel Circle
  Knoxville, TN 37934
  (865)966-9040
  FAX: (865)675-3787
  pastor@unioncpchurch.com
CL: Hugh Turpin
  101 E Passmore Lane
  Oak Ridge, TN 37830
  (865)272-5116
  FAX: (865)675-3787
  turpinhk@cs.com

Virtue   (4MWC)SEET2316
  725 Virtue Road

Knoxville, TN 37934
  (865)966-1491   <Knox>
  FAX: (865)966-0558
  virtuecpchurch@tds.net
PA: Steve Graham   <M1>
  804 Sky Blue Drive
  Knoxville, TN 37923
  (865)206-0012
  eve1ts@hotmail.com
CL: Jack A Watson
  12309 Turkey Creek Road
  Knoxville, TN 37934
  (865)966-5998
  jwatson423@aol.com

Walkertown   (4C)SEET2222
  6885 Kingsport Highway
  Afton, TN 37616
  (423)639-1333   <Greene>
OD: Kevin McAmis   <M5>
  94 Faith Court
  Greeneville, TN 37745
  (423)638-3671
  mcamiskevinr@johndeere.com
CL: Debbie Smith
  4833 Landon Court
  Kingsport, TN 37664
  (423)288-6396

Willoughby   (4C)SEET2219
  240 Wheeler Road (mailing)
  220 Willoughby Road (physical)
  Bulls Gap, TN 37711
  ( )   <Greene>
SS: Chris Franklin   <M2>
  310 Yellow Springs Road
  Midway, TN 37809
  (423)638-5600
  chrisfranklin104@comcast.net
CL: Charles Clowers
  240 Wheeler Road
  Bulls Gap, TN 37711
  (423)235-5249

Young's Chapel   (4WC)SEET2317
  1705 Lawnville Road
  Kingston, TN 37763
  (865)376-2192   <Roane>
  FAX: (865)376-2196
  info@youngschapel.net
PA: Dale Watson   <M1>
  1705 Lawnville Road
  Kingston, TN 37763
  (865)376-2192
  revdwatson@comcast.net
CL: Paul McCallie
  3340 Kingston Highway
  Kingston, TN 37763
  (865)376-9199
  pt57466@bellsouth.net

OTHERS ON MINISTERIAL ROLL:

Brown, Whitney   <M1 OM>
  137 Roberta Drive
  Memphis, TN 38112
  (865)387-0002
  whitneymbrown@gmail.com
Choi, Ezra   <M1 WC>
  605 Arbor Hollow Circle #203
  Cordova, TN 38018

PRESBYTERY OF EAST TENNESSEE CONTINUED

(901)236-82635

Choi, Sean <M1 WC>
7565 Macon Road
Cordova, TN 38016
(901)826-2993
esloveh2@hotmail.com

Coker, Robert N <M1 WC>
721 Lakeview Drive
Loudon, TN 37774
(865)458-8791
FAX: (865)458-5360
nickcoker@bellsouth.net

Creamer, Jennifer <M1 WC>
22 Oakhurst Avenue
Ipswich, MA 01938
(831)809-9890
jencreamer@gmail.com

Harper, Carlton <M1 WC>
255 Glenview Circle
Lenoir City, TN 37771
(865)317-1296
carltonharperone@gmail.com

Fly, William <M1 OM>
3002 Trowbridge Drive
Paragould, AR 72450
(865)938-6273
billyfly3@gmail.com

Franco, Ricardo <M1 WC>
7 Hancock Street
Melrose, MA 02176
(781)605-5900
casadefericardo@verizon.net

Freeman, A Daniel <M1 WC>
210 Dogwood Drive
Greeneville, TN 37743
(423)638-5925

Gillis, Ernest H <M1 WC>
3273 Bruckner Boulevard
Snellville, GA 30078
(770)982-6587
professorgil64@hotmail.com

Greenwell, James C <M1 WC>
7165 Wind Whisper Boulevard
Knoxville, TN 37924
(865)742-1653
FAX: (865)742-1653
greenwelljc@comcast.net

Hartman, Gary <M1 WC>
3001 Hines Valley Road
Lenoir City, TN 37771
(865)986-4949
g37771@att.net

Hester, Mark S <M1 WC>
763 Finn Long Road
Friendsville, TN 37737
(865)995-1541
markshester@att.net

Hubbard, Donald <M1 RT>
2128 N Campbell Station Road
Knoxville, TN 37932
(865)693-0264
djhubbard@mindspring.com

Ivey, Billy F <M1 RT>
409 Rodeo Drive
Knoxville, TN 37922
(865)966-5946
iveybe@tds.net

Johnson, Beverly B <M1 RT>
801 Riverhill Drive Apt 308
Athens, GA 30606
(865)977-0405

bevloujohnson@aol.com

Kelly, Patrick L <M1 M9>
1449 Rainbow Road
Mountain City, TN 37681
(423)727-4067

Keown, Gale J <M1 RT>
1025 Cason Lane
Murfreesboro, TN 37128
(865)805-5451

Malinoski, T J <M1 DE>
9087 Fenmore Cove
Cordova, TN 38016
(901)276-4572
mlmalinoski@comcast.net

McBeth, David <M1 WC>
109 Gloria Place
Jacksonville, NC 28540
(910)238-4279
dsj3mcbeth@gmail.com

McConnell, Donald R <M1 RT>
147 Confederacy Circle
Knoxville, TN 37934
(865)288-0230
donjoyce515@hotmail.com

McGuire, James D <M1 WC>
220 Southwind Circle #2
Greenville, TN 37745
(423)638-6380
jmcguire915@comcast.net

Melson, Glenda <M1 M9>
331 Tickle Weed Road
Swansea, SC 29160
(417)588-2758
gmelson@fidnet.com

Nicholson, Casey <M1 WC>
1020 Tusculum Boulevard
Greeneville, TN 37745
(423)639-0268
caseynicholson@mac.com

Ortiz, Milton <M1 DE>
8846 N Cortona Circle
Cordova, TN 38018
(901)486-6679
mortiz@cumberland.org

Peterson, Lisa <M1 WC>
7778 Cedar Creek Road
Townsend, TN 37882
(901)604-0737
petersonli@aol.com

Pickard, Ronald <M1 WC>
6292 Golden Drive
Morristown, TN 37814
(423)587-9735

Prenshaw, Rebecca <M1 WC>
1100 Albemarie Lane
Knoxville, TN 37923
(865)531-1954
bprenshaw@yahoo.com

Richardson, W Jean <M1 RT>
7533 Lancashire Boulevard
Powell, TN 37849
(865)947-3111
jeanandregena@frontier.com

Scott, Jerry <M1 M9>
2310 Sentell Drive
Maryville, TN 37803
(865)803-3669
dmjlscott@yahoo.com

Sledge, Jeff <M1 WC>
241 Long Bow Road
Knoxville, TN 37934

(865)318-5565
jeffsledge@charter.net

Sweet Brockman, Anna <M1>
210 E Main Street Apt B
Greenfield, TN 38230
(865)803-8582
amsweet@memphisseminary.edu

Sweet, Don <M1 RT>
3008 Shropshire Boulevard
Powell, TN 37849
(865)938-7435
mariondon77@netscape.com

West, Fred E, Jr <M1 WC>
510 Cedaredge Drive
New Smyrna, FL 32168
(206)409-8321
jwest616@earthlink.net

Winn, Don <M1 WC>
375 Cumberland Mountain Circle
Sunbright, TN 37872
(615)478-9910
dwinn_ky@yahoo.com

OTHER LICENTIATES ON ROLL:

Craig, Aaron <M2>
325 Cherry Avenue
McKenzie, TN 38201
(731)352-6718

OTHER CANDIDATES ON ROLL:

Caldwell, Chris <M3>
829 Chateaugay Road
Knoxville, TN 37923
(865)599-1044
luke64345@yahoo.com

Johnson, Kris <M3>
130 Essex Street Box 192B
South Hamilton, MA 01982
(808)741-3370
kris.johnson2198@gmail.com

Peach, John <M3>
221 Geronimo Road
Knoxville, TN 37934
(865)675-5956
peachroot@aol.com

Emaus Presbytery
MISSION SYNOD

	1.Church Number	2.Active	3.Total	4.Church School	5.Prof. of Faith	6.Gains	7.Losses	8.Children Baptized	9. OUR UNITED OUT-REACH	10. Total Out-Reach Giving	11. All Other Expenses	12. Total Income Received	13. Value Church Prop. 1=1000
	1	2	3	4	5	6	7	8	9	10	11	12	13
Horeb-Central*	8915	99	119	35	8	21	17	0		5,792	20,498	26,313	111
La Rosa*	8911	77	82	45	5	11	2	0		3,562	6,753	18,248	28
Senda de Libertad	8919	57	58	0	4	3	0	0		5,271	5,296	14,451	0
Zamora	8918	98	104	60	3	8	13	0		0	24,111	21,159	130
Presbytery	A8900												
TOTALS	4	331	363	140	16	44	35	0	0	14,625	56.658	80,171	269

*Math error corrected. **Purged roll..

CHURCHES, PASTORS, AND CLERKS:

Horeb-Central   (4WMC)MSAN8915
Carrera 50D #62-69, Prado Centro
Medellin, Antioquia
Colombia, South America
(574)263-2154   <S America>
ipchoreb@hotmail.com
SS: Rene Wilgen Porras   <M3>
Cra 50 D #62-69
Medellin
Colombia, South America
(321)637-3089
renewilgen@hotmail.com
CL: Johana Daza Rivera
Direccion Cra 50D #62-69
Colombia, South America
(312)834-7999
johadaza@gmail.com

La Rosa de Saron   (4C)MSAN8911
Calle 100 #50C-09
Barrio Santa Cruz Sector La Rosa
Medellin, Antioquia
Colombia, South America
(574)236-6509   <S America>
SS: Andres Giraldo   <M2>
Calle 76 #87-14 Apto 202
Medellin, Antioquia
Colombia, South America
(574)422-6669
andresgiraldo@une.net.co
CL: Claudia Cordoba
Calle 100 #50C-35
Barrio Santa Cruz Sector La Rosa
Medellin, Antioquia
Colombia, South America
57(315)605-0011

Senda de Libertad   (C)MSAN8919
Cra 120 #39 F-91
Medellin, Antioquia
Colombia, South America
(574)496-1681
ipcsaladomedellin@gmail.com
PA: Josue Guerrero   <M1>
Calle 76 #88-65

Medellin, Antioquia
Colombia, South America
(574)412-3504
josueggutierrez@yahoo.es
AP: Cruzana Guerrero   <M1>
Cra 120 #39 F-91
Medellin, Antioquia
Colombia, South America
(574)496-1681
ipcsaladomedellin@gmail.com
CL: Session Clerk
Cra 120 #39 F-91
Medellin, Antioquia
Colombia, South America
(574)496-1681
ipcsaladomedellin@gmail.com

Zamora   (4WC)MSAN8918
Calle 20D #42C-56 (physical)
Cra 58 #32A-41 Apt 420 (mailing)
Bello, Antioquia
Colombia, South America
(574)461-0069   <S America>
ipczamora@gmail.com
PA: Alejandro Vasquez   <M1>
Cra 58 #32A-41 Apt 420
Bello, Antioquia
Colombia, South America
(574)451-4816
almaesda@une.net.co
CL: Cecilia Taborda
Direccion calle 20 #42c-56
Colombia, South America
(300)783-5638
chilalu1147@hotmail.com

OTHERS ON MINISTERIAL ROLL:

Daza, Edilberto   <M1 HR>
Cra 12 #8-47
Cartago, Valle
Colombia, South America
57(314)794-1905
presbicartago@gmail.com
Daza, Johan   <M1 DE>
8148 Yellow Stone Drive
Cordova, TN 38016
(281)793-3869

jdaza@cumberland.org
Martinez, Dagoberto   <M1 RT>
Cra 62D #71-113
Bello, Antioquia
Colombia, South America
(574)452-3466
Rivera, Zenobia   <M1 WC>
Cra 12 #8-47
Cartago, Valle
Colombia, South America
57(310)500-1791
zenobiadedaza@yahoo.com.mx

OTHER LICENTIATES ON ROLL:

Varilla, Adan Manuel   <M2>
Calle 44 94-68 Barrio La America
Medellin
Colombia, South America
(300)241-1896
adanvarilla@hotmail.com

OTHER CANDIDATES ON ROLL:

Lopez, Yeison   <M3>
Barrio San Francisco
Istmina (Choco)
Colombia, South America
(315)290-1817
Morales, Juan Fernando   <M3>
Calle 38 Sur #40-45
Envigado
Colombia, South America
(574)236-6509
Vargas, Lida Patricia   <M3>
Calle 44 94-68 Barrio La America
Medellin
Colombia, South America
(301)657-4906
lidapavargas@hotmail.com
Velez, Gloria Patricia   <M3>
Cra 50D #62-69
Medellin
Colombia, South America
(310)890-1655
gloriapvelez14@gmail.com

Grace Presbytery
SOUTHEAST SYNOD

	GENERAL	MEMBERSHIP			CHANGES				FINANCES				
	1. Church Number	2. Active	3. Total	4. Church School	5. Prof. of Faith	6. Gains	7. Losses	8. Children Baptized	9. OUR UNITED OUT-REACH	10. Total Out-Reach Giving	11. All Other Expenses	12. Total Income Received	13. Value Church Prop. 1=1000
	1	2	3	4	5	6	7	8	9	10	11	12	13
Antioch	0701	30	37	23	0	0	1	0	1,733	5,290	10,355	17,321	150
Beersheba	0702	168	206	94	0	8	4	1	19,200	51,288	164,598	217,200	1,200
Branchville	0106	153	219	40	No Report Received			0	0	0	0	0	1,650
Cairo	0704	10	23	7	0	0	0	0	0	2,825	14,574	19,871	150
Christ	0303	49	89	12	0	3	10	1	1,065	3,800	90,300	92,750	1,200
Coker*	0705	44	94	20	2	2	7	1	650	2,710	34,679	56,812	1,935
Columbus*	0706	154	154	45	0	22	1	0	1,540	2,400	155,058	146,169	1,500
Crestline	0102	30	30	18	No Report Received			0	6,000	0	0	0	1,500
El Camino	0310	80	80	25	3	6	2	1	2,000	3,000	72,120	68,679	530
Enon	0707	149	262	148	4	9	8	2	1,200	16,867	222,276	238,631	1,050
Erin	0601	66	107	45	0	2	1	1	0	8,596	60,393	60,812	218
First Hispanic+	0307	76	76	39	No Report Received			0	0	0	0	0	175
Forrest Avenue	0403	17	113	7	0	0	2	0	1,817	3,502	24,513	20,482	240
Gadsden	0402	98	160	48	0	7	5	0	11,908	10,992	126,072	139,334	800
Glencoe	0404	85	247	70	No Report Received			0	0	0	0	0	2,000
Grace Commun	0407	80	129	40	No Report Received			0	8,062	0	0	0	1,200
Greens Chapel	0208	37	70	20	0	0	0	0	8,125	15,148	40,887	74,106	819
Groverton**	0602	22	22	9	0	1	21	0	0	520	5,490	6,010	0
Helena	0108	58	61	33	1	3	1	0	5,799	18,722	70,373	100,404	700
Homewood	0111	78	115	45	No Report Received			0	10,500	0	0	0	2,025
Hope	0308	78	127	20	No Report Received			0	4,150	0	0	0	1,985
Hopewell	0101	32	36	32	3	17	3	1	1,120	2,200	48,226	54,484	1,254
House of Prayer	0214	180	180	180	No Report Received			0	0	0	0	0	450
Hueytown 1st	0109	20	102	6	CLOSED 2016								
Immanuel	0311	20	23	9	No Report Received			0	2,142	0	0	0	0
McLeod Chapel	0708	15	20	10	No Report Received			0	0	0	0	0	350
Mt. Zion	0709	21	21	12	0	0	2	0	6,042	15,112	22,108	60,428	812
New Hope	0104	195	226	75	0	0	7	2	34,895	88,089	258,805	346,894	2,400
Piedmont	0406	74	74	56	0	0	2	0	1,200	7,500	79,099	92,229	1,101
Pleasant Hill	0710	14	32	5	No Report Received			0	0	0	0	0	160
Roca DeSalvacion	0115	23	70	23	8	23	18	0	0	3,528	52,396	69,261	5
Rocky Ridge	0105	69	222	36	1	9	1	1	19,452	33,033	152,062	201,232	1,200
Salem	0607	20	20	10	0	0	35	0	0	4,175	41,826	16,984	150
Spring Creek	0113	123	167	75	5	5	1	1	4,400	57,600	223,000	265,000	1,250
Steam Mill	0608	42	55	60	0	2	14	1	0	12,290	98,337	101,076	400
Union	0114	45	63	35	No Report Received			0	835	0	0	0	500
TOTALS	35	2,513	3,774	1,405	27	119	146	13	153,835	369,187	2,077,547	2,466,169	30,799

*Math error corrected. **Purged roll (x)Closed 2013 +Union church

GRACE PRESBYTERY CONTINUED

CHURCHES, PASTORS, AND CLERKS:

Antioch (2C)SEGR0701
2994 Antioch Church Road
Reform, AL 35481
( ) <Pickens>
CL: Reba Carpenter
3951 County Road 45
Reform, AL 35481
(205)375-6042
rebcar0228@gmail.com

Beersheba (4MEWC)SEGR0702
1736 Beersheba Road
Columbus, MS 39702
(662)327-9615 <Lowndes>
FAX: (662)324-8320
officebeersheba@att.net
PA: Timothy Daniel Lee <M1>
186 Blasingame Drive
Columbus, MS 39702
(601)433-3714
pastor@beershebachurch.com
CL: Charles Studdard
95 Studdard Drive
Columbus, MS 39702
(662)328-8844
FAX: (662)327-8773
clstuddard@cableone.net

Branchville (4MWC)SEGR0106
80 Hurst Road
Odenville, AL 35120
(205)629-3258 <St Clair>
FAX: (205)629-3258
session@branchvillechurch.org
PA: Keith L. Mariott <M1>
155 Ridgewood Lane
Odenville, AL 35120
(205)903-5251
kjmariott@windstream.net
CL: Steve Smith
80 Hurst Road
Odenville, AL 35120
session@branchvillechurch.org

Cairo (4MC)SEGR0704
3836 Highway 50 W (mailing)
West Point, MS 39773
Cairo Road (physical)
Cedar Bluff, MS 39741
( ) <Clay>
CL: Judy Chrismond
3836 Highway 50 W
West Point, MS 39773
(662)494-7290
tjchrismond@gmail.com

Christ (4EWC)SEGR0303
19501 Holly Lane
Lutz, FL 33548
(813)909-9789 <Hillsborough>
ccpclutz@verizon.net
PA: Joshua Murray <M1>
3714 Landings Way Drive Apt 305
Tampa, FL 33624
(870)723-3286
jdm4428@yahoo.com
CL: Jeannie Vaughn
16107 Carden Drive
Odessa, FL 33556

(813)926-6631
jvaughn1@tampabay.rr.com

Coker (4MEWC)SEGR0705
PO Box 262 (mailing)
14705 Romulus Road (physical)
Coker, AL 35452
(205)339-1178 <Tuscaloosa>
cokercpgreg@att.net
SS: Greg Tucker <M2>
PO Box 262
Coker, AL 35452
(205)541-7484
cokercpgreg@att.net
CL: Retha Channell
15535 Lisenba Drive
Coker, AL 35452
(205)339-8125

Columbus (4EWC)SEGR0706
2698 Ridge Road
Columbus, MS 39705
(662)328-2692 <Lowndes>
fcpcsecretary@att.net
PA: Luke Lawson <M1>
270 N Ridgeland Circle
Columbus, MS 39705
(662)295-9322
luke_lawson03@hotmail.com
CL: Carol Carley
71 Little Tom Road
Columbus, MS 39705
(662)328-4589
carleyr@bellsouth.net

Crestline (4MWC)SEGR0102
605 Hagood Street
Birmingham, AL 35213
(205)879-6001 <Jefferson>
FAX: (205)968-8105
jan@crestlinechurch.org
PA: Janice M Overton <M1>
3320 Pipeline Road
Birmingham, AL 35243
(205)281-6819
FAX: (205)968-8105
jan@crestlinechurch.org
CL: Birki Cvacho
1214 Regal Avenue
Birmingham, AL 35213
(205)592-3023
blcvacho@bellsouth.net

El Camino (C)SEGR0310
6248 SW 14th Street (mailing)
6790 SW 12th Street (physical)
West Miami, FL 33144
(305)261-6200 <Dade>
lucatha@aol.com
PA: Luciano Jaramillo <M1>
6249 SW 14th Street
West Miami, FL 33144
(305)264-1074
ljara@aol.com
CL: Hedemarrie Dussan
6248 SW 14th Street
Miami, FL 33144
(054)812-0613

Enon (4MWC)SEGR0707
PO Box 294 (mailing)
9000 Highway 12 (physical)

Ackerman, MS 39735
(662)285-3303 <Choctaw>
enoncpchurch@dtcweb.net
PA: Jerry L Lawson <M1>
6039 MS Highway 415
Ackerman, MS 39735
(662)285-8295
lawson@dtcweb.net
CL: Raymond D Gillon Jr
PO Box 294
Ackerman, MS 39735
(601)916-3589
rgillon@dtcweb.net

Erin (4WC)SEGR0601
PO Box 574, Carthage, MS (mailing)
590 Pete Freeman Road (physical)
Union, MS 39051
( ) <Newton>
OD: Scott Engle <M5>
308 D Byrum Road
Decatur, MS 39327
(601)683-9586
CL: Lynn Federick
PO Box 574
Carthage, MS 39051
(601)267-4954

First Hispanic (4MWU)SEGR0307
2828 W Kirby Street
Tampa, FL 33614
(813)932-9684 <Hillsborough>
FAX: (813)932-9700
fhpctampafla@aol.com
PA: Alexandri Sosa <M1>
2828 W Kirby Street
Tampa, FL 33614
(813)960-1473
FAX: (813)932-9700
sosapcus@gmail.com
CL: Martha Lezama
8510 Kings Rail Way
Tampa, FL 33647

Forrest Avenue (4MWC)SEGR0403
2316 Forrest Avenue
Gadsden, AL 35904
(256)547-2833 <Etowah>
SS: Lem Lockmiller Jr <M1>
PO Box 348
Leesburg, AL 35983
(256)490-3021
CL: Joe Neal
1110 Cabot Avenue
Gadsden, AL 35904
(256)547-2833
jnwr996@gmail.com

Gadsden (4MWC)SEGR0402
PO Box 2055 (mailing)
1200 Piedmont Cutoff (physical)
Gadsden, AL 35903
(256)492-2556 <Etowah>
FAX: (256)492-2525
office@gadsdencp.com
PA: Daniel Barkley <M1>
2732 Rexford Street
Hokes Bluff, AL 35903
daniel@gadsdencp.com
(256)478-0397
CL: Tinley Kirby
714 Reynolds Circle

GRACE PRESBYTERY CONTINUED

Gadsden, AL 35901
(256)490-4159
tinleykirby@gmail.com

_____

Glencoe   (4WC)SEGR0404
200 N College Street
Glencoe, AL 35905
(256)492-1584   <Etowah>
FAX: (256)492-1584
glencoecpchurch@yahoo.com
PA: Rodney McInnis   <M1>
6589 Harbor Place
Gadsden, AL 35907
(256)454-2399
mcinnisrodneyand@bellsouth.net
CL: Scott Stewart
200 N College Street
Gadsden, AL 35905
(256)492-1584
stewie242@hotmail.com

_____

Grace Community   (4C)SEGR0407
3515 Highway 14
Millbrook, AL 36054
(334)285-4655   < >
millbrookgcc@gmail.com
SS: Albert Russell   <M2>
375 Ashton Park Drive
Millbrook, AL 36054
(334)290-0399
chemistry.russell@gmail.com
CL: Debbie Silva
3515 Highway 14
Millbrook, AL 36054
(334)290-3884
quilter.deb@gmx.com

_____

Greens Chapel   (4WC)SEGR0208
PO Box 729 (mailing)
81 Greens Chapel Road (physical)
Cleveland, AL 35049
(205)559-7671   <Blount>
PA: David Linski   <M1>
202 Green's Chapel Road
Cleveland, AL 35049
(205)240-943
pastor@greenschapelcpc.org
CL: Ben Royal
148 Truman Drive
Cleveland, AL 35049
(205)274-7503
broyal@otelco.net

_____

Groverton   (2C)SEGR0602
222 Leon Harrell Road
Morton, MS 39117
( )   <Scott>
SS: Ronnie Spears   <M5>
101 Shirley Drive
Pelahatchie, MS 39145
CL: Joel Lingle
6266 Highway 481 N
Morton, MS 39117
(601)942-1927

_____

Helena   (4MC)SEGR0108
PO Box 418 (mailing)
3396 Helena Road (physical)
Helena, AL 35080
(205)663-2174   <Shelby>
helenacpchurch@bellsouth.net
SS: Mike Ensminger   <M2>

188 Grande View Lane
Maylene, AL 35114
(205)620-4699
me0573@att.com
CL: Betty Barron
1263 Siskin Drive
Alabaster, AL 35007
205-664-9251
barron1263@asi-web.com

_____

Homewood   (4WC)SEGR0111
513 Columbiana Road
Homewood, AL 35209
(205)942-3051   <Jefferson>
FAX: (205)945-0677
hcpc@homewoodcpc.com
PA: Mathew Derek Jacks   <M1>
341 Shadeswood Drive
Hoover, AL 35226
(205)903-8469
pastorderek@homewoodcpc.com
AP: Sherrad Hayes
4655 Vintage Lane
Birmingham, AL 35244
(706)773-5201
sherrad.hayes@gmail.com
CL: Melissa Dameron-Vines
1517 Astre Circle
Hoover, AL 35226
(205)422-1253
mdvines73@hotmail.com

_____

Hope   (4WC)SEGR0308
826 S Miller Road
Valrico, FL 33594
(813)684-4689   <Hillsborough>
FAX: (813)655-7919
hopecpc@verizon.net
PA: William E (Eddie) Jenkins   <M1>
1836 S Ridge Drive
Valrico, FL 33594
(813)651-3802
hopechurch4@aol.com
CL: Donna Cachia
4122 Helene Place
Valrico, FL 33594
(813)684-8391
djc1948@msn.com

_____

Hopewell   (4MWC)SEGR0101
2139 Cumberland Drive SE
Bessemer, AL 35023
(205)425-2126   <Jefferson>
SS: James Scott Edwards   <M3>
226 Jasmine Drive
Alabaster, AL 35007
(205)837-4069
jedwards53163@bellsouth.net
CL: Beverly Edwards
226 Jasmine Drive
Alabaster, AL 35007
(205)529-4507
bedwards@primehydraulic.net

_____

House of Prayer   (4C)SEGR0214
405 E Moulton Street (mailing)
Decatur, AL 35601
170 County Road 730 (physical)
Decatur, AL 35601
(256)355-0947   <Cullman>
FAX: (256)355-0947
nlajap@yahoo.com

PA: Neil Aguiar   <M1>
405 E Moulton Street
Decatur, AL 35601
(256)616-1318
nlajap@yahoo.com
AP: Antonio Mena Rojas   <M1>
1421 1st Street NW
Cullman, AL 35055
(256)531-8193
antonio.mena.7@facebook.com
CL: Andres Esteban
405 E Moulton Street
Decatur, AL 35601
(256)355-0947
FAX: (256)355-0947

_____

Hueytown First   (4MWC)SEGR0109
4846 15th Street Road
Hueytown, AL 35023
( )   <Jefferson>
CLOSED 4/3/2016

_____

Immanuel   (4MC)SEGR0311
10235 US Highway 301 (mailing)
36839 Indian Lake Cemetary Road (physical)
Dade City, FL 33525
(352)567-7427   <Pasco>
PA: Charles Reed   <M1>
10235 US Highway 301
Dade City, FL 33525
estchuck12@embarqmail.com
(352)567-7427
CL: Chad Reed
36821 Indian Lake Cemetary Road
Dade City, FL 33523
(352)567-8755
chadrreed@embarqmail.com

_____

McLeod Chapel   (4MC)SEGR0708
305 E Minor Street (mailing)
Macon-Lynn Creek Road (physical)
Macon, MS 39341
(662)726-4609   <Noxubee>
CL: James B Moore III
305 E Minor Street
Macon, MS 39341
(662)726-4609

_____

Mt Zion   (4C)SEGR0709
3044 Wolfe Road
Columbus, MS 39705
(662)328-3778   <Lowndes>
mjmims@muw.edu
CL: Martha Jo Mims
3011 Wolfe Road
Columbus, MS 39705
(662)328-3778
mjmims@muw.edu

_____

New Hope   (4EWC)SEGR0104
5521 Double Oak Lane
Birmingham, AL 35242
(205)937-3684   <Shelby>
FAX: (205)991-5159
jessie@newhopecpc.org
PA: Donny Acton   <M1>
5521 Double Oak Lane
Birmingham, AL 35242
(205)991-5252
FAX: (205)991-5259
donny@newhopecpc.org
AP: Mindy Acton   <M1>

GRACE PRESBYTERY CONTINUED

1413 Oak Ridge Drive
Birmingham, AL 35242
(205)991-3204
FAX: (205)991-5259
mindy@newhopecpc.org
AP: Sherrlyn Frost   <M1>
  5557 Surrey Lane
  Birmingham, AL 35242
  (205)408-0729
  FAX: (205)991-5259
  sherrlyn@newhopecpc.org
CL: Jessie R Dunnaway
  120 Virginia Way
  Birmingham, AL 35242
  (205)991-7434
  FAX: (205)991-5259
  jessie@newhopecpc.org
_____
Piedmont   (4MWC)SEGR0406
  23746 AL Highway 9 N
  Piedmont, AL 36272
  (256)447-7275   <Calhoun>
PA: Ken Byford   <M1>
  58 Quincy Lane
  Montevallo, AL 35115
  (205)665-5753
  kenabyford@gmail.com
CL: Charles Needham
  537 County Road 176
  Piedmont, AL 37282
  (256)405-5661
  number1teacher26@aol.com
_____
Pleasant Hill   (4MC)SEGR0710
  115 Westwood Drive SW (mailing)
  7782 CR 181, Eutaw, AL (physical)
  Bessemer, AL 35022
  (205)425-9659   <Greene>
  williambetts7177@gmail.com
LS: William H Betts   <M6>
  115 Westwood Drive SW
  Bessemer, AL 35022
  (205)425-9659
CL: Greg Espey
  12034 County Road 60
  Eutaw, AL 35462
  (205)372-2260
  gregandmichel@bellsouth.net
_____
Roca De Salvacion   (C)SEGR0115
  2404 Altadena Road
  Birmingham, AL 35243
  (205)705-3145   <Jefferson>
  cpcrocadesalvacion@gmail.com
PA: William Alas   <M1>
  105 Waterford Cove Drive
  Calera, AL 7655
  (205)966-9411
  alas3542085@yahoo.es
CL: Arely Torres
  1902 Chandalar Court
  Pelham, AL 35124
  (205)994-1978
  arelymartinez07@live.com
_____
Rocky Ridge   (4WC)SEGR0105
  2404 Altadena Road
  Birmingham, AL 35243
  (205)823-2719   <Jefferson>
  rockyridgechurch@bellsouth.net
PA: James DuWayne Pounds   <M1>
  364 Vincent Street
  Alabaster, AL 35007

(205)540-4284
duwaynelbs50@gmail.com
AP: Don H Thomas   <M1 RT>
  4829 Caldwell Mill Road
  Birmingham, AL 35242
  (256)742-0785
  dhtatn4ybc@cs.com
CL: Jaclyn Tow
  1913 Creek Trace
  Hoover, AL 35244
  (205)910-3758
  jackietow13@gmail.com
_____
Salem   (4WC)SEGR0607
  PO Box 121 (mailing)
  Sebastopol, MS 39359
  1220 Highway 487 E (physical)
  Walnut Grove, MS 39189
  (601)253-2678   <Leake>
  sondragould@att.net
PA: Angela Halford   <M1>
  PO Box 404
  Sebastopol, MS 39359
  (501)251-4668
  angelahalford1@gmail.com
CL: Virginia Gould
  1220 Highway 487 E
  Walnut Grove, MS 39189
  (601)253-2678
  sondragould@att.net
_____
Spring Creek   (4MWC)SEGR0113
  3411 Spring Creek Road (mailing)
  3455 Spring Creek Road (physical)
  Montevallo, AL 35115
  (205)665-4184   <Shelby>
  springcreekcp@aol.com
PA: Scott Fowler   <M1>
  1900 Alex Mill Road
  Montevallo, AL 35115
  (205)901-8478
  springcreekcp@aol.com
CL: Ben Ingram
  15 Quincy Lane
  Montevallo, AL 35115
  (205)665-4145
  ben_ingram@msn.com
_____
Steam Mill   (4WC)SEGR0608
  593 Pine Grove Road (mailing)
  Walnut Grove, MS 39189
  11551 Road 101 (physical)
  Union, MS 39365
  ( )   <Neshoba>
  nchambers@hughes.net
PA: Nicholas Chambers   <M1>
  11300 Road 101
  Union, MS 39365
  (601)697-4470
  nachambrs@hotmail.com
CL: Myra Bankston
  6517 Highway 492
  Union, MS 39365
  (601)616-0436
  mbankston@ecmhci.com
_____
Union   (4MWC)SEGR0114
  PO Box 64 (mailing)
  11633 Bama Rock Garden Road (physical)
  Vance, AL 35490
  ( )   <Tuscaloosa>
LS: Herbie Gray   <M6>

2554 A Rocky Ridge
Birmingham, AL 35226
CL: Clifford Odell
  11491 Bama Rock Garden Road
  Vance, AL 35490
  wjsrabbit@aol.com
_____
OTHERS ON MINISTERIAL ROLL:

Acton, Wade   <M1 RT>
  1615 Estes Drive
  Glencoe, AL 35905
  (256)492-8542
  ginnyacton@juno.com
Black, Gary G   <M1 WC>
  503 S Main Street
  Piedmont, AL 36272
  (205)447-7142
Brasher, Karen   <M1 WC>
  2931 Barker Cypress Road, Apt 415
  Houston, TX 77084
  (205)777-2420
  ekb077@gmail.com
Carter, Patricia   <M1 M9>
  2509 Decatur Stratton Road
  Decatur, MS 39327
  (601)604-3813
  revtree@yahoo.com
Chuquimia, Walter   <M5 OM>
  18240 S US Highway 301
  Winauma, FL 33598
  (813)399-4050
  walter@beth-el.info
Clark, J Don   <M1 RT>
  1601 Lake Ridge Circle
  Birmingham, AL 35216
  (205)942-4054
  jdsjcl@charter.net
Crawford, Roger B   <M1 RT>
  541 Highway 25 N
  Carthage, MS 39051
  (601)298-1899
Davis, C Timothy   <M1 WC>
  8880 Childress Road
  West Paducah, KY 42086
  (850)995-8383
  FAX: (904)994-6003
  charles0828@earthlink.net
Edmonds, Wayne   <M1 RT>
  112 Dogwood Trail
  Eclectic, AL 36024
  (334)857-2202
  sweetpea@comlinkinc.net
English, Don W   <M1 WC>
  4311 Guys Court
  Bessemer, AL 35022
  (205)428-4790
Foreman, Samuel L   <M1 WC>
  2811 Laredo Drive
  Hattiesburg, MS 39402
  (601)562-1415
  slfcpc@yahoo.com
Gaither, Randy   <M1 WC>
  No 3 Pacific Street
  Belmopan City
  Belize, Central America
  rgaither@valuelinx.net
Garcia, Ramon   <M1 OM>
  2714 Callista Court Apt 104
  Naples, FL 34114
  (239)200-5714
  revga@hotmail.com

GRACE PRESBYTERY CONTINUED

Hartung, J Thomas   \<M1 M9\>
2291 Americus Boulevard W Apt 1
Clearwater, FL 33763
(727)797-2882
revtom6@aol.com

Headrick, Anthony   \<M1 M8\>
3327 N Eagle Road Ste 110-132
Meridian, ID 83646
(619)524-8821
chaps2a@yahoo.com

Headrick, Christopher   \<M1 WC\>
1913 Vestavia Court Apt B
Vestavia Hills, AL 35216
(205)240-0979
bravespop@gmail.com

Headrick, Jerry   \<M1 RT\>
9950 Old Stage Road
Stockton, AL 36579
(251)377-9744
willjheadrick@gmail.com

Hunley, Jearl   \<M1 RT\>
2618 Canterbury Road
Columbus, MS 39705
(662)329-1516
jdhunley@cableone.net

Ingram, Matthew   \<M1 WC\>
29 Quincy Lane
Montevallo, AL 35115
(205)914-0829
mbingram80@gmail.com

Johnson, Thomas (Tommy) C   \<M1 RT\>
PO Box 566
Helena, AL 35080
(205)936-1350
revtomjohnson@aol.com

Laperche, Michael   \<M1 WC\>
9317 Moondancer Circle
Roseville, CA 95747
(813)948-8016
pastor-mike@earthlink.net

Lathem, W Ray   \<M1 WC\>
452 County Road 1462
Cullman, AL 35055
(256)708-1247
lathemray@bellsouth.net

Lefavor, David   \<M1 M8\>
414 S Monroe Siding Road
Xenia, OH 45385
(813)613-4133
david.lefavor@med.va.gov

Moore, James R, Sr   \<M1 RT\>
2778 Marguerite Street S
Hokes Bluff, AL 35903
(256)494-9030
jmoore@microxl.com

Mora, Wilfredo   \<M1 WC\>
17512 SW 153rd Court
Miami, FL 33187
(786)554-1478
moraw68@gmail.com

Morrow, Charles   \<M1 RT\>
5032 Pine Grove Road
Union, MS 39365
(601)479-0288
morrowp7@yahoo.com

Payne, Robert (Bob)   \<M1 WC\>
PO Box 11
Lauderdale, MS 39335
(205)856-2427
payne.bob.emmet@gmail.com

Ros, Ramiro   \<M1 WC\>
107 Bracken Lane
Brandon, FL 33511
(813)633-1548
bethel@gte.net

Rowlett, Ron   \<M1 WC\>
22 Diana Drive
Savannah, GA 31406
(912)351-0736

Schultz, Don   \<M1 RT\>
708 Gateway Lane
Tampa, FL 33613
(813)960-1473

Sims, Jacob   \<M1 WC\>
23716 Alabama Highway 9 N
Piedmont, AL 36272
(205)907-8273
jacobdsims@gmail.com

Talley, Ed   \<M1 WC\>
404 Serenity Circle
Walland, TN 37886
(205)854-1886

Thomas, Lynn   \<M1 DE\>
4833 Caldwell Mill Lane
Birmingham, AL 35242
(205)601-5770
lynndont@gmail.com

Tobler, Garth   \<M1 WC\>
136 Boat Landing Road
Oneonta, AL 35121
(205)683-0298
gatobler@gmail.com

Travieso, Julio   \<M1 WC\>
15910 Countrybrook Street
Tampa, FL 33624
(813)963-3727
jutra98@aol.com

Weldon, Mark   \<M1 WC\>
1515 Chambliss Drive
Birmingham, AL 35226
(205)913-3033
weldonm@bellsouth.net

Yarce, Omar   \<M1 WC\>
10925 Neptune Drive
Cooper City, FL 33026
omaryarce@gmail.com
(205)919-9685

OTHER LICENTIATES ON ROLL:

Diego, Aida Melendez   \<M2\>
412 SW 87 Place
Miami, FL 33174
(305)815-1197
revaidamd@yahoo.com

Munoz, Mardoqueo   \<M2\>
816 NW 87th Avenue #101
Miami, FL 33172
(305)801-6424
tonymarda@comcast.net

Sumerlin, Larkin   \<M2\>
174 Brookgreen Lane
Indian Springs, AL 35124
(334)357-00007
larkin_sumerlin72@hotmail.com

Tanck, Brian   \<M2\>
64 Mercer Street
Princeton, NJ 08540
(630)730-1577
brian.tanck@gmail.com

OTHER CANDIDATES ON ROLL:

Barrios, Janina   \<M3\>
6751 SW 16th Street
Miami, FL 33155
(786)757-0369
janina83@hotmail.com

Hernandez, Jhonathan   \<M3\>
10090 NW 80th Court
Hialeah Gardens, FL 33016
jhoto2006@hotmail.com

Marquez, Jose Ignacio   \<M3\>
8976 W Flagler Street
Miami, FL 33174
jimarquez.aviation@gmail.com

Myers, Bill   \<M3\>
145 G Morgan Road
Laurel, MS 39443
(601)425-1929

Seva, Judith   \<M3\>
7685 Tara Circle Apt 204
Naples, FL 34104
(239)269-3917
jclthgirl12@gmail.com

Solito, Carlos   \<M3\>
106 Highway 63
Calera, AL 35040
(205)329-8514
fcg9700@gmail.com

Yarce, Virginia   \<M3\>
10925 Neptune Drive
Cooper City, Fl 33026
(954)850-7111
ginnyyarce@gmail.com

Hong Kong Presbytery
MISSION SYNOD

GENERAL		MEMBERSHIP			CHANGES				FINANCES			
	1.Church Number	2.Active	3.Total 4.Church School		5.Prof. of Faith 6.Gains 7.Losses 8.Children Baptized				9. OUR UNITED OUT-REACH	10. Total Out-Reach Giving	11. All Other Expenses	12. Total Income Received	13. Value Church Prop. 1=1000
	1	2	3	4	5	6	7	8	9	10	11	12	13
Cheung Chau	8801	39	39	21	0	0	0	0	64	1,699	41,056	36,972	128
Kowloon	8803	109	294	82	2	4	2	2	1,538	39,200	192,000	191,000	155
Macau	8804	85	151	20	10	6	0	3	1,600	12,162	144,417	180,263	787
Mu Min*	8810	228	342	70	15	32	5	15	1,282	9,030	444,986	470,535	0
North Point	8805	47	114	32	1	1	4	0	2,416	27,677	131,697	168,151	13
Po Lam	8808	77	134	7	1	2	4	0	385	10,000	132,313	180,250	0
Shatin	8807	234	247	60	10	13	5	1	175	6,340	254,058	260,454	385
Tao Hsien	8806	400	556	200	0	10	2	0	2,563	162,882	593,841	817,773	2,898
Xi Lin	8809	120	168	0	5	9	7	5	1,922	12,704	285,977	283,776	0
Yao Dao	8811	187	206	25	8	13	0	0	1,922	3,866	181,177	204,290	0
TOTALS	10	1,526	2,251	517	52	90	29	14	13,867	285,560	2,401,522	2,793,464	4,366

CHURCHES, PASTORS, AND CLERKS:

Cheung Chau   (4C)MSHK8801
11 On Wing Centre 2/F
Pak She Back Street
Cheung Chau, HONG KONG
(852)2981-4933   <Hong Kong>
cccpcmail@yahoo.com.hk
SS: Kelvin Ho   <M2>
11 On Wing Centre 2/F
Pak She Back Street
Cheung Chau, HONG KONG
(852)2981-4933
kelvinskho@gmail.com
CL: Kelvin Ho
11 On Wing Centre 2/F
Pak She Back Street
Cheung Chau, HONG KONG
(852)2981-4933
kelvinskho@gmail.com

Kowloon   (4WC)MSHK8803
338-340 Castle Peak Road
Flat D 2/FL
Kowloon, HONG KONG
(852)2386-6563   <Hong Kong>
FAX: (852)3020-0365
kcumber@biznetvigator.com
SS: Ting Bong Ha   <M2>
338-340 Castle Peak Road
Flat D 2/FL
Kowloon, HONG KONG
(852)2386-6563
FAX: (852)3020-0365
kcumber@biznetvigator.com
CL: Lai Seung AU
338-340 Castle Peak Road
Flat D 2/FL
Kowloon, HONG KONG
(852)2386-6563
FAX: (852)3020-0365
kcumber@biznetvigator.com

Macau   (4WC)MSHK8804
258 Carlos D'Assumpcao
Ed Kin Heng Long 4 Andar LMNP
MACAU
(853)2892-1702   <Macau>
cpc_macau@yahoo.com.hk
PA: Eva Watt   <M4>
258 Carlos D'Assumpcao
Ed Kin Heng Long 4 Andar LMN
MACAU
(853)2892-1702
eva6e@hotmail.com
CL: Mei Teng Lio
258 Carlos D'Assumpcao
Ed Kin Heng Long 4 Andar LMN
MACAU
(853)2892-1702
cpc_macau@yahoo.com.hk

Mu Min   (C)MSHK8810
2/F Fu Tung Shopping Center
Tung Chung
Lantau Island, HONG KONG
(852)2109-1738   <Hong Kong>
FAX: (852)2109-1737
mmcpc@cumberland.org.hk
PA: Patrick Tat Wing So   <M1>
2/F Fu Tung Shopping Center
Tung Chung
Lantau Island, HONG KONG
(852)2109-1738
FAX: (852)2109-1737
cpctwso@yahoo.com.hk
CL: Kong Shing Chan
2/F Fu Tung Shopping Center
Tung Chung
Lantau Island, HONG KONG
(852)2109-1738
FAX: (852)2109-1737
mmcpc@cumberland.org.hk

North Point   (4WC)MSHK8805
14-16 Tsat Tsz Mui Road
1/Fl Block B
North Point, HONG KONG
(852)2562-2148   <Hong Kong>
FAX: (852)2564-2898
cpc.northpoint@gmail.com
SS: Eliza Yuk Lan Yau   <M2>
14-16 TsatTsz Mui Road
1/Fl Block B
North Point, HONG KONG
(852)2562-2148
FAX: (852)2564-2898
elizaylyau@yahoo.com.hk
CL: Queenie Tang
14-16 Tsat Tsz Mui Road
1/Fl Block B
North Point, HONG KONG
(852)2562-2148
FAX: (852)2564-2898
cpc.northpoint@gmail.com

Po Lam   (ARC)MSHK8808
Wing B&C, G/F, Ming Wik House
Kin Ming Estate
Tseung Kwan O NT, HONG KONG
(852)2706-0111   <Hong Kong>
FAX: (852)2706-0114
polamcpc@yahoo.com.hk
SS: Yim Ngar Wong   <M2>
Wing B&C G/F Ming Wik House
Kin Ming Estate
Tseung Kwan O NT, HONG KONG
(852)2706-0111
FAX: (852)2706-0114
yimngar@yahoo.com.hk
CL: Oi Lin Lai
Wing B&C G/F Ming Wik House
Kin Ming Estate
Tseung Kwan O NT, HONG KONG
(852)2706-0111
FAX: (852)2706-0114
yimngar@yahoo.com.hk

HONG KONG PRESBYTERY CONTINUED

Shatin   (ARC)MSHK8807
  G/1F 251 Tin Sam Village
  Shatin NT, HONG KONG
  (852)2693-3444   <Hong Kong>
  FAX: (852)2607-2245
  cpcshatin@yahoo.com.hk
PA: Jonathan Chor K Siu   <M1>
  G/1F 251 Tin Sam Village
  Shatin NT, HONG KONG
  (852)2693-3444
  FAX: (852)2607-2245
  cpccksiu@yahoo.com.hk
CL: Angelo Chui
  G/1F 251 Tin Sam Village
  Shatin NT, HONG KONG
  (852)2693-3444
  FAX: (852)2607-2245
  cpcshatin@yahoo.com.hk

Tao Hsien   (4F)MSHK8806
  2/F Welland Plaza
  188 Nam Cheong Street
  Sham Shui Po, Kowloon, HONG KONG
  (852)2783-8923   <Hong Kong>
  FAX: (852)2771-2726
  thchurch@taohsien.org.hk
PA: Amos Pui Chung Yuen   <M1>
  2/F Welland Plaza
  188 Nam Cheong Street
  Sham Shui Po, Kowloon, HONG KONG
  (852)2783-8923
  FAX: (852)2771-2726
  revyuen@taohsien.org.hk
CL: Adays Lee
  2/F Welland Plaza
  188 Nam Cheong Street
  Sham Shui Po, Kowloon, HONG KONG
  (852)2783-8923
  FAX: (852)2771-2726
  thchurch@taohsien.org.hk

Xi Lin   (4C)MSHK8809
  28 Hong Yip Street
  Yuen Long, HONG KONG
  (852)2639-9176   <Hong Kong>
  FAX: (853)2639-5620
  info@yuenlongchurch.org
PA: William Kin Keung Yeung   <M1>
  28 Hong Yip Street
  Yuen Long, HONG KONG
  (852)2639-9176
  FAX: (852)2639-5620
  william@yuenlongchurch.org
CL: Loarinne Tang
  28 Hong Yip Street
  Yuen Long, HONG KONG
  (852)2639-9176
  FAX: (852)2639-5620
  loarinne@yuenlongchurch.org

Yao Dao   (4C)MSHK8811
  CPC Yao Dao Primary School
  Tin Yuet Estate
  Tin Shui Wai, NT, HONG KONG
  (852)2617-7872   <Hong Kong>
  FAX: (852)2617-0287
  ydgrowth@gmail.com
SS: Antony Cheng   <M2>
  CPC Yao Dao Primary School
  Tin Yuet Estate

  Tin Shui Wai, NT, HONG KONG
  (852)2617-7872
  FAX: (852)2617-0287
  antonycycheng@yahoo.com.hk
CL: Sum Lam
  CPC Yao Dao Primary School
  Tin Yuet Estate
  Tin Shui Wai, NT, HONG KONG
  (852)2617-7872
  FAX: (852)2617-0287
  ydgrowth@gmail.com

OTHERS ON MINISTERIAL ROLL:

Cheung, Luke   <M1 WC>
  2/F Welland Plaza
  188 Nam Cheong Street
  Sham Shui Po Kowloon, HONG KONG
  (852)2783-8923
  FAX: (852)2771-2726
  luke.cheung@cgst.edu
Hung, Ella Siu Kei   <M1 WC>
  2/F Welland Plaza
  188 Nam Cheong Street
  Sham Shui Po, Kowloon, HONG KONG
  (852)2783-8923
  FAX: (852)2771-2726
  ellahung@yahoo.com
Lee, Ted Shu Tak   <M1 WC>
  2/F Welland Plaza
  188 Nam Cheong Street
  Sham Shui Po, Kowloon, HONG KONG
  (852)2783-8923
  FAX: (852)2771-2726
  tedlee@taohsien.org.hk
Leung, Grace Siu Tim Yu <M1 WC>
  2/F Welland Plaza
  188 Nam Cheong Street
  Sham Shui Po, Kowloon, HONG KONG
  (852)2783-8923
  FAX: (852)2771-2726
  yuleungsiutim@netvigator.com
Wong, So Li   <M1 WC>
  2/F Fu Tung Shopping Center
  Tung Chung
  Lantau Island, HONG KONG
  (852)2109-1738
  FAX: (852)2109-1737
  soliwong@gmail.com
Yu, Carver Tat Sum   <M1 WC>
  2/F Welland Plaza
  188 Nam Cheong Street
  Sham Shui Po, Kowloon, HONG KONG
  (852)2783-8923
  FAX: (852)2771-2726
  carver.yu@cgst.edu

OTHER LICENTIATES ON ROLL:

Ho, Carmen   <M2>
  Tin Yuet Estate
  Tin Shui Wai NT, HONG KONG
  (852)2617-7872
  FAX: (852)2617-0287
  ho_carcar@yahoo.com.hk
Lam, Janice   <M2>
  G/F & 1/F 251 Tin Sum Village
  Tai Wai, Shatin NT, HONG KONG
  (852)2693-3444
  FAX: (852)2607-2245
  janiceyeung929@gmail.com

Li, Chun Wai   <M2>
  1/Fl Block B
  14 TsatTsz Mui Road
  North Point, HONG KONG
  (852)2562-2148
  FAX: (852)2564-2898
  cwli2000hk@gmail.com
Liu, Lai Yuet   <M2>
  2/F Fu Tung Shopping Centre
  Tung Chung
  Lantau Island NT, HONG KONG
  (852)2109-1738
  FAX: (852)2109-1737
  laiyuet0914@gmail.com
Mak, Daphne Suet Chung   <M2>
  2/F Welland Plaza
  188 Nam Cheong Street
  Sham Shui Po, Kowloon, HONG KONG
  (852)2783-8923
  FAX: (852)2771-2726
  daphne@taohsien.org.hk
Tang, Po Kau   <M2>
  G/1F, 251 Tin Sam Village
  Shatin, NT, HONG KONG
  (852)2693-3444
  FAX: (852)2607-2245
  cpc_pokau@yahoo.com.hk
Tsui, Jackson   <M2>
  258 Carlos D'Assumpcao
  Ed King Heng Long 4 Andar LMNP
  MACAU
  (853)2882-1702
  tsuih@yahoo.com
Tsui, Sukie   <M2>
  Wing B & C
  G/F Ming Wik House
  Kin Ming Es
  (852)2706-0111
  FAX: (852)2706-0114
  sukiecpc@yahoo.com.hk Wong, Sam-
Son Chi   <M2>
  2/F Fu Tung Shopping Centre
  Tung Chung
  Lantau Island NT, HONG KONG
  (852)2109-1738
  FAX: (852)2109-1737
  wongchishui@yahoo.com.hk
Yau, Chat Ming   <M2>
  G/F 251 Tin Sum Village
  Shatin NT, HONG KONG
  (852)2693-3444
  FAX: (852)2607-2245
  summerycm@yahoo.com.hk
Yuen, Susanna   <M2>
  28 Hong Yip Street
  Yuen Long, NT, HONG KONG
  (522)639-9176
  FAX: (522)639-5620
  susanna@yuenlongchurch.org
Yung, Karen Wing Man   <M2>
  Flat D 2/F
  338-340 Castle Peak Road
  Kowloon, HONG KONG
  (852)2386-6563
  FAX: (852)3020-0365
  yungyungmiss@yahoo.com.hk

HONG KONG PRESBYTERY CONTINUED

OTHER CANDIDATES ON ROLL:

Cheung, Agnes   \<M3\>
 2/F Welland Plaza
 188 Nam Cheong Street
 Sam Shui Po
 Kowloon, HONG KONG
 (852)2783-8923
 FAX: (852)2771-2726
 agnes@taoshien.org.hk

Ho, Jessie   \<M3\>
 2/F Welland Plaza
 188 Nam Cheong Street
 Sam Shui Po
 Kowloon, HONG KONG
 (852)2783-8923
 FAX: (852)2771-2726
 jesse@taoshien.org.hk

Hung, Kevin   \<M3\>
 28 Hong Yip Street
 Yuen Long NT, HONG KONG

(852)2639-9176
FAX: (852)2639-5620
kevinhk0627@gmail.com

Lam, Chris   \<M3\>
 2/F Welland Plaza
 188 Nam Cheong Street
 Shamshuipo, Kowloon, HONG KONG
 (852)2783-8923
 FAX: (852)2771-2726
 chrislam@taoshien.org.hk

Lam, Dicky   \<M3\>
 Flat D 2/F
 338-340 Castle Peak Road
 Kowloon, HONG KONG
 (852)2386-6563
 FAX (852)3020-0365
 lamdicky912@gmail.com

Lam, Mercy   \<M3\>
 28 Hong Yip Street
 Yuen Long NT, HONG KONG
 (852)2639-9176
 FAX: (852)263-5620

thlammercy@gmail.com
Li, Siu Fun   \<M3\>
 Tin Yuet Estate
 Tin Shui Wai NT, HONG KONG
 (852)2617-7872
 FAX: (852)2617-0287
 spyaodao@yahoo.com

Sze, Yat Sung   \<M3\>
 Tin Yuet Estate
 Tin Shui Wai NT, HONG KONG
 (852)2617-7872
 FAX: (852)2617-0287
 yatsungs@yahoo.com.hk

Tam, Wai Sun   \<M3\>
 Wing B & C
 G/F Ming Wik House
 Kin Ming Es
 Tseung Kwan O, HONG KONG
 (852)2706-0111
 FAX: (852)2706-0114
 tsw428@gmail.com

Hope Presbytery
SOUTHEAST SYNOD

GENERAL		MEMBERSHIP			CHANGES				FINANCES				
	1.Church Number	2.Active	3.Total	4.Church School	5.Prof. of Faith	6.Gains	7.Losses	8.Children Baptized	9. OUR UNITED OUT-REACH	10. Total Out-Reach Giving	11. All Other Expenses	12. Total Income Received	13. Value Church Prop. 1=1000
	1	2	3	4	5	6	7	8	9	10	11	12	13
Allsboro	0501	43	83	21	0	0	1	0	0	9,930	75,699	76,979	300
Baldwin Chapel	0202	38	65	14	2	1	1	2	0	4,573	34,846	41,039	200
Faith	0213	49	107	31	No Report Received			0	0	0	0	0	600
Florence 1st	0506	85	122	55	1	6	9	1	13,868	21,637	130,939	159,966	1,000
Hickory Grove	0507	26	37	16	No Report Received			0	1,200	0	0	0	150
Hurricane*	0508	35	35	20	2	2	59	0	100	6,146	70,647	74,057	300
Maud	0509	10	4	0	No Report Received			0	100	0	0	0	90
Mt. Hester	0510	6	6	0	0	0	4	0	100	640	10,282	16,473	200
Mt. Pleasant	0511	7	7	7	0	0	0	0	100	610	6,333	6,943	280
Nebo	0512	30	30	23	0	1	3	0	400	2,587	41,7987	53,616	1,225
Old Mt Bethel	0513	35	35	26	0	0	1	1	100	4,741	22,589	26,779	55
Park Terrace	0514	34	34	25	No Report Received			0	0	0	0	0	671
Rogersville 1st	0517	130	271	87	3	9	12	4	15,125	52,594	270,160	191,263	1,074
Springfield*	0515	85	169	52	0	0	2	0	0	17,103	101,438	126,225	1,200
Union Hill	0516	97	132	42	8	14	2	0	200	17,031	78,271	92,825	1,500
Welti	0212	122	199	68	1	2	4	0	18,810	45,717	159,171	189,390	925
TOTALS	16	840	1,336	482	17	35	98	8	50,103	183,309	1,002,362	1,055,555	9,404

*Math error corrected. **Purged roll.

CHURCHES, PASTORS, AND CLERKS:

Allsboro   (4MEWC)SEHO0501
 515 Iuka Road (mailing)
 1925 Allsboro Road (physical)
 Cherokee, AL 35616
 (256)360-2919   \<Colbert\>
SS: Don F Thomas   \<M1 OP\>
 743 Rain Dance Way
 Cordova, TN 38018
 (901)412-3695

thomas63981@comcast.net
CL: Dale Johnson
 515 Iuka Road
 Cherokee, AL 35616
 (256)360-2973
 djohnson@bibank.com

Baldwin Chapel   (4MEWC)SEHO0202
 381 County Road 404 (mailing)
 126 County Road 1153 (physical)
 Cullman, AL 35057
 (256)737-1850   \<Cullman\>

PA: Gary Carter   \<M1\>
 8311 County Road 1082
 Vinemont, AL 35179
 (256)443-8389
 garycarter51@gmail.com
CL: Bonnie Marty
 381 County Road 404
 Cullman, AL 35057
 (256)734-6399
 brmarty45@yahoo.com

Faith   (4WC)SEHO0213

HOPE PRESBYTERY CONTINUED

5821 County Road 1114 (mailing)
Vinemont, AL 35179
6880 AL Highway 157 (physical)
Cullman, AL 35057
(256)734-0893   <Cullman>
PA: Dudley Brock   <M1>
490 County Road 1184
Cullman, AL 35057
(256)734-0893
preacherbrock@att.net
CL: Philip Nickles
5821 County Road 1114
Vinemont, AL 35179
(256)620-1977
nickles.phil@yahoo.com

Florence First   (4WC)SEHO0506
2422 Darby Drive
Florence, AL 35630
(256)766-0471   <Lauderdale>
FAX: (256)766-0736
fcpoffice@comcast.net
PA: Dwayne McDuff   <M1>
9770 County Road 5
Florence, AL 35633
(256)764-6354
FAX: (256)766-0736
fcpdmcduff@comcast.net
CL: Chris Cassel
1317 Cypress Mill Road
Florence, AL 35630
(256)740-1199
chriscassel1199@gmail.com

Hickory Grove   (4MC)SECU0507
75 County Road 59
Moulton, AL 35650
(256)306-0025   <Lawrence>
dhtatn4ybc@cs.com
CL: Noah Williamson
655 County Road 38
Mount Hope, AL 35651
(256)974-9413
mwilliamson@lawrenceal.org

Hurricane   (4EWC)SEHO0508
1331 County Road 86 (mailing)
1000 County Road 156 (physical)
Rogersville, AL 35652
(256)247-7483   <Lauderdale>
PA: Jimmy R Cox   <M1>
2250 County Road 156
Anderson, AL 35610
(256)710-1702
dcox01@msn.com
CL: Bryan Belue
1331 County Road 86
Rogersville, AL 35652
(256)247-7175
rbeluebigboy@aol.com

Maud   (4MWC)SEHO0509
2280 Maud Road (mailing)
Gypsy Loop (physical)
Cherokee, AL 35616
(256)360-2811   <Colbert>
CL: Paula Pardue
2280 Maud Road
Cherokee, AL 35616
(256)360-2811

Mt Hester   (4MEWC)SEHO0510
PO Box 174 (mailing)
14720 Mount Hester Road (physical)
Cherokee, AL 35616
(   )   <Colbert>
CL: Leigh Ann Malone
2625 Sutton Hill Road
Cherokee, AL 35616
(256)359-6134
leighmalone05@yahoo.com

Mt Pleasant   (4MC)SEHO0511
30 Carolyn Road (mailing)
13575 County Line Road (physical)
Muscle Shoals, AL 35661
(256)446-5397   <Colbert>
CL: James Letsinger
8285 2nd Street
Leighton, AL 35646
(256)446-9367

Nebo   (4MEWC)SEHO0512
8630 Highway 101
Lexington, AL 35648
(256)577-5952   <Lauderdale>
nebo9491@gmail.com
PA: Terry Herston   <M1>
390 County Road 95
Rogersville, AL 35652
(256)247-3004
tpaw51@gmail.com
CL: Steve Littrell
9491 Highway 101
Lexington, AL 35648
(256)577-5952
nebo9491@gmail.com

Old Mt Bethel   (4C)SEHO0513
County Road 51
Rogersville, AL 35652
(   )   <Lauderdale>
PA: Terry Herston   <M1>
390 County Road 95
Rogersville, AL 35652
(256)247-3004
tpaw51@gmail.com
CL: Tommy Word
620 County Road 521
Lexington, AL 35648
(256)247-3182
tword1956@gmail.com

Park Terrace   (4MEWC)SEHO0514
100 E Wheeler Avenue
Sheffield, AL 35660
(256)383-8052   <Colbert>
pastor@parkterracechurch.org
PA: George Lee   <M1>
314 Kingston Drive
Florence, AL 35633
(256)740-0809
butchleeautos@yahoo.com
CL: Peggy Vickers
112 Pasadena Avenue
Muscle Shoals, AL 35661
(256)383-1992

Rogersville First   (4WC)SEHO0517
16751 Highway 72
Rogersville, AL 35652
(256)247-3339   <Lauderdale>

fcprogersville@yahoo.com
PA: James P Driskell   <M1>
16751 Highway 72
Rogersville, AL 35652
(256)648-6758
patprespax@yahoo.com
CL: Suzanne Christopher
16751 Highway 72
Rogersville, AL 35652
(256)710-7432
19scd59@gmail.com

Springfield   (4MWC)SEHO0515
5400 Highway 101
Rogersville, AL 35652
(256)247-1424   <Lauderdale>
FAX: (256)247-1424
kennymorgan330@hotmail.com
PA: Kenneth P Morgan   <M1>
5400 Highway 101
Rogersville, AL 35652
(256)247-3890
FAX: (256)247-1424
kennymorgan330@hotmail.com
CL: Charles G Lash
170 Meadow Ridge Lane
Rogersville, AL 35652
(256)247-0040

Union Hill   (4MEWC)SEHO0516
6535 Bailey Road
Anderson, AL 35610
(256)233-1841   <Limestone>
PA: Charles Hood   <M1>
1200 County Road 519
Anderson, AL 35610
(256)229-6251
hooddad11@gmail.com
CL: Curtis Usery
28341 Easter Ferry Road
Lester, AL 35647
(256)232-9237

Welti   (4MWC)SEHO0212
8817 County Road 747
Cullman, AL 35055
(256)737-9138   <Cullman>
weltipastor@welticpchurch.com
PA: James L Peyton   <M1>
1455 County Road 643
Cullman, AL 35055
(256)735-3620
jakjpeyton@att.net
AP: Abigail Prevost   <M1>
4731 Lafayette Road
Hopkinsville, KY 42240
(731)343-5386
abbyprevost@gmail.com
CL: Lee Holder
6589 County Road 747
Cullman, AL 35055
(256)739-5136
lholder@tvpinc.com

OTHERS ON MINISTERIAL ROLL:

Deaton, John   <M1 WC>
277 School Lane
Springfield, PA 19064
(215)906-7067
deatonjr11@gmail.com

HOPE PRESBYTERY CONTINUED

Malone, John W   <M1 RT>
  3693 Highway 67 South
  Sommerville, AL 35670
  (256)778-8237

Parker, Susan   <M1 WC>
  655 York Drive
  Rogersville, AL 35652
  (256)247-3877
  park9301@bellsouth.net

Rodgers, Howard   <M1 RT>
  336 County Road 1216
  Vinemont, AL 35179
  (256)739-6296
  djbr421@yahoo.com

OTHER LICENTIATES ON ROLL:

OTHER CANDIDATES ON ROLL:

Japan Presbytery
MISSION SYNOD

GENERAL		MEMBERSHIP			CHANGES				FINANCES				
1.Church Number	2.Active	3.Total	4.Church School	5.Prof. of Faith	6.Gains	7.Losses	8.Children Baptized	9. OUR UNITED OUT-REACH	10. Total Out-Reach Giving	11. All Other Expenses	12. Total Income Received	13. Value Church Prop. 1=1000	
	1	2	3	4	5	6	7	8	9	10	11	12	13
Asahi Mission	8315	26	27	10	0	0	1	2	962	2,369	21,657	44,486	25
Den-en Mission	8310	14	35	10	0	0	2	0	301	1,043	44,392	29,338	70
EbinaShionNoOka	8311	108	166	40	0	2	7	0	2,794	19,012	77,576	94,803	74
Higashi Koganei	8301	30	35	4	0	0	1	0	1,046	5,344	54,548	61,314	130
Ichikawa Grace	8314	21	27	10	0	5	1	0	416	1,009	54,339	34,279	45
Izumi	8312	28	42	9	0	0	0	0	546	2,206	35,683	37,889	36
Kibougaoka	8302	173	334	60	7	8	2	0	4,783	32,939	133,777	166,922	479
Koza	8303	524	1,116	404	14	20	26	1	17,058	126,038	473,458	599,496	1,512
KunitachiNozomi	8306	59	103	75	0	1	2	0	2,014	9,125	78,301	85,165	170
Megumi	8309	41	49	5	0	1	1	0	1,698	7,993	56,304	60,617	71
Naruse	8305	59	122	12	3	7	1	0	1,903	9,150	66,107	75,257	98
Sagamino	8304	29	56	9	0	1	1	0	709	6,081	47,259	44,209	174
Shibusawa*	8307	38	99	11	0	1	3	0	2,030	9,135	62,554	75,964	245
TOTALS	13	1,150	2,211	659	24	46	48	4	36,260	231,444	1,205,955	1,409,739	3,129

*Math error corrected. **Purged roll.

CHURCHES, PASTORS, AND CLERKS:

Asahi Mission   (4F)MSJA8315
  1F Miyabi-Bldg
  1-19-21 Honcho Tsurugamine
  Asahi-ku Yokohama, Kanagawa-Ken
  241-0021 JAPAN
  (045)489-3720   <Japan>
  FAX: (045)953-2588
  info@asahi-ch.com
PA: Atsushi Suzuki   <M1>
  53-17 Higashi Kibogaoka Asahi-ku
  Yokohama, Kanagawa-ken
  241-0826 JAPAN
  (045)362-2603
  FAX: (045)362-2603
  asyuwa98@m10.alpha-net.ne.jp
CL: Session Clerk Asahi Mission Point

1F Miyabi-Bldg
1-19-21 Honcho Tsurugamine
Asahi-ku Yokohama, Kanagawa-Ken
241-0021 JAPAN
(045)489-3720
FAX: (045)953-2588
info@asahi-ch.com

Den-en Mission   (4MC)MSJA8310
9-41-2 Kamitsuruma-honcho
Sagamihara-Shi, Kanagawa-Ken
228-0818 JAPAN
(042)744-6804   <Japan>
FAX: (042)744-6804
den-en.church@pc5.so-net.ne.jp
PA: Kazuhiko Furuhata   <M1>
  #310, 9-41-15 Kamitsurumahoncho
  Sagamihara-shi, Kanagawa-ken
  252-0318 JAPAN

(042)814-7802
FAX: (042)814-7802
cpc.furuhata@gmail.com
CL: Takashi Kanazashi
  3-6-406 Shimoyuzuki
  Hachiouji-shi, Tokyo
  197-0732 JAPAN
  (042)675-6895
  fredericfchopin@gmail.com

Ebina Shion No Oka   (4MWC)MSJA8311
3-17-57 Nakashinden
Ebina-shi, Kanagawa-ken
243-0422 JAPAN
(046)234-3426   <Japan>
ebinazion@gmail.com
PA: Yukio Tamai   <M1>
  3-17-57 Nakashinden
  Ebina-shi, Kanagawa-ken

JAPAN PRESBYTERY CONTINUED

243-0422 JAPAN
(046)234-3426
yukiotamai@icloud.com
CL: Hiroko Fushimi
2-4-7 Rinkan Yamato-shi
Kanagawa-ken
242-0003 JAPAN
(046)275-3801
FAX: (046)725-3801
hrkfsm@hotmail.com

Higashi Koganei   (4MWC)MSJA8301
2-14-16 Higashi-cho
Koganei-shi, Tokyo
184-0011 JAPAN
(042)231-1279   <Japan>
FAX: (042)231-1279
PA: Nobuko Seki   <M1>
2-14-16 Higashi-cho Koganei-Shi
Tokyo
184-0011 JAPAN
(042)231-1279
seki@koza-church.jp
CL: Jyunko Kuchiki
2-14-16 Higashi-cho
Koganei-shi, Tokyo
184-0011 JAPAN
(042)251-7781
FAX: (042)251-7781

Ichikawa Grace Mission (4MF)MSJA8314
1-11-20 Kokubu
Ichikawa-shi, Chiba-ken
272-0834 JAPAN
(047)369-7540   <Japan>
FAX: (047)369-7540
ichikawa-grace@mbi.nifty.com
PA: Yasuo Masuda   <M1>
1-11-20 Kokubu
Ichikawa-shi, Chiba-ken
272-0834 JAPAN
(047)369-7540
FAX: (047)369-7540
fwgc6854@mb.infoweb.ne.jp
CL: Session Clerk Ichikawa Grace Mission
1-11-20 Kokubu
Ichikawa-shi, Chiba-ken
272-0834 JAPAN
(047)369-7540
FAX: (047)369-7540
ichikawa-grace@mbi.nifty.com

Izumi   (4WC)MSJA8312
4194-13 Izumi-cho Izumi-ku
Yokohama, Kanagawa-ken
245-0016 JAPAN
(045)803-1749   <Japan>
FAX: (045)361-4351
izumi@kyokai.org
PA: Kenji Ushioda   <M1>
2-47-3 Akuwa-higashi Seya-ku
Yokohama, Kanagawa-ken
243-0023 JAPAN
(046)361-4351
ushioda@jc.ejnet.ne.jp
CL: Takeshi Yohena
7-7-44 Ryokuen Isumi-ku
Yokohama-shi
246-0023 JAPAN
(045)814-4537
ayohena@uc.catv-yokohama.ne.jp

Kibougaoka   (4WMC)MSJA8302
72-2 Naka Kibogaoka
Asahi-ku Yokohama, Kanagawa-ken
241-0825 JAPAN
(045)391-6038   <Japan>
FAX: (045)391-6653
PA: Ryuzo Matsuya   <M1>
72-2 Naka Kibogaoka Asahi-ku
Yokohama, Kanagawa-ken
241-0825 JAPAN
(045)364-8297
matsuya.r@woody.ocn.ne.jp
CL: Kazuhiro Ohashi
2-50-16 Akuwa-Higashi
Seya-ku Yokohama, Kanagawa-ken
246-0023 JAPAN
(045)363-4923
k_0084@nifty.com

Koza   (4MWC)MSJA8303
2-14-1 Minami Rinkan
Yamato-shi, Kanagawa-ken
242-0006 JAPAN
(046)724-1370   <Japan>
FAX: (046)276-9685
cpckoza@koza-church.jp
PA: Masahiro Matsumoto   <M1>
2-14-1 Minami Rinkan
Yamato-shi, Kanagawa-ken
242-0006 JAPAN
(046)275-2767
matsumoto@koza-church.jp
AP: Nobuko Seki   <M1>
2-14-16 Higashi-cho Koganei-Shi
Tokyo
184-0011 JAPAN
(042)231-1279
seki@koza-church.jp
CL: Yutaka Shibata
1-18-3 Rinkan Yamato-shi
Kanagawa-ken
241-0003 JAPAN
(046)272-0579
shibata@koza-church.jp

Kunitachi Nozomi   (4MWC)MSJA8306
3-15-9 Higashi
Kunitachi-shi, Tokyo
186-0002 JAPAN
(042)572-7616   <Japan>
FAX: (042)572-7616
nozomi-ch@ceres.ocn.ne.jp
PA: Kenta Karasawa   <M1>
3-15-10 Higashi
Kunitachi-shi, Tokyo
186-0002 JAPAN
(042)575-5549
FAX: (042)575-5549
smbno6@gmail.com
CL: Shigekazu Osawa
3-15-9 Higashi
Kunitachi-shi, Tokyo
186-0002 JAPAN
(042)572-7776
s-osawa@mub.biglobe.ne.jp

Megumi   (4MWC)MSJA8309
3-355-4 Kami Kitadai Higashi
Yamato-shi, Tokyo
207-0023 JAPAN

(042)564-0593   <Japan>
megumikyokai@gmail.com
PA: Makihiko Arase   <M1>
3-355-4 Kamikitadai Higashi
Yamato-shi, Tokyo
207-0023 JAPAN
(080)6636-1960
viator@cb3.so-net.ne.jp
CL: Shigeru Yanagawa
2-68-25 Sunagawa-cho
Tachikawa-shi, Tokyo
190-003 JAPAN

Naruse   (4WC)MSJA8305
7-20-12 Tamagawa Gakuen
Machida-shi, Tokyo
194-0041 JAPAN
(042)725-9909   <Japan>
FAX: (042)725-9909
cpc-naruse@nifty.com
PA: Yoshimasa Niwa   <M1>
15-402 Narakita Danchi
2913 Naramachi Aoba-ku
Kanagawa-ken, Yokohama
227-0036 JAPAN
(045)961-1540
FAX: (045)961-1540
rsb09335@nifty.com
CL: Hiroshi Yoshizaki
7-20-12 Tamagawa Gakuen
Machida-shi, Tokyo
194-0041 JAPAN
(046)384-5332
hs-2703-9427@nifty.com

Sagamino   (4MWC)MSJA8304
4-13-24 Higashihara
Zama-shi, Kanagawa-ken
228-0004 JAPAN
(046)255-6441   <Japan>
FAX: (046)255-6441
kyokai@sagamino.org
PA: Takehiko Miyai   <M1>
A-201 2-2-48 Higashihara Zama-shi
Kanagawa-ken
228-0004 JAPAN
(046)207-6558
FAX: (046)207-6558
tacke.m@gmail.com
CL: Akimasa Nakano
1-105 Sagaminosakura 5-1
Higashihara Zama-shi
Kanagawa-ken
228-0004 JAPAN
(046)254-8564
nakano.a.ipt@gmail.com

Shibusawa   (4MWC)MSJA8307
1-8-50 Magarimatsu
Hadano-shi, Kanagawa-ken
259-1321 JAPAN
(046)387-1203   <Japan>
FAX: (046)387-1203
keitaro_o@hotmail.com
PA: Keitaro Ohi   <M1>
1-8-50 Magarimatsu
Hadano-shi, Kanagawa-ken
259-1321 JAPAN
(046)387-1203
FAX: (046)387-1203
keitaro_o@hotmail.com

JAPAN PRESBYTERY CONTINUED

CL: Shinobu Araki
313 Daia Paresu Hontsugi Dai2
779-1 Mita Atsugi-shi, Kanagawa-ken
243-0211 JAPAN
araki_shinobu@yahoo.co.jp

OTHERS ON MINISTERIAL ROLL:

Asayama, Masaharu   <M1 RT>
6-3-2-308 Toyogaoka
Tama-shi, Tokyo
206-0031 JAPAN
(042)373-2710
asa@ipcc-21.com

Hamazaki, Takashi   <M1 RT>
1551-1-202 Inokuchi
Nakai-cho Ashigarakami-gun
Kanagawa-ken
259-0151 JAPAN
(046)541-8550
gen22-14@qf7.so-net.ne.jp

Ikushima, Michinobu   <M1 RT>
2074 Nakashinden
Ebina-Shi, Kanagawa-Ken
243-0422 JAPAN
(046)232-9888
m.ikushima@tbz.t-com.ne.jp

Katsuki, Shigeru   <M1 WC>
2-14-16 Higashi-cho

Koganei-shi, Tokyo
184-0011 JAPAN
(042)232-3640
FAX: (042)231-1279
shigeru.katsuki@nifty.com

Satoh, Iwao   <M1 OM>
8710 Hickory Falls Lane
Pewee Valley, KY 40056
iwaosatoh@gmail.com
(502)210-0852

Yano, Fumitsuta   <M1 WC>
424-4 Kamide, Fjinomiya-shi
Shuizuika-ken   JAPAN
(054)454-0313

OTHER LICENTIATES ON ROLL:

Inou, Yuki   <M2>
Tokyo Christian University
3-301-5 Uchino Inzai-shi, Chiba
270-1347 JAPAN
(047)646-1141
yuki_inoh0615@yahoo.co.jp

Miyajima, Atsushi   <M2>
Rua Araja
58 Paraiso Sao Joa
48280-000, Bahia, BRAZIL
(5571)3664-1037
ariel.atsushi@gmail.com

Suzuki, Temote   <M2>
9-41-15-310 Honcho Kamitsuruma
Sagamihara-shi, Kanagawa-ken
228-0818 JAPAN
timocsuzuki@gmail.com

Taira, Masanori   <M2>
Japan Biblical Theological Seminary
2-14-1 Minami Rinkan
Yamoto-shi, Kanagawa-ken
242-0006 JAPAN

Wada, Ichiro   <M2>
Tokyo Christian University
3-301-5 Uchino Inzai-shi, Chiba
270-1347 JAPAN
(047)646-1141
ichirowada@gmail.com

OTHER CANDIDATES ON ROLL:

Miyagi, Ken   <M3>
Tokyo Christian University
3-301-5 Uchino Inzai-shi, Chiba
270-1347 JAPAN
ken1818@hotmail.co.jp

Missouri Presbytery
GREAT RIVERS SYNOD

	1.Church Number	2.Active	3.Total	4.Church School	5.Prof. of Faith	6.Gains	7.Losses	8.Children Baptized	9. OUR UNITED OUT-REACH	10. Total Out-Reach Giving	11. All Other Expenses	12. Total Income Received	13. Value Church Prop. 1=1000
	1	2	3	4	5	6	7	8	9	10	11	12	13
Bethel	4102	6	6	6	0	0	0	0	0	1,856	4,951	11,951	10
Elk Creek*	4304	19	19	11	0	0	0	0	0	300	22,447	27,424	75
God's Grace	4104	48	57	12	17	33	10	17	0	1,225	11,127	12,000	120
Happy Home	4306	20	23	0	0	0	0	0	2,344	6,013	19,510	28,018	175
Harmony	4203	18	41	7	5	2	3	0	3,503	8,638	27,297	44,362	80
Hopewell*	4105	34	37	17	1	0	0	0	3,202	15,359	38,282	35,597	310
Korean	4316												
Lobb	4209				CLOSED 9/17/2016				0	0	0	0	170
Mansfield	4308	54	73	30	No Report Received			0	0	0	0	0	75
Marshall	4210	86	203	34	0	5	3	2	12,429	35,741	127,744	124,817	1,050
New Hope (DeC)	4309	17	17	9	No Report Received			0	0	0	0	0	60
Orange	4108	52	52	52	1	8	1	0	5,000	18,105	77,301	76,553	780
Phillipsburg	4311	9	13	6	No Report Received			0	0	0	0	0	150
Pierson*	4312	8	12	6	0	5	0	0	743	8,148	4,505	13,390	150
Pleasant Grove*	4109	10	55	6	1	1	5	0	0	100	3,917	3,862	30
Salem	4216	10	10	0	No Report Received			0	0	0	0	0	150
Seymour	4313	15	29	6	No Report Received			0	0	0	0	0	50
Shawnee Mound	4111	4	37	6	0	0	0	1	0	703	1,230	5,415	7,026	60
Spring Creek*	4113	28	37	14	0	0	10	0	3,530	3,625	27,565	29,067	182
Springfield 1st	4314	41	72	60	3	6	3	0	6,356	14,675	112,475	87,886	1,500
Warrensburg*	4115	54	58	24	0	0	14	0	1,125	5,717	51,833	45,161	500
White Oak Pond	4315	112	204	89	2	5	2	0	16,743	27,710	140,276	167,437	2,150
TOTALS	20	647	1,064	402	30	65	52	19	55,678	319,442	673,897	715,329	7,769

*Math error corrected. **Purged roll.

CHURCHES, PASTORS, AND CLERKS:

Bethel (2C)GRMI4102
14621 Lawrence 1032 (mailing)
Sarcoxie, MO 64862
Crossroads Lawrence 1030 & Lawrence 2170 (physical)
Wentworth, MO
(417)285-6571   <Lawrence>
SS: Tim Steeley   <M2>
PO Box 281
Mt Vernon, MO 65712
(417)466-4345
tsteeley@swr5.k12.mo.us
CL: Lana Moore
14621 Lawrence 1032
Sarcoxie, MO 64862
(417)285-6571
lanajeanmoore@hotmail.com

Elk Creek (4MEC)GRMI4304
7423 County Road 3730 (mailing)
Peace Valley, MO 65788
US Highway 160 E (physical)
West Plains, MO 65775
(417)257-0983   <Howell>
pastorbrown44@yahoo.com
PA: Dale M Brown   <M1 HR>
HC 61 Box 4740
West Plains, MO 65775
(417)257-0983

pastorbrown44@yahoo.com
CL: Cindy Rasor
7423 County Road 3730
Peace Valley, MO 65788
(417)256-7353
rrasor@centurytel.net

God's Grace (4MC)GRMI4104
415 Water Street (mailing)
417 W Water Street (physical)
Greenfield, MO 65661
( )   <Dade>
CL: Debra Kay Bartlett
423 Water Street
Greenfield, MO 65661
(417)637-5678
debrakaybartlett@gmail.com

Happy Home (4C)GRMI4306
510 S Newport Avenue (mailing)
5604 State Highway ZZ (physical)
Conway, MO 65632
( )   <Webster>
CL: Rex Luallin
510 S Newport Avenue
Conway, MO 65632
(417)589-3804

Harmony (4WC)GRMI4203
3508 Scott Street (mailing)
Saint Joseph, MO 64507

SE State Road Z (physical)
San Antonio, MO 64443
(816)279-0733   <Buchanan>
orvalschafer@aol.com
OD: Marion Cannon   <M5>
4248 SW State Route N
Stewartsville, MO 64490
(816)449-2437
orvalschafer@aol.com
CL: Viola Schafer
3508 Scott Street
Saint Joseph, MO 64507
(816)279-0733
orvalschafer@aol.com

Hopewell (4EWC)GRMI4105
248 NE 50th Road (mailing)
273 NE 50th Road (physical)
Lamar, MO 64759
(417)682-2396   <Barton>
FAX: (417)682-3514
parrishron@att.net
OD: George Haag   <M5>
301 Gulf Street
Lamar, MO 64759
(417)682-3876
CL: Reba Simmons
63 E Highway C
Lamar, MO 64759
(417)884-2810

MISSOURI PRESBYTERY CONTINUED

Korean   (4C)GRMI4316
4216 Charleston Avenue
Springfield, MO 65408
(417)888-0442
hesed-park@hanmail.net
PA: Sang Hoon Park   <M1>
2980 W Melbourne Street
Springfield, MO 65810
(417)888-0442
hesed-park@hanmail.net
CL: Session Clerk Korean
4216 Charleston Avenue
Springfield, MO 65408

Lobb   (4MC)GRMI4209
Flynn Road & 7-Highway
Independence, MO 64050
( )   <Jackson>
CLOSED 9/17/2016

Mansfield   (4MEC)GRMI4308
PO Box 673 (mailing)
307 S Phelps Avenue (physical)
Mansfield, MO 65704
( )   <Wright>
OD: S Larry Scott   <M5>
2211 Airport Road
Mansfield, MO 65704
(417)924-4390
revslscott@gmail.com
CL: Leon Veenstra
4680 Highway F
Hartville, MO 65667
(417)741-7408
veenstra@getgoin.net

Marshall   (4MWC)GRMI4210
1000 S Miami
Marshall, MO 65340
(660)886-2402   <Saline>
pastor_randy_shannon@yahoo.com
PA: Randy Shannon   <M1>
30282 Highway H
Marshall, MO 65340
(660)886-9454
pastor_randy.shannon@yahoo.com
CL: Karen Guthrie
1506 Broadmoor Lane
Marshall, MO 65340
(660)886-5797
kguthrie7878@gmail.com

New Hope (DeC)   (4WC)GRMI4309
230 County Road 2630 (mailing)
Dent County Road 6200 (physical)
Salem, MO 65560
( )   <Dent>
PA: Michael Reno   <M1>
52 Rolla Gardens
Rolla, MO 65401
(573)578-5321
rollarenomike@gmail.com
CL: Kim Moser
1862 Highway BB
Jadwin, MO 65501
(573)729-2780

Orange   (4WC)GRMI4108
109 Agnes (mailing)
Crane, MO 65633
15743 Highway K (physical)

Aurora, MO 65605
(417)678-5220   <Lawrence>
PA: D Kevin Vanderlaan   <M1>
17246 Highway K
Aurora, MO 65605
(217)620-2723
pastorkevin2@gmail.com
CL: Leah Estes
501 S Western
Marionville, MO 65705
(417)723-8033
lestesx5@centurytel.net

Phillipsburg   (4WC)GRMI4311
11187 Cuba Road (mailing)
Grovespring, MO 65662
Grover Street (physical)
Phillipsburg, MO 65722
( )   <Laclede>
OD: Chris Wilson   <M5>
745 Birchwood
Marshfield, MO 65706
(417)425-0863
chris@springfieldbsu.org
CL: Cheryl Brown
11187 Cuba Drive
Grovespring, MO 65662
(417)462-0813
brownc@hartville.k12.mo.us

Pierson   (4C)GRMI4312
12754 State Highway M (mailing)
Billings, MO 65610
45129 State Highway 413 (physical)
Billings, MO 65610
(417)369-2104   <Stone>
OD: Jon White   <M5>
12754 State Highway M
Billings, MO 65610
(417)890-1533
CL: Kary Crumpley
1513 Crumpley Drive
Marionville, MO 65705
(417)839-3552
karycrumpley@gmail.com

Pleasant Grove   (4C)GRMI4109
PO Box 97 (mailing)
891 SE Y Highway (physical)
Knob Noster, MO 65336
( )   <Johnson>
CL: Dana Smith
836 Southeast Y Highway
Knob Noster, MO 65536
(660)563-9739
dsmith@knobnoster.k12.mo.us

Salem   (4WC)GRMI4216
211 NW County Road OO (mailing)
382 NW County Road H (physical)
Warrensburg, MO 64093
( )   <Johnson>
CL: Anne Patrick
211 NW County Road OO
Warrensburg, MO 64093
(660)747-8902
apatrick52@hotmail.com

Seymour   (4C)GRMI4313
PO Box 40 (mailing)
222 Main Street (physical)

Seymour, MO 65746
(417)935-2235   <Webster>
OD: Sam Burt   <M5>
102 E Summit Avenue
Seymour, MO 65746
(417)735-2759
CL: Denise Burt
102 E Summit Avenue
Seymour, MO 65746
(417)300-6451
gerrydburt@gmail.com

Shawnee Mound   (4WC)GRMI4111
72 NW 1150 Road
Chilhowee, MO 64733
( )   <Henry>
SS: Mary Anna Townsend   <M2>
1123 Tyler Avenue
Warrensburg, MO 64093
(660)909-5966
wrenhse1123@gmail.com
CL: Doris Hunter
62 NW 1150 Road
Chilhowee, MO 64733
(660)885-3709
dfhunter@embarqmail.com

Spring Creek   (4EWC)GRMI4113
307 E 365th Road (mailing)
Hwy 123 & Hwy A Junction (physical)
Dunnegan, MO 65640
(417)754-8498   <Polk>
OD: Scott Garner   <M5>
1403 E Primrose Lane
Republic, MO 65738
(417)732-4218
CL: Gary M Roetto
307 E 365th Road
Dunnegan, MO 65640
(417)754-8498

Springfield First   (4MWC)GRMI4314
4216 S Charleston Avenue
Springfield, MO 65804
(417)862-6434
reformedminister@yahoo.com
PA: Andrew (Andy) Eppard
1427 W McGee Street
Springfield, MO 65807
(417)862-6434
reformedminister@yahoo.com
CL: Carol Fare
302 N Market Street
Nixa, MO 65714
(417)725-2775
cjfare52@sbcglobal.net

Warrensburg   (4WC)GRMI4115
201 Grover Street
Warrensburg, MO 64093
(660)747-3021   <Johnson>
PA: Randy Crawshaw   <M1>
136 NE 1271 Road
Knob Noster, MO 65336
(660)563-5149
randy_crawshaw@yahoo.com
CL: Dana Moore
113 Larkin Street
Warrensburg, MO 64093
(660)747-8777
dmoore@ucmo.edu

MISSOURI PRESBYTERY CONTINUED

White Oak Pond   (4MWC)GRMI4315
  16549 Highway 5 (mailing)
  16551 Highway 5 (physical)
  Lebanon, MO 65536
  (417)532-5049   <Laclede>
  wopcpc@whiteoakpond.org
PA: Richard Plachte   <M1 HR>
  615 Grover Street
  Warrensburg, MO 64093
  (660)441-4427
  rap@aerobiz.org
AP: Jill Carr   <M1>
  PO Box 1547
  Lebanon, MO 65536
  (417)532-6760
  dig.micah.6.8@gmail.com
CL: Janie Lewis
  1931 King James Drive
  Lebanon, MO 65536
  (417)664-6357

OTHERS ON MINISTERIAL ROLL:

Ang, John   <M1 HR>
  5843 S Farm Road 157
  Springfield, MO 65810
  (417)886-3487
  pastorcares@yahoo.com
Appling, John   <M1 WC>
  1722 S Fairway Avenue
  Springfield, MO 65804
  (417)877-4643
  pegblessings@sbcglobal.net
Appling, Peggy   <M1 WC>
  1722 S Fairway
  Springfield, MO 65804
  (417)877-4643
  pegblessings@sbcglobal.net
Bone, Leslie   <M1 M9>
  16504 E George Franklin Drive
  Independence, MO 64055
  (816)373-6625
  lesliebone@comcast.net

Campbell, Gordon C   <M1 RT>
  1469 E Wayland Street
  Springfield, MO 65804
  (417)823-9567
  gofor12@gmail.com
Hansen, Terry   <M1 WC>
  16549 Highway 5
  Lebanon, MO 65536
  (417)533-8106
  thansen@whiteoakpond.org
Harris, Edward   <M1 HR>
  10000 Wornall Road Apt 2315
  Kansas City, MO 64114
  (816)214-8977
  ed121@kcrr.com
Rodden, Linda   <M1 WC>
  363 Cornelison Street
  Lebanon, MO 65536
  (417)588-2207
  linda.rodden@mercy.net
Roedder, Unhui Grace   <M1 WC>
  419 S Jonathan Avenue
  Springfield, MO 65802
  (417)494-6491
  kimroedder@hotmail.com
Wieland, Jack G, Jr   <M1 WC>
  PO Box 116
  Napoleon, MO 64074
  (217)823-4331
  jgwieland@hotmail.com

OTHER LICENTIATES ON ROLL:

OTHER CANDIDATES ON ROLL:

Cintro, Eddie   <M3>
  5695 S Franklin
  Springfield, MO 65810
  (417)894-1480
  eddiecintron7@gmail.com
Hudson, Jennifer   <M3>
  716 Apache Drive
  Marshall, MO 65340
  (660)631-3893

Murfreesboro Presbytery
TENNESSEE SYNOD

GENERAL		MEMBERSHIP			CHANGES				FINANCES				
	1.Church Number	2.Active	3.Total	4.Church School	5.Prof. of Faith	6.Gains	7.Losses	8.Children Baptized	9. OUR UNITED OUT-REACH	10. Total Out-Reach Giving	11. All Other Expenses	12. Total Income Received	13. Value Church Prop. 1=1000
	1	2	3	4	5	6	7	8	9	10	11	12	13
Algood	7201	21	29	6	No Report Received			0	0	0	0	0	180
Banks	7202	15	17	13	2	2	2	2	1,300	3,930	29,653	29,975	344
Bates Hill	7203	66	103	37	No Report Received			0	4,840	0	0	0	325
Beech Grove*	7204	22	22	10	1	3	1	1	0	6,232	39,274	39,672	423
Belvidere*	7205	4	5	5	0	0	35	0	0	320	6,380	9,048	60
Blues Hill*	7207	18	18	14	0	0	13	0	6,191	9,938	22,096	37,467	80
Cloyd's	7208	97	97	45	No Report Received			0	4,800	0	0	0	2,500
Commerce	7209	53	53	35	1	4	12	0	3,000	5,017	58,006	63,023	425
Cookeville 1st	7210	564	642	240	3	12	5	2	42,275	106,960	399,531	546,747	4,600
Cowan	7211	60	78	44	0	7	0	0	10,964	21,851	102,980	109,664	1,880
Dibrell	7212	9	9	9	0	0	0	0	500	0	10,890	12,442	35
Dry Valley	7213	8	10	10	No Report Received			0	250	0	0	0	10
Goshen	7214	95	95	45	No Report Received			0	3,208	0	0	0	874
Gum Creek	7215	22	22	12	0	0	1	0	500	2,604	23,933	26,016	130
Harmony	7216	62	99	54	1	3	3	0	10,205	25,002	82,122	114,009	1,041
Hickory Valley	7251	9	9	21	No Report Received			0	0	0	0	0	0
Hillsboro	7217	16	18	6	No Report Received			0	0	0	0	0	250
Jerusalem	7218	43	48	24	0	0	0	0	9,429	20,250	102,394	94,299	275
Joywood	7250	25	36	12	No Report Received			0	0	0	0	0	375
LaGuardo	7219	25	25	3	No Report Received			0	0	0	0	0	150
Lebanon	7220	280	497	208	5	14	8	1	25,542	35,494	451,209	423,496	4,000
Liberty	7222	96	146	52	2	3	4	0	12,184	31,542	99,527	129,212	989
Livingston 1st	7223	10	42	3	No Report Received			0	0	0	0	0	250
LuzD.L.Naciones	7252	9	20	23	No Report Received			0	0	0	0	0	0
Manchester	7224	78	215	65	0	0	4	0	19,341	29,907	156,344	193,411	1,300
McMinnville*	7225	6	6	9	1	0	0	0	627	1,585	13,322	9,414	200
Monteagle	7227	5	5	0	0	0	0	0	0	0	7,225	7,305	70
Mt. Carmel*	7228	12	20	0	0	0	3	0	0	1,200	10,690	14,700	350
Mt. Hermon	7229	9	18	10	No Report Received			0	0	0	0	0	200
Mt. Tabor	7230	25	25	15	1	3	15	0	4,182	8,709	37,999	45,081	138
Mt. Vernon	7231	32	37	26	No Report Received			0	0	0	0	0	410
Murfreesboro	7232	148	388	92	0	0	13	1	13,380	30,839	243,995	306,438	3,245
New Hope*	7233	72	78	22	0	10	0	0	0	2,980	74,740	92,464	1,022
Old Zion	7234	7	9	5	0	1	1	0	2,718	4,173	18,201	27,174	300
Owens Chapel	7235	53	70	18	5	0	2	0	500	5,515	86,786	92,576	210
Providence	7238	14	14	38	No Report Received			0	0	0	0	0	150
Rock Island	7274												
Rockvale	7239	68	149	31	0	0	4	0	9,520	14,308	75,735	162,718	1,310
Rocky Glade	7240	62	74	68	0	0	1	0	3,500	12,200	45,100	65,050	375
Ruth Chapel	7241	2	5	0	No Report Received			0	0	0	0	0	3
Sewanee	7242	22	28	12	No Report Received			0	2,037	0	0	0	225
Smithville	7243	144	144	101	3	8	15	0	23,700	54,781	0	237,943	1,700
Suggs Creek	7244	10	9	0	0	1	0	1	3,152	4,524	19,449	25,241	120
Union Hill	7246	49	71	41	No Report Received			0	1,038	0	0	0	250
Watertown	7247	10	10	7	0	0	2	0	1,000	1,608	15,142	15,422	479
Winchester 1st	7249	513	948	450	11	22	13	2	59,993	98,595	593,414	601,048	3,500
TOTALS	45	3,028	4,517	2,033	34	90	153	8	248,876	508,522	2,719,385	3,394,543	34,168

*Math error corrected. **Purged roll.

MURFREESBORO PRESBYTERY CONTINUED

CHURCHES, PASTORS, AND CLERKS:

Algood (4WC)TNMU7201
3617 Burton Cove Road (mailing)
Cookeville, TN 38506
Corner Harp & Main Street (physical)
Algood, TN 38506
( ) <Putnam>
PA: Richard Bond <M1>
2425 Fisk Road, Lot 0
Cookeville, TN 38506
(931)526-7610
erbond@frontier.net
CL: E Burton
3617 Burton Cove Road
Cookeville, TN 38506
(931)537-6661
e_burton@frontier.com

Banks (4MWC)TNMU7202
846 Avenue (mailing)
2933 Banks Pisgah Road (physical)
Smithville, TN 37166
( ) <DeKalb>
SS: Greg Whaley <M2>
4970 Comstock Road
Chapel Hill, TN 37034
(931)364-7637
grewha@mail.com
CL: Robert Joins
846 Lutrell Avenue
Smithville, TN 37166
(615)597-6366
b_joins@hotmail.com

Bates Hill (4MEWC)TNMU7203
9957 Nashville Highway (mailing)
6111 Old Nashville Highway (physical)
Mc Minnville, TN 37110
(931)939-3235 <Warren>
cavecrew1979@gmail.com
CL: William R Black
9980 Nashville Highway
Mc Minnville, TN 37110
(931)743-9809
cavecrew1979@gmail.com

Beech Grove (4MC)TNMU7204
PO Box 26 (mailing)
471 Oscar Crowell Road (physical)
Beechgrove, TN 37018
(931)394-2387 <Coffee>
CL: Crystal B Brandon
269 French Brantley Road
Wartrace, TN 37183
(931)394-2387
no_tenn@hotmail.com

Belvidere (4WC)TNMU7205
Walnut Hill Road
Belvidere, TN 37306
( ) <Franklin>
PA: Joseph H Butler <M1>
56 Cline Ridge Road
Winchester, TN 37398
(931)224-8423
jhbu737@bellsouth.net
CL: Alton Smith
123 Post Oak Road
Belvidere, TN 37306
starsmith53@hotmail.com

Blues Hill (4MWC)TNMU7207
7292 Short Mountain Road
Mc Minnville, TN 37110
( ) <Warren>
SS: Lyon Walkup <M1>
225 Bertha Owen Road
Morrison, TN 37357
(931)607-3233
dirtroad@blomand.net
CL: Naomi Smith
522 Smith Town Road
Mc Minnville, TN 37110
(931)939-2435
memesmith@blomand.net

Cloyd's (4WC)TNMU7208
PO Box 277 (mailing)
595 West Division (physical)
Mt Juliet, TN 37121
(615)758-7434 <Wilson>
PA: Michael Reese <M1>
114 Palmer Road
Lebanon, TN 37090
(615)443-0457
michaelhreese@bellsouth.net
CL: Vickie Hibdon
7141 Lebanon Road
Mount Juliet, TN 37122
(615)444-6498

Commerce (4WC)TNMU7209
351 Borum Road (mailing)
4260 S Commerce Road (physical)
Watertown, TN 37184
(615)237-9409 <Wilson>
crutchmckinwater@aol.com
SS: Denny C Shepard <M1>
8514 Newsom Station Road
Nashville, TN 37221
(615)662-1114
CL: Jacki Crutcher
351 Borum Road
Watertown, TN 37184
(615)237-3310
crutchmckinwater@aol.com

Cookeville First (4WC)TNMU7210
565 E 10th Street
Cookeville, TN 38501
(931)526-6585 <Putnam>
FAX: (931)528-2270
charles@cookevillecpchurch.org
PA: Christian Smith <M1>
2017 Grademere Drive
Cookeville, TN 38501
(931)265-8896
csmith2490@gmail.com
CL: Lanny Knight
521 Chad Lane
Cookeville, TN 38501
(931)528-7800
alknight2@msn.com

Cowan (4MC)TNMU7211
PO Box 277 (mailing)
206 Cowan Street W (physical)
Cowan, TN 37318
(931)967-7431 <Franklin>
cowancpchurch@bellsouth.net
PA: Ronnie M Pittenger <M1>

207 Cowan Street W
Cowan, TN 37318
(615)832-8832
CL: Cindy Henn
PO Box 277
Cowan, TN 37318
(931)967-7431
cowancpchurch@bellsouth.net

Dibrell (4C)TNMU7212
128 Mitchell Road (mailing)
Mike Muncey Road (physical)
McMinnville, TN 37110
( ) <Warren>
CL: Jacqulyn S Boyd
128 Mitchell Road
McMinnville, TN 37110
(931)934-2088

Dry Valley (4C)TNMU7213
5196 Shady Lane (mailing)
4415 Highway 70 N (physical)
Cookeville, TN 38506
( ) <Putnam>
PA: Richard Bond <M1>
2425 Fisk Road Lot 0
Cookeville, TN 38506
(931)854-0979
CL: Janice F Bohannon
5196 Shady Lane
Cookeville, TN 38506
(931)528-7894
jandan80@gmail.com

Goshen (4MWC)TNMU7214
PO Box 881 (mailing)
1262 Williams Cove Road (physical)
Winchester, TN 37398
(931)967-0245 <Franklin>
goshenchurch@cafes.net
PA: Richard Morgan <M1>
1468 Williams Cove Road
Winchester, TN 37398
(931)349-4474
icthuse3@gmail.com
CL: Frances Hanger
251 Whipperwill Lane
Winchester, TN 37398
(931)967-7730
FAX: (931)967-7730
bhanger@bellsouth.net

Gum Creek (4C)TNMU7215
1063 Franklin Heights Drive
Winchester, TN 37398
(931)967-6539 <Franklin>
PA: Coyle Campbell <M1>
186 Old Limestone Road
New Market, AL 35761
(256)379-4392
CL: Molly Perry
1063 Franklin Heights Drive
Winchester, TN 37398
(931)967-6539

Harmony (4MWC)TNMU7216
8891 Lynchburg Road
Winchester, TN 37398
(931)962-0842 <Franklin>
PA: Joseph H Butler, Jr <M1>
261 Ridgefield Drive

MURFREESBORO PRESBYTERY CONTINUED

Winchester, TN 37398
(931)224-8423
jhbu737@live.com
CL: Clare Wiseman
8555 Lynchburg Road
Winchester, TN 37398
(931)967-3932
wisrc9802@gmail.com

Hickory Valley   (4U)TNMU7251
Sparta, TN 38583
(931)738-5812   <White>
PA: Richard Bond   <M1>
1528 Eastlake Drive
Cookeville, TN 38506
(931)526-7610
CL: Kathryn Adcock
1450 Oak Grove Road
Sparta, TN 38583
(931)761-5858
kadcock@blomand.net

Hillsboro   (4EC)TNMU7217
PO Box 4
Hillsboro, TN 37342
(931)394-2415   <Coffee>
CL: Robert L Jenkins
68 Hillsboro Viola Road
Hillsboro, TN 37342
(931)596-2745

Jerusalem   (4MWC)TNMU7218
7192 Mona Road
Murfreesboro, TN 37129
(615)895-8118   <Rutherford>
PA: Brent Wills   <M1>
4607 E Richmond Shop Road
Lebanon, TN 37090
(615)449-3258
bwills9185@yahoo.com
CL: Jimmy C Francis
4657 W Jefferson Pike
Murfreesboro, TN 37129
(615)893-8311
jcfjimmy@aol.com

Joywood   (4MWC)TNMU7250
7120 Old Nashville Highway
Murfreesboro, TN 37129
(615)459-6518   <Rutherford>
joywoodchurch@yahoo.com
PA: Jeff Clark   <M1>
327 Haynes Haven Lane
Murfreesboro, TN 37129
(615)896-7733
jclark7733@aol.com
CL: Mark Tharp
5018 Willowbend Drive
Murfreesboro, TN 37128
(615)895-4772
markat52@comcast.net

LaGuardo   (4WC)TNMU7219
7320 Highway 109 N
Lebanon, TN 37087
(615)444-0419   <Wilson>
OD: Gary Mraz   <M5>
8630 Highway 109 N
Lebanon, TN 37087
CL: Nancy Voight
500 Woods Ferry Pike

Lebanon, TN 37087

Lebanon   (4MWC)TNMU7220
522 Castle Heights Avenue
Lebanon, TN 37087
(615)444-7453   <Wilson>
FAX: (615)444-6671
lcpsecretary@hotmail.com
PA: Kevin Medlin   <M1>
316 Dandelion Drive
Lebanon, TN 37087
(615)444-7453
FAX: (615)444-6671
kmedlin12@hotmail.com
CL: Kelly Hendricks
464 Locust Grove Road
Watertown, TN 37184
(615)443-0226
FAX: (615)444-6671

Liberty   (4MWC)TNMU7222
317 Liberty Lane
McMinnville, TN 37110
(931)473-3813   <Warren>
libertycpc@gmail.com
PA: Marcus Hayes   <M1>
2901 Sandage Avenue Apt 304
Fort Worth, TX 76109
(270)841-7576
marcus.hayes@att.net
AP: Jennifer Hayes   <M1>
2901 Sandage Avenue Apt 304
Fort Worth, TX 76109
(205)533-1018
hayesj712@gmail.com
CL: Patty Boyd
35 Lonsvale Drive
McMinnville, TN 37110
(931)473-8059
pattyboyd@blomand.net

Livingston First   (4WC)TNMU7223
PO Box 393 (mailing)
110 Byrdstown Highway (physical)
Livingston, TN 38570
(931)823-5115   <Overton>
SS: Donald Ray Fossey, II   <M3>
328 Waterloo Road
Cookeville, TN 38506
(931)498-2149
dfossey@twlakes.net
CL: Janice Ledbetter
311 Garrett Mills Road
Livingston, TN 38570

Luz D L Naciones   (4F)TNMU7252
114 Northwood Lane
Mc Minnville, TN 37110
( )   <Warren>
PA: Jose Perez   <M1>
89 Northwood Lane Apt A102
Mc Minnville, TN 37110
(931)743-5585
CL: Session Clerk
114 Northwood Lane
Mc Minnville, TN 37110
(931)815-9502

Manchester   (4MWEC)TNMU7224
838 McArthur Street
Manchester, TN 37355

(931)728-2975   <Coffee>
FAX: (931)728-2975
mancp@cafes.net
PA: Mark Barron   <M1>
836 McArthur Street
Manchester, TN 37355
(931)728-2975
FAX: (931)728-2975
mbarron@cafes.net
CL: Debbie Shelton
1255 M G England Road
Manchester, TN 37355
(931)728-9422
debbiebl@cafes.net

McMinnville   (4MWC)TNMU7225
115 Peers Street
McMinnville, TN 37110
(931)474-4255   <Warren>
dwalhart@aol.com
PA: Daryl Alhart   <M1>
2187 Rutledge Ford Road
Decherd, TN 37324
(931)349-7104
dwalhart@aol.com
CL: Leota Watson
804 W Main Street
Mc Minnville, TN 37110
(931)473-7561
leotaw@blomand.net

Monteagle   (4C)TNMU7227
PO Bos 243 (mailing)
343 College Street (physical)
Monteagle, TN 37356
( )   <Grundy>
CL: Billie Faye Terrill
PO Box 243
Monteagle, TN 37356
(931)924-2787

Mt Carmel   (4MEWC)TNMU7228
1484 Elora Road
Huntland, TN 37345
(931)469-7394   <Franklin>
PA: Richard, "Rocky" Whray   <M1>
201 8th Avenue SE
Winchester, TN 37398
(931)636-4844
rocklex1017@att.net
CL: Tina M Morrow
714 Baxter Hollow Road
Belvidere, TN 37306
(931)967-3853
ramtmm@netzero.net

Mt Hermon   (4MEWC)TNMU7229
5544 Mt Hermon Road
Cookeville, TN 38506
( )   <Putnam>
SS: Maury A Norman   <M1 OP>
1750 Shipley Road
Cookeville, TN 38501
(931)526-1644
maurynorman@yahoo.com
CL: Ruth Shubert
6799 Cherry Creek Road
Cookeville, TN 38506
(931)526-5109

Mt Tabor   (4EC)TNMU7230

MURFREESBORO PRESBYTERY CONTINUED

3122 Donard Court (mailing)
6000 Manchester Highway (physical)
Murfreesboro, TN 37127
(615)545-4695   <Rutherford>
sheila.mcclain4695@gmail.com
PA: Brent Wills   <M1>
4607 E Richmond Shop Road
Lebanon, TN 37090
(615)449-3258
bwills9185@yahoo.com
CL: Sheila McClain
3122 Donard Court
Murfreesboro, TN 37128
(615)545-4695
sheila.mcclain4695@gmail.com

Mt Vernon   (4C)TNMU7231
131 Hickory Hills Drive (mailing)
Murfreesboro, TN 37128)
11915 Mt Vernon Road (physical)
Rockvale, TN 37153
(615)890-9125   <Rutherford>
PA: Judy Taylor Sides   <M1>
534 Bethany Circle
Murfreesboro, TN 37128
(615)895-1627
CL: Gregory L Sides
534 Bethany Circle
Murfreesboro, TN 37128
(615)895-1627

Murfreesboro   (4MEWC)TNMU7232
907 E Main Street
Murfreesboro, TN 37130
(615)893-6755   <Rutherford>
FAX: (615)893-4553
firstcp@comcast.net
PA: Christopher Warren   <M1>
906 Prince Lane
Murfreesboro, TN 37129
(615)828-8719
chris@murfreesborocpc.org
AP: Joy Warren   <M1>
907 W Main Street
Murfreesboro, TN 37129
(615)828-8719
revjoywarren@gmail.com
CL: Margaret Barlow
4965 Steeplechase Road
Christiana, TN 37037
(615)895-4918
mbarlow@viammfg.com

New Hope   (4EWC)TNMU7233
PO Box 1215 (mailing)
7845 Coles Ferry Pike (physical)
Lebanon, TN 37087
(615)449-7020   <Wilson>
PA: Paul Hancock   <M1>
107 Highland Ridge
Hendersonville, TN 37075
(615)429-4331
pah4331@gmail.com
CL: Mary Ann Smith
423 Stonegate Drive
Lebanon, TN 37090
(615)444-0102
nwhpchrch0@gmail.com

Old Zion   (4C)TNMU7234
395 Coventry Drive (mailing)

Nashville, TN 37211
7489 Old Kentucky Road (physical)
Sparta, TN 38583
(   )   <White>
PA: James A McGill   <M1>
433 S Walnut Avenue
Cookeville, TN 38501
(931)526-6936
jam7235@frontiernet.net
CL: Kay Armstrong
268 Tulip Drive
Sparta, TN 38583
(615)406-3976

Owens Chapel   (4C)TNMU7235
1310 Liberty Road (mailing)
3058 Liberty Road (physical)
Winchester, TN 37398
(931)636-8076   <Franklin>
ferguea9@gmail.com
PA: Blake Stephens   <M1>
2559 Holders Cove Road
Winchester, TN 37398
(931)939-2628
blsteph@edge.net
CL: Jimmy McKinney
1310 Liberty Road
Winchester, TN 37398
(931)967-3679
bigmacj37@comcast.net

Providence   (3C)TNMU7238
c/o Pierce Dodson(mailing)
106 Bartonwood Drive
Lebanon, TN 37087
Providence Road (physical)
Hartsville, TN 37074
(   )   <Trousdale>
CL: Session Clerk
c/o Pierce Dodson(mailing)
106 Bartonwood Drive
Lebanon, TN 37087

Rock Island   (4C)TNMU7274
PO Box 146
Rock Island, TN 38581
(931)979-1701
PA:Barry Boggs   <M1>
1039 Johnnie Bud Lane
Cookeville, TN 38501
(931)979-1701
boggsone@hotmail.com
CL: Mike Cornett
125 Great Oak Drive
Rock Island, TN 38581

Rockvale   (4MEWC)TNMU7239
PO Box 67 (mailing)
8769 Rockvale Road (physical)
Rockvale, TN 37153
(615)274-3143   <Rutherford>
PA: Jonathan Watson   <M1>
4017 Claude Drive
Smyrna, TN 37167
watsonjonathan@bellsouth.net
(615)630-9153
CL: Martha A Lannom
903 Sunset Avenue
Murfreesboro, TN 37129
(615)896-1348
malannom@bellsouth.net

Rocky Glade   (4C)TNMU7240
PO Box 8 (mailing)
2017 Rocky Glade Road (physical)
Eagleville, TN 37060
(   )   <Rutherford>
PA: J. Tommy Jobe   <M1>
PO Box 8
Eagleville, TN 37060
(615)776-7755
cppreacher@united.net
CL: Bill Lamb
425 River Eagleville Road
Eagleville, TN 37060
(615)274-2275
billlamb1@bellsouth.net

Ruth Chapel   (2C)TNMU7241
347 Windle Community Road (mailing)
146 Windle Community Road (physical)
Livingston, TN 38570
(   )   <Overton>
SS: Donald Fossey II   <M3>
328 Waterloo Road
Cookeville, TN 38506
(931)498-2149
dfossey@twlakes.net
CL: Jo K Smith
347 Windle Community Road
Livingston, TN 38570
(931)823-5916

Sewanee   (4WC)TNMU7242
Box 11
Sewanee, TN 37375
(931)598-0766   <Franklin>
smdiam@hotmail.com
CL: Paul E Mooney
Box 11
Sewanee, TN 37375
(931)598-0766

Smithville   (4MWC)TNMU7243
201 S College Street
Smithville, TN 37166
(615)597-4197   <DeKalb>
FAX: (615)597-4397
office@smithvillecpc.com
PA: Isaac Gray   <M1>
512 Ed Taft Drive
Smithville, TN 37166
(870)373-4731
revgray08@gmail.com
CL: Wesley A Rogers
305 S College Street
Smithville, TN 37166
(615)597-5549
wesrogers305@gmail.com

Suggs Creek   (4MWC)TNMU7244
405 Corinth Road
Mount Juliet, TN 37122
(   )   <Wilson>
IP: Larry Green   <M1>
525 Dearman Street
Smithville, TN 37166
(615)597-5832
larrylgreen24@aol.com
CL: Dianna Huff
167 Eakes Thompson Road
Mount Juliet, TN 37122

MURFREESBORO PRESBYTERY CONTINUED

dhuff1983@bellsouth.net

Union Hill   (4MWC)TNMU7246
235 Sykes Road
Brush Creek, TN 38547
(615)683-8327   <Smith>
brotherperry@msn.com
SS: Dennis Croslin   <M3>
165 Maple Street
Gordonsville, TN 38563
(615)934-2383
CL: Robin L Nixon
237 Temperance Hall Highway
Hickman, TN 38567
(615)418-5074
robinlpn@hotmail.com

Watertown   (4WC)TNMU7247
510 W Main Street
Watertown, TN 37184
( )   <Wilson>
OD: Rodger McCann   <M5>
352 Winding River Lane
Sparta, TN 38563
(931)738-0352
CL: Emily Nix
305 Cornwell Avenue
Watertown, TN 37184
(615)237-3488
emilymckin_1@juno.com

Winchester First   (4WC)TNMU7249
PO Box 176 (mailing)
200 2nd Avenue NW (physical)
Winchester, TN 37398
(931)967-2121   <Franklin>
FAX: (931)967-8444
wintncp@bellsouth.net
PA: Michael Clark   <M1>
80 Bryan Drive
Winchester, TN 37398
(931)967-2121
book_worm35@comcast.net
AP: Amber Clark   <M1>
80 Bryan Drive
Winchester, TN 37398
(931)967-2121
revamber@comcast.net
AP: Anna Sweet-Brockman   <M1>
112 2nd Avenue NW
Winchester, TN 37398
(931)967-2121
aannasweetbrockman@gmail.com
CL: Karen Zarecor
260 Harris Chapel Road
Estill Springs, TN 37330
(931)962-4465
zarecor@bellsouth.net

OTHERS ON MINISTERIAL ROLL:

Benedict, Mary McCaskey   <M1 WC>
892 Pen Oak Drive
Cookeville, TN 38501
(931)260-1422
marykat_61@hotmail.com
Burrow, Vernon   <M1 RT>
603 Saratoga Drive
Murfreesboro, TN 37130
(615)406-6385
vernonburrow@comcast.net

Clark, Jonathan   <M1 RT>
88 Woodcrest Drive
Winchester, TN 37398
(931)967-9613
FAX: (931)967-8444
clark3568@bellsouth.net
Estep, William   <M1 RT>
239 Skyline Drive
Harriman, TN 37748
(865)882-5114
Ferguson, Elizabeth   <M1 WC>
PO Box 839
Sewanee, TN 37375
(931)636-8076
ferguea9@gmail.com
Ferry, Aaron   <M1 WC>
5360 Summer Rose Boulevard
Knoxville, TN 37918
(615)946-3078
amferry815@gmail.com
Green, Harry   <M1 WC>
45 Wood Way
McMinnville, TN 37110
(931)815-9190
Hackman-Truhan, Deborah   <M1 WC>
7314 N Miramar Drive
Peoria, IL 61614
(931)537-9040
cprevdeb@hotmail.com
Hancock, B. J.   <M1 RT>
103 W Cowan Street
Cowan, TN 37318
(931)967-8491
Harper, Josh   <M1 WC>
227 LaCroix Drive #1
Collierville, TN 38017
(615)934-7940
jdharperministry@hotmail.com
Johnson, Lanny   <M1 RT>
120 S Mill Street
Morrison, TN 37357
(931)212-1658
ljohnson37357@gmail.com
Labrada, Hector   <M1 WC>
74 Cumberland Drive
McMinnville, TN 37110
Logan, Jason   <M1 M8>
212 Saddlebag Court
Rineyville, KY 40162
(502)626-0722
jason.b.logan.mil@mail.mil
Matlock, Robert   <M1 RT>
156 Dovenshire Drive
Fairfield Glade, TN 38558
(931)210-0614
revbobm@msn.com
McCaskey, Charles   <M1 RT>
679 Canter Lane
Cookeville, TN 38501
(931)526-4885
charles@cookevillecpchurch.org
Merritt, Joyce   <M1 WC>
3929 Snail Shell Cave Road
Rockvale, TN 37153
(615)574-3047
Nye, John   <M1 WC>
210 Crestview Drive
Mount Juliet, TN 37122
Oliver, Lisa   <M1 M9 OM>
110 Allen Drive
Hendersonville, TN 37075

(615)319-6466
lisa.oliver316@gmail.com
Parks, Sam   <M1 WC>
10 Lila Way
Cartersville, GA 60120
(615)529-2465
wsamparks@aol.com
Salisbury, Rebecca   <M1 WC>
1033 Twin Oaks Drive
Murfreesboro, TN 37130
(615)410-7801
rebsalisbury@yahoo.com

OTHER LICENTIATES ON ROLL:

Kerner, Leanne   <M2 ST>
156 State Route 348
W Symsonia, KY 42082
(270)851-9709
cooldoll@bellsouth.net
White, Mack   <M2>
408 W Main Street
Smithville, TN 37166
(615)318-9863
wmax408@yahoo.com

OTHER CANDIDATES ON ROLL:

Quevedo, Mariano   <M3>
289 Golf Club Lane
McMinnville, TN 37110
Ramiriz, Araceli   <M3>
234 Vinewood Road Apt DG
McMinnville, TN 37110
Twilla, Kevin   <M3>
287 Owl Cirle
Lebanon,TN 37087
Watson, Micah   <M3>
2529 Middle Tennessee Boulevard
Murfreesboro, TN 37130
(615)692-2742
mwatson4289@gmail.com
Wills, Robin   <M3>
4607 E Richmond Shop Road
Lebanon, TN 37090
(615)870-4773
robinrush24@aol.com
Wright, John   <M3>

Nashville Presbytery
TENNESSEE SYNOD

	1.Church Number	2.Active	3.Total	4.Church School	5.Prof. of Faith	6.Gains	7.Losses	8.Children Baptized	9. OUR UNITED OUT-REACH	10. Total Out-Reach Giving	11. All Other Expenses	12. Total Income Received	13. Value Church Prop. 1=1000
	1	2	3	4	5	6	7	8	9	10	11	12	13
Arlington	7311	19	39	25	0	0	0	0	0	9,900	83,888	49,136	445
Beech	7301	196	196	110	13	23	4	3	12,583	27,087	292,252	395,711	2,990
Bethel	7302	76	88	40	15	17	2	1	0	4,632	140,738	133,291	141
Brenthaven**	7331	223	316	161	0	12	180	1	34,000	81,000	455,000	431,232	7,000
Brush Hill+	7325	136	204	66	2	8	13	2	7,364	17,106	197,268	202,406	5,600
Calvary	7342	11	11	0	0	0	1	0	300	300	44,769	47,034	500
Camp Ground*	7312	17	17	12	0	0	0	0	0	5,026	41,115	43,109	450
Cane Ridge	7326	17	17	5	0	0	1	0	0	0	35,349	26,538	275
Charlotte+	7303	25	55	16	0	0	1	0	3,586	5,324	31,956	35,546	541
Clarksville	7304	284	284	254	4	12	9	0	38,790	54,704	357,826	412,430	4,600
Concord	7306	30	30	35	0	0	1	1	1,000	1,000	34,075	35,234	90
Cristo Vive	7314				No Report Received			0	0	0	0	0	0
Cumberland Valle	7307	26	41	18	0	0	2	0	3,040	6,513	25,150	30,893	250
Dickson	7308	333	410	113	5	7	4	2	13,000	36,762	179,977	229,172	1,500
Donelson	7327	43	114	65	1	1	4	0	2,400	10,308	76,356	91,597	1,650
Dry Fork	7309	14	26	0	0	2	1	0	0	3,300	12,900	26,919	100
Erin	7310	11	11	0	0	0	2	0	0	431	20,784	24,393	350
Goodlettsville	7328	315	315	356	14	21	5	2	0	28,029	490,519	518,548	3,500
Halls Creek*	7313	31	41	26	0	0	16	0	0	8,189	26,072	40,300	505
Hendersonville	7340	19	19	19	0	0	0	0	0	915	30,851	37,045	50
Liberty	7315	51	53	51	3	5	4	1	3,520	15,002	117,980	104,561	600
Locust Grove	7316	12	38	5	1	1	1	0	1,621	4,841	34,850	37,849	313
Madison 1st	7329	23	51	19	1	2	2	0	4,201	12,964	27,620	40,584	340
Mariah	7317	41	41	25	0	2	1	0	0	1,925	36,367	51,500	150
McAdoo	7318	36	36	17	0	0	2	0	6,393	8,888	66,514	72,678	646
Mt. Denson**	7319	41	87	17	0	1	85	0	7,297	12,874	89,558	81,610	730
Mt. Liberty	7320	90	164	48	1	1	1	1	4,390	10,656	92,400	102,318	1,300
Mt. Sharon	7321	67	200	45	0	1	7	1	8,750	15,399	128,013	169,388	1,750
Mt. Sinai*	7330	13	13	5	2	2	4	0	0	300	11,165	12,454	266
Mt. View**	7322	42	63	24	5	5	32	0	0	2,888	83,472	88,066	475
New Hope*	7337	5	6	6	0	0	1	0	0	575	2,964	4,297	20
New Providence	7305	24	24	10	0	0	4	0	2,759	3,746	56,117	93,910	900
Shiloh	7338	21	38	6	1	1	30	0	300	3,528	46,367	31,374	1,000
St. Luke	7332	114	302	53	0	1	4	1	18,652	33,450	172,140	205,590	3,525
Sudanese	7341	38	38	0	No Report Received			0	0	0	0	0	24
Tusculum	7333	179	688	125	9	9	8	0	10,611	106,414	409,643	420,576	3,405
Waverly	7339	20	21	2	0	0	4	0	0	978	36,987	40,803	667
West Nashville*	7334	111	408	84	0	9	0	1	18,170	29,996	313,838	2659091	3,894
TOTALS	38	2,754	4,505	1,872	77	145	437	17	202,727	564,950	4,302,845	4,627,183	51,082

*Math error corrected. **Purged roll.

NASHVILLE PRESBYTERY CONTINUED

CHURCHES, PASTORS, AND CLERKS:

_____

Arlington   (4WC)TNNA7311
PO Box 624 (mailing)
7 Knight Street (physical)
Erin, TN 37061
(931)289-3597   <Houston>
CL: Andrea Dillard
85 Victor Lane
Erin, TN 37061
(931)289-4004
adillard@workforceessentials.com

_____

Beech   (4MWC)TNNA7301
3216 Long Hollow Pike
Hendersonville, TN 37075
(615)824-3990   <Sumner>
FAX: (615)824-6507
office@beechcp.com
PA: Jeff DeWees   <M1>
116 Lancaster Court
Gallatin, TN 37066
(931)209-3331
pastorjeff@beechcp.com
CL: Jim Crews
1008 Stirlingshire Drive
Hendersonville, TN 37075
(615)824-7206
jimcrews@bellsouth.net

_____

Bethel   (4MC)TNNA7302
3375 Sango Road
Clarksville, TN 37043
(931)358-3295   <Montgomery>
PA: Stewart Salyer   <M1>
2211 Foxfire Road
Clarksville, TN 37043
(931)980-2829
stewart.salyer@gmail.com
CL: Chris Davis
632 Eastwood Court
Clarksville, TN 37043
(931)624-9449
cdavis@cemc.org

_____

Brenthaven   (4C)TNNA7331
516 Franklin Road
Brentwood, TN 37027
(615)373-4826   <Williamson>
FAX: (615)373-4869
secretary@brenthaven.org
PA: Kip J Rush   <M1>
513 Meadowlark Lane
Brentwood, TN 37027
(615)376-4563
pastor@brenthaven.org
AP: Sandra Shepherd   <M1>
525 Summit Oaks Court
Nashville, TN 37221
(615)772-5358
woolywagon@gmail.com
CL: Christi Peppers
5008 Woodland Hills Drive
Brentwood, TN 37027
(615)376-9977
christi.peppers@gmail.com

_____

Brush Hill   (4MEWC)TNNA7325
3705 Brush Hill Road
Nashville, TN 37216

(615)227-2504   <Davidson>
FAX: (615)227-0039
bhcpc@birch.net
PA: Kenny Butcher   <M1>
4608 Cather Court
Nashville, TN 37214
(615)719-1887
bhpastor@birch.net
AP: Paul Tucker   <M1>
3801 Brush Hill Pike
Nashville, TN 37216
(615)430-9158
paultucker@gmail.com
CL: Terri Peltier
403 Cunniff Parkway
Goodlettsville, TN 37072
(615)227-2504
tp1260@aol.com

_____

Calvary   (4C)TNNA7342
340 Ringgold Road
Clarksville, TN 37042
(931)645-9200   <Montgomery>
2ourchurch@gmail.com
SS: Choil Ma   <M1>
300 Ringgold Road Apt 503
Clarksville, TN 37042
(931)824-2443
choilma@yahoo.com
CL: Session Clerk
340 Ringgold Road
Clarksville, TN 37042

_____

Camp Ground   (4MWC)TNNA7312
88 Campground Road
Erin, TN 37061
(931)289-4605   <Houston>
LS: Terry Mathis   <M6>
88 Campground Road
Erin, TN 37061
(931)289-3602
ttmathis@peoplestel.net
CL: Tammy Simmons
5970 Highway 13
Erin, TN 37061
(931)289-3727
tsimmons3658@yahoo.com

_____

Cane Ridge   (4EC)TNNA7326
6867 Burkitt Road (mailing)
13412 Old Hickory Boulevard (physical)
Cane Ridge, TN 37013
(615)941-8317   <Davidson>
FAX: (615)941-2985
gdunn6867@comcast.net
LS: Gregory (Greg) Dunn   <M6>
6867 Burkitt Road
Cane Ridge, TN 37013
(615)941-8317
FAX: (615)941-2985
gdunn6867@comast.net
CL: Eleanor Willett
145 Greenwood Drive
La Vergne, TN 37086
(615)793-5016
tuffyw9@comcast.net

_____

Charlotte   (4WC)TNNA7303
515 Mt Hebron Road (mailing)
3 Court Square (physical)
Charlotte, TN 37036

( )   <Dickson>
PA: Steve Jones   <M1>
PO Box 368
Burns, TN 37029
(615)441-6159
stevenejones@bellsouth.net
CL: Eloise Jones
515 Mount Hebron Road
Charlotte, TN 37036
(615)789-5353
joneseloise515@bellsouth.net

_____

Clarksville   (4WC)TNNA7304
1410 Golf Club Lane
Clarksville, TN 37040
(931)648-0817   <Montgomery>
office@clarksvillecpc.com
PA: Stephen L Louder   <M1>
98 Gallant Court
Clarksville, TN 37043
(931)217-0369
pastorsteve@clarksvillecpc.com
AP: Paula Louder   <M1>
98 Gallant Court
Clarksville, TN 37043
(931)804-4809
paula@clarksvillecpc.com
AP: Taylor Young   <M1>
2651 Holt Lane
Clarksville, TN 37043
(615)830-3344
brandontayloryoung@yahoo.com
CL: Ashley Kettle
205 Bullock Drive
Clarksville, TN 37040
(931)624-8769
ashleykettle@gmail.com

_____

Concord   (4MC)TNNA7306
63 Gander Branch Road
Waverly, TN 37185
( )   <Humphreys>
CL: Phyllis Webb
3571 Fire Tower Road
Erin, TN 37061
(931)289-4601

_____

Cristo Vive   (4C)TNNA7314
611 Cheron Road
Madison, TN 37115
( )   <Davidson>
PA: Carlos Cinco   <M1>
611 Cheron Road
Madison, TN 37115
(615)586-1269
pastorcinco2020@gmail.com
CL: Session Clerk
611 Cheron Road
Madison, TN 37115

_____

Cumberland Valley   (4WC)TNNA7307
285 Cumberland Valley Road
Mc Ewen, TN 37101
(931)582-8050   <Houston>
PA: Jesse L Freeman, Jr   <M1>
270 Eastside Road
Burns, TN 37029
(615)202-4594
mptc@bellsouth.net
CL: June R Hicks
1339 Highway 13 S

NASHVILLE PRESBYTERY CONTINUED

Waverly, TN 37185
(931)296-4284

_____
Dickson   (4WC)TNNA7308
500 Highway 70 E
Dickson, TN 37055
(615)446-8511   <Dickson>
FAX: (615)446-7827
office@cumberlandpresbyterian.org
PA: Robert D Truitt   <M1>
1238 Old East Side Road
Burns, TN 37029
(615)740-9180
FAX: (615)446-7827
rdtjct@aol.com
AP: Dean Guye   <M1>
2759 Highway 70 E
Dickson, TN 37055
(615)446-7687
deanjoy@att.net
CL: Andrew Bullington
355 Twin Oaks Drive
Kingston Spring, TN 37082
(615)840-5473
thebullington@gmail.com

_____
Donelson   (4WC)TNNA7327
2914 Lebanon Road
Nashville, TN 37214
(615)516-9427   <Davidson>
email@donelsoncpchurch.com
PA: Michael Bertsch   <M1>
204 Buckleigh Point
Gallatin, TN 37066
(423)763-8314
mikebertsch14@gmail.com
CL: Keith C Vanstone
3803 Plantation Drive
Hermitage, TN 37076
(615)210-5010
keithv@bellsouth.net

_____
Dry Fork   (4C)TNNA7309
174 Dry Fork Creek Road (mailing)
1050 Dry Fork Creek Road (physical)
Bethpage, TN 37022
(615)841-3169   <Sumner>
PA: Ted Bane   <M1>
903 W Old Hickory Boulevard
Madison, TN 37115
(615)975-9343
tedjan95@aol.com
CL: Sue Carr
174 Dry Fork Creek Road
Bethpage, TN 37022
(615)841-3169
suekencarr@nctc.com

_____
Erin   (4MWC)TNNA7310
PO Box 307 (mailing)
4793 E Main Street (physical)
Erin, TN 37061
( )   <Houston>
erincpchurch@gmail.com
SS: Timothy W Ferrell   <M1>
1850 Dunbar Road
Woodlawn, TN 37191
(931)920-2662
ferrelltw@aol.com
CL: Carolyn Zurawski
978 Scotts Chapel Road

Cumberland City, TN 37050
(931)827-3111

_____
Goodlettsville   (4MWC)TNNA7328
226 South Main Street
Goodlettsville, TN 37072
(615)859-5888   <Davidson>
FAX: (615)859-8820
gcpc@goodlettsvillechurch.com
PA: Tim Stutler   <M1>
1044 Mansker Farm Boulevard
Hendersonville, TN 37075
(615)859-5888
tim@goodletttsvillechurch.com
CL: Dillard Tutor
292 Lake Terrace Drive
Hendersonville, TN 37075
dillardtutor@msn.com

_____
Halls Creek   (4EC)TNNA7313
3650 Perrywinkle Branch Road (mailing)
2803 Halls Creek Road (physical)
Waverly, TN 37185
(931)296-7758   <Humphreys>
CL: Jeremy Tolene
PO Box 54
Waverly, TN 37185
tolenej@hcss.com

_____
Hendersonville   (4WC)TNNA7340
453 Walton Ferry Road
Hendersonville, TN 37075
(615)822-6091   <Sumner>
CL: Susan Wyatt
115 Elissa Drive
Hendersonville, TN 37075
(615)948-8242
FAX: (615)824-0195
susandwyatt@comcast.net

_____
Liberty   (4MWC)TNNA7315
725 S Liberty Church Road
Clarksville, TN 37042
( )   <Montgomery>
PA: Rocky Johnson   <M1>
1208 Redwood Drive
Clarksville, TN 37042
(423)620-7753
rockyj1960@gmail.com
CL: Bob Del Giorno
1510 S Freestone Court
Clarksville, TN 37042
(931)647-1086
bodeno@charter.net

_____
Locust Grove   (4WC)TNNA7316
3449 Locust Church Road
Cunningham, TN 37052
( )   <Montgomery>
SS: Timothy W Ferrell   <M1>
1850 Dunbar Road
Woodlawn, TN 37191
(931)920-2662
ferrelltw@aol.com
CL: Lawanda Black
3192 Budds Creek Road
Palmyra, TN 37142
(931)326-5298
jobee39@hughes.net

_____
Madison First   (4MWC)TNNA7329

735 Argyle Avenue
Madison, TN 37115
(615)868-2888   <Davidson>
FAX: (615)868-2888
madisonfirst@yahoo.com
PA: Johnny Parish   <M1>
114 Savo Bay
Hendersonville, TN 37075
(615)824-5842
johnnyparish@bellsouth.net
CL: Edith Marlin
112 Becker Avenue
Old Hickory, TN 37138
(615)847-4148
edithmarlin@outlook.com

_____
Mariah   (4MWC)TNNA7317
43 Mariah Church Lane
Waverly, TN 37185
(931)296-5546   <Humphreys>
SS: Nathaniel Mathews   <M2>
1006 Woodland Drive
New Johnsonville, TN 37134
(931)209-6645
bro.nate-mathews@hotmail.com
CL: Anita Gehring
65 Warden Road
Waverly, TN 37185
(931)296-8059

_____
McAdoo   (4WC)TNNA7318
3724 Ashland City Road
Clarksville, TN 37043
(931)362-3091   <Montgomery>
CL: Nancy Rhinehart
1601 Harville Road
Clarksville, TN 37043
(931)362-3105
rhinehart.nancy@yahoo.com

_____
Mt Denson   (4MWC)TNNA7319
4558 Highway 161
Springfield, TN 37172
(615)384-3613   <Robertson>
PA: Patricia (Pat) Pickett   <M1 M9>
1460 Cheatham Dam Road
Ashland City, TN 37015
(615)792-4973
tovahtoo@aol.com
CL: Ashley Wilks
4028 Wilks Road
Springfield, TN 37172
ashleywilks@bellsouth.net

_____
Mt Liberty   (4MWC)TNNA7320
3655 Highway 49 E
Charlotte, TN 37036
(615)789-5916   <Dickson>
PA: Justin Griffin   <M1>
3655 Highway 49 E
Charlotte, TN 37036
(615)969-2426
jjjjgriff@gmail.com
CL: Cindy Simpson
3378 Highway 49 E
Charlotte, TN 37036
(615)945-0010
cindyrsimpson@hotmail.com

_____
Mt Sharon   (4MWC)TNNA7321
4634 Mount Sharon Road

NASHVILLE PRESBYTERY CONTINUED

Greenbrier, TN 37073
(615)384-8569   <Robertson>
pastor@mtsharoncpchurch.org
CL: James D Jordan
2100 W End Avenue Ste 1150
Nashville, TN 37203
(615)329-2100
FAX: (615)329-2187
jdjordan@gjplaw.com

Mt Sinai   (4WC)TNNA7330
3738 Hydes Ferry Road
Nashville, TN 37218
(615)586-7886   <Davidson>
SS: David Lomax   <M3>
1501 Robert Cartwright Drive
Goodlettsville, TN 37072
(615)753-2493
lomaxdavid53@yahoo.com
CL: Katherine B Pleas
555 Church Street #801
Nashville, TN 37219
(615)251-4037
pleas5@hotmail.com

Mt View   (4C)TNNA7322
2359 Leatherwood Road (mailing)
Stewart, TN 37175
282 Hickman Creek Road (physical)
Dover, TN 37058
(931)217-0893   <Stewart>
mvcpchurch@gmail.com
PA: Ronald D Burgess   <M1>
116 Harris Ridge Road
Dover, TN 37058
(931)232-5151
revron4@bellsouth.net
CL: Michelle Sills
126 Ralls Road
Dover, TN 37058
(931)305-8893
michellesills@gmail.com

New Hope   (4C)TNNA7337
c/o Sharon Cook (mailing)
8009 White Oak Road
Stewart, TN 37175
60 New Hope Road (physical)
Stewart, TN 37175
( )   <Houston>
LS: G Ray Mayo
3019 Lights Chapel Road
Clarksville, TN 37040
CL: Sharon E Cook
8009 White Oak Road
Stewart, TN 37175
(931)721-2513
ricsha55@yahoo.com

New Providence   (4MWC)TNNA7305
1307 Fort Campbell Boulevard
Clarksville, TN 37042
(931)647-4455   <Montgomery>
PA: John Adam Smith   <M1 M9>
916 Allen Road
Nashville, TN 37214
(615)545-6486
john.a.smith.81@gmail.com
CL: Toni Boothe
1260 Dotsonville Road
Clarksville, TN 37042

(931)647-8297
alchvic1059@hotmail.com

Shiloh   (4C)TNNA7338
4812 Shiloh-Canaan Road
Palmyra, TN 37142
(931)387-4198   <Montgomery>
greg1013@aol.com
SS: Rick Purcell   <M3>
895 Branch Road
Clarksville, TN 37043
(269)277-7277
rickkpurcell@sbcglobal.net
CL: Dianne Harris
400 Attaway Road
Clarksville, TN 37040
(931)206-8415
dharrisx2@acepipe.net

St Luke   (4MWC)TNNA7332
901 W Old Hickory Boulevard
Madison, TN 37115
(615)868-1982   <Davidson>
stlukecpchurch@gmail.com
PA: Dwayne Tyus   <M1>
901 W Old Hickory Boulevard
Madison, TN 37115
(615)720-2564
dwayne.tyus@gmail.com
CL: Angie Pinson
901 W Old Hickory Boulevard
Madison, TN 37115
(615)337-7311
stlukecpchurch@gmail.com

Sudanese   (F)TNNA7341
c/o First UMC (mailing)
149 W Main Street
407 Owen Drive (physical)
Gallatin, TN 37066
(615)585-2842   <Sumner>
CL: John Tiang Ping
49 Millwood Drive
Nashville, TN 37217
(615)365-3274

Tusculum   (4MWC)TNNA7333
477 McMurray Drive
Nashville, TN 37211
(615)833-0742   <Davidson>
tusculumchurch@gmail.com
PA: Roger Patton, Jr   <M1>
1534 Eden Rose Place
Nolensville, TN 37135
(615)975-5526
rogerlpatton@att.net
CL: Dawn Gannon
3417 County Hill Road
Antioch, TN 37013
(615)399-2782
dawngannon0317@yahoo.com

Waverly   (4MWC)TNNA7339
109 N Church Street
Waverly, TN 37185
(931)296-3232   <Humphreys>
FAX: (931)296-3232
waverlycpc@att.net
CL: Charles Stanton
1551 Baptist Branch Road
McEwen, TN 37101

(931)582-8449
cstanton@bellsouth.net

West Nashville   (4MWC)TNNA7334
6849 Charlotte Pike
Nashville, TN 37209
(615)352-2800   <Davidson>
FAX: (615)352-2801
info@wncp.org
PA: Rickey Page   <M1>
736 Rodney Drive
Nashville, TN 37205
(615)353-7850
FAX: (615)352-2801
rickey.page@wncp.org
CL: Nancy Crowell
707 Newberry Road
Nashville, TN 37205
nancydcrowell@gmail.com

OTHERS ON MINISTERIAL ROLL:

Acuff, David   <M1 M8>
4969 Quail Lane
Columbia, SC 29206
(803)727-3910
david.acuff@us.army.mil
Barna, Clifton   <M1 OM>
1012 Adam Court
Cottontown, TN 37066
(352)598-3246
cliff.barna@gmail.com
Baranoski, Timothy   <M1 M8>
1205 Tomahawk Drive B
Jber, AK 99505
(615)440-3499
timothy.i.baranoski.mil@mail.mil
Bennett, Alfred J   <M1 HR>
7286 Nolensville Road
Nolensville, TN 37135
(615)776-5181
Carlton, Gary   <M1 RT>
108 Greenbrier Street
Dickson, TN 37055
(615)441-8963
gwcarlton@yahoo.com
Cook, Lisa   <M1 M9>
4101 Dalemere Court
Nashville, TN 37207
(615)830-6217
tgoose@comcast.net
Corbin, William   <M1 HR>
7300 N Lamar Road
Mount Juliet, TN 37122
(615)459-8998
raven.rest@comcast.net
De Vries, Raymond   <M1 HR>
2080 Stanford Village Drive
Antioch, TN 37013
(615)332-3587
ray.devries@comcast.net
Duke, Michael E   <M1 WC>
106 Friar Tuck Drive
Dickson, TN 37055
(615)446-6515
Dumas, Byron   <M1 OM>
1775 Theresa Drive
Clarksville, TN 37043
(931)552-8772
bdumas7346@aol.com
Earheart-Brown, Daniel   <M1 PR>

NASHVILLE PRESBYTERY CONTINUED

475 N Highland Street Apt 9L
Memphis, TN 38122
jebrown@memphisseminary.edu
(901)278-0367

Ferguson, E Blant   <M1 RT>
704 Bear Run
Hiawassee, GA 30546
(706)896-9296
blantferg@yahoo.com

Goodwill, James L   <M1 RT>
7317 Tanbark Way
Raleigh, NC 27615
(704)526-8729
jim@jimgoodwill.com

Gough, Ernest E   <M1 WC>
8366 Highway 70
Nashville, TN 37221
(615)646-4372
eegough@bellsouth.net

Hurley, E C   <M1 HR>
#2 Killard Road, Killard
Doonbeg, County Clare
IRELAND
(931)551-6173
hurleyec@gmail.com

Jones, Gregory   <M1 WC>
400 Adam Wood Drive Apt D12
Nashville, TN 37211
(931)249-9512
greg1013@aol.com

Miller, Carol   <M1 WC>
101 Park Avenue
Dickson, TN 37055
(615)441-6656
lcarolmiller@comcast.net

Norton, Kitty   <M1 WC>
251 Westchase Drive
Nashville, TN 37205
(615)584-1464
kitty.a.norton@vanderbilt.edu

Parrish, Steven   <M1 PR>
4610 Dunn Avenue
Memphis, TN 38117
(901)743-9545
sparrish@memphisseminary.edu

Patton, Malcolm   <M1 RT>
921 Harris Drive
Gallatin, TN 37066
(615)452-5557
FAX: (615)824-6507
bpatton11@comcast.net

Polacek, Fred E   <M1 WC>
907 Graham Drive
Old Hickory, TN 37138
(615)754-5328
revfredp@gmail.com

Rippy, James G   <M1 WC>
442 Trina Street
Gallatin, TN 37066
(615)681-7086
lrippy@live.com

Roddy, Lowell G   <M1 RT>
2583 Hedgerow Lane
Clarksville, TN 37043
(931)368-1081
FAX: (931)221-1032
lgroddy@yahoo.com

Schott, Fred, Jr   <M1 HR>
606 Taylor Trail
Springfield, TN 37172
(615)384-8572
fws195@aol.com

Sims, Edward G   <M1 RT>
2161 N Meadow Drive
Clarksville, TN 37043
(931)206-5759
simseg@aol.com

Stefan, Gregory   <M1 WC>
1917 Birchwood Street
East Pearl, PA 17519
(717)838-1171
pastorstefan@att.net

Stovall, Jeff   <M1 WC>
2829 Trelawny Drive
Clarksville, TN 37043
(931)993-6104
jeffstovall@juno.com

Tabor, Don M   <M1 RT>
9611 Mitchell Place
Brentwood, TN 37027
(615)776-7292
FAX: (615)373-3356
dontabor@comcast.net

Vick, Joe   <M1 RT>
6064 Old Hickory Boulevard
Whites Creek, TN 37189
(615)519-5249
joervick@gmail.com

Ward, Andrew   <M1 WC>
407 Rose Hill Court
Goodlettsville, TN 37072
(615)456-9136
andrewbward@aol.com

West, David   <M1 M9>
2027 Lucille Street
Lebanon, TN 37087
(217)732-7568

Whitworth, Gary W   <M1 RT>
1706 Old Hickory Boulevard
Brentwood, TN 37027
(615)915-4180

OTHER LICENTIATES ON ROLL:

Cassell, C J   <M2 ST>
825 Aimes Court
Nashville, TN 37221
(615)594-2693
n4cjc@comcast.net

Chall-Hutchinson, Deborah   <M2>
190 Ussery Road
Clarksville, TN 37043
(931)905-1671
challhut@gmail.com

Moore, Kimberly   <M2>
1025 Three Island Ford Road
Charlotte, TN 37036
(615)545-1595
kimberly.a.moore@vanderbilt.edu

Wilkinson, Neal   <M2>
1174 Tanglewood Street
Memphis, TN 38114
(615)934-7342
nwilkinson@memphisseminary.edu

OTHER CANDIDATES ON ROLL:

Bourque, Leo   <M3>
1620 Sarahs Cove
Hermitage, TN 37076
(615)767-2428
bourque120@gmail.com

Everett, William   <M3>
1906 Cogburn Road
Clarksville, TN 37042
weverett62@hotmail.com

Lomax, David   <M3>
1501 Robert Cartwright Drive
Goodlettsville, TN 37072
(615)753-2493
lomaxdavid53@yahoo.com

Norris, Dakota   <M3>
4750 Highway 431 N
Springfield, TN 37172
(615)681-6346
volsfan2011@gmail.com

Stevens, Brittany   <M3>
606 Huntington Parkway
Nashville, TN 37211
(615)719-3362
bstevens5@my.apsu.edu

North Central Presbytery
MIDWEST SYNOD

GENERAL		MEMBERSHIP			CHANGES				FINANCES				
	1.Church Number	2.Active	3.Total	4.Church School	5.Prof. of Faith	6.Gains	7.Losses	8.Children Baptized	9. OUR UNITED OUT-REACH	10. Total Out-Reach Giving	11. All Other Expenses	12. Total Income Received	13. Value Church Prop. 1=1000
	1	2	3	4	5	6	7	8	9	10	11	12	13
Bethany	5401	64	330	65	0	0	6	0	11,279	40,711	91,874	112,804	560
Burnt Prairie	5102	16	34	6	No Report Received			0	0	0	0	0	63
Campground	5402	13	15	15	No Report Received			0	0	0	0	0	50
Casey	5201	16	26	17	0	0	10	0	2,915	5,009	26,673	32,838	50
Christ	5305	8	11	7	No Report Received			0	624	0	0	0	150
Comunidad	5212				Dropped from roll 10/23/2016								
Cumb. Chapel	5104	7	7	5	0	0	0	0	0	10,550	8,208	20,475	4
Ebenezer	5203	38	38	30	No Report Received			0	4,095	0	0	0	1,000
Elm River*	5107	52	52	69	2	4	1	2	7,198	9,887	45,400	80,093	250
Fairfield	5108	188	327	93	No Report Received			0	122	0	0	0	1,000
Faith	5501	5	13	4	0	0	0	0	15,010	5,647	25,516	141,837	500
Fullerton	5404	27	27	20	0	0	0	0	2,103	1,406	22,205	29,606	50
Georgetown	5204	30	65	15	2	2	0	1	4,745	8,055	43,788	51,962	113
Good Prospect	5205	84	84	113	0	0	6	5	6,397	25,673	66,345	99,565	1,200
Grace	5502	12	29	16	No Report Received			0	0	0	0	0	245
Knights Chapel	5306	29	36	38	No Report Received			0	0	0	0	0	100
Lebanon North	5113	66	87	63	6	5	3	5	100	10,835	69,298	84,684	200
Lebanon South	5114				No Report Received			0	0	0	0	0	0
Lincoln 1st	5405	39	91	12	2	2	2	2	5,400	6,372	66,040	69,208	575
Monroe City	5307	8	8	0	No Report Received			0	0	0	0	0	200
Morningside	5304	58	80	21	No Report Received			0	712	0	0	0	1,600
Mt. Gilead	5406	29	49	42	0	0	0	0	1,250	3,625	25,925	34,005	145
Mt. Olivet	5308	12	26	11	0	0	0	0	500	3,651	16,372	21,080	75
New Hope	5208	41	104	34	3	0	4	0	7,510	14,266	46,034	69,476	400
Pleasant Grove	5210	27	27	20	0	0	0	0	3,088	21,165	23,444	32,604	150
Shiloh	5409	28	102	26	0	4	2	0	1,000	8,365	37,827	47,314	310
Shinar	5410	31	38	0	No Report Received			0	0	0	0	0	237
Spring Hill	5411	5	5	3	No Report Received			0	0	0	0	0	379
Union North	5124	30	30	20	0	0	5	0	0	7,714	36,877	44,889	120
United	5119	50	99	20	No Report Received			0	0	0	0	0	503
Willow Creek	5211	71	94	90	0	1	7	1	11,057	32,510	79,186	110,567	1,000
TOTALS	31	1,110	1,963	897	15	18	46	16	85,105	215,441	731,012	1,083,007	10,910

*Math error corrected. **Purged roll.

NORTH CENTRAL PRESBYTERY CONTINUED

CHURCHES, PASTORS, AND CLERKS:

Bethany   (4MWC)MINC5401
  PO Box 384 (mailing)
  219 S Lincoln Street (physical)
  Bethany, IL 61914
  (217)665-3034   <Moultrie>
  bethanycpc@yahoo.com
CL: Dean McReynolds
  399 County Road 1600 N
  Bethany, IL 61914
  (217)665-3420
  wdeanmcreynolds@yahoo.com

Burnt Prairie   (4MWC)MINC5102
  RR 3 Box 947 (mailing)
  Fairfield, IL 62837
  Church Street (physical)
  Burnt Prairie, IL 62820
  (618)925-1185   <White>
LS: Scott D Smothers   <M6>
  RR 5 Box 573
  Fairfield, IL 62837
  (618)842-6009
  lsmothers@myfrontiermail.com
CL: Andy Pottorff
  RR 3 Box 947
  Fairfield, IL 62837
  (618)925-1185
  andypottorff@yahoo.com

Campground   (4WEC)MINC5402
  1497 Hookdale Avenue (mailing)
  Route 4 (physical)
  Greenville, IL 62246
  (618)664-1547   <Bond>
CL: Rodney Reavis
  1497 Hookdale Avenue
  Greenville, IL 62246
  (618)664-1547
  rcreavis@yahoo.com

Casey   (4C)MINC5201
  PO Box 21 (mailing)
  16 N Central (physical)
  Casey, IL 62420
  (217)932-5404   <Clark>
CL: Mary Gard
  7810 N 400th Street
  Casey, IL 62420
  (217)932-2971
  thetoymaker@wildblue.net

Christ   (4MC)MINC5305
  6140 S Meridian
  Indianapolis, IN 46217
  (317)787-9585   <Marion>
CL: Paula Price
  892 Geagan Street
  Greenwood, IN 46143
  (317)709-8138

Cumberland Chapel   (4C)MINC5104
  1075 County Road 2400E (mailing)
  Route 2 CR 1300 N, CR 1200 E (physical)
  Fairfield, IL 62837
  ( )   <Wayne>
PA: J B Gates   <M1>
  PO Box 289
  Enfield, IL 62835

  (618)963-2306
  rjjbgate@hamiltoncom.net
CL: Ronald E Huffman
  1075 County Road 2400E
  Fairfield, IL 62837
  (618)842-9518
  huffmanrj@hotmail.com

Ebenezer   (4WF)MINC5203
  1941 W Belmont Avenue
  Chicago, IL 60657
  (773)528-8218   <Cook>
PA: Eduardo Montoya   <M1>
  270 Windsor Drive
  Roselle, IL 60172
  (630)980-1577
  edmontoya@hotmail.com
CL: Samuel Alvarez
  3740 W Leland Avenue
  Chicago, IL 60625
  (773)509-9165

Elm River   (4EC)MINC5107
  2212 County Highway 2 (mailing)
  2250 County Highway 2 (physical)
  Cisne, IL 62823
  ( )   <Wayne>
SS: Ralph Blevins   <M1>
  1623 County Road 2375 E
  Geff, IL 62842
  (618)854-2494
  pastorreblevins@gmail.com
CL: Jack Enlow
  2212 County Highway 2
  Cisne, IL 62823
  (618)854-2492
  enlow@wabash.net

Fairfield   (4MEWC)MINC5108
  1700 W Delaware
  Fairfield, IL 62837
  (618)847-5281   <Wayne>
  FAX: (618)842-2608
PA: Jeff Biggs   <M1>
  1504 Cumberland Drive
  Fairfield, IL 62837
  (618)842-2219
  jeffbiggsonline@gmail.com
CL: Kevan Stum
  15 Brock Lane
  Fairfield, IL 62837
  (618)842-2705

Faith   (4C)MINC5501
  20301 E Ten Mile Road
  St Clair Shores, MI 48080
  (586)775-1524   <Macomb>
CL: Christopher D McMacken
  20396 Erben Street
  St Clair Shores, MI 48081
  (586)771-7855
  cmcmacken@itctransco.com

Fullerton   (4WC)MINC5404
  1105 E Allen Street (mailing)
  Route 48 (physical)
  Farmer City, IL 61848
  ( )   <DeWitt>
CL: Duane Runyon
  1105 E Allen Street
  Farmer City, IL 61848

  (309)825-3324
  dprunyon@yahoo.com

Georgetown   (4EWC)MINC5204
  201 Frazier Street
  Georgetown, IL 61846
  (217)662-6988   <Vermilion>
CL: Stephen K Hughes
  1011 E 14th Street
  Georgetown, IL 61846
  (217)662-6988
  hughesst@sbcglobal.net

Good Prospect   (4MWC)MINC5205
  PO Box 5 (mailing)
  301 E Trilla Road (physical)
  Trilla, IL 62469
  (217)234-8529   <Coles>
  trillacp@yahoo.com
CL: Jedd Tolen
  PO Box 8
  Trilla, IL 62469
  trillatolens@gmail.com

Grace   (4C)MINC5502
  1122 Harrison Boulevard
  Lincoln Park, MI 48146
  (313)381-3456   <Wayne>
CL: Dorinda Boyer
  21625 Knights Lane
  Brownstown, MI 48183
  (734)675-7322

Knights Chapel   (4WC)MINC5306
  1285 S County Road 375 W
  Petersburg, IN 47567
  ( )   <Pike>
CL: Janet Church
  5541 W County Road 100 S
  Petersburg, IN 47567
  (812)749-3242

Lebanon North   (4C)MINC5113
  Route 5
  Fairfield, IL 62837
  (618)842-5205
  FAX: (618)842-5205   <Wayne>
PA: J C McDuffie   <M1>
  RR 3 Box 574
  Fairfield, IL 62837
  (618)842-5624
  mactrapper4@frontier.com
CL: De Young
  107 W King Street
  Fairfield, IL 62837
  (618)516-1736

Lebanon South   (4C)MINC5114
  Route 3
  Galatia, IL 62935
  ( )   <Saline>
OD: Robert D Craig   <M5>
  46030 Sunset Drive
  Bay Minette, AL 36507
CL: James Patterson
  RR 2
  Galatia, IL 62935
  (618)268-4471

Lincoln First   (4MEWC)MINC5405
  PO Box 596 (mailing)

NORTH CENTRAL PRESBYTERY CONTINUED

110 Broadway (physical)
Lincoln, IL 62656
(217)732-7568   \<Logan\>
cumberland@frontier.com
PA: Steven Blaum   \<M1\>
184 900 Street
Middletown, IL 62666
(217)871-3339
strab2010@yahoo.com
CL: Janet Brosamer
1402 1500th Street
Lincoln, IL 62656
(217)737-9125

Monroe City   (4MWC)MINC5307
PO Box 167 (mailing)
8th & Cleveland Streets (physical)
Monroe City, IN 47557
(812)743-5171   \<Knox\>
FAX: (812)743-5171
PA: David Parman   \<M1\>
5034 S Monroe School Road
Monroe City, IN 47557
(812)743-2646
FAX: (812)743-5171
CL: Mary Welton
1278 S Welton Chapel Road
Vicennes, IN 47591
(812)726-5338

Morningside   (4WC)MINC5304
8419 Newburgh Road
Evansville, IN 47715
(812)473-4700   \<Vanderburgh\>
FAX: (812)473-4765
morningsidechurch@sbcglobal.net
PA: James Messer   \<M1 M8\>
3653 Old Madisonville Road
Henderson, KY 42420
(270)827-0711
jcmess@hotmail.com
CL: Karen Gossman
5077 Kenosha Drive
Newburgh, IN 47630
(812)490-6522
km56gossman@yahoo.com

Mt Gilead   (4C)MINC5406
PO Box 494 (mailing)
1077 Mt Gilead Road (physical)
Greenville, IL 62246
( )   \<Bond\>
CL: Elizabeth File
547 IL Route 140
Pocahontas, IL 62275
(618)664-3216

Mt Olivet   (4C)MINC5308
3153 S State Road 257 (mailing)
4299 S State Road 57 (physical)
Washington, IN 47501
(812)254-4077   \<Daviess\>
g9barnard@yahoo.com
CL: Karen Barnard
3153 S State Road 257
Washington, IN 47501
(812)254-4077
g9barnard@yahoo.com

New Hope   (4EC)MINC5208
3997 N 100th Street (mailing)

Casey, IL 62420
20955 E 2100th Avenue (physical)
Yale, IL 62481
( )   \<Jasper\>
royndebbie@hotmail.com
LS: Chris Parr   \<M6\>
9956 E 2100th Avenue
Hidalgo, IL 62438
(618)793-2704
parpar62432@yahoo.com
CL: Roy Shanks
3997 N 100th Street
Casey, IL 62420
(217)932-2995
royndebbie@hotmail.com

Pleasant Grove   (4EC)MINC5210
6360 E 2100th Avenue (mailing)
Martinsville, IL 62442
4125 E 200th Avenue (physical)
Annapolis, IL 62413
(618)569-4588   \<Crawford\>
donnie.bailey62@yahoo.com
LS: Bill Ulery   \<M6\>
10725 E 1500th Road
Marshall, IL 62441
(217)382-4593
CL: Donnie B Bailey
7970 E 1625th Avenue
Robinson, IL 62454
(618)569-4588
donnie.bailey62@yahoo.com

Shiloh   (4MWC)MINC5409
7722 Shiloh Road
Virginia, IL 62691
(217)452-3802   \<Cass\>
CL: Anna Ruth Long
6614 IL Route 78
Virginia, IL 62691
(217)883-2654
hjlong@casscomm.com

Shinar   (4WC)MINC5410
11383 147th Avenue (mailing)
West Burlington, IA 52655
19705 185th Avenue (physical)
New London, IA 52645
(319)457-2652   \<Des Moines\>
OD: Shane McCampbell   \<M5\>
109 Indian Terrace
Burlington, IA 52601
(319)457-2652
revshane777@yahoo.com
CL: Carolyn Schenk
11383 147th Avenue
West Burlington, IA 52655
(319)754-8274
carolynschenk@yahoo.com

Spring Hill   (4C)MINC5411
690 E 1800th Avenue (mailing)
9 miles SW of Beecher City (physical)
Beecher City, IL 62414
( )   \<Fayette\>
OD: Donald Ray Miller   \<M5\>
Route 2 Box 136C
Beecher City, IL 62414
(618)487-5648
CL: Nelda Kline
690 E 1800th Avenue

Beecher City, IL 62414
(618)487-5363

Union North   (4C)MINC5124
506 Lakeview Drive (mailing)
635 County Road 2400 E (physical)
Fairfield, IL 62837
(618)847-4061   \<Wayne\>
CL: Sandra Beckel
506 W Lakeview Drive
Fairfield, IL 62837
(618)842-6400
gonqwik@fairfieldwireless.net

United   (4MC)MINC5119
204 S Powell Street
Norris City, IL 62869
(618)378-3341   \<White\>
FAX: (618)378-3064
tc_5854@yahoo.com
CL: Nellie Shepard
206 E Eubanks Street
Norris City, IL 62869
(618)378-3997

Willow Creek   (4MWC)MINC5211
6492 E 400th Road
Martinsville, IL 62442
(618)569-4955   \<Clark\>
PA: Kevin Small   \<M1\>
6492 E 400th Road
Martinsville, IL 62442
(618)562-1463
revkev61@gmail.com
CL: Norma Calvert
6313 E 400th Road
Martinsville, IL 62442
(618)569-3035
norma.calvert@yahoo.com

OTHERS ON MINISTERIAL ROLL:

Allen, Gail   \<M1 WC\>
488 County Road 1650 N
Bethany, IL 61914
(217)665-3387
kallen1_61914@yahoo.com
Aros, Jeremias   \<M1 RT\>
5649 W Roscoe Street
Chicago, IL 60634
(773)685-4395
jeremiasaros@sbcglobal.net
Barnett, Rudolph   \<M1 RT\>
RR 5 Box 267
McLeansboro, IL 62859
(618)643-3253
Bender, Richard J   \<M1 WC\>
5297 Normandy Place
Evansville, IN 47715
(812)983-9597
richardjbenderjr@yahoo.com
Bunting, Geoff   \<M1 WC\>
9229 Hedgewood Court
Evansville, IN 47725
(812)925-6630
geoff.bunting@yahoo.com
Compton, Marcia   \<M1 ST\>
6276 Cascade Circle
Indianapolis, IN 46234
(317)209-9798
mcomptonma@yahoo.com
Craig, Robert A   \<M1 RT\>

NORTH CENTRAL PRESBYTERY CONTINUED

1711 Bellevue Avenue Apt D-706
Richmond, VA 23227
(573)219-8051
robertacraig1954@gmail.com

Dallwig, Roger   <M1 RT>
1661 Hickory Lane
Corydon, IN 47112
(812)705-5071
rcd129@hotmail.com

Furr, Wayne   <M1 WC>
706 E 6th Street
Coal Valley, IL 61240
(309)791-1691
prespreacher@gmail.com

Korb, Leon C   <M1 RT>
15360 E 350 North Road
Ridge Farm, IL 61870
(217)662-8398

Lovelace, John G   <M1 RT>
1202 E Cedar Street
New Baden, IL 62265
(812)476-5879
jlove1234@aol.com

Nichols, Oscar Lee   <M1 RT>
1035 N County Road 650E
Trilla, IL 62469
(217)234-6551

Oliveira, Jose   <M1 WC>
7310 Jasmine Drive
Hanover Park, IL 60133
(630)855-0870
valdirsoares@yahoo.com

Richards, Carroll R   <M1 RT M9>
210 Allison Drive
Lincoln, IL 62656
(217)732-7894
FAX: (217)732-7894
dr_cr@comcast.net

Scott, Lisa   <M1 WC>
ADDRESS ON FILE
(816)332-0604
lascott1979@att.net

Shirley, Betty L   <M1 RT>
811 Rotherham Drive
Ballwin, MO 63011
(636)386-3174
therevbls@prodigy.net

Topar, Shirley   <M1 WC>
2233 Cambridge Drive SE
Grand Rapids, MI 49506
(616)245-0625
s_j_topar@yahoo.com

Watkins, Robert B   <M1 RT DE>
235 Misty Drive
Somerset, KY 42503
(319)431-0990
watkr@mac.com

Yarce, Janeth   <M1 WC>
3019 W Calavar Road
Phoenix, AZ 85053
(630)518-0295
janethyarce@yahoo.com

_____

OTHER LICENTIATES ON ROLL:

Sandiford, Holton   <M2>
4227 E 300th Road
Casey, IL 62420
(217)259-3773

Stephenson, Joseph   <M2>
PO Box 129
Bethany, IL 61914
(217)853-7819

_____

OTHER CANDIDATES ON ROLL:

Red River Presbytery
MISSION SYNOD

GENERAL		MEMBERSHIP			CHANGES			FINANCES				
1.Church Number	2.Active	3.Total	4.Church School	5.Prof. of Faith	6.Gains	7.Losses	8.Children Baptized	9. OUR UNITED OUT-REACH	10. Total Out-Reach Giving	11. All Other Expenses	12. Total Income Received	13. Value Church Prop. 1=1000
1	2	3	4	5	6	7	8	9	10	11	12	13
Burns Flat*	6301	93	93	60	14	14	18	2	3,000	26,140	95,415	113,381	1,500
Clinton**	6302	60	70	41	0	0	50	0	5,230	13,741	113,641	127,355	1,500
Covenant	6304	83	106	81	2	4	5	2	6,000	37,267	157,785	184,241	1,250
Denton**	8404	49	49	20	1	11	157	0	10,096	17,400	85,730	131,061	2,500
Eastlake	6205	63	154	31	1	2	3	0	10,203	14,383	84,970	106,612	1,300
Faith	6201	39	39	0	0	5	2	0	5,591	5,606	114,864	91,363	450
Hubbard	8410	8	8	0	No Report Received			0	0	0	0	0	200
Lake Highlands+	8411	109	109	67	1	4	7	2	2,925	5,098	287,586	267,596	3,510
Locust Grove	6203	7	11	5	No Report Received			0	0	0	0	0	150
Marlow	6305	38	71	18	0	3	1	0	7,314	13,936	112,497	76,536	580
Mesquite	8412	35	35	12	0	0	4	0	0	3,316	104,351	95,143	1,200
Mt. Zion*	8414	7	8	25	0	3	0	0	1,307	2,400	8,705	13,036	100
Newberry*	8415	31	31	5	0	18	3	1	800	5,133	23,614	25,813	470
Olney*	8416	61	92	36	0	1	0	0	8,925	13,143	88,989	89,252	600
Pathway	8418	1,200	2,260	804	65	181	13	7	0	346,437	2,637,715	2,624,891	10,100
Sandy Springs	8420	35	35	8	0	0	0	0	0	3,065	17,768	31,606	200
Shiloh	8421	99	214	54	0	3	4	0	22,119	58,944	150,859	225,064	950
St. John	8413	30	33	0	0	0	6	0	4,784	13,554	62,444	67,768	916
St. Luke	8407	56	56	40	0	0	13	0	0	10,265	247,270	228,684	1,910
St. Mark (TX)	8408	20	20	6	0	0	1	0	449	4,620	0	53,595	1,048
St. Timothy	8419	145	245	117	0	7	12	0	21,972	50,669	223,387	289,566	2,000
Stonegate	6307	50	50	22	0	1	0	0	690	1,576	156,543	105,021	866
Trinity	8409	68	72	28	0	4	21	0	8,934	23,437	155,243	138,804	1,300
Zion Valley	8425	13	13	3	0	0	0	0	500	5,415	15,600	21,009	180
TOTALS	24	2,405	3,877	1,484	84	261	319	17	120,839	675,545	2,309,899	2,873,417	34,580

*Math error corrected. **Purged roll. +Union church

CHURCHES, PASTORS, AND CLERKS:

Burns Flat   (4WMC)MSRR6301
  PO Box 8 (mailing)
  205 Highway 44 (physical)
  Burns Flat, OK 73624
  (580)562-4706   <Washita>
  burnsflatcpc@windstream.net
  PA: Thomas R Spence   <M1>
  PO Box 802
  Burns Flat, OK 73624
  (580)562-4531
  tomspence0302@gmail.com
  CL: Gene Reeves
  11649 N 2160 Road
  Dill City, OK 73641
  (580)674-3763
  patsyreeves@windstream.net

Clinton   (4WMC)MSRR6302
  500 S 30th Street
  Clinton, OK 73601
  (580)323-3440   <Custer>
  PA: Dale Nease   <M1>
  500 S 30th Street
  Clinton, OK 73601
  (580)323-7557
  CL: Dave Felch

500 S 30th Street
Clinton, OK 73601
(580)323-3111

Covenant   (4MEWC)MSRR6304
  15791 State Highway 1W
  Ada, OK 74820
  (580)332-0799   <Pontotoc>
  PA: Duawn Mearns   <M1>
  15791 State Highway 1W
  Ada, OK 74820
  (580)332-0799
  duawn@covenantcpc.org
  CL: Randy C Davidson
  PO Box 880
  Ada, OK 74821
  (580)421-6969
  randy@d-son.com

Denton   (4MWC)MSRR8404
  PO Box 236 (mailing)
  1424 Stuart Road (physical)
  Denton, TX 76202
  (940)387-6811   <Denton>
  gacakee12@verizon.net
  CL: Kathy McIntire
  304 Surveyors Road
  Aubrey, TX 76227
  (940)365-2087

kcm1@att.net

Eastlake   (4C)MSRR6205
  700 SW 134th Street
  Oklahoma City, OK 73170
  (405)799-8987   <Oklahoma>
  eastlakecumberland@att.net
  PA: Leslie A Johnson   <M1>
  11716 Price Drive
  Oklahoma City, OK 73170
  (405)248-4232
  ljohnson275@cox.net
  CL: Paulette Geeslin
  5505 S Villa Avenue
  Oklahoma City, OK 73119
  pgeeslin4701@yahoo.com

Faith   (4WC)MSRR6201
  PO Box 690715 (mailing)
  2801 S 129th East Avenue (physical)
  Tulsa, OK 74169
  (918)437-2190   <Tulsa>
  FAX: (918)437-2199
  tulsafaith@att.net
  PA: Thomas R Sanders   <M1 DE>
  4201 W Kent Street
  Broken Arrow, OK 74012
  (918)269-0043
  FAX: (918)437-2199

RED RIVER PRESBYTERY CONTINUED

trsncf@msn.com
CL: Georgia Stevens
   29605 S River Ridge Drive
   Catoosa, OK 74015
   FAX: (918)437-2199
   stevenscabinets@yahoo.com

Hubbard   (4MWC)MSRR8410
   404 N Magnolia
   Hubbard, TX 76648
   (   )   <Hill>
CL: Brenard Nunnelley
   475 H County Road 3350 N
   Hubbard, TX 76648
   (254)576-2468
   bfn76648@aol.com

Lake Highlands   (4WU)MSRR8411
   8525 Audelia Road
   Dallas, TX 75238
   (214)348-2133   <Dallas>
   lhpc@lhpres.org
PA: Perryn Rice   <M4>
   10802 Hayfield Drive
   Dallas, TX 75238
   (931)526-6585
   perryn@lhpres.org
CL: Maureen Ramsay
   8935 Larchwood Drive
   Dallas, TX 75238
   (214)542-6173
   FAX: (214)348-2408
   msramsay@hotmail.com

Locust Grove   (4MWC)MSRR6203
   PO Box 577 (mailing)
   203 E Harriett Avenue (physical)
   Locust Grove, OK 74352
   (918)479-5613   <Mayes>
CL: Mayme Miley
   7847 S 438 Road
   Locust Grove, OK 74352
   (918)479-2575

Marlow   (4MWC)MSRR6305
   202 N Sixth
   Marlow, OK 73055
   (580)658-2892   <Stephens>
PA: Terra Sisco   <M1>
   811 W Cheyenne Street
   Marlow, OK 73055
   (618)384-6126
   terrasisco@hotmail.com
CL: Gayle Kemmerer
   2019 Crestline
   Duncan, OK 73533
   (580)255-5829

Mesquite   (4C)MSRR8412
   819 N Town East Boulevard
   Mesquite, TX 75150
   (972)270-6923   <Dallas>
   FAX: (972)270-6923
   mcpchurch@gmail.com
IP: Wesley H Johnson   <M1>
   6222 Crestmoor Lane
   Sachse, TX 75048
   (972)429-6129
   wjohnson@transitionconsulting.com
CL: Patricia Chatt
   1705 Windmire Drive

Mesquite, TX 75181
   (214)394-6513
   pbchatt@sbcglobal.net

Mt Zion   (2C)MSRR8414
   691 County Road 4108 (mailing)
   Greeneville, TX 75401
   15175 Texas Highway 11 W (physical)
   Cumby, TX 75433
   (903)454-3444   <Hopkins>
   bvwood10@yahoo.com
CL: Brenda McDaniel
   14366 State Highway 11 W
   Cumby, TX 75433
   (903)886-2503
   brendamcdaniel49@yahoo.com

Newberry   (2C)MSRR8415
   PO Box 253 (mailing)
   1301 Newberry Road (physical)
   Millsap, TX 76066
   (   )   <Parker>
PA: Tim Dewhirst   <M1>
   3609 Oakbriar Lane
   Colleyville, TX 76034
   (817)605-8147
   timdew@sbcglobal.net
CL: Joel Young
   2902 Old Milsap Road
   Weatherford, TX 76088
   (817)341-0800
   joelyoung@aol.com

Olney   (4MEWC)MSRR8416
   PO Box 756 (mailing)
   210 S Avenue M (physical)
   Olney, TX 76374
   (940)564-2882   <Young>
   olneycpc@brazosnet.comt
PA: David Carpenter   <M1>
   909 W Elm Street
   Olney, TX 76374
   (940)564-2339
   olneycpc@brazosnet.com
CL: Clifton W Key
   PO Box 615
   Olney, TX 76374
   (940)564-2979
   barkey8@brazosnet.com

Pathway   (4EC)MSRR8418
   (previously named St Matthew)
   PO Box 182 (mailing)
   825 NW Renfro(physical)
   Burleson, TX 76097
   (817)295-5832   <Johnson>
   FAX: (817)295-2576
   info@pathway.church
PA: Rick Owen   <M1>
   3305 Wild Oaks Court
   Burleson, TX 76028
   (817)295-5832
   FAX: (817)295-2576
   rowen@pathway.church
AP: Josh Fortney   <M1>
   765 Windridge Lane
   Burleson, TX 76028
   (214)794-9912
   jfortney@pathway.church
AP: Jeffrey A Gehle   <M1>
   PO Box 182

Burleson, TX 76097
   (817)295-5832
   jeff.gehle@pathway.church
AP: Judith Ellen Madden   <M1>
   100 SW Brushy Mound
   Burleson, TX 76028
   (817)295-5832
   jmadden@pathway.church
AP: R Allan Mink   <M1>
   1113 Hidden Glen Court
   Burleson, TX 76028
   (817)295-5832
   FAX: (817)295-2576
   alan.mink@pathway.church
CL: Kim Perkey
   2600 Embry Lane
   Burleson, TX 76028
   (817)235-9061
   kimberley.k.perkey@wellsfargo.com

Sandy Springs   (4C)MSRR8420
   1865 Bones Chapel Road (mailing)
   Rease Road (physical)
   Whitesboro, TX 76273
   (   )   <Grayson>
CL: Eddie Vidrine
   1865 Bones Chapel Road
   Whitesboro, TX 76273
   (902)584-5148
   eddievid@gmail.com

Shiloh   (4MEWC)MSRR8421
   7810 Shiloh Road
   Midlothian, TX 76065
   (972)723-3758   <Ellis>
   vernon@sansom.us
PA: Vernon Sansom   <M1>
   104 Cockrell Hill Road
   Ovilla, TX 75154
   (972)825-6887
   vernon@sansom.us
CL: Georgia Williams
   1425 Black Champ Road
   Waxahachie, TX 75167
   (214)949-7228
   georgia@reliablegokarts.net

St John   (4WC)MSRR8413
   6007 W Pleasant Ridge Road
   Arlington, TX 76016
   (817)478-6219   <Tarrant>
   FAX: (817)478-8684
   stjohncpc@att.net
PA: Adrian Scott   <M1>
   4101 Way Road
   Fort Worth, TX 76133
   (817)205-7760
   scott.adrian@zoho.com
CL: Barbara Harrell
   6207 W Poly Webb Road
   Arlington, TX 76016
   (817)229-1796
   baharrell@tx.rr.com

St Luke   (4C)MSRR8407
   1404 Sycamore School Road
   Fort Worth, TX 76134
   (817)293-3778   <Tarrant>
   FAX: (817)293-2750
   office@stlukecpc.org
PA: David Kurtz   <M1>

RED RIVER PRESBYTERY CONTINUED

4700 Elkwood Lane
Arlington, TX 76016
(817)683-4783
davidk36@yahoo.com
CL: Beth McLaughlin
5462 Rutland Avenue
Fort Worth, TX 76133
(817)292-5471
mcbeth1951@att.net

St Mark (TX)   (4MWC)MSRR8408
4101 Hardeman Street
Fort Worth, TX 76119
(817)536-1315   <Tarrant>
PA: Roosevelt Baugh   <M1>
4101 Hardeman Street
Fort Worth, TX 76119
(817)536-1315
gmf1220@charter.net
CL: Hazel F Wilson
2801 Sarah Jane Lane
Fort Worth, TX 76119
(817)536-4892
jesseewilson@charter.net

St Timothy   (4WC)MSRR8419
PO Box 210338 (mailing)
3001 Forest Ridge Drive (physical)
Bedford, TX 76095
(817)571-7474   <Tarrant>
FAX: (817)571-7714
SS: Kevin R Henson   <M1>
1101 Bear Creek Parkway Ste 3210
Keller, TX 76248
(817)354-1182
kevin.r.henson@gmail.com
CL: Danny Washmon
PO Box 210338
Bedford, TX 76095
(817)571-7474
washmon@rocketmail.com

Stonegate   (ARC)MSRR6307
17101 North Western Avenue
Edmond, OK 73012
(405)340-7281   <Oklahoma>
stonegatecpc@gmail.com
PA: Marian Sontowski   <M1>
17101 North Western Avenue
Edmond, OK 73012
(405)340-7281
stonegatecpc@gmail.com
CL: Jeanette Silman
17101 North Western Avenue
Edmond, OK 73012
(405)340-7281
stonegate.clerk@gmail.com

Trinity   (4MEWC)MSRR8409
7120 W Cleburne Road
Fort Worth, TX 76133
(817)292-6149   <Tarrant>
trinitycpc@sbcglobal.net
PA: Randy L Hardisty   <M1>
4908 Redondo Street
Fort Worth, TX 76180
(817)428-3513
rhardisty@sbcglobal.net
CL: Betty Jean Cooper
1108 Trinity Trail
Saginaw, TX 76131

(817)306-4877
bjjacoop@sbcglobal.net

Zion Valley   (4C)MSRR8425
2684 South FM 1655
Chico, TX 76431
(   )   <Wise>
PA: Barney Hudson   <M1>
10541 Fossil Hill Drive
Fort Worth, TX 76131
(817)851-2960
barneyrev@gmail.com
CL: Priscilla Moreland
1177 N State Highway 101
Chico, TX 76431
(940)644-2462
hdpjmoreland@hotmail.com

OTHERS ON MINISTERIAL ROLL:

Aden, Marty   <M1 M9>
202 Bennington Place
Wilmington, NC 28412
(910)274-8465
maadretny@gmail.com
Baltimore, Claud G   <M1 RT>
PO Box 1358
1430 Lakehurst Drive
Ada, OK 74821
(580)332-2679
baltimorejb@earthlink.net
Brown, Chuck   <M1 DE>
475 N Highland Street 6B
Memphis, TN 38122
(817)915-2907
cbrown@cumberland.org
Brown, Stephanie S   <M1 M9>
475 N Highland Street 6B
Memphis, TN 38122
(817)915-1317
scrudderbrown7@gmail.com
Condon, Jr, Thomas W   <M1 RT>
6508 Victoria Avenue
N Richland Hills, TX 76180
(817)656-9334
Ferrol, Ruben   <M1 M9 RT>
13018 E 28th Street
Tulsa, OK 74134
(610)966-7289
rubeferrol@msn.com
Fowler, Emily   <M1 M9>
5225 Maple Avenue Apt 5304
Dallas, TX 75235
(817)9853-3559
emilykaye.fowler@gmail.com
Gardner, Charles   <M1 RT>
PO Box 1035
Elephant Butte, NM 87035
(719)784-7744
Harris, Wendell   <M1 WC>
329 N Louis Tittle Avenue
Mangum, OK 73554
(580)782-2142
wendellharris@itlnet.net
Hayes, Jennifer   <M1 M9>
2901 Sandage Avenue Apt 304
Fort Worth, TX 76109
(205)533-1018
hayesj712@gmail.com
Hayes, Marcus   <M1 WC>
2901 Sandage Avenue Apt 304

Fort Worth, TX 76109
(270)841-7576
marcus.hayes@att.net
Hendershot, Charles A   <M1 WC>
122 Tree Shadow
Whitney, TX 76692
(254)694-3852
Hong, Soon Gab   <M1 WC>
13600 Doty Avenue Apt 4
Hawthorne, CA 90250
(972)446-0350
lemuelhong@hotmail.com
Howell, Linda   <M1 WC>
PO Box 80050
Keller, TX 76244
(601)942-2015
lshowell885@yahoo.com
Kays, Michael   <M1 WC>
2505 Canterbury Avenue
Muskogee, OK 74403
(918)577-6255
msppk@suddenlink.net
Lain, Judy   <M1 WC>
1928 Pine Ridge Drive
Bedford, TX 76021
(817)909-6702
judylaine5@gmail.com
Lombard, Kristi   <M1 M9>
902 Clearview
Krum, TX 76249
(940)435-5077
pastorkristi@yahoo.com
Martinez, Soledad   <M1 WC>
2801 Biway Street
Fort Worth, TX 76114
(817)812-8247
shirleymartinez1252@gmail.com
McGee, Charles Randall   <M1 WC>
9037 Groveland Drive
Dallas, TX 75218
(214)328-2488
randallmcgee@sbcglobal.net
Nelson, Charles E   <M1 WC>
209 Classic Court
Springtown, TX 76082
(903)641-5466
dundeal10@aol.com
Petty, Linda Lee   <M1 WC>
8601 S Mingo Road Apt 3115
Tulsa, OK 74133
(918)252-4741
Rice, Keith   <M1 HR>
PO Box 582
Itasca, TX 76055
(254)087-2418
rsvkeith@yahoo.com
Rivera, Carlos A   <M1 WC>
Calle Dr Jose Maria Vertiz 1410
Departmento 202B, Colonia Portales
Delegacion Benito
Juarez, C.P. 03300 MEXICO
(52)1-55-31058377
caralrifra@une.net.co
Ruggia, Mario (Bud)   <M1 M9 RT>
603 Rumsey Street
Kiowa, KS 67070
(620)825-4076
ruggia@aol.com
Schmoyer, Donna Marie   <M1 WC>
613 Mound Street
Monongahela, PA 15063

RED RIVER PRESBYTERY CONTINUED

(817)266-6572
schmoyerdm@yahoo.com
Scrudder, Norlan   <M1 RT>
  29688 S 534 Road
  Park Hill, OK 74451
  (918)949-1326
  ndscrudder@gmail.com
Scott, Adrian
  4101 Willow Way Road
  Fort Worth, TX 76133
  (817)205-7760
  scott.adrian@zoho.com
Sharpe, Michael G   <M1 DE>
  3423 Summerdale Drive
  Bartlett, TN 38133
  (901)276-4572
Shelton, Robert M   <M1 RT>
  7128 Lakehurst Avenue
  Dallas, TX 75230
  (214)696-3237
Shugert, Richard   <M1 WC>
  5208 Bellis Drive
  Fort Worth, TX 76244
  (817)913-7211
  shugertr@yahoo.com
Smith, Robert H   <M1 WC>
  5055 S 76th East Avenue Apt D
  Tulsa, OK 74145
  (918)671-5520
  rhsmith@sstelco.com
Snelling, Linda   <M1 WC>
  431 Windemere
  Ada, OK 74820
  (580)332-0329
  lsnelling50@gmail.com
Thomas, Cassandra   <M1 RT>
  1920 Dancy Street
  Fayetteville, NC 28301
  (910)488-4897
  chcothomas@yahoo.com
Wagner, Hugh   <M1 RT>

12556 Timberline Drive
Garfield, AR 72732
(479)359-0021
hughawagner@gmail.com
Webb, Lonnie, Sr   <M1 WC>
  500 S 300th Street
  Clinton, OK 73601
  (970)682-8025
  lgwebb.sr@gmail.com
Webb, William G   <M1 OM>
  7926 S 78th East Avenue
  Tulsa, OK 74133
  (918)294-9117
Youngman, Betty   <M1 RT>
  1471 Creekview Court
  Fort Worth, TX 76112
  (817)492-4100
  bettyy@swbell.net
Zumbrunnen, Craig H   <M1 WC>
  1210 Country Club Road Apt 3
  Santa Teresa, NM 88008
  (580)471-0308
  craigzum1@yahoo.com

OTHER LICENIATES ON ROLL:

King, Keith   <M2 ST>
  3341 S 137th East Avenue
  Tulsa, OK 74134
  (918)437-5464
  cpkking@yahoo.com

OTHER CANDIDATES ON ROLL:

Bohon, Chris Michael   <M3>
  505 Edgehill Road
  Joshua, TX 76058
  (817)228-9494
  cbohon@pathway.church
Brown, Houston   <M3>
  866 N McLean

Memphis, TN 38107
(817)915-9090
hpbrown95@gmail.com

Butler, Alan   <M3>
  866 N McLean Boulevard
  Memphis, TN 38107
  (817)937-8488
  afbutler@memphisseminary.edu
Lofton, Kathy   <M3>
  10636 County Road 1500
  Ada, OK 74820
  (580)332-0898
  kdnlofton@gmail.com
Rice, Nathan   <M3>
  5205 Kelso Lane
  Garland, TX 75043
  (972)400-0675
  nathanerice@gmail.com
Rosales, David   <M3>
  101 N Lowe
  Hobart, OK 73651
  (580)682-0722
  sagradalut@gmail.com
Tucker, Dave   <M3>
  329 Miss Mary Road
  Cleburne, TX 76031
  (817)602-3874
  digtucker@gmail.com

Robert Donnell Presbytery
SOUTHEAST SYNOD

	1.Church Number	2.Active	3.Total	4.Church School	5.Prof. of Faith	6.Gains	7.Losses	8.Children Baptized	9. OUR UNITED OUT-REACH	10. Total Out-Reach Giving	11. All Other Expenses	12. Total Income Received	13. Value Church Prop. 1=1000
	1	2	3	4	5	6	7	8	9	10	11	12	13
Alabaster	0107	160	282	40	4	4	2	3	5,833	27,936	163,213	191,257	2,300
Big Cove*	0801	21	21	11	4	5	1	1	0	230	25,103	25,840	330
Christ Church	0814	63	112	15	0	4	0	0	10,531	14,368	98,332	106,420	650
Concord	0802	20	81	17	3	3	0	0	1,792	2,037	18,250	16,577	286
East Point	0206	17	19	20	0	2	2	0	600	1,904	29,626	29,727	859
Edgefield	0813	3	3	0	0	0	0	0	0	200	6,413	6,500	127
Eidson Chapel	0207	20	51	17	No Report Received			0	0	0	0	0	140
Goosepond*	0803	23	48	6	0	4	4	0	1,800	6,576	25,686	32,262	250
Gurley	0804	61	61	25	0	1	0	0	5,664	25,508	102,909	128,626	751
Hope+	0812	28	28	5	0	0	10	0	0	1,119	55,339	56,458	600
Huntsville, 1st	0806	45	112	25	0	1	1	0	1,200	10,712	105,010	94,610	1,463
Meridianville	0808	41	41	18	0	0	0	0	0	525	60,783	61,451	1,350
Scottsboro	0809	257	457	115	3	4	2	0	23,839	87,874	248,829	323,708	2,780
Stevenson	0810	37	140	13	0	1	2	0	8,496	21,878	76,398	84,986	1,200
Union Grove	0211	20	27	15	No Report Received			0	0	0	0	0	200
Walnut Grove	0811	14	14	4	0	2	1	0	25	1,525	4,902	5,146	14
TOTALS	15	831	1,543	346	14	31	25	4	59,780	202,392	1,020,793	1,163,568	13,270

*Math error corrected. **Purged roll. +Union church

CHURCHES, PASTORS, AND CLERKS:

Alabaster   (4WC)SERD0107
   8828 Highway 119
   Alabaster, AL 35007
   (205)663-3152   <Shelby>
   FAX: (205)663-8323
   fpcalabaster@bellsouth.net
PA: Darren Kennemer   <M1>
   8828 Highway 119
   Alabaster, AL 35007
   (205)663-3152
   FAX: (205)663-8323
   dlkennemer@gmail.com
AP: Earl Goodwin   <M1>
   1012 Windsor Parkway
   Moody, AL 35004
   (205)222-1741
   FAX: (205)664-8323
   earlgoodwin@yahoo.com
CL: Margaret Russo
   8828 Highway 119
   Alabaster, AL 35007
   (205)663-3152
   mrusso@harbert.net

Big Cove   (4MWC)SERD0801
   5984 Highway 431 S
   Brownsboro, AL 35741
   (256)518-9657   <Madison>
SS: Donald Reeves   <M1 HR>
   PO Box 528
   Rainsville, AL 35986
   (256)228-4057
   reevesd@nacc.edu
CL: Kay Tidwell

730 Old Big Cove Road
Owens Cross Roads, AL 35763
(256)288-6651
greenthumbkt@gmail.com

Christ Church   (4WC)SERD0814
   1580 Jeff Road
   Huntsville, AL 35806
   (256)837-6014   <Madison>
PA: Cardelia Howell Diamond   <M1>
   1580 Jeff Road
   Huntsville, AL 35806
   (256)837-6014
   cpclergymama@gmail.com
CL: Frances Dawson
   PO Box 904
   Scottsboro, AL 35768
   (256)259-0904
   francesdawson@gmail.com

Concord   (4MWC)SERD0802
   1827 Joe Quick Road
   New Market, AL 35761
   (256)828-4503   <Madison>
CL: Richard Dixon
   626 Briar Fork Road
   Hazel Green, AL 35761
   (256)828-0002
\   dixonelec16@gmail.com

East Point   (4WC)SERD0206
   1441 US Highway 278 E
   Cullman, AL 35055
   (256)734-0900   <Cullman>
SS: Philip Nickles   <M1 OP>
   5821 County Road 1114

Vinemont, AL 35179
(256)734-9847
nickles.phil@yahoo.com
CL: Karen Munger
   PO Box 1773
   Cullman, AL 35056
   (256)739-0746
   karenamunger@bellsouth.net

Edgefield   (4UC)SERD0813
   411 McMahan Cove Road (mailing)
   Stevenson, AL 35772
   311 County Road 158 (physical)
   Stevenson, AL 35772
   ( )   <Jackson>
CL: Christie Nunley
   411 McMahan Cove Road
   Stevenson, AL 35772
   (256)437-9011

Eidson Chapel   (4C)SERD0207
   2680 County Road 1725
   Holly Pond, AL 35083
   ( )   <Cullman>
OD: Floyd Bradford   <M5>
   351 Piney Grove Road W
   Falkville, AL 35622
   (256)784-6510
   FAX: (415)864-1543
CL: Linda Harris
   5910 County Road 747
   Cullman, AL 35058
   (256)734-6697

Goosepond   (4MWC)SERD0803
   1155 East Hancock Drive
   Scottsboro, AL 35769

ROBERT DONNELL PRESBYTERY CONTINUED

(256)259-4386   <Jackson>
betrich76@gmail.com
CL: Bettie M Jordan
   198 County Road 46
   Hollywood, AL 35752
   (256)437-1546
   betrich76@gmail.com

_____

Gurley   (4MEWC)SERD0804
   223 Section Line Road
   Gurley, AL 35748
   (256)776-2331   <Madison>
PA: Toy E Brindley   <M1>
   PO Box 335
   Gurley, AL 35748
   (256)776-2331
   gurleycpc@gmail.com
CL: Becky Arnold
   423 Sharps Cove Road
   Gurley, AL 35748
   (256)776-6950
   bailey@darnold.net

_____

Hope   (4WU)SERD0812
   10001 Bailey Cove Road SE
   Huntsville, AL 35803
   (256)881-4673   <Madison>
   hopepresby@comcast.net
OD: Christie Ashton   <M5>
   10001 Bailey Cove Road SE
   Huntsville, AL 35803
   (256)881-4673
   pastorhope@comcast.net
CL: Joanna Sterling-Clutts
   10001 Bailey Cove Road SE
   Huntsville, AL 35803
   (256)479-9899
   alabamahoosier@gmail.com

_____

Huntsville First   (4EWC)SERD0806
   PO Box 777 (mailing)
   1802 Bankhead Parkway (physical)
   Huntsville, AL 35804
   (256)536-9371   <Madison>
   hsvfcpc@att.net
PA: Richard W Hughes   <M1>
   2954 Bob Wade Lane
   Harvest, AL 35749
   (256)859-3178
   hughesrichard23@gmail.com
CL: Steve Rowley
   PO Box 777
   2012 Brandy Court
   Huntsville, AL 35811
   (256)651-5916
   steve.rowley35@gmail.com

_____

Meridianville   (4MWC)SERD0808
   PO Box 188 (mailing)
   11696 Highway 231/431 N (physical)
   Meridianville, AL 35759
   (256)828-0160   <Madison>
   dptalley@hotmail.com
PA: Keith Lorick   <M1>
   127 Chesapeake Boulevard
   Madison, AL 35757
   (256)325-3865
   keithlorick@knology.net
CL: Donna Talley
   360 Monroe Road
   Meridianville, AL 35759

(256)683-6111
dptalley@hotmail.com

_____

Scottsboro   (4WC)SERD0809
   PO Box 639 (mailing)
   315 S Kyle Street (physical)
   Scottsboro, AL 35768
   FAX: (256)259-2809
   cumberland@scottsboro.org
   (256)574-2575   <Jackson>
PA: Micaiah Thomas Tanck   <M1>
   2912 S Broad Street Apt B3
   Scottsboro, AL 35769
   (205)478-5985
   micaiah.thomas@gmail.com
CL: Gene Gossett
   1707 Brandon Street
   Scottsboro, AL 35769
   256)574-6334
   ggossett@scottsboro.org

_____

Stevenson   (4MEWC)SERD0810
   112 College Street
   Stevenson, AL 35772
   (256)437-8632   <Jackson>
PA: Perry Whitaker
   202 College Street
   Stevenson, AL 35772
   (256)437-8632
   brotherperry@msn.com
CL: Jen Stewart
   112 College Street
   Stevenson, AL 35772
   (256)437-3116
   jstewart306@hotmail.com

_____

Union Grove   (4WC)SERD0211
   91 County Road 1734 (mailing)
   2760 County Road 1742 (physical)
   Holly Pond, AL 35803
   (256)796-1023   <Cullman>
   johnson9983@att.net
PS: David Hooper   <M6>
   115 County Road 682
   Cullman, AL 35055
   (256)775-2419
   davidhoop165@yahoo.com
CL: Glen Johnson
   91 County Road 1734
   Holly Pond, AL 35083
   (256)796-1023
   johnson9983@att.net

_____

Walnut Grove   (4WC)SERD0811
   PO Box 403 (mailing)
   711 New Hope/Cedar Point Road (physical)
   New Hope, AL 35760
   ( )   <Madison>
CL: Kathy Pegues
   211 Butler Lane
   New Hope, AL 35760
   (256)723-8740
   mcwoodpeg@nehp.net

_____

OTHERS ON MINISTERIAL ROLL:
Alverson, Elmer L   <M1 HR>
   354 Roy Davis Road
   New Market, AL 35761
   (256)828-4503
   1941buddy@att.net
Babcock, Edward S, Jr   <M1 HR>

1007 San Ramone Avenue
   Huntsville, AL 35802
   (256)882-9339
   ejsb1@aol.com
Bynum, Ronald H   <M1 WC>
   121 Sycamore Road
   Gurley, AL 35748
   (256)776-9313
   ronaldbynum@bellsouth.net
Gillis, Aubrey Thomas   <M1 WC>
   110 Blue Sky Lane
   Alabaster, AL 35007
   (251)947-1638
   FAX: (205)664-8323
   tomgillis63@hotmail.com
Hall, Brad   <M1 WC>
   1602 Toll Gate Road SE
   Huntsville, AL 35801
   (256)533-4845
Hall, John D   <M1 WC>
   109 Oddo Lane SE
   Huntsville, AL 35802
   (256)880-5129
   johnhall33@comcast.net
Hall, Roy W   <M1 RT>
   87 Lee Hall Street
   Scottsboro, AL 35769
   (256)259-9340
   royhall@scottsboro.org
Herring, C E (Ed) Jr   <M1 RT>
   969 Campground Circle
   Scottsboro, AL 35769
   (256)259-2721
   edherring@scottsboro.org
Howell-Diamond, Steven   <M1 WC>
   106 Ultimate Court
   Madison, AL 35757
   smdiam@hotmail.com
   (931)636-7336
Howton, Orvie Ray   <M1 RT>
   4928 Montauk Trail SE
   Owens Cross Road, AL 35763
   (256)533-9224
   orphowton@yahoo.com
Hughes, Charles   <M1 HR>
   114 Gaul Street
   Estill Springs, TN 37330
   (931)649-5189
   cphugs@cafes.net
Lambert, James   <M1 RT>
   224 Peabody Road
   Meridianville, AL 35759
   (256)828-6850
Livingston, Ronald L   <M1 HR>
   11314 Maplecrest Drive
   Huntsville, AL 35803
   hairy404@outlook.com
Matthews, James N   <M1 HR>
   241 Morning Star Drive
   Huntsville, AL 35811
   (256)337-2765
   brojim10@att.net
Murphree, Hughlen   <M1 HR>
   4298 County Road 1719
   Holly Pond, AL 35083
   (256)796-5352
   hmurph@hiwaay.net
Phillips-Burk, Pam   <M1 DE>
   3325 Bailey Creek Cove N
   Collierville, TN 38017
   (256)684-5247

ROBERT DONNELL PRESBYTERY CONTINUED

pam@cumberland.org
Smith, James   <M1 WC>
  1949 Little Cove Road
  Owens Cross Roads, AL 35763
  dr.james.smith42@gmail.com

OTHER CANDIDATES ON ROLL:

Tennessee-Georgia Presbytery
SOUTHEAST SYNOD

	1.Church Number	2.Active	3.Total	4.Church School	5.Prof. of Faith	6.Gains	7.Losses	8.Children Baptized	9. OUR UNITED OUT-REACH	10. Total Out-Reach Giving	11. All Other Expenses	12. Total Income Received	13. Value Church Prop. 1=1000
	1	2	3	4	5	6	7	8	9	10	11	12	13
Bartow	2101	86	154	60	0	1	0	0	5,000	28,966	122,490	138,718	913
Cedar Springs	2119	8	17	0	0	0	1	0	960	2,238	20,015	16,168	323
Charleston	2102	42	48	20	0	4	10	0	4,000	9,582	46,878	65,710	800
Chattanooga 1st	2104	548	548	153	0	15	12	2	10,000	31,595	560,648	514,045	1,250
Cleveland*	2108	142	180	63	0	0	2	0	14,473	60,937	227,874	252,660	5,000
Cornerstone Com	2107	12	42	9	No Report Received			0	0	0	0	0	675
Ebenezer	2110	5	6	0	No Report Received			0	0	0	0	0	75
El Redill*	2149	50	50	36	5	0	3	0	1,009	4,355	59,221	61,637	850
Falling Water	2111	62	71	34	2	8	6	2	1,000	34,232	98,717	120,557	890
Flint Springs	2112	24	24	0	No Report Received			0	0	0	0	0	150
Glory Church	2144	55	55	7	No Report Received			0	0	0	0	0	2,300
Jasper	2113	29	42	13	0	0	1	0	3,868	4,693	42,405	34,655	750
Kelly's Chapel*	2120	10	10	10	0	0	11	0	0	1,579	17,281	63,824	100
Korean Livingsto	2130	30	30	8	Provisional Church			0	0	0	0	0	0
New Hope	2115	54	84	31	4	6	0	0	3,000	7,325	70,107	77,432	800
Oak Grove	2121	16	30	0	1	2	0	0	0	1,320	12,693	9,211	110
Pine Hill	2117	13	13	14	No Report Received			0	0	0	0	0	70
Prospect United**	2116	44	44	14	0	1	29	0	1,500	1,715	50,247	63,253	1,400
Red Bank	2105	168	168	62	0	2	10	0	12.240	12,240	215,208	227,448	2,000
Richard City	2118	20	64	10	0	0	1	0	900	2,016	44,316	43,735	900
Silverdale*	2106	135	152	40	1	11	0	1	7,660	14,155	134,046	162,982	1,200
South Pittsburg	2123	17	61	0	0	0	1	0	150	438	22,255	22,346	825
Sumach	2124	110	214	80	1	3	4	2	5,417	12,582	141,635	151,407	675
Whitwell	2122	8	9	10	No Report Received			0	0	0	0	0	25
Tennessee-Georgia Presbytery									250				
TOTALS	25	1,778	2,205	687	14	54	90	7	71,177	229,968	1,886,037	2,025,788	21,081

*Math error corrected. **Purged roll.

TENNESSEE-GEORGIA PRESBYTERY CONTINUED

CHURCHES, PASTORS, AND CLERKS:

Bartow (4MWEC)SETG2101
1078 Cassville White Road (mailing)
Cartersville, GA 30121
2851 Highway 140 NE (physical)
Rydal, GA 30171
(770)382-3896 <Bartow>
pastormarkbcpcga@gmail.com
PA: Mark Rackley <M1>
3060 Highway 140 NE
Rydal, GA 30171
(770)382-3790
pastormarkbcpcga@gmail.com
CL: Susan Turner
1129 Richards Road
Rydal, GA 30171
(770)547-0266
susan.turner318@gmail.com

Cedar Springs (4C)SETG2119
495 Cedar Springs Loop (mailing)
6665 Old Dunlap Road (physical)
Whitwell, TN 37397
( ) <Marion>
PA: Kriss McGowan <M1>
885 Mount Calvary Road
Whitwell, TN 37397
(423)463-8609
krissmcg658@gmail.com
CL: Sarah Way
4595 Old Dunlap Road
Whitwell, TN 37397
(423)580-7685
sarahway1958@aol.com

Charleston (4MEWC)SETG2102
PO Box 476 (mailing)
Charleston, TN 37310
8267 N Lee Highway (physical)
Cleveland, TN 37312
(423)336-5004 <Bradley>
PA: Bill Bond <M1>
205 Windmere Drive
Chattanooga, TN 37411
(423)316-0867
bill@wcbj.net
CL: Vivian McCormack
5502 Mouse Creek Road NW
Cleveland, TN 37312
(423)479-8230
mcco6868@bellsouth.net

Chattanooga First (4WC)SETG2104
1505 N Moore Road
Chattanooga, TN 37411
(423)698-2556 <Hamilton>
FAX: (423)629-6683
office@firstcumberland.com
PA: Courtney Krueger <M2>
1505 N Moore Road
Chattanooga, TN 37411
CL: Christy Miller
7853 Legacy Park Court
Chattanooga, TN 37421
(423)894-8220
christymiller62@epbfi.com

Cleveland (4WC)SETG2108
161 2nd Street NE Ste 3 (mailing)

200 Church Street NE (physical)
Cleveland, TN 37311
(423)476-6751 <Bradley>
FAX: (423)476-6423
gchudson3@gmail.com
PA: Jennifer Newell <M1>
2322 Maraco Circle
Chattanooga, TN 37421
(423)892-5834
FAX: (423)476-6423
newelljennifer3@gmail.com
CL: Rodney Curvin
2508 Overbrook Circle NW
Cleveland, TN 37312
rodneycurvin@hotmail.com

Cornerstone Com (4MWC)SETG2107
9632 E Brainerd Road
Chattanooga, TN 37421
(423)892-3027 <Hamilton>
cornerstone3cp@gmail.com
SS: Jerry (Butch) Hullander <M1>
767 Rifle Range Road
Ringgold, GA 30736
(706)935-4878
jerryihs@catt.com
CL: Session Clerk
9632 E Brainerd Road
Chattanooga, TN 37421
(423)892-3027
cornerstone3cp@gmail.com

Ebenezer (4C)SETG2110
10699 Griffith Highway (mailing)
2400 Highway 108(physical)
Whitwell, TN 37397
(423)942-1939 <Marion>
cprevinsv@bellsouth.net
PA: Phillip Layne <M1>
10699 Griffith Highway
Whitwell, TN 37397
(423)658-5849
44philliplayne@gmail.com
CL: Lloyd Shadrick
3412 Sequatchie Mountain Road
Sequatchie, TN 37374
(423)942-1939

El Redill (C)SETG2149
875 Scenic Highway
Lawrenceville, GA 30045
(678)698-7971 <Monmouth>
FAX: (678)225-0127
mabega@juno.com
PA: Maria (Mabe) Garcia <M1>
875 Scenic Highway
Lawrenceville, GA 30045
(678)698-7971
mabega@juno.com
CL: Francia Bryon
3315 Crooked Stick Drive
Cumming, GA 30041
(678)977-8606
elenabry1@yahoo.com

Falling Water (4WC)SETG2111
PO Box 2027 (mailing)
6534 Old Dayton Pike (physical)
Hixson, TN 37343
(423)843-3050 <Hamilton>
CL: Libby Ingalls

1037 Nest Trail
Chattanooga, TN 37415
(802)734-2321
muddypotter13@gmail.com

Flint Springs (4WC)SETG2112
2225 North East Road SE (mailing)
Flint Springs Road (physical)
Cleveland, TN 37311
( ) <Bradley>
PA: Kevin Wilson <M1>
2225 North East Road SE
Cleveland, TN 37311
(423)284-6397
revkev1000@hotmail.com
CL: James F Mitchell, Jr
517 Mitchell Road SE
Cleveland, TN 37323
(423)479-7649

Glory Church of Jesus Christ(C)SETG2144
3480 Summit Ridge Parkway
Duluth, GA 30096
( ) < >
PA: David Lee <M1>
3480 Summit Ridge Parkway
Duluth, GA 30096
(404)641-4359
gcjcatl@gmail.com
CL: Session Clerk Glory Church
3480 Summit Ridge Parkway
Duluth, GA 30096

Jasper (4MWC)SETG2113
PO Box 877 (mailing)
148 College Street (physical)
Jasper, TN 37347
(423)942-2188 <Marion>
FAX: (423)942-2188
SS: James H. Patterson <M1>
6705 Ballard Drive #211
Chattanooga, TN 37421
(423)267-8568
FAX: (423)942-2188
CL: Dorris G Ross
214 Hancock Road
Jasper, TN 37347
(423)942-5224
FAX: (423)942-2188
ross37347@charter.net

Kelly's Chapel (4MC)SETG2120
3748 Alvin York Highway (mailing)
470 Highway 27 (physical)
Whitwell, TN 37397
( ) <Marion>
carolb8667@bellsouth.net
OD: Anthony Tucker <M5>
209 Rock City Trail
Lookout Mountain, GA 30750
CL: Session Clerk
3748 Alvin York Highway
Whitwell, TN 37397

Korean Livingstone (P)SETG2130
3340 Bentbill Crossing
Cumming, GA 30041
(770)912-7710
barkmoksa@hanmail.net
PA: Yang Rae Park <M1>
3340 Bentbill Crossing

TENNESSEE-GEORGIA PRESBYTERY CONTINUED

Cumming, GA 30041
(770)912-7710
barkmoksa@hanmail.net
CL: Session Clerk Korean Livingstone
3340 Bentbill Crossing
Cumming, GA 30041
(770)912-7710
barkmoksa@hanmail.net

New Hope   (4MWC)SETG2115
176 E Valley Road (mailing)
196 E Valley Road (physical)
Whitwell, TN 37397
(423)949-3951   <Sequatchie>
PA: Jimmy Byrd   <M1>
176 E Valley Road
Whitwell, TN 37397
(615)289-3347
revjimmybyrd@hotmail.com
CL: James Condra
PO Box 1001
Dunlap, TN 37327
(423)447-8126
jwcondra@bledsoe.net

Oak Grove   (4C)SETG2121
872 Alvin York Highway (mailing)
8150 Griffith Highway (physical)
Whitwell, TN 37397
( )   <Marion>
PA: Phillip H Layne   <M1>
10699 Griffith Highway
Whitwell, TN 37397
(423)658-6421
44philliplayne@gmail.com
CL: Martha S Layne
872 Alvin York Highway
Whitwell, TN 37397
(423)658-6421

Pine Hill   (4MC)SETG2117
Rt 2 Box 220 (mailing)
146 Pine Hill Road SW (physical)
McDonald, TN 37353
(423)339-2816   <Bradley>
OD: Russell Maroon   <M5>
7103 Snow Hill Road
Ooltewah, TN 37363
(423)472-1094
CL: Session Clerk
Rt 2 Box 220
McDonald, TN 37353

Prospect United   (4MC)SETG2116
310 New Murraytown Road NW
Cleveland, TN 37312
(423)476-6181   <Bradley>
prospectucpc@att.net
PA: Philip (Phil) Sumrall   <M1>
107 Barnhardt Circle
Fort Oglethorpe, GA 30742
(423)903-1938
phil.sumrall@gmail.com
CL: Patricia Stonecipher
607 Davis Road NW
Cleveland, TN 37312
(423)336-2295
g.l.stonecipher@att.net

Red Bank   (4WC)SETG2105
115 Morrison Springs Road

Chattanooga, TN 37415
(423)877-1383   <Hamilton>
rbcpchurch@gmail.com
PA: Jim Buttram   <M1>
5385 Bungalow Circle
Hixson, TN 37343
(865)938-7418
FAX: (865)483-8445
littlejimb@gmail.com
CL: Sylvia Hall
930 Sherry Circle
Hixson, TN 37343
(423)875-3668
hallcad1946@epbfi.com

Richard City   (4MWC)SETG2118
1706 Marion Avenue
South Pittsburg, TN 37380
(423)837-6533   <Marion>
CL: Bill Norman
624 19th Street
South Pittsburg, TN 37380
(423)837-6693
FAX: (423)837-8903
billnorman@catcore.com

Silverdale   (4MEWC)SETG2106
7407 Bonny Oaks Drive
Chattanooga, TN 37421
(423)892-8710   <Hamilton>
FAX: (423)892-7751
PA: George Cliff Hudson   <M1 DE>
4782 Waverly Court
Ooltewah, TN 37363
(423)238-6333
gchudson3@gmail.com
CL: Dotty Manis
7939 Clara Chase Drive
Ooltewah, TN 37363
(423)238-4021
dottmae@centurylink.net

South Pittsburg   (4MWC)SETG2123
PO Box 327 (mailing)
400 Elm Avenue (physical)
South Pittsburg, TN 37380
(423)837-6488   <Marion>
spcpc1@yahoo.com
PA: Kriss McGowan   <M1>
885 Mount Calvary Road
Whitwell, TN 37397
(423)463-8609
krissmcg658@gmail.com
CL: George Holland
214 Dixie Avenue
South Pittsburg, TN 37380
(423)837-7113
georgehollandsp@att.net

Sumach   (4MWC)SETG2124
PO Box 804 (mailing)
9203 Highway 225 N (physical)
Chatsworth, GA 30705
(706)695-4773   <Murray>
FAX: (706)695-4773
sumachcpchurch@windstream.net
PA: Tom Clark   <M1>
2089 Sumach Church Road
Chatsworth, GA 30705
(270)469-4377
CL: Carolyn Luffman

926 Long Avenue
Chatsworth, GA 30705
(706)695-4346
cizzle44@hotmail.com

Whitwell   (4C)SETG2122
7390 Highway 108
Whitwell, TN 37397
(423)658-5849   <Marion>
PA: Phillip Layne   <M1>
10699 Griffith Highway
Whitwell, TN 37397
(423)658-5849
44philliplayne@gmail.com
CL: Session Clerk
7390 Highway 108
Whitwell, TN 37397
(423)658-5849

OTHERS ON MINISTERIAL ROLL:

Barry, James C   <M1 WC>
49 Smitty's Circle
Chattanooga, TN 37415
(903)315-7998
james_barry@bellsouth.net
Brister, Glenn   <M1 WC>
3004 Delaware Avenue
McComb, MS 39648
(706)934-8629
bearmountainpenworks@gmail.com
Carver, Gary   <M1 HR>
2810 Cabin Road
Chattanooga, TN 37404
(423)698-2556
FAX: (423)629-6683
sandgatthecabin@epbfi.com
Han, Seung Chon   <M0>
3075 Landington Way
Duluth, GA 30096
kpc0191@gmail.com
(678)469-5015
Jackson, Lamar   <M1 HR>
280 Deer Ridge Drive Apt D
Dayton, TN 37321
(423)570-9348
hljaxn@charter.net
Jones, Harold   <M1 HR>
4123 Wilkesview Drive Apt A
Chattanooga, TN 37416
(478)320-4222
harold@personalcharacter.com
Kang, Jin Koo   <M1 OM>
2310 Hisway
Lawrenceville, GA 30044
(678)462-7526
agatopia@hanmail.net
Kelso, James H   <M1 HR>
131 Lords Way
Dawsonville, GA 30534
(706)216-7513
elgato@alltel.net
Kim, Mi Young   <M1 WC>
IN KOREA
Kim, Min Soo   <M1 OM>
5350 Taylor Road
Johns Creek, GA 30022
samil2110@yahoo.com
(678)622-2717
Kim, Yoong S   <M1 WC>
225 Bayswater Drive
Suwanee, GA 30024
(678)765-7018

TENNESSEE-GEORGIA PRESBYTERY CONTINUED

yoongkim1934@yahoo.com

Lee, Sarah   <M1 WC>
  (no address on file)

March, Kevin   <M1 HR>
  1701 Ray Jo Circle
  Chattanooga, TN 37421
  (423)499-4180
  kmadm1@aol.com

Martin, Theresa   <M1 WC>
  116 Crisman Street
  Chattanooga, TN 37415
  (423)903-7260 (cell)
  choochootm@usa.net

Martin, Tom   <M1 WC>
  116 Crisman Street
  Chattanooga, TN 37415
  (423)903-7260 (cell)
  choochootm@usa.net

McGowan, Rhonda   <M1 OM>
  885 Mount Calvary Road
  Whitwell, TN 37397
  (423)619-5679
  rhondam658@gmail.com

Melton, Samuel D   <M1 HR>
  2249 Bucks Pocket Road SE
  Oldfort, TN 37362
  (423)472-8467

Potter, Bruce   <M1 WC>
  1712 Marion Avenue
  South Pittsburg, TN 37380
  (423)228-4485
  brucepotter@charter.net

Prosser, Forest   <M1 RT>
  1157 Mountain Creek Road
  Chattanooga, TN 37405
  (423)877-4114
  forestprosser@comcast.net

Tolley, Robert (Butch)   <M1 WC>
  1445 New Murraytown Road NW
  Cleveland, TN 37312
  (423)837-6488
  butchtolley@hotmail.com

Turner, Glyn   <M1 M8>
  5005 Eagle Drive
  Gulfport, MS 39501
  (585)307-7715
  glynturner@outlook.com

Wright, B J   <M1 WC>
  301 25th Street
  Phenix City, AL 36867
  (334)298-2896
  bojobo3@yahoo.com

OTHER LICENTIATES ON ROLL:

Craven, Mark   <M2>
  21 Kingston Street
  Chattanooga, TN 37415
  (4230618-0169
  craven.ma@gmail.com

Garcia, Lucas   <M2>
  875 Scenic Highway
  Lawrenceville, GA 30045
  (678)698-7971
  lgvplola@hotmail.com

Hollingshed, Lee   <M2 ST>
  3612 Harmony Church Grove Road
  Dallas, GA 30132
  (770)548-0152
  leearmstrong@bellsouth.net

Kennedy, Jim   <M2>
  613 English Ivy Way
  Aberdeen, MD 21001
  jpkak@comcast.net

OTHER CANDIDATES ON ROLL:

Park, Young   <M3 ST>
  3340 Bentbill Crossing
  Cummings, GA 30041
  (404)661-6117
  barkmogun@gmail.com

Trinity Presbytery
MISSION SYNOD

GENERAL		MEMBERSHIP			CHANGES				FINANCES				
	1.Church Number	2.Active	3.Total	4.Church School	5.Prof. of Faith	6.Gains	7.Losses	8.Children Baptized	9. OUR UNITED OUT-REACH	10. Total Out-Reach Giving	11. All Other Expenses	12. Total Income Received	13. Value Church Prop. 1=1000
	1	2	3	4	5	6	7	8	9	10	11	12	13
Antioch	8101	16	16	11	0	0	0	0	1,000	18,449	11,427	14,479	325
Austin, First*	8601	43	43	7	0	0	4	0	100	1,200	675	132,604	3,000
Bertram	8605	63	171	15	0	2	2	1	1,925	17,111	132,627	88,365	1,093
Concord	8104	51	60	37	0	0	0	1	10,624	29,998	96,894	126,892	805
Daingerfield*	8106	8	9	6	0	0	1	0	0	4,367	19,193	21,263	112
Elmira Chapel	8111	60	104	45	0	0	17	0	500	54,909	178,185	165,595	2,500
Freeport	8103	24	24	4	0	0	5	0	1,200	9,416	39,248	61,269	933
Houston 1st	8606	68	110	75	0	4	0	0	51,323	115,839	355,628	513,233	3,000
Jefferson**	8109	32	35	24	0	0	24	2	0	2,746	51,285	48,016	900
Longview, 1st	8112	37	161	17	2	2	4	0	8,389	10,264	79,012	85,997	428
Marshall	8115	155	317	117	0	0	13	3	29,879	85,777	430,804	526,459	3,037
Mt. Hope	8117	1	1	6	0	0	1	0	0	333	3,867	4,200	178
Northminster+**	8610	226	226	70	0	8	57	4	0	5,616	282.787	294,695	3,628
Nueva Vida	8612	89	134	26	No Report Received			0	0	0	0	0	0
Oak Grove	8607	12	12	6	0	2	1	0	565	2,915	10,200	10,030	200
Pine Hill	8122	17	54	15	0	0	2	0	1,550	12,265	21,987	33,773	85
Pine Tree**	8113	20	28	6	0	0	44	0	0	4,212	44,988	28,537	400
Progress	8123	6	7	6	No Report Received			0	0	0	0	0	0
Round Rock+*	8611	144	144	89	1	38	7	7	300	21,500	171,134	183,667	1,445
Shepherd/Hills+**	8604	349	349	141	4	74	0	4	0	111,619	525,344	506,760	1,693
Shiloh	8125	7	41	0	0	0	1	0	0	3,288	18,056	20,261	66
Stone Oak	8608	80	143	30	0	5	2	3	0	14,400	282,746	297,146	2,500
TOTALS	22	1,511	2,191	756	7	135	184	25	107,355	526,225	2,756,087	3,163,241	26,328

*Math error corrected. **Purged roll. +Union Church

CHURCHES, PASTORS, AND CLERKS:

Antioch   (4MWC)MSTR8101
PO Box 42 (mailing)
518 N Antioch Road (physical)
Quitman, LA 71268
(318)259-7069   <Jackson>
CL: Jerry L Hanes
5104 Beech Springs Road
Quitman, LA 71268
(318)259-4246
lindaameme@hotmail.com

Austin First   (4WC)MSTR8601
6800 Woodrow Avenue
Austin, TX 78757
(512)453-8434   <Travis>
cpaustin@prodigy.net
OD: Ron Stevenson   <M5>
6800 Woodrow Avenue
Austin, TX 78757
(512)453-8434
austinfirstcp@prodigy.net
CL: Nick Hadden
6800 Woodrow Avenue
Austin, TX 78757
(512)453-8434
cpaustin@prodigy.net

Bertram   (4MEWC)MSTR8605
PO Box 242 (mailing)
430 Highway 29 (physical)
Bertram, TX 78605
(512)355-2182   <Burnet>
PA: Daryl Johnson   <M1>
425 W Vaughan Street
Bertram, TX 78605
(512)355-2182
djchurch@earthlink.net
CL: Mary Richmond
1700 Thousand Oaks Trail
Liberty Hill, TX 78642
(936)443-4765
mlrwrich@ecpi.com

Concord   (4MWC)MSTR8104
212 County Road 4705
Troup, TX 75789
(903)842-4745   <Cherokee>
FAX: (903)842-4745
revdad.duane@gmail.com
PA: Duane A Dougherty Jr   <M1>
212 County Road 4705
Troup, TX 75789
(903)842-4745
revdad.duane@gmail.com
CL: Sandy Mager
356 County Road 4629
Troup, TX 75789
(903)842-4745
stmager@yahoo.com

Daingerfield   (4MC)MSTR8106
PO Box 645 (mailing)
307 Broadnak (physical)
Daingerfield, TX 75638
(903)645-2183   <Morris>
sharjohn@windstream.net
SS: John C Lawson   <M2>
PO Box 645
Daingerfield, TX 75638
(903)645-2183
sharjohn@windstream.net
CL: John C Lawson
PO Box 645
Daingerfield, TX 75638
(903)645-2183
sharjohn@windstream.net

Elmira Chapel   (4MWC)MSTR8111
3501 Elmira Drive
Longview, TX 75605
(903)759-2069   <Gregg>
elmirachapel@aol.com
PA: James M Cantey   <M1>
3505 Elmira Drive
Longview, TX 75605
(903)452-6049
CL: Carol McDowell
3501 Elmira Drive
Longview, TX 75605
(903)759-2069
elmirachapel@aol.com

Freeport   (4C)MSTR8103
1402 W Broad Street
Freeport, TX 77541
CL: Cathy Bettoney

TRINITY PRESBYTERY CONTINUED

1149 Ash Street
Clute, TX 77531
(979)265-7630
cathybettoney@yahoo.com

Houston First   (4EWC)MSTR8606
2119 Avalon Place
Houston, TX 77019
(713)522-7821   <Harris>
FAX: (713)522-8869
firstcp@cphouston.org
PA: J Geoffrey Knight   <M1>
2119 Avalon Place
Houston, TX 77019
(713)522-7821
FAX: (713)522-8869
geoff@family.net
AP: Freddy Diaz   <M1>
2425 Holly Hall Apt B42
Houston, TX 77054
(832)305-2379
fredglobeus@yahoo.com
CL: Linda Trajo
2119 Avalon Place
Houston, TX 77019
(713)522-7821
FAX: (713)522-8869
firstcp@cphouston.org

Jefferson   (4EC)MSTR8109
501 E Jefferson Street
Jefferson, TX 75657
(903)665-2883   <Marion>
office@jeffersonpresbyterian.org
PA: Robert (Toby) Davis   <M1>
1211 AR 223 Highway
Pineville, AR 72566
(901)826-5755
pastortobydavis@gmail.com
CL: Shannon Kuhn
879 Big Cypress Marina Road
Jefferson, TX 75657
(903)407-3409
shannonkuhn1968@gmail.com

Longview First   (4WC)MSTR8112
PO Box 2349 (mailing)
2401 Alpine Street (physical)
Longview, TX 75601
(903)758-5184   <Gregg>
FAX: (903)757-2572
fcpclongview@sbcglobal.net
PA: Donald W Nunn   <M1>
203 Bridgers Hill Road
Longview, TX 75604
(903)297-6074
dwnunn@earthlink.net
CL: Mollie Benson
567 Hidden Forest
Longview, TX 75601
(903)663-0443
FAX: (903)757-2572
fcpclongview@sbcglobal.net

Marshall   (4EWC)MSTR8115
PO Box 1303 (mailing)
501 Indian Spring Road (physical)
Marshall, TX 75671
(903)935-3787   <Harrison>
FAX: (903)935-3193
info@cumberlandofmarshall.org
PA: William Rustenhaven III   <M1>
PO Box 1303
Marshall, TX 75671
(903)935-7275

FAX: (903)935-3193
rusty@cumberlandofmarshall.org
AP: Mary Kathryn Kirkpatrick   <M1>
401 1/2 Henley-Perry Drive
Marshall, TX 75670
(903)930-6236
mkkirpartick@gmail.com
CL: Shirley Jones
104 Hillcrest Terrace
Marshall, TX 75672
(903)938-3980
shopfarm75672@yahoo.com

Mt Hope (CLOSING) (4MC)MSTR8117
Box 66
Joinerville, TX 75658
(903)847-3451   <Rusk>
CL: Anna J Holman
PO Box 115
Joinerville, TX 75658
(903)847-3801

Northminster   (4U)MSTR8610
6800 Tezel Road
San Antonio, TX 78250
(210)680-4825   <Bexar>
FAX: (210)680-4826
npcoffice@npcsatx.org
CL: Marsha Schendel
8730 Prince Heights
San Antonio, TX 78254
(210)681-4231

Nueva Vida   (F)MSTR8612
18060 Keith Harrow Road
Houston, TX 77084
(832)593-8355   <Harris>
PA: Ruben D Albarracin   <M1>
7411 Magnolia Shadows Lane
Houston, TX 77095
(281)463-8617
FAX: (281)463-8617
confiaendios@hotmail.com
CL: Patricia Nunez
7303 Hollow Field W
Cypress, TX 77433
(281)855-1881
FAX: (713)533-9735

Oak Grove   (4C)MSTR8607
12951 Ranch Road 2338
Georgetown, TX 78633
( )   <Williamson>
CL: Wanda Shelton
2355 County Road 226
Florence, TX 76527
(512)579-1325

Pine Hill   (4C)MSTR8122
8236 Farm Road 3019 (mailing)
FM 3019 County Road 3281 (physical)
Winnsboro, TX 75494
( )   <Hopkins>
CL: Elizabeth Aden
404 Yates Street
Mount Vernon, TX 75457
(903)537-7288
libbya1@suddenlink.net

Pine Tree   (4MWC)MSTR8113
PO Box 5340 (mailing)
1805 Pine Tree Road (physical)
Longview, TX 75608
(903)759-2685   <Gregg>
ptcpc@sbcglobal.net

PA: John V Lindsay   <M1>
401 Greenwood Avenue
Marshall, TX 75670
(940)391-1213
CL: Darlynn Jones
1819 Flagstone Drive
Longview, TX 75605
(903)236-7310
darlynnj@att.net

Progress   (4C)MSTR8123
722 Gewin Lane (mailing)
3643 Progress Church Road (physical)
Pleasant Hill, LA 71065
(318)796-3725   <Sabine>
mamacgewin@yahoo.com
CL: Carolyn W Gewin
722 Gewin Lane
Pleasant Hill, LA 71065
(318)796-3703
mamacgewin@yahoo.com

Round Rock   (4U)MSTR8611
4010 Sam Bass Road
Round Rock, TX 78681
(512)544-2152   <Travis>
rrpc_info@roundrockpresbyterian.org
OD: Catherine Craley   <M5>
4010 Sam Bass Road
Round Rock, TX 78681
CL: Elaine B Dodd
1805 Castleguard Way
Cedar Park, TX 78613
(512)260-0310
doddeb@sbcglobal.net

Shepherd of the Hills   (4U)MSTR8604
5226 W William Cannon Drive
Austin, TX 78749
(512)892-3580   <Travis>
FAX: (512)892-6307
church@shpc.org
OD: Jim Capps   <M5>
5226 W William Cannon Drive
Austin, TX 78749
(512)892-3580
FAX: (512)358-0879
jim@shpc.org
AP: Michael Killeen   <M1>
5226 W William Cannon Drive
Austin, TX 78749
(512)560-0423
FAX: (512)358-0879
mike@shpc.org
AP: Britta Dukes   <M1>
5226 W William Cannon Drive
Austin, TX 78749
(512)892-3580
FAX: (512)358-0879
britta@shpc.org
CL: Clift Bowman
5226 W William Cannon Drive
Austin, TX 78749
(512)288-5839
FAX: (512)358-0879
cbowman24@austin.rr.com

Shiloh   (4C)MSTR8125
4928 County Road 3275 (mailing)
2467 County Road 3205 (physical)
Clarksville, TX 75426
(903)427-3785   <Red River>
shiloh.presbyterian@yahoo.com
PA: Billy Jack Holt   <M1>
5039 Highway 37 N

TRINITY PRESBYTERY CONTINUED

Clarksville, TX 75426
(903)428-9909
jackdora@windstream.net
CL: Mary Jo McGill
4928 County Road 3275
Clarksville, TX 75426
(903)427-3785
hoopnmj@yahoo.com

Stone Oak (4C)MSTR8608
20024 Crescent Oaks
San Antonio, TX 78258
(210)497-7974 <Bexar>
FAX: (210)497-8724
officemanager@satx.rr.com
PA: Kevin Colvard <M1>
27027 Harmony Hills
San Antonio, TX 78260
(205)267-9372
FAX: (210)497-8724
rev_kev@satx.rr.com
CL: Barry Elliott
2204 Sunderidge
San Antonio, TX 78260
(210)884-1749
FAX: (210)497-8724
barrydeanelliott@gmail.com

OTHERS ON MINISTERIAL ROLL:

Attema, Lee <M1 WC>
PO Box 138
San Ignacio Town, Cayo District
BELIZE
(281)728-6263
lattema@icloud.com
Attema, Leslie <M1 WC>
PO Box 138
San Ignacio Town, Cayo District
BELIZE
(281)728-6263
leslieattema@icloud.com
Bone, W Harold <M1 WC>
315 Joey Drive
Bourne, TX 78006
(210)859-5560
revdocbone@yahoo.com
Bowers, Sharon G <M1 M9>
201 Wild Buffalo Drive
Kyle, TX 78640
(512)230-7078
sharon.bowers@gmail.com
Bozeman, Robert <M1 HR>
582 Bozeman Loop
Belmont, LA 71406
(318)256-5781
bo@bozemanengineering.com
Chancellor, Hilton <M1 HR>
11905 Preserve Vista
Austin, TX 78738
(512)382-1972
hiltontex@aol.com
Davenport, Mark A <M1 WC>
323 Chimney Rock Drive #1314
Tyler, TX 75703
(205)427-4941
hoginbama@yahoo.com
Diaz, Gloria Villa <M1 OM>
2425 Holly Hall Apt B42
Houston, TX 77054
(832)758-5871
gloria@newdayinchrist.org
Gonzalez, Nora <M1 OM>
2515 Blueberry Lane
Pasadena, TX 77502
(832)202-5572

Hannah, Hugh <M1 HR>
217 Mitchell Road SE
Cleveland, TN 37323
(423)473-7852
pjhannah23@hotmail.com
Harris, Ernest <M1 HR>
610 Turtle Creek Drive
Reno, TX 75462
(903)782-9712
ernie.jeri@yahoo.com
Hoke, Walter <M1 WC>
215 Navajo Trail
Georgetown, TX 78633
(512)869-1948
Jarnagin, Mary <M1 WC>
PO Box 49102
Austin, TX 78765
(512)709-4787
marjar@yahoo.com
Kessie, John Paul <M1 HR>
138 Pony Grass Lane
Bastrop, TX 78602
(512)585-1617
jplmkessie@verizon.com
Magrill Jr, J Richard <M1 HR>
500 Miller Drive
Marshall, TX 75672
(901)685-9454
rmmagrill@gmail.com
McCarty, John <M1 M9 HR>
305 W Martindale Drive
Marshall, TX 75672
(423)650-8788
mtsjohn@gmail.com
McNeese, Mark <M1 WC>
3306 Greenlawn Parkway
Austin, TX 78757
(512)517-1042
2mam53@gmail.com
Mills, David M <M1 WC>
60 Huge Oak Street
Bertram, TX 78605
(512)355-3511
Park, Sung In <M1 OM>
10109 Loxley Lane
Austin, TX 78717
Parsons, Hugh L <M1 HR>
1526 Welch
Houston, TX 77006
(713)522-6126
p-h-parsons@comcast.net
Peters, David J <M1 IT>
4010 Sam Bass Road
Round Rock, TX 78681
(512)244-2152
Rush, Robert D <M1 OM>
12935 Quail Park Drive
Cypress, TX 77429
(832-559-1500)
robertrush832@gmail.com
Rustenhaven, William, Jr <M1 HR>
703 W Burleson Street
Marshall, TX 75670
(903)935-7056
rustenhavendolores@yahoo.com
Santillano, Ray Paul <M1 M8>
1270 Polo Road Apt 618
Columbia, SC 29223
(808)349-3308
ray.santillano@us.army.mil
Smith, David R <M1 HR>
PO Box 892
Rosepine, LA 70659
(903)297-6074

ogreyfox@att.net
Suenram, Timothy <M1 WC>
117 Saint Andrews Street
Rockport, TX 78382
(832)217-6367
9tdsdt9@gmail.com
Turner, Steven W <M1 WC>
7622 Snider Road
Gilmer, TX 75645
(903)738-8831
juxtaposition47@yahoo.com
Wayman, Sam <M1 HR OM>
707 High Hill Creek Road
LaGrange, TX 78945
(979)968-3734
samndonnawayman@gmail.com
Weston, Robert E <M1 HR>
11 Summer Bluff
San Antonio, TX 78254
(210)347-0232
FAX: (210)680-4826
rjaweston@gmail.com

OTHER LICENTIATES ON ROLL

OTHER CANDIDATES ON ROLL

Montoya, David <M3>
20900 FM 1093 Apt 11208
Richmond, TX 77407
(823)366-6897
davinay@hotmail.com

West Tennessee Presbytery
GREAT RIVERS SYNOD

	GENERAL		MEMBERSHIP			CHANGES				FINANCES			
	1.Church Number	2.Active	3.Total	4.Church School	5.Prof. of Faith	6.Gains	7.Losses	8.Children Baptized	9. OUR UNITED OUT-REACH	10. Total Out-Reach Giving	11. All Other Expenses	12. Total Income Received	13. Value Church Prop. 1=1000
	1	2	3	4	5	6	7	8	9	10	11	12	13
ACTS Korean	9436	151	171	41	81	77	5	4	800	57,620	267,117	275,518	730
Antioch Union	9401	26	27	21	No Report Received			0	0	0	0	0	343
Atwood	9101	4	6	6	0	0	1	0	350	780	5,995	9,339	200
Barren Springs	9102	0	0	0	DEFUNCT			0	0	0	0	0	25
Beech	9402	73	73	18	1	1	4	0	2,198	9,899	43,550	64,709	400
Bells Chapel*	9403	21	58	16	0	0	13	0	747	1,306	19,288	17,746	500
Bethel (TC)	9301	23	34	15	No Report Received			0	0	0	0	0	300
Bethesda	9404	25	40	20	0	0	0	0	1,700	2,000	22,354	29,209	360
Bethlehem	9405	0	0	0	DEFUNCT			0	0	0	0	0	70
Bolivar	9202	30	47	6	No Report Received			0	3,322	0	0	0	350
Bradford	9104	49	131	31	No Report Received			0	2,057	0	0	0	175
Brunswick	9302	25	60	0	0	0	1	0	908	3,013	24,129	28,727	418
Camden	9105	55	117	40	No Report Received			0	125	0	0	0	900
Camp Ground	9204	16	29	30	No Report Received			0	1,000	0	0	0	175
Claybrook	9205	8	8	8	0	0	0	0	150	1,937	11,180	14,871	10
Cloverdale	9407	0	0	0	CLOSED 10/2016			0	0	0	0	0	5
Colonial	9305	47	126	29	7	10	4	1	5,917	12,980	67,658	79,771	800
Concord*	9106	50	55	20	0	0	0	0	0	1,562	59,334	53,571	500
Cool Springs CC	9107	60	70	40	0	4	1	1	0	6,558	47,590	58,110	150
Cool Springs GC	9408	61	61	40	No Report Received			0	4,402	0	0	0	300
Davidson Chapel	9108	42	151	41	0	1	2	1	480	6,930	63,750	64,905	450
Double Springs	9109	42	60	31	0	1	2	1	3,914	6,743	32,976	39,852	565
Dresden	9110	31	39	20	2	2	2	0	3,519	6,065	26,898	35,368	315
Dyer	9409	115	115	70	1	1	2	0	13,421	22,802	107,367	134,209	1,085
Dyersburg, 1st	9410	367	597	111	7	33	12	1	43,000	160,552	592,826	711,155	5,996
Ebenezer (MC)	9206	6	6	7	No Report Received			0	200	0	0	0	50
Ebenezer (TC)	9303	128	128	60	No Report Received			0	3,000	0	0	0	380
Faith	9308	189	332	92	0	0	6	2	11,094	17,322	282,780	307,658	2,575
Fulton	9412	100	177	60	0	2	2	0	0	24,184	113,919	149,564	850
Germantown*	9310	130	166	98	7	10	0	3	17,798	32,170	223,650	253,202	1,000
Gleason	9111	21	34	15	0	2	1	0	0	0	20,523	19,942	400
Good Springs	9112	28	28	16	0	0	2	0	0	215	25,010	28,646	266
Holly Grove	9304	327	756	251	4	9	14	2	0	42,975	270,336	402,442	1,300
Hopewell (BC)	9207	34	34	34	0	0	1	0	1,871	275	17,294	15,239	30
Hopewell (WC)	9115	14	14	18	0	0	0	0	2,879	3,617	17,967	22,657	90
Humboldt	9116	70	114	35	0	0	1	0	0	17,544	74,906	94,341	1,000
Hurricane Hill	9413	25	52	12	No Report Received			0	0	0	0	0	130
Jackson, 1st	9208	269	432	176	0	3	10	0	9,646	20,791	301,376	331,969	3,000
Kenton	9414	23	38	21	2	2	0	0	3,999	9,026	38,273	39,999	475
Korean	9322	37	37	11	0	3	4	0	100	4,236	40,930	45,166	500
Lexington First	9209	65	122	14	9	13	6	7	4,397	8,220	39,236	45,655	900
Maple Springs*	9210	66	115	15	0	0	30	1	0	6,213	27,732	82,826	485
Martin	9117	41	41	41	0	0	1	0	0	50	49,151	47,355	175
Mason Hall	9415	7	20	4	No Report Received			0	0	0	0	0	100
McKenzie	9118	319	388	220	5	18	6	0	33,298	57,714	275,377	339,959	3,000
Medina	9119	13	31	13	0	0	1	0	2,571	13,194	21,991	35,816	161
Meridian	9120	65	141	35	No Report Received			0	0	0	0	0	175
Milan	9121	224	345	80	7	23	8	0	0	12,585	291,978	335,639	2,500
Mill Creek	9122	23	23	8	3	3	1	3	1,600	9,100	12,908	21,725	50
Morella	9416	6	26	6	No Report Received			0	0	0	0	0	125
Morning Sun	9314	56	78	10	0	0	3	0	3,090	8,815	74,175	79,753	750
Mt. Ararat	9417	94	224	70	5	5	49	0	0	22,911	46,510	78,698	500
Mt. Carmel	9315	27	44	12	0	0	1	0	2,259	5,806	16,908	23,091	150
Mt. Olive	9418	10	25	9	No Report Received			0	0	0	0	0	205
Mt. Vernon	9213	28	40	17	0	0	1	0	3,907	9,309	37,202	39,438	380
Mt. Zion	9214	92	196	81	3	3	2	1	15,750	34,187	239,633	255,998	2,000
New Beginning	9306	68	186	14	No Report Received			0	0	0	0	0	124
New Bethel*	9215	41	112	20	0	0	2	3	400	1,250	0	23,437	90
New Bethlehem	9420	4	4	4	0	0	0	0	225	5,470	127	2,355	8
New Ebenezer	9422	71	71	63	4	8	0	4	4,019	13,845	78,009	80,748	450
New Salem (MC)	9216	8	8	3	0	0	0	0	0	0	8,903	7,451	95

West Tennessee Presbytery   (Continued)
GREAT RIVERS SYNOD

	GENERAL		MEMBERSHIP			CHANGES			FINANCES			
	1.Church Number	2.Active	3.Total	4.Church School	5.Prof. of Faith	6.Gains	7.Losses	8.Children Baptized	9. OUR UNITED OUT-REACH	10. Total Out-Reach Giving	11. All Other Expenses	12. Total Income Received	13. Value Church Prop. 1=1000
	1	2	3	4	5	6	7	8	9	10	11	12	13
New Salem (SC)	9316	70	70	15	0	0	0	0	300	2,505	65,851	79,043	98
New Salem (WC)	9124	17	17	22	0	0	0	0	4,777	20,495	61,103	48,810	100
Newbern	9419	49	59	25	0	0	2	0	8,319	28,760	191,651	134,080	709
North Union	9423	68	75	40	No Report Received			0	0	0	0	0	360
Nuevo Empezar	9324	23	25	17	No Report Received			0	2,967	0	30,817	31,718	0
Oak Grove	9217	32	108	22	No Report Received			0	200	0	0	0	300
Oak Hill	9125	11	11	10	0	0	0	0	386	1,098	3,700	3,859	0
Olive Branch**	9312	166	241	143	5	14	269	1	2,194	16,140	202,245	248,340	1,950
Oliver's Chapel	9127	30	74	30	No Report Received			0	0	0	0	0	314
Olivet	9220	193	332	100	0	1	5	1	6,581	27,763	296,067	296,830	2,108
Palestine (DC)	9424	5	5	7	No Report Received			0	0	0	0	0	50
Palestine (HC)	9221	49	107	30	1	0	2	1	4,992	7,061	52,680	54,906	150
Parsons, First	9222	29	50	8	0	1	0	0	0	0	34,040	32,218	550
Pleasant Green	9129	10	20	8	No Report Received			0	0	0	0	0	100
Pleasant Grove	9317	10	22		No Report Received			0	0	0	0	0	32
Pleasant Union	9318	138	138	20	0	0	2	1	0	6,888	93,142	106,170	300
Poplar Grove*	9425	42	76	11	0	5	0	1	4,683	9,230	30,100	46,830	350
Protemus	9426	40	45	52	1	1	7	0	6,120	18,478	41,632	61,197	125
Ramer	9223	16	16	12	No Report Received			0	532	0	0	0	100
Roellen	9428	6	6	12	0	0	1	0	500	1,972	9,750	10,165	60
Rutherford	9429	24	30	18	2	3	1	0	4,497	11,310	173,852	42,142	300
Salem	9430	8	17	16	No Report Received			0	0	0	0	0	135
Savannah 1st*	9224	101	134	59	7	7	16	1	31,787	36,371	219,542	226,071	2,500
Selmer, Ct. Ave.	9225	61	82	16	No Report Received			0	2,400	0	0	0	550
Sharon	9130	16	29	12	0	0	1	0	1,000	6,895	28,733	24,075	589
Shiloh (AC)	9226	35	35	23	0	2	2	0	2,055	6,572	18,674	29,779	95
Shiloh (CC)	9131	31	46	0	0	0	4	0	2,137	7,022	36,062	36,850	175
Trezevant	9132	9	9	9	0	0	18	0	0	0	7,782	13,855	150
Troy	9432	17	24	15	No Report Received			0	69	0	0	0	100
Union City	9433	105	203	69	No Report Received			0	0	0	0	0	2,000
Walnut Grove	9320	14	28	18	No Report Received			0	0	0	0	0	300
West Union*	9321	90	224	58	0	0	3	0	2,200	5,335	112,099	127,368	1,500
Woodward's Ch	9434	12	12	20	No Report Received			0	0	0	0	0	30
Yorkville	9435	26	59	22	No Report Received			0	500	0	0	0	575
Zion	9133	4	14	5	No Report Received			0	400	0	0	0	98
TOTALS	93	5,554	8,948	3,288	83	205	516	35	298,909	837,986	5,450,303	6,174,899	56,919

*Math error corrected. **Purged roll.

CHURCHES, PASTORS, AND CLERKS:

ACTS Korean   (Provisional)GRWT9436
  6524 Summer Avenue
  Memphis, TN 38134
  (901)381-4790
  usyoun61@hotmail.com
PA: Daniel Youn   <M1>
  6524 Summer Avenue
  Memphis, TN 38134
  (901)381-4790
  usyoun61@hotmail.com
CL: Session Clerk
  6524 Summer Avenue
  Memphis, TN 38134
  (901)381-4790
  usyoun61@hotmail.com

Antioch Union   (4C)GRWT9401
  6765 Mount Olive Road (mailing)
  486 W Newman Glover Road (physical)
  Union City, TN 38261
  (731)885-6435   <Obion>
PA: Mitch Boulton   <M1>
  80 Topsy Lane
  Savannah, TN 38372
  (731)487-2318
  steelermitch@gmail.com
CL: Sharon Barnes
  5765 Mount Olive Road
  Union City, TN 38261
  (731)885-2521

Atwood   (4MWC)GRWT9101
  PO Box 203 (mailing)
  14010 Church Street (physical)
  Atwood, TN 38220

(731)662-7692   <Carroll>
rickylong@tennesseetel.net
SS: Richard Reed   <M2>
  236 Madison Street
  Dyer, TN 38330
  (731)692-3604
CL: Ricky Long
  230 Brooks Road
  Atwood, TN 38220
  (731)662-7692
  rickylong@tennesseetel.net

Barren Springs   (4C)GRWT9102
  1860 Barren Spring Church Road
  Hollow Rock, TN 38342
  ( )   <Carroll>
(DEFUNCT)

Beech   (4MEC)GRWT9402

WEST TENNESSEE PRESBYTERY CONTINUED

PO Box 553 (mailing)
880 Beech Chapel Road (physical)
Union City, TN 38261
(731)885-1710   <Obion>
bethcooks54@hotmail.com
PA: Bobby D Williams   <M1>
844 W Highway 22
Union City, TN 38261
(731)885-1710
CL: Beth Williams
844 W Highway 22
Union City, TN 38281
(731)885-1710
bethcooks54@hotmail.com

Bells Chapel   (2WC)GRWT9403
309 Bells Chapel Road
Dyer, TN 38330
(731)643-6729   <Gibson>
LS: Dennis Emerson   <M6>
137 Midway Road Apt 25
Dyer, TN 38330
(731)643-6539
dennied53@hotmail.com
CL: Dennis Emerson
137 Midway Road Apt 25
Dyer, TN 38330
(731)643-6539
dennied53@hotmail.com

Bethel (TC)   (1WC)GRWT9301
PO Box 114 (mailing)
Tipton, TN 38071
3406 Tracy Road (physical)
Atoka, TN 38004
(901)837-0343   <Tipton>
SS: Kenneth L McCoy   <M1>
1422 Walton Road
Memphis, TN 38117
(901)682-0891
CL: Cindy Rhodes
PO Box 114
Tipton, TN 38071
(901)837-7793

Bethesda   (4MWC)GRWT9404
10755 State Highway 188 (mailing)
9651 State Highway 188 (physical)
Friendship, TN 38034
(   )   <Crockett>
jirvin527@yahoo.com
CL: Jim Irvin
10755 State Highway 188
Friendship, TN 38034
(731)414-7180
jirvin527@yahoo.com

Bethlehem   (4C)GRWT9405
1469 Bethlehem Road
Union City, TN 38261
(   )   <Obion>
(DEFUNCT)

Bolivar   (4MWC)GRWT9202
PO Box 413 (mailing)
448 Nuckolls Road (physical)
Bolivar, TN 38008
(731)658-5459   <Hardeman>
CL: Faye Cromwell
2995 Naylor Road
Toone, TN 38381

(731)658-5329
cromwellr@bellsouth.net

Bradford   (4MWC)GRWT9104
PO Box 186 (mailing)
117 Highway 45 S (physical)
Bradford, TN 38316
(731)742-3397   <Gibson>
CL: Don Lannom
PO Box 85
Bradford, TN 38316
(731)742-3838

Brunswick   (4MWC)GRWT9302
PO Box 67 (mailing)
4976 Brunswick Road (physical)
Brunswick, TN 38014
(901)386-0105   <Shelby>
CL: Mary Ellen Starks
PO Box 142
Brunswick, TN 38014
(901)388-9862

Camden   (4MWC)GRWT9105
239 W Main Street
Camden, TN 38320
(731)584-7598   <Benton>
FAX: (731)584-7598
camdencpoffice@bellsouth.net
SS: Carey Womack   <M1>
114 Doris Street
Camden, TN 38320
(731)220-3900
FAX: (731)584-7598
camdencppastor@bellsouth.net
CL: Nancy D Arnold
PO Box 214
Camden, TN 38320
(731)441-2778
FAX: (731)584-7598
arnldnnc@aol.com

Camp Ground   ,(4C)GRWT9204
2535 Middleburg Road
Decaturville, TN 38329
(   )   <Decatur>
SS: David Hawley   <M1>
127 John Holt Road
Beech Bluff, TN 38313
(731)427-7284
dhpreach@aol.com
CL: Fred Brasher
771 Middleburg Road
Decaturville, TN 38329
(731)852-4400

Claybrook   (C)GRWT9205
1300 US Highway 412 E (mailing)
1364 US Highway 412 E (physical)
Jackson, TN 38305
(   )   <Madison>
SS: Jerald D Smith   <M1>
2625 Beech Bluff Road
Beech Bluff, TN 38313
(731)427-9316
jergensmith@aol.com
CL: Martha Wolfe
1300 US Highway 412 E
Jackson, TN 38305
(731)424-4979
jergensmith@aol.com

Cloverdale   (2C)GRWT9407
3541 Cloverdale Road
Obion, TN 38240
(   )   <Obion>
CLOSED 10/2016

Colonial   (4MWC)GRWT9305
1500 S Perkins Road
Memphis, TN 38117
(901)682-4747   <Shelby>
SS: Lisa Anderson   <M1 M9>
1790 Faxon Avenue
Memphis, TN 38112
(901)246-8052
anderli90@gmail.com
AP: Emily Trapp   <M3>
4750 Harvest Knoll Cove N
Memphis, TN 38125
(901)756-4738
CL: George R Marston
1042 LaRue Place
Memphis, TN 38122
(901)685-1488
put11599@bellsouth.net

Concord   (3MWC)GRWT9106
153 Herd Law Road
Trenton, TN 38382
(   )   <Gibson>
PA: Don McCurley   <M1>
4036 McAllister Street
Milan, TN 38358
(731)723-3623
dcmccurley@hotmail.com
CL: Don Gibson
4225 Christmasville Road
Medina, TN 38355
(731)783-0992

Cool Springs CC   (4C)GRWT9107
240 Little Grove Road
Lavinia, TN 38348
(   )   <Carroll>
LS: Robert Barger   <M6>
7127 Highway 104 W
Lavinia, TN 38348
(731)987-2477
rbarger104@att.net
CL: Ann Hammett
8725 US Highway 70
Cedar Grove, TN 38321
(731)987-2516

Cool Springs GC   (4MWC)GRWT9408
37 Cool Spring Road
Trimble, TN 38259
(731)643-6153   <Gibson>
SS: Steve Rogers   <M3>
119 East Drive
Newbern, TN 38059
(731)882-2229
srtn68@yahoo.com
CL: Mike Pruett
119 Heritage Drive
Rutherford, TN 38369
(731)665-6348
mdpruett@tennesseetel.net

Davidson Chapel   (4MWC)GRWT9108
399 Laneview Concord Road

WEST TENNESSEE PRESBYTERY CONTINUED

Trenton, TN 38382
(731)618-1521
FAX: (731)664-3735
dale.cavaness@horne-llp.com <Gibson>
PA: Corey Cummings   <M1>
   1023 W Woodrow Street
   Milan, TN 38358
   (731)686-1851
   corey@milancp.org
CL: Dale Cavaness
   2093 Brentwood Drive
   Milan, TN 38358
   (731)618-1521
   FAX: (731)664-3735
   dale.cavaness@horne-llp.com

Double Springs   (4WC)GRWT9109
   18 Double Springs Road
   Humboldt, TN 38343
   (731)787-6422   <Gibson>
PA: Russell Little   <M1>
   29 Cotton Row
   Medina, TN 38355
   (731)783-3565
   russelllittle@bellsouth.net
CL: Linda Fisher
   65 Spencer Drive
   Medina, TN 38355
   (731)613-8355
   lfisher@eplus.net

Dresden   (4MWC)GRWT9110
   PO Box 131 (mailing)
   121 S Wilson Street (physical)
   Dresden, TN 38225
   ( )   <Weakley>
CL: Martha Killebrew
   PO Box 131
   Dresden, TN 38225
   (731)364-3294
   FAX: (731)364-3500
   killebrewm@frontiernet.net

Dyer   (4MEWC)GRWT9409
   PO Box 181 (mailing)
   256 E College Street (physical)
   Dyer, TN 38330
   (731)692-2594   <Gibson>
   dyercpchurch@gmail.com
PA: Johnny E Watson   <M1>
   7 Hickory Lane
   Metropolis, IL 62960
   (731)414-3065
   jewatson01@gmail.com
CL: Johnny Ward
   46 Old Dyer Trenton Road
   Dyer, TN 38330
   (731)692-2594
   ward3363@bellsouth.net

Dyersburg First   (4WC)GRWT9410
   2280 Parr Avenue
   Dyersburg, TN 38024
   (731)285-5703   <Dyer>
   FAX: (731)285-5792
   cpoffice@cumberlandchurch.com
PA: Cory Williams   <M1>
   585 Tater Hill Road
   Newbern, TN 38059
   (901)486-5981
   coromis@hotmail.com

AP: Annetta Camp   <M1>
   2303 Mill Creek Road
   Halls, TN 38040
   (731)285-5703
   FAX: (731)285-5792
   annetta@cumberlandchurch.com
CL: William Mallard
   198 Walnut Lane Ext
   Dyersburg, TN 38024
   (731)285-0837
   FAX: (731)287-0873
   wem1950@bellsouth.net

Ebenezer (MC)   (2EWC)GRWT9206
   Main Street
   Mercer, TN 38392
   (731)935-2391   <Madison>
CL: Pope Mulherin
   8 Prestwick Drive
   Jackson, TN 38305
   (731)427-3113

Ebenezer (TC)   (4WC)GRWT9303
   70 Witherington Road
   Mason, TN 38049
   ( )   <Tipton>
CL: Ann Burlison
   564 Baskin Road
   Burlison, TN 38015
   (901)294-3614
   aburlison@tipton-county.com

Faith   (4WC)GRWT9308
   3427 Appling Road
   Bartlett, TN 38133
   (901)377-0526   <Shelby>
   FAX: (901)382-2600
   faithcumberlandp@bellsouth.net
PA: Steven Shelton   <M1>
   7886 Farmhill Cove
   Bartlett, TN 38135
   (901)377-0526
   faithcpcpastor@gmail.com
CL: Karen Patten
   5728 North Street
   Bartlett, TN 38134
   (901)237-0535
   mkpatten@outlook.com

Fulton   (4MWC)GRWT9412
   PO Box 5343 (mailing)
   1159 Parker Road (physical)
   South Fulton, TN 38257
   (731)479-9912   <Obion>
PA: David Bayer   <M1>
   3090 Tom Counce Road
   South Fulton, TN 38257
   (731)479-3060
   dbayer9060@gmail.com
CL: Donald R Moore
   155 Cox Road
   Fulton, KY 42041
   (270)436-2723
   donaldmoore9@aol.com

Germantown   (4EWC)GRWT9310
   2385 Riverdale
   Germantown, TN 38138
   (901)755-3884   <Shelby>
   FAX: (901)759-3653
   cpcgww@aol.com

PA: William Warren   <M1>
   7139 Toro Cove
   Germantown, TN 38138
   (901)755-8058
   cpcgww@aol.com
CL: Iva McCutchen
   1240 Bristol Drive
   Memphis, TN 38119
   (901)761-0575
   ivesmc@att.net

Gleason   (4MC)GRWT9111
   190 David Court (mailing)
   McKenzie, TN 38201
   171 Smyth Lane (physical)
   Gleason, TN 38229
   (731)648-5343   <Weakley>
PA: James (Jim) Pinnell   <M1>
   1525 Parks Well Road
   Gleason, TN 38229
   (731)648-5078
   revpinnell@hotmail.com
CL: Donald Ray Stephens
   190 David Court
   McKenzie, TN 38201
   (731)352-5852
   tuvart@charter.net

Good Springs   (4WC)GRWT9112
   180 Barham Road (mailing)
   Good Springs Road (physical)
   Dukedom, TN 38226
   ( )   <Weakley>
SS: Dennis Weaver   <M2 ST>
   1750 Government Road
   Princeton, KY 42245
   (731)592-9054
   dsweaver@memphisseminary.edu
CL: Loretta Barham
   180 Barham Road
   Dukedom, TN 38226
   (731)469-9555

Holly Grove   (4MWC)GRWT9304
   4538 Holly Grove Road
   Brighton, TN 38011
   (901)476-8379   <Tipton>
   FAX: (901)476-3324
   hollygrovecpchurch@att.net
PA: Peter Jeffrey   <M1>
   61 Northwood Drive
   McKenzie, TN 38201
   (731)352-0792
   jeffreyp@bethelu.edu
AP: Debbie Marshall   <M1>
   1494 Bucksnort Road
   Covington, TN 38019
   (901)494-1251
   dsmarshall05@att.net
CL: Donna E Lindley
   4538 Holly Grove Road
   Brighton, TN 38011
   (901)476-8379
   FAX: (901)476-3324
   hollygrovecpchurch@att.net

Hopewell (BC)   (2EWC)GRWT9207
   2309 Saulsbury Road (mailing)
   289 Hopewell Road (physical)
   Walnut, MS 38683
   ( )   <Benton>

WEST TENNESSEE PRESBYTERY CONTINUED

PA: Byron Forester   <M1>
2376 Eastwood Place
Memphis, TN 38112
(901)324-1707
bforester@bellsouth.net
CL: Kathy D Wilburn
2309 Saulsbury Road
Walnut, MS 38683
(662)223-6447
kwilburn@fareselaw.com

Hopewell (WC)   (2WC)GRWT9115
1061 Gaylord Road (mailing)
Route 1 Box 91 (physical)
Sharon, TN 38255
( )   <Weakley>
CL: Lonnie Hazlewood
1061 Gaylord Road
Sharon, TN 38255
(731)973-2426
lonminh@citlink.net

Humboldt   (4MEWC)GRWT9116
2375 E Mitchell Street
Humboldt, TN 38343
(731)784-2703   <Gibson>
pastor@humboldtcpc.org
PA: Robert Harris   <M1>
619 N 24th Avenue
Humboldt, TN 38343
(731)420-6067
pastor@humboldtcpc.org
CL: Carolyn Hunley
6 Clinton Road
Humboldt, TN 38343
(731)784-2031
carolynhunley16@yahoo.com

Hurricane Hill   (4C)GRWT9413
Newbern, TN 38059
( )   <Dyer>
CL: Holly Powers
684 Hurricane Hill Road
Dyersburg, TN 38024
(731)285-4436

Jackson First   (4WC)GRWT9208
1730 US Highway 45 Bypass
Jackson, TN 38305
(731)664-1632   <Madison>
FAX: (731)664-1633
fcpc1730@bellsouth.net
PA: Terry M Hunley   <M1>
48 Charleston Square
Jackson, TN 38305
(731)660-5685
thunley1@charter.net
CL: Glenn Fesmire
7 Broadfield Drive
Jackson, TN 38301
(731)234-9959
glennfes@aol.com

Kenton   (4MEWC)GRWT9414
301 W College Street
Kenton, TN 38233
( )   <Obion>
LS: Charles McCall   <M6>
549 Mason Hall Road
Trimble, TN 38259
(731)297-3288

cmccall@ycinet.net
CL: Paul E Williams
206 Hillside Street
Kenton, TN 38233
(731)749-5656

Korean   (P)GRWT9322
7565 Macon Road
Cordova, TN 38018
(901)755-9101   <Shelby>
kcomemphis@gmail.com
PA: Ho-Jin Lee   <M1>
7565 Macon Road
Cordova, TN 38018
(901)754-7070
hojin.lee70@gmail.com
CL: Gong Dickens
7565 Macon Road
Cordova, TN 38018
(901)758-1130

Lexington First   (4MWC)GRWT9209
PO Box 11 (mailing)
931 N Broad Street (physical)
Lexington, TN 38351
(731)968-7176   <Henderson>
patfreelandjones@yahoo.com
PA: C William Jones Jr   <M1>
109 Lakewood Drive
Lexington, TN 38351
(731)967-7618
patfreelandjones@yahoo.com
CL: Teresa Ferguson
7747 Middleburg Road
Scotts Hill, TN 38374
(731)968-9079

Maple Springs   (4MWC)GRWT9210
2625 Beech Bluff Road (mailing)
2005 Beech Bluff Road (physical)
Beech Bluff, TN 38313
(731)424-4065   <Henderson>
PA: Jerald D Smith   <M1>
2625 Beech Bluff Road
Beech Bluff, TN 38313
(731)427-9316
jergensmith@aol.com
CL: Tricia Fowler
37 Fowler Cut Off Road
Beech Bluff, TN 38313
(731)423-1255
tfowler@firstbankonline.com

Martin   (4MWC)GRWT9117
312 E Main Street
Martin, TN 38237
(731)587-3222   <Weakley>
FAX: (731)487-6484
cathyjahr@charter.net
PA: Michael T Lavender   (M1)
308 Main Street
Martin, TN 38237
(731)431-9127
mike_lavender@yahoo.com
CL: Cathy Jahr
142 Rolling Meadows
Martin, TN 38237
(731)587-6484
cathyjahr@charter.net

Mason Hall   (2EWC)GRWT9415

549 Mason Hall Road (mailing)
Trimble, TN 38259
1861 CP Church Road (physical)
Kenton, TN 38233
( )   <Obion>
mccall.cmccall@gmail.com
CL: Charles McCall
549 Mason Hall Road
Trimble, TN 38259
(731)431-8195
mccall.cmccall@gmail.com

McKenzie   (4WC)GRWT9118
PO Box 133 (mailing)
16835 Highland Drive (physical)
McKenzie, TN 38201
(731)352-2440   <Carroll>
FAX: (731)352-3101
church@mckenziecpc.org
PA: Kevin L Wood   <M1>
339 David Street
McKenzie, TN 38201
(865)228-0710
FAX: (865)588-8581
revkevbuford1972@gmail.com
AP: Garrett Burns   <M1>
387 Forrest Avenue
McKenzie. TN 38201
(731)535-3126
gburns2888@gmail.com
CL: June Perritt
PO Box 133
McKenzie, TN 38201
(731)352-2440
FAX: (731)352-3101
church@mckenziecpc.org

Medina   (4EC)GRWT9119
104 Cumberland Street
Medina, TN 38355
(731)618-0192   <Gibson>
PA: Linda H Glenn   <M1>
49 Mason Road
Threeway, TN 38343
(731)618-0192
lindahglenn@click1.net
CL: Kiara Castleman
307 W Main Street
Greenfield, TN 38230
(731)487-3363
kiascham@gmail.com

Meridian   (4C)GRWT9120
1099 Adams Road (mailing)
2590 Meridian Road (physical)
Greenfield, TN 38230
( )   <Weakley>
CL: David McBride
1099 Adams Road
Greenfield, TN 38230
(731)235-3058

Milan   (4WC)GRWT9121
6083 S First Street
Milan, TN 38358
(731)686-1851
office@milancp.org
PA: Doy L Daniels Jr   <M1>
1095 Crestview Drive
Milan, TN 38358
(731)686-1851

WEST TENNESSEE PRESBYTERY CONTINUED

FAX: (731)723-9324
revdrdoy@gmail.com
CL: Ronnie Parks
62 Hughes Loop
Milan, TN 38358
(731)686-3065
ronnieparks@bellsouth.net

Mill Creek   (4C)GRWT9122
239 Smith Street (mailing)
434 Mill Creek Road (physical)
Puryear, TN 38251
( )   <Henry>
PA: Anne Hames   <M1 M9>
118 Paris Street
McKenzie, TN 38201
(731)352-4066
FAX: (731)352-4069
hamesa@bethelu.edu
CL: Richard E Vincent
239 Smith Street
Puryear, TN 38251
(731)247-5211
richardearlvincent@yahoo.com

Morella   (2EWC)GRWT9416
51 Morella Road
Kenton, TN 38233
( )   <Gibson>
CL: J C Reed
121 Tull Road
Kenton, TN 38233
(731)749-5545

Morning Sun   (4MC)GRWT9314
2682 Morning Sun Road
Cordova, TN 38016
(901)382-3439   <Shelby>
mscpc13@gmail.com
CL: Gwen Hromada
4350 Thorpe Drive
Mason, TN 38049
(901)466-1154
gwen247@aceweb.com

Mt Ararat   (4WC)GRWT9417
1465 Troy-Hickman Road
Union City, TN 38261
(731)536-5406   <Obion>
PA: Robert A Smith   <M1>
PO Box 501
Newbern, TN 38059
(731)627-3332
ras1957@bellsouth.net
CL: Bobby Hall
664 Mill Creek Road
Troy, TN 38260
(731)536-4798

Mt Carmel   (4C)GRWT9315
106 E Marginal Street (mailing)
2355 Union Drive (physical)
Somerville, TN 38068
( )   <Fayette>
PA: Clinton Buck   <M1>
PO Box 770068
Memphis, TN 38117
(901)682-2358
clintonbuck@aol.com
CL: Harry N Wiles
106 E Marginal Street

Somerville, TN 38068
(901)465-9733

Mt Olive   (4MEC)GRWT9418
76 Yorkville Highway (mailing)
42 Mt Olive Road (physical)
Dyer, TN 38330
( )   <Gibson>
PA: Charles Fike   <M1>
2070 N 1st Street
Milan, TN 38358
(731)686-0224
CL: Carolyn Martin
76 Yorkville Highway
Dyer, TN 38330
(731)692-2773

Mt Vernon   (4MC)GRWT9213
3101 Mt Vernon Road
Ramer, TN 38367
(731)645-6420   <McNairy>
CL: Larry Gage
130 Shiloh Terrace Drive
Selmer, TN 38375
(731)645-6828
lgage6828@charter.net

Mt Zion   (4MWC)GRWT9214
480 County Road 401
Falkner, MS 38629
(662)837-7013   <Tippah>
FAX: (662)837-7969
info@mtzioncpc.org
PA: Thomas Richie Lockhart   <M1>
700 County Road 343
Falkner, MS 38629
(662)837-4281
nmsdiamonddawgs@yahoo.com
CL: Dennis Bogue
105 Gowdy Drive
Ripley, MS 38663
(662)837-0265
dennis.bogue@yahoo.com

New Beginning   (4C)GRWT9306
2300 Frayser Boulevard
Memphis, TN 38127
(901)353-4011
PA: Craig Wilson   <M1>
2300 Frayser Boulevard
Memphis, TN 38127
(901)277-4066
craigwilson2300@yahoo.com
SC: Elnora McKinzie
1111 Holmes Street
Memphis, TN 38122
(870)377-2174

New Bethel   (4C)GRWT9215
3708 New Bethel Road
Selmer, TN 38375
( )   <McNairy>
CL: Preston King
3708 New Bethel Road
Selmer, TN 38375
(731)645-3150
kingpreston2828@yahoo.com

New Bethlehem   (2EWC)GRWT9420
1585 Bethlehem Road (mailing)
825 Bethlehem Road (physical)

Newbern, TN 38059
( )   <Dyer>
CL: Mary Bell Murray
1585 Bethlehem Road
Newbern, TN 38059
(731)627-2332
murrayc2@juno.com

New Ebenezer   (4MEWC)GRWT9422
PO Box 364 (mailing)
1606 Ebenezer Road (physical)
Troy, TN 38260
(731)536-4936   <Obion>
PA: Mitch Boulton   <M1>
80 Topsy Lane
Savannah, TN 38372
(731)487-2318
steelermitch@gmail.com
CL: Lisa Hamm
656 Ebenezer Road
Troy, TN 38260
lhammnewebenezer@hotmail.com

New Salem (MC)   (4C)GRWT9216
453 New Salem Road
Bethel Springs, TN 38315
( )   <McNairy>
CL: Malcolm Dickson
153 Harris Road
Bethel Springs, TN 38315
(731)934-7282
FAX: (731)934-0736
robert.dickson@aol.com

New Salem (SC)   (4MWC)GRWT9316
6813 Salem Road
Lakeland, TN 38002
(901)829-3241   <Shelby>
FAX: (901)829-3241
ptcriss@hotmail.com
PA: Paul T Criss   <M1>
6831 Salem Road
Lakeland, TN 38002
(901)626-8462
ptcriss@hotmail.com
CL: Patty Butler Little
6909 Salem Road
Lakeland, TN 38002
(901)829-3218

New Salem (WC)   (3C)GRWT9124
3220 Sharon Highway 89 (mailing)
Highway 89 (physical)
Sharon, TN 38255
( )   <Weakley>
SS: Kermit Travis   <M1>
3220 Sharon Highway 89
Dresden, TN 38225
(731)364-2315
CL: John C Clark
215 Rambo Road
Sharon, TN 38255
(731)364-3921
jcjclark@frontiernet.net

Newbern   (4MWC)GRWT9419
310 E Main
Newbern, TN 38059
(731)627-3646   <Dyer>
SS: Steve Rogers   <M3>
119 East Drive

WEST TENNESSEE PRESBYTERY CONTINUED

Newbern, TN 38059
(731)882-2229
srtn68@yahoo.com
CL: Jamie Kay Berkley
403 E Main Street
Newbern, TN 38059
(731)676-8626
jamiekayb@hotmail.com

North Union   (4EC)GRWT9423
15 Cardwell Road (mailing)
Dyer, TN 38330
78 Preacher Dowland Road (physical)
Kenton, TN 38233
(731)673-4122   <Gibson>
CL: Chad Murray
2067 Locust Grove Road
Newbern, TN 38059
(731)676-6027
chadgfc@gmail.com

Nuevo Empezar   (4EC)GRWT9324
3442 Tutwiler
Memphis, TN 38122
(901)644-0513
PA: Bertha Davis   <M1>
2242 Slocum Avenue
Memphis, TN 38127
(901)644-0513
CL: Lydia Langbein
4675 Glenmore Lane
Millington, TN 38053
(901)487-6336
lile@rittermail.com

Oak Grove   (4MC)GRWT9217
3655 Talley Store Road
Henderson, TN 38340
(731)989-3825   <Chester>
PA: Laura Todd   <M1>
3303 Decker Street
Bartlett, TN 38134
(901)496-1443
littlelaurarose@yahoo.com
CL: Don Terry
1450 Braund Road
Henderson, TN 38340
(731)989-7982
FAX: (731)989-7982

Oak Hill   (1C)GRWT9125
5820 Highway 69 N (mailing)
5135 Highway 59 N (physical)
Paris, TN 38242
(   )   <Henry>
CL: Theresa Rushing
5820 Highway 69 N
Paris, TN 38242
(731)642-3499
trushing@utm.edu

Olive Branch   (4MWC)GRWT9312
8161 Germantown Road
Olive Branch, MS 38654
(662)893-7347   <Desoto>
FAX: (901)893-7347
officefcpc@yahoo.com
PA: James L Ratliff   <M1>
4027 Club View Drive
Memphis, TN 38125
(901)758-0125
pastorjimfcpc@yahoo.com
CL: Charlie Trapp

4750 Harvest Knoll Cove N
Memphis, TN 38125
(901)626-2952
charliebethtrapp@bellsouth.net

Oliver's Chapel   (4WC)GRWT9127
85 Olivers Chapel Road (mailing)
22 Olivers Chapel Road (physical)
Bradford, TN 38316
(731)742-3559   <Gibson>
FAX: (731)742-3994
mpybas@yahoo.com
PA: Sam Harwell   <M1>
23 Lake Hayes Estates Road
Trenton, TN 38382
(731)414-2153
sambharl@yahoo.com
CL: Marcy Tahmazian
85 Olivers Chapel Road
Bradford, TN 38316
(731)742-3097
FAX: (731)742-3994
mpybas@yahoo.com

Olivet   (4MWC)GRWT9220
6095 Highway 226
Savannah, TN 38372
(731)925-2685   <Hardin>
olivetcp@bellsouth.net
CL: Walton Williams
10875 Highway 64
Savannah, TN 38372
(731)412-7569

Palestine (DC)   (4C)GRWT9424
985 Palestine Road (mailing)
Route 2 (physical)
Newbern, TN 38059
(   )   <Dyer>
SS: Donnie Ragsdale   <M1>
915 S Olive Street
Union City, TN 38261
(731)885-0014

CL: Session Clerk Palestine CP Church
985 Palestine Road
Newbern, TN 38059
(731)627-9227

Palestine (HC)   (4MWC)GRWT9221
1010 Nobles Road (mailing)
6835 Highway 22A (physical)
Lexington, TN 38351
(   )   <Henderson>
mcadamsjc@bellsouth.net
PA: Wayne Tompkins   <M1>
548 E Columbia Road 23
Emerson, AR 71740
(870)807-2874
waynetompkinsministries@yahoo.com
CL: Cheri McAdams
1010 Nobles Road
Luray, TN 38352
(731)614-0433
mcadamsjc@bellsouth.net

Parsons First   (4MEWC)GRWT9222
PO Box 141 (mailing)
114 Virginia Avenue N (physical)
Parsons, TN 38363
(731)847-7148   <Decatur>
PA: David Hawley   <M1>
127 John Holt Road

Beech Bluff, TN 38313
(731)427-7284
haw177@aol.com
CL: Tony Collett
6636 Rockhouse Road
Linden, TN 37096
(931)589-5103
tacollett@tds.net

Pleasant Green   (4C)GRWT9129
c/o Helen Watkins (mailing)
2776 Highway 105
Trezevant, TN 38258
712 Idlewild-Holly Leaf (physical)
Atwood, TN 38220
(   )   <Gibson>
OD: Keith Pence   <M5>
PO Box 703
Gleason, TN 38229
(731)819-2553
CL: Helen Watkins
2776 Highway 105
Trezevant, TN 38258
(731)669-1601
hjoy1@charter.net

Pleasant Grove   (2C)GRWT9317
2625 Pleasant Grove Road (mailing)
2320 Pleasant Grove Road (physical)
Moscow, TN 38057
(901)877-3287   <Fayette>
CL: Jack Joyner
2625 Pleasant Grove Road
Moscow, TN 38057
(901)877-3287

Pleasant Union   (4MWC)GRWT9318
9251 Brunswick Road
Millington, TN 38053
(901)829-3262   <Shelby>
PA: Matthew Dean Cunningham   <M1>
1646 Brighton-Clopton Road
Brighton, TN 38011
(901)475-4252
mcunningham0528@comcast.net
CL: Patricia Parks
8995 Mulberry Road
Atoka, TN 38004
(901)829-3012
pittypat28@aol.com

Poplar Grove   (4C)GRWT9425
492 Church Road
Halls, TN 38040
(731)627-2445   <Lauderdale>
2Orrs.mn@charter.net
PA: Johnnie Welch   <M1>
PO Box 1506
Dyersburg, TN 38025
(731)287-9008
johnniewelch@msn.com
CL: Larry Keen
323 Pennington Road
Halls, TN 38040
(731)836-5546
lkeen@lctn.com

Protemus   (4EWC)GRWT9426
2372 W Shawtown Road (mailing)
2033 W Shawtown Road (physical)
Troy, TN 38260
(   )   <Obion>

WEST TENNESSEE PRESBYTERY CONTINUED

LS: James R Gunter   \<M6\>
6997 Bud Barker Road
Obion, TN 38240
(731)538-9252
CL: Betty Rhamy
2372 W Shawtown Road
Troy, TN 38260
(731)538-9458

_____

Ramer   (4MEWC)GRWT9223
4096 Highway 57 W
Ramer, TN 38367
( )   \<McNairy\>
OD: Albert Brown   \<M5\>
1772 Buena Vista Road
Bethel Springs, TN 38315
(731)934-7349
CL: George Armstrong
216 Ballpark Road E
Ramer, TN 38367
(731)645-3987

_____

Roellen   (2C)GRWT9428
6040 Highway 104 E (mailing)
Highway 104 E (physical)
Dyersburg, TN 38024
(731)285-0300   \<Dyer\>
krector@cableone.net
PA: Dennis Vance   \<M1\>
1320 Valleywood Drive
Paris, TN 38242
(731)644-3627
rvdvance@hotmail.com
CL: Hal Rector
6040 Highway 104 E
Dyersburg, TN 38024
(731)285-0300
krector@cableone.net

_____

Rutherford   (4MEWC)GRWT9429
945 S Trenton Street (mailing)
113 N Trenton Street (physical)
Rutherford, TN 38369
(731)665-6487   \<Gibson\>
PA: Hobert Walker   \<M1\>
PO Box 66
Rutherford, TN 38369
(731)665-7236
rutherfordcpchurch@gmail.com
CL: Joe Bone
945 S Trenton Street
Rutherford, TN 38369
(731)665-7253
jobne@msn.com

_____

Salem   (4MC)GRWT9430
174 Franklin Street (mailing)
184 Franklin Street(physical)
Gadsden, TN 38337
( )   \<Crockett\>
SS: Karl Schwarz   \<M1\>
83 W Curtis Street
Bells, TN 38006
(731)663-3987
schw8651@bellsouth.net
CL: Ann Davis
174 Franklin Street
Gadsden, TN 38337
(731)784-4713
cloud31@bellsouth.net

_____

Savannah First   (4WC)GRWT9224

300 Tennessee Street
Savannah, TN 38372
(731)925-4493   \<Hardin\>
savannah1stcp@hotmail.com
LS: Helen Hamilton   \<M6\>
245 Elm Street
Savannah, TN 38372
(731)925-7338
helmackham@aol.com
CL: Levin Edwards
300 Tennessee Street
Savannah, TN 38372
(731)925-4493
levinedwards@gmail.com

_____

Selmer Court Ave   (4MWC)GRWT9225
PO Box 741 (mailing)
234 Court Avenue (physical)
Selmer, TN 38375
(731)645-5257   \<McNairy\>
CL: Gwelda W Treece
299 Country Club Lane
Selmer, TN 38375
(731)645-5519
gweldat@bellsouth.net

_____

Sharon   (4MEC)GRWT9130
PO Box 588 (mailing)
5414 US Highway 45 (physical)
Sharon, TN 38255
( )   \<Weakley\>
SS: David Lancaster   \<M1 PR\>
426 Fugua Road
Martin, TN 38237
(731)588-5895
lancasterd@bethel-college.edu
CL: Patricia Elam
2275 Mount Vernon Road
Sharon, TN 38255
(731)456-2882
jimelam@frontiernet.net

_____

Shiloh (AC)   (4WC)GRWT9226
c/o Scott Coleman (mailing)
5 County Road 617A
164 County Road 634 (physical)
Corinth, MS 38834
( )   \<Alcorn\>
CL: LaWanda Burns
37 County Road 750
Corinth, MS 38834
(662)415-1038
ljmburns@gmail.com

_____

Shiloh (CC)   (4C)GRWT9131
2880 Highway 423
McKenzie, TN 38201
( )   \<Carroll\>
church@shilohcp.org
PA: Melissa Reid Goodloe   \<M1\>
225 Macedonia Road
McKenzie, TN 38201
(731)412-9657
rev.mgoodloe@shilohcp.org
CL: Vickie Summers
2880 Highway 423
McKenzie, TN 38201
(731)225-6714
vsum1956@gmail.com

_____

Trezevant   (3EC)GRWT9132
PO Box 160 (mailing)

98 Church Street (physical)
Trezevant, TN 38258
(731)669-4525   \<Carroll\>
CL: Bobby Argo
PO Box 160
Trezevant, TN 38258
(731)669-6926

_____

Troy   (4WC)GRWT9432
PO Box 454 (mailing)
308 Main Street (physical)
Troy, TN 38260
( )   \<Obion\>
CL: Alan Thompson
171 Country Valley Drive
Troy, TN 38260
(731)536-1107
atthompson2@netzero.com

_____

Union City   (4MW C)GRWT9433
631 E Church Street
Union City, TN 38261
(731)885-9773   \<Obion\>
FAX: (731)885-9766
uccpc@yahoo.com
CL: Session Clerk
631 E Church Street
Union City, TN 38261
(731)885-9773   \<Obion\>
FAX: (731)885-9766
uccpc@yahoo.com

_____

Walnut Grove   (4MWC)GRWT9320
1383 Walnut Grove Road
Burlison, TN 38015
(901)476-5533   \<Tipton\>
billyshires@bellsouth.net
SS: Christopher Todd   \<M1\>
3303 Decker Street
Bartlett, TN 38134
(901)848-9*913
catodd1964@gmail.com
CL: Denise Shires
681 Highway 179
Covington, TN 38019
(901)476-4590
billyshires@bellsouth.net

_____

West Union   (4MWC)GRWT9321
3099 W Union Road
Millington, TN 38053
(901)876-5757   \<Shelby\>
westunionoffice@bigriver.net
PA: James R Hamblin   \<M1\>
60 Rolling Meadow Drive
Drummonds, TN 38023
(901)840-4747
brojim391@gmail.com
CL: Bobbie Roberts
8931 Bass Road
Millington, TN 38053
bobbiemroberts@gmail.com

_____

Woodward's Chapel   (2C)GRWT9434
1357 Webster Street (mailing)
Union City, TN 38261
3054 Bud O Yates Road (physical)
Obion, TN 38240
(731)431-9127   \<Obion\>
FAX: (731)623-4226
SS: Mike Lavender   \<M3 ST\>
308 Main Street
Martin, TN 38237

WEST TENNESSEE PRESBYTERY CONTINUED

(731)253-7308
FAX: (731)623-4226
mikelavender@alumni.vanderbilt.edu
CL: Alvin Minnick
1357 Webster Street
Union City, TN 38261
(731)442-1130
alviniraq2004@yahoo.com

Yorkville　　　　　(4MEC)GRWT9435
PO Box 156 (mailing)
17 Newbern Highway (physical)
Yorkville, TN 38389
(731)643-6594　　　　　<Gibson>
CL: Mike Roberts
PO Box 213
Yorkville, TN 38389
(731)643-6237
roberts8@ycinet.net

Zion　　　　　(4C)GRWT9133
8670 Highway 436 (mailing)
3890 New Zion Road (physical)
McKenzie, TN 38201
( )　　　　　<Carroll>
SS: Jon T Carlock　　　　　<M1>
248 Cherry Avenue
McKenzie, TN 38201
(731)693-0003
carlockj@bethelu.edu
SS: Richard Reed　　　　　<M2>
236 Madison Street
Dyer, TN 38330
(731)692-3604
CL: Stan Welch
3670 New Zion Road
McKenzie, TN 38201
(731)358-2238

OTHERS ON MINISTERIAL ROLL:

Akin, Hershel W　　　　　<M1 WC>
388 Mysen Drive
Cordova, TN 38018
(901)744-8980
Alexander, Merlyn A　　　　　<M1 HR>
80 N Hampton Lane
Jackson, TN 38305
m_j_alexander@eplus.net
(731)668-8185
Anderson, Barry L　　　　　<M1 DE>
1790 Faxon Avenue
Memphis, TN 38112
(901)725-0924
wa4mff@aol.com
Bagby, Larry　　　　　<M1 WC>
3189 Northwood Drive
Memphis, TN 38111
(901)452-1952
Brown, Elinor　　　　　<M1 DE>
752 Hawthorne Street
Memphis, TN 38107
(901)274-1474
esb@cumberland.org
Brown, Mark　　　　　<M1 M9>
752 Hawthorne Street
Memphis, TN 38107
(901)274-1474
dmbrown@utmem.edu
Burns, J B, Jr　　　　　<M1 WC>
1020 Maud Road
Cherokee, AL 35616
(256)360-2252
Caperton, Donald　　　　　<M1 RT>

285 Britton Ford Road
Springville, TN 38256
(731)593-5096
dandjcaperton@vol.com
Coleman, Don L　　　　　<M1 WC>
85 Orchard Lane
Savannah, TN 38372
(731)925-9710
Condron, Dudley　　　　　<M1 RT>
1360 Harbert Avenue
Memphis, TN 38104
(901)726-1488
dudleywcondron@aol.com
Corbin, Eric　　　　　<M1 WC>
816 Bluegrass Lane
Champaign, IL 61822
(217)239-9945
eric@corbinzone.com
Crisp, Gregory W　　　　　<M1 WC>
635 Eden Brook Lane
Cordova, TN 38018
(901)266-0406
DeBerry, Martha　　　　　<M1 WC>
PO Box 243
McKenzie, TN 38201
(731)393-5033
1spiritualdirector@earthlink.net
Dyer, Stuart　　　　　<M1 WC>
3574 Foxfield Trail
Bartlett, TN 38135
(901)388-0612
Eddleman, Keith　　　　　<M1 WC>
2787 Stage Park Drive
Memphis, TN 38134
(901)388-9885
Edwards, Joey　　　　　<M1 WC>
5279 Ivy Creek Lane
Lakeland, TN 38002
(901)573-7579
edwardsjoey@bellsouth.net
Gam, John　　　　　<M1 WC>
1235 Sanders Street
Auburn, AL 36830
Gillock, Ed　　　　　<M1 WC>
PO Box 157
Savannah, TN 38372
(731)609-6744
Grimsley, Roger　　　　　<M1 WC>
215 N Oak Street
Springfield, TN 37172
Harwell, Keith　　　　　<M1 WC>
13132 Stinson Street
Milan, TN 38358
(731)613-3780
Heflin, Donna S　　　　　<M1 WC>
4144 Meadow Court Drive
Bartlett, TN 38135
(901)382-8198
rdheflin@bellsouth.net
Hill, Jody　　　　　<M1 WC>
4030 St Andrew Circle
Corinth, MS 38834
(662)512-8226
jody.hill34@gmail.com
Holmes, Aaron G　　　　　<M1 WC>
PO Box 171
Atwood, TN 38220
(731)662-7595
agholmes@charter.net
Howe, Francis　　　　　<M1 WC>
129 Manley Street
McKenzie, TN 38201
(731)352-5551
Hubbard, Pratt　　　　　<M1 WC>
1565 Eli Brown Road

McKenzie, TN 38201
(731)352-9178
Jackson, Terry　　　　　<M1 M9>
1461 Mount Pleasant Road
Hernando, MS 38632
(662)429-9741
James, William F　　　　　<M1 WC>
4090 Meadow Field Lane
Bartlett, TN 38135
(615)653-1396
billjames1954@gmail.com
Janner, Tony　　　　　<M1 WC>
104 Northwood Drive
McKenzie, TN 38201
(731)352-8055
drtonyjanner@yahoo.com
Jett, Mace T Jr　　　　　<M1 WC>
109 Park Street
Martin, TN 38237
(731)587-0805
Kleinjan, Lori　　　　　<M1 WC>
6516 Farnell Avenue
Memphis, TN 38134
(901)372-8413
lkleinj@prodigy.net
Latimer, James M　　　　　<M1 WC>
7621 Richmond
Memphis, TN 38125
(901)787-7875
jimmylatimer@redeemerevangelical.com
Laurence, Brenda　　　　　<M1 WC>
2823 Nine Mile Road
Enville, TN 38332
(731)687-2022
southernmoma@hotmail.com
Magliolo, Sam　　　　　<M1 WC>
14352 Fairview
Byhalia, MS 38611
(662)838-7720
samagliolo@fedex.com
Malinoski, Melissa　　　　　<M1 WC>
9087 Fenmore Cove
Cordova, TN 38016
(420)620-0089
FAX: (423)636-1017
mmalinoski@memphisseminary.edu
Maynard, Geoffery　　　　　<M1 WC>
1356 Marcia Road
Memphis, TN 38117
(901)409-5269
McClanahan, Jo Ann　　　　　<M1 WC>
215 White Brothers Road
Humboldt, TN 38343
(731)784-1176
joannmcclanahan@hughes.net
McClanahan, H Walter　　　　　<M1 WC>
215 White Bros Road
Humboldt, TN 38343
(731)784-1176
waltermac2@hughes.net
McClung, Andy　　　　　<M1 WC>
919 Dickinson Street
Memphis, TN 38107
(901)606-6615
scubarev@att.net
McClung, Tiffany　　　　　<M1 M9>
919 Dickinson Street
Memphis, TN 38107
(901)606-6615
tmcclung@memphisseminary.edu
McMillan, L Ronald　　　　　<M1 WC>
675 Kimberly Drive
Atoka, TN 38004
(901)837-1101
mcmillanron@bellsouth.net
Meeks, Brittany　　　　　<M1 WC>

WEST TENNESSEE PRESBYTERY CONTINUED

710 N Avalon Street
Memphis, TN 38107
(901)336-9024
bpmeeks@memphisseminary.edu

Minor, Mitzi   \<M1 PR\>
875 S Cox
Memphis, TN 38104
(901)278-6115

Mosley, Karen   \<M1 WC\>
PO Box 172154
Memphis, TN 38187

Nash, Zachary   \<M1 M8\>
(on file in General Assembly Office)
zachary.nash@us.af.mil

Ndoro, Wonder   \<M1 WC\>
111 Roberta Avenue
Memphis, TN 38112
(901)334-5861
gusungo@yahoo.com

Norton, Thomas H   \<M1 RT\>
1049 Lakemont Circle
Winter Park, FL 32792
tomnorton33@gmail.com
(270)505-5218

Orr, Melvin   \<M1 HR\>
806 Washington Street
Newbern, TN 38059
(731)627-2445
2Orrs.mn@charter.net

Perkins, Ed   \<M1 RT\>
721 E Paris Avenue
McKenzie, TN 38201
(731)352-2754

Pinion, Phillip   \<M1 WC\>
PO Box 87
Union City, TN 38281
(731)885-9175

Pounds, James D   \<M1 WC\>
40 Nellie Lane
Savannah, TN 38372
(731)925-2685
olivetcp@bellsouth.net

Powell, Jeff   \<M1 WC\>
547B Fawn Drive
Henderson, TN 38340
(731)608-2040
jfpowell2003@yahoo.com

Prosser, Robert   \<M1 DE\>
1021 Old State Route 76
Henry, TN 38231
(731)243-4467

Qualls, Michael   \<M1 DE\>
5355 June Cove
Horn Lake, MS 38637
(901)377-0526
FAX: (901)382-2600
mqualls1@yahoo.com

Quinton, Noah   \<M1 WC\>
2912 Waller Omer Road
Sturgis, KY 42459
(270)952-3875
noah.quinton@gmail.com

Ridgely, Michael   \<M1 WC\>
5195 Broad Street S
Trezevant, TN 38258
(731)669-3767

Rietz, Allen   \<M1 WC\>
1239 Hopewell Church Road
Finger, TN 38334
(731)989-7872

Scrivener, Carol   \<M1 WC\>
746 Willowsprings Boulevard
Franklin, TN 37064
(731)660-6469
csscriv@juno.com

Searcy, James M   \<M1 WC\>
1307 Lucy Way

Knoxville, TN 37912
(817)293-6132
gsearcy@earthlink.net

Thomas, Don F   \<M1 WC\>
743 Rain Dance Way
Cordova, TN 38018
(901)412-3695
thomas63981@comcast.net

Thompson, Tommy   \<M1 WC\>
9160 Tchulahoma Road
Southaven, MS 38671
(662)393-2552

Truax, Robert Lee, Jr   \<M1 M9 RT\>
2989 Champions Drive Apt 204
Lakeland, TN 38002
(901)266-5927

Turner, O Gene   \<M1 WC\>
5160 McSpadden Road
Rives, TN 38253
(731)536-0189

Walker, Michael C   \<M1 WC\>
1404 Wilshire Drive
Odessa, TX 79761
(731)643-6730
mworator@gmail.com

Ward, Frank   \<M1 WC\>
46 Henderson Cove
Atoka, TN 38004
(901)837-1972
bamaguy68@xipline.com

Westbrook, James   \<M1 RT\>
1717 Wedgewood Drive
Union City, TN 38261
(731)884-0918
westbrook731@bellsouth.net

Wheeler, Nathan   \<M1 DE\>
2084 Linden Avenue
Memphis, TN 38104
(901)606-9535
nathantyac@gmail.com

White, Diann   \<M1 WC\>
9394 Alex Dickson Cove
Bartlett, TN 38133
(901)377-7776
diannwhite12@yahoo.com

Wilson, Thomas   \<M1 WC\>
4543 Lake Vista
Memphis, TN 38128
(901)382-6190
tomjw217@gmail.com

OTHER LICENTIATES ON ROLL:

Jett-Rand, Dana   \<M2\>
78 Lester Lane
Martin, TN 38237
(731)587-0805
msdanajett@yahoo.com

OTHER CANDIDATES ON ROLL:

Adams, Jamie   \<M3 ST\>
403 W Washington
Union City, TN 38261
(731)885-1217
adamsj2@k12tn.net

Dimo, Urelia   \<M3\>
171 Roberta Drive
Memphis, TN 38112

Earheart-Brown, Paul   \<M3\>
502 E Lamar Alexander Parkway
Box 2519
Maryville, TN 37804

Hudson, Ellen   \<M3\>
301 N Royal Oaks Blvd Apt 2614
Franklin, TN 37067
(731)780-1004
ellen.hudson17@icloud.com

Puluc, Paul   \<M3\>

1421 Greentree Valley Court Apt 5
Memphis, TN 38119
paul-tuba@hotmail.com
(830)872-6090

Sprenkle, David   \<M3\>
5733 Stone Street
Olive Branch, MS 38654
(901)604-8707
dsprenkle@memphisseminary.edu

ALPHABETICAL ROLL OF MINISTERS

Symbols in this roll:

(M0) - Mentored Minister
(M1) - Ordained Minister
(M2) - Licentiate
(M3) - Candidate
(M4) - Minister of another denomination who through reciprocal agreement is enrolled as a member of presbytery and has temporarily the rights and privileges of such membership according to the Constitution, Article 5.3.

--=≪ A ≫=--

Acton, Donald W (M1)
1186 Jenkins Lane
Knoxville, TN 37922
(865)966-5132 SEET#2310

Acton, Donny (M1)
1413 Oak Ridge Drive
Birmingham, AL 35242
FAX: (205)991-5259
donny@newhopecpc.org
(205)991-3204 SEGR#0104

Acton, Mindy (M1)
1413 Oak Ridge Drive
Birmingham, AL 35242
FAX: (205)991-5259
mindy@newhopecpc.org
(205)991-3204 SEGR#0104

Acton, Wade (M1)
1615 Estes Drive
Glencoe, AL 35905
ginnyacton@juno.com
(256)492-8542 SEGR#0406

Acuff, David (M1)
4969 Quail Lane
Columbia, SC 29206
david.acuff@us.army.mil
(803)727-3910 TNNA#7300

Adams, Fred Michael (M1)
42 Julies Way
Somerset, KY 42503
fma46@twc.com
(606)451-9155 MICU#3314

Adams, Jamie (M3)
403 W Washington
Union City, TN 38261
adamsj2@k12tn.net
(731)885-1217 GRWT#9100

Aden, Dare (M1)
1280 Kimber Road
Dongola, IL 62926
FAX: (618)827-4612
dare_aden@hotmail.com
(618)827-3625 MICO#3400

Aden, Marty (M1)
202 Bennington Place
Wilmington, NC 28412
maadretny@gmail.com
(910)274-8465 MSRR#8400

Agudelo, Gildardo (M1)
Cra 73C # 1A-54
Cali, COLOMBIA, SA
( ) MSCA#8223

Aguiar, Neil (M1)
405 E Moulton Street
Decatur, AL 35601
nlajap@yahoo.com
(256)616-1318 SEGR#0214

Ahn, Da-Wit (David) (M1)
1304 Kakyeng-Dong
Sangdang-Gu Cheongju-City
Choongbook, KOREA
(043)235-0219 MMT

Akai, Anum (M1)
458 Dean Taylor Court
Simpsonville, KY 40067
(502)405-3120 MICU#3100

Akin, Hershel W (M1)
388 Mysen Drive
Cordova, TN 38018
(901)744-8980 GRWT#9100

Alas, William (M1)
105 Waterford Drive Cove
Calera, AL 35040
alas3542085@yahoo.es
(205)966-9411 SEGR#0115

Albarracin, Ruben D (M1)
7411 Magnolia Shadows Lane
Houston, TX 77095
FAX: (281)463-8617
confiaendios@hotmail.com
(281)463-8617 MSTR#8612

Alderson, Cameron (M3)
122 E Cherry Street
Chandler, IN 47610
(812)925-6475 MICO#3400

Alexander, Merlyn A (M1)
80 N Hampton Lane
Jackson, TN 38305
m_j_alexander@eplus.net
(731)668-8185 GRWT#9100

Alhart, Daryl (M1)
2187 Rutledge Ford Road
Decherd, TN 37324
dwalhart@aol.com
(931)349-7104 TNMU#7225

Allen, Gail (M1)
488 County Road 1650 N
Bethany, IL 61914
kallen1_61914@yahoo.com
(217)665-3387 MINC#5200

Alverson, Elmer L (M1)
354 Roy Davis Road
New Market, AL 35761
1941buddy@att.net
(256)828-4503 SERD#7108

Anderson, Barry L (M1)
1790 Faxon Avenue
Memphis, TN 38112
wa4mff@aol.com
(901)725-0924 GRWT#9100

Anderson, Christopher (M1)
14 Indian Springs Road
Batesville, AR 72501
csanderson@memphisseminary.edu
(870)805-0886 GRAR#1517

Anderson, Kyle (M3)
828 E Main Street
Batesville, AR 72501
kanderson@mempisseminary.edu
(870)834-5799

Anderson, Lisa (M1)
1790 Faxon Avenue
Memphis, TN 38112

anderli60@gmail.com
(901)246-8052 GRWT#9305

Ang, John (M1)
5843 S Farm Road 157
Springfield, MO 65810
pastorcares@yahoo.com
(417)886-3487 GRMI#4100

Appling, John (M1)
1722 S Fairway Avenue
Springfield, MO 65804
pegblessings@sbcglobal.net
(417)877-4643 GRMI#4100

Appling, Peggy (M1)
1722 S Fairway Avenue
Springfield, MO 65804
pegblessings@sbcglobal.net
(417)877-4643 GRMI#4100

Arase, Makihiko (M1)
3-355-4 Kamikitadai Higashi
Yamato-shi, Tokyo
207-0023, JAPAN
FAX: (042)567-2977
viator@cb3.so-net.ne.jp
(042)567-2977 MSJA#8309

Arias, John Jairo (M1)
Calle 144 Sur #496-08 / Apto 202
Caldas, Antioquia
COLOMBIA, SA
(57)317-693-1162 MSAN#8900

Ariza, Fabiola (M1)
COLOMBIA, SA
fatvioleta@hotmail.com
(316)419-8414 MSCA#8200

Aros, Jeremias (M1)
5649 W Roscoe Street
Chicago, IL 60634
jeremiasaros@sbcglobal.net
(773)685-4395 MINC#5200

Arteaga, Gilberto (M3)
Aereo 794
Buenaventura, COLOMBIA, SA
pastorgilbertoa@hotmail.com
( )256-4261 MSCA#8210

Asayama, Masaharu (M1)
6-3-2-308 Toyogaoka
Tama-shi, Tokyo
206-0031, JAPAN
asa@ipcc-21.com
(042)373-2710 MSJA#8300

Ashley, Jack (Nick) (M2)
2625A Raleigh Drive
Evansville, IN 47715
edencateringusa@aol.com
(812)204-1422 MICO#3400

Ashton, Christie (M5)
10001 Bailey Cove Road SE
Huntsville, AL 35803
FAX: (256)881-0031
pastorhope@bellsouth.net
(256)881-4673 SERD#0800

Attema, Lee (M1)
PO Box 138

MINISTERS CONTINUED

San Ignacio Town, Cayo District
BELIZE
lattema@icloud.com
(281)728-6263 MSTR#8100
Attena, Leslie (M1)
PO Box 138
San Ignacio Town, Cayo District
BELIZE
leslieattema@icloud.com
(281)728-6263 MSTR#8100
Atwell, Keith G (M1)
7688 Hardyville Road
Hardyville, KY 42746
FAX: (270)524-9100
(270)528-3667 MICU#3102

--==<< B >>==--

Babcock, Edward S, Jr (M1)
1007 San Ramone Avenue
Huntsville, AL 35802
ejsb1@aol.com
(256)882-9339 SERD#0800
Bagby, Larry (M1)
3189 Northwood Drive
Memphis, TN 38111
(901)452-1952 GRWT#9100
Ballow, Brent (M1)
715 Highland Church Road
Paducah, KY 42001
hcppastor@bellsouth.net
(270)564-8891 MICO#3400
Baltimore, Claud G (M1)
PO Box 1358
1430 Lakehurst Drive
Ada, OK 74821
baltimorejb@earthlink.net
(580)332-2679 MSRR#8400
Bane, Ted (M1)
903 W Old Hickory Boulevard
Madison, TN 37115
tedjan95@aol.com
(615)975-9343 TNNA#7309
Baranoski, Timothy (M1)
1205 Tomahawk Drive B
Jber, AK 99505
timothy.i.baranoski.mil@mail.mil
(615)440-3499 TNNA#7300
Barkley, Daniel (M1)
2732 Rexford Street
Hokes Bluff, AL 35903
daniel@gadsdencp.com
(256)478-0397 SEGR#0402
Barna, Clifton (M1)
1012 Adam Court
Cottontown, tn 37066
cliff.barna@gmail.com
(352)598-3246 TNNA#7300
Barnett, Rudolph (M1)
RR 5 Box 267
McLeansboro, IL 62859
(618)643-3253 MINC#5200
Barnhouse, Donald Grey, Jr (M1)
51 Harristown Road
Paradise, PA 17562
donaldbarnhouse@gmail.com
(610)337-4015 MICU#3131
Barrett, Geoff (M1)
155 Maude Lane
Harrodsburg, KY 40330
FAX: (256)881-0031
glbarrett@live.com
(859)748-8373 MICU#3100

Barricklow, Gary (M3)
3012 Winston Meadows
Rio Rancho, NM 87144
garysr@barricklow.com
(505)417-0331 MSDC#8700
Barrios, Janina (M3)
6751 SW 16th Street
Miami, FL 33155
janina83@hotmail.com
(786)757-0369 SEGR#0100
Barron, Mark (M1)
836 McArthur Street
Manchester, TN 37355
FAX: (931)728-2975
mbarron@cafes.net
(931)728-2975 TNMU#7224
Barry, James (M1)
49 Smitty's Circle
Chattanooga, TN 37415
james_barry@bellsouth.net
(903)315-7998 SETG#2100
Barton, Cindy (M2)
83426 Argus Avenue
Trona, CA 93562
cbarton53@hotmail.com
(760)372-4033 MSDC#8700
Barton, Robert (M1)
22460 Klines Resort Road Lot #290
Three Rivers, MI 49093
csm2ndinfbde2002@yahoo.com
(859)613-2686 MICU#3100
Baugh, Roosevelt (M1)
4101 Hademan Street
Fort Worth, TX 76119
FAX: (817)534-1339
gmf1220@charter.net
(817)536-1315 MSRR#8408
Bautista, Juan (M1)
Tranv 30 No 17F-122
Cali
Colombia, South America
( )442-4562 MSCA#8217
Bayer, David (M1)
9060 Tom Counce Road
South Fulton, TN 38257
dbayer9060@gmail.com
(731)479-3060 GRWT#9412
Bell, Marc (M1)
3467 State Route 175 N
Bremen, KY 42325
marc.bell1@att.net
(270)846-4203 MICU#3503
Bell, Michelle (M2)
8643 Dry Creek Road Unit 1226
Centennial, CO 80112
mabbell@comcast.net
(720)344-4040 MSDC#8700
Benadom, Dennis (M1)
13314 Sage Street
Trona, CA 93562
galerose91@msn.com
(760)372-4536 MSDC#8503
Bender, Richard J (M1)
5297 Normandy Place
Evansville, IN 47715
richardjbenderjr@yahoo.com
(812)983-9597 MINC#5200
Benedict, Mary McCaskey (M1)
892 Pen Oak Drive
Cookeville, TN 38501
marykat_61@hotmail.com
(931)260-1422 TNMU#7200
Bennett, Alfred J (M1)

7286 Nolensville Road
Nolensville, TN 37135
(615)776-5181 TNNA#7300
Bertsch, Michael (M1)
204 Buckleigh Point
Gallatin, TN 37066
mikebertsch14@gmail.com
(423)763-8314 TNNA#7327
Betancur, Sergio (M1)
Iglesia El Rebano
Calle 128 sur #48-13
Caldas, Antioquia, COLOMBIA, SA
sergiobetancurposada@hotmail.com
(574)278-0787 MSCA#8208
Biggs, Jeff (M1)
1504 Cumberland Drive
Fairfield, IL 62837
jeffbiggsonline@gmail.com
(618)842-2219 MINC#5108
Black, Gary G (M1)
503 S Main Street
Piedmont, AL 36272
(205)447-7142 SEGR#0400
Blackburn, Samuel N (M1)
6706 S 6th Street
Fort Smith, AR 72908
(479)649-9436 GRAR#1100
Blair, Fonda (M1)
PO Box 11093
Murfreesboro, TN 37129
fblair4334@gmail.com
(615)605-9755 TNCO#7100
Blair, John (M1)
108 Cliff Drive
Lawrenceburg, TN 38464
jnbblair@charter.net
(931)766-2480 TNCO#7111
Blakeburn, Larry A (M1)
790 Emory Valley Road Apt 714
Oak Ridge, TN 37830
larry@1stcpc.org
(731)676-2978 SEET#2313
Blandon, Juan Esteban (M1)
Calle 51 #15-32
barrio Los Naranjos
Dosquebradas, Risaralda
COLOMBIA, SA
juanestebanblandon@yahoo.com
57(314)680-2246 MSAN#8907
Blanton, D B (M1)
ADDRESS UNKNOWN
( ) GRAR#1100
Blaum, Steve R (M1)
184 900 Street
Middletown, IL 62666
cumberland@frontier.com
(217)871-3339 MINC#5405
Blevins, Ralph (M1)
1623 County Road 2375 E
Geff, IL 62842
pastorreblevins@gmail.com
(618)854-2494 MINC#5107
Blevins, Tom (M1)
50 Blevins Road
Center, KY 42214
(270)565-1792 MICU#3100
Board, N Ray (M1)
267 State Route 293 N
Princeton, KY 42445
rayboard@att.net
(270)365-0006 MICO#3400
Boggs, Barry (M1)
1039 Johnnie Bud Lane

MINISTERS CONTINUED

Cookeville, TN 38501
boggsone@hotmail.com
(931)979-1701   TNMU#7274
Boggs, Robert   (M1)
   89 Maple Leaf Lane
   Leitchfield, KY 42754
   (270)259-5546   MICU#3100
Bohon, Chris Michael   (M3)
   505 Edgehill Road
   Joshua, TX 76058
   cbohon@pathway.church
   (817)228-9494   MSRR#8400
Bond, Bill   (M1)
   205 Windmere Drive
   Chattanooga, TN 37411
   bill@wcbj.net
   (423)316-0867   SETG#2102
Bond, Richard   (M1)
   2425 Fisk Road Lot 0
   Cookeville, TN 38506
   erbond@frontier.net
   (931)854-0979   TNMU#7213
Bondurant, Lee   (M1)
   1453 Paseo Del Sur Court
   El Paso, TX 79928
   lee_b5217@yahoo.com
   (915)309-7269   MSDC#8700
Bone, Leslie   (M1)
   16504 George Franklyn Drive
   Independence, MO 64055
   lesliebone@comcast.net
   (816)373-6625   GRMI#4100
Bone, W Harold   (M1)
   315 Joey Drive
   Bourne, TX 78006
   ruaha1@sbcglobal.net
   (210)859-5560   MSTR#8100
Boulton, Mitch   (M1)
   80 Topsy Lane
   Savannah, TN 38372
   steelermitch@gmail.com
   (731)487-2318   GRWT#9422
Bourque, Leo
   1620 Sarahs Cove
   Hermitage, TN 37076
   bourque120@gmail.com
   (615)767-2428   TNNA#7300
Bower, Clay   (M1)
   221 Waterlemon Way
   Monroe, NC 28110
   cbrev.9497@gmail.com
   (704)575-9497   MSDC#8700
Bowers, Sharon G   (M1)
   201 Wild Buffalo Drive
   Kyle, TX 78640
   sharon.bowers@gmail.com
   (512)230-7078   MSTR#8100
Bowling, Andrew   (M1)
   20945 Highway 16 E
   Siloam Springs, AR 72761
   (479)524-6576   GRAR#1100
Bowman, Greg   (M3)
   3241 South Fork Road
   Glasgow, KY 42141
   ( )   MICU#3217
Bozeman, Robert   (M1)
   582 Bozeman Loop
   Belmont, LA 71406
   bo@bozemanengineering.com
   (318)256-5781   MSTR#8100
Bradberry, Jim   (M3)
   120 Hummingbird Lane
   Searcy, AR 72143

(501)278-9750   GRAR#1205
Bradshaw, James (Jim)   (M1)
   415 S Red Street
   Sheridan, AR 72150
   (870)942-2525   GRAR#1105
Brantley, Kevin T   (M1)
   308 A Chestnut Street
   Sacremento, KY 42372
   ktbrantley1971@gmail.com
   (270)405-2222   MICU#3100
Brasher, Karen   (M1)
   2931 Barker Cypress Road Apt 415
   Houston, TX 77084
   ekb077@gmail.com
   (205)777-2420   SEGR#0100
Braswell, Jimmy   (M1)
   1514 E 10th
   Odessa, TX 79761
   jjcgbraz@cableone.net
   (432)335-9346   MSDC#8703
Brewer, Barbara Jean   (M1)
   1360 White Oak Bluff Road
   Rison, AR 71665
   (870)325-6449   GRAR#1100
Brindley, Toy   (M1)
   PO Box 225
   Gurley, AL 35748
   (256)776-2331   SERD#0804
Brister, Glenn   (M1)
   3004 Delaware Avenue
   McComb, MS 39648
   bearmountainpenworks@gmail.com
   (706)934-8629   SETG#2100
Brock, Dudley   (M1)
   490 County Road 1184
   Cullman, AL 35057
   preacherbrock@att.net
   (256)734-0893   SEHO#0213
Brooks, Wayne E   (M1)
   1505 Parkview Drive
   Campbellsville, KY 42718
   webrooks@windstream.net
   (270)465-9235   MICU#3104
Brown, Amy   (M1)
   679 Freeze Bend Road
   Newport, AR 72112
   ( )   GRAR#1100
Brown, Charles R   (M1)
   475 N Highland Street 6B
   Memphis, TN 38122
   cbrown@cumberland.org
   (817)915-2907   MSRR#8400
Brown, Dale M   (M1)
   HC 61 Box 4740
   West Plains, MO 65775
   pastorbrown44@yahoo.com
   (417)257-0983   GRMI#4304
Brown, Elinor   (M1)
   752 Hawthorne Street
   Memphis, TN 38107
   esb@cumberland.org
   (901)274-1474   GRWT#9100
Brown, Houston   (M3)
   866 N McLean
   Memphis, TN 38107
   hpbrown95@gmail.com
   (817)915-9090   MSRR#8400
Brown, Mark   (M1)
   752 Hawthorne Street
   Memphis, TN 38107
   dmbrown@utmem.edu
   (901)274-1474   GRWT#9100
Brown, Philip   (M1)

540 Mt Pisgah Road
Dongola, IL 62926
brownlp75@yahoo.com
(618)827-3516   MICO#5115
Brown, Rex   (M1)
   134 Everhart Drive
   Greeneville, TN 37745
   firstcumberland@gmail.com
   (423)639-4298   SEET#2205
Brown, Stephanie S   (M1)
   475 N Highland Street 6B
   Memphis, TN 38122
   scrudderbrown7@gmail.com
   (817)915-1317   MSRR#8400
Brown, Whitney   (M1)
   137 Roberta Drive
   Memphis, TN 38112
   (865)387-0002   SEET#2200
Broyles, Byrd   (M1)
   295 Davy Crockett Road
   Limestone, TN 37681
   b3broyles@outlook.com
   (423)257-4578   SEET#2212
Bruington, Don   (M1)
   PO Box 105
   Falls of Rough, KY 40119
   (270)257-2228   MICU#3100
Bryan, Hannah   (M1)
   32 Trenton Lane
   Mead, OK 73449
   hbryan@choctawnation.com
   (580)775-4955   MSCH#6105
Buchanan, Larry   (M1)
   720 Shelby Road
   Salem, KY 42078
   (270)988-1880   MICO#3610
Buck, Clinton   (M1)
   PO Box 770068
   Memphis, TN 38117
   clintobuck@aol.com
   (901)682-2358   GRWT#9315
Bunnell, Robert (Bob)   (M1)
   329 Lexington Drive
   Glasgow, KY 42141
   bob_bunnell@yahoo.com
   (270)629-6209   MICU#3312
Bunting, Geoff   (M1)
   9229 Hedgewood Court
   Evansville, IN 47725
   geoff.bunting@yahoo.com
   (812)925-6630   MINC#5200
Burgess, Ronald D   (M1)
   116 Harris Ridge Road
   Dover, TN 37058
   revron4@bellsouth.net
   (931)232-5151   TNNA#7322
Burns, Garrett   (M1)
   387 Forrest Avenue
   McKenzie, TN 38201
   gburns2888@gmail.com
   (731)535-3126   GRWT#9118
Burns, J B, Jr   (M1)
   1020 Maud Road
   Cherokee, AL 35616
   (256)360-2252   GRWT#9100
Burrow, Vernon   (M1)
   603 Saratoga Drive
   Murfreesboro, TN 37130
   vernonburrow@comcast.net
   (615)406-6385   TNMU#7200
Burrows, Arthur L, Jr   (M1)
   PO Box 511
   Hopkinsville, KY 42241

MINISTERS CONTINUED

(270)886-1301   MICU#3505
Butcher, Kenny   (M1)
4608 Cather Court
Nashville, TN 37214
bhpastor@birch.net
(615)719-1887   TNNA#7325
Butler, Alan   (M3)
866 N McLean Boulevard
Memphis, TN 38107
afbutler@memphisseminary.edu
(817)937-8488   MSRR#8400
Butler, Jim   (M1)
507 W Chestnut Street
Leitchfield, KY 42754
jbutler54@insightbb.com
(502)635-8587   MICU#3211
Butler, John   (M1)
501 Cherokee Drive
Campbellsville, KY 42718
rev.butlerj8134@gmail.com
(270)403-7602   MICU#3104
Butler, Joseph H, Jr   (M1)
56 Cline Ridge Road
Winchester, TN 37398
jhbu737@bellsouth.net
(931)224-8423   TNMU#7205
Buttram, Jim   (M1)
5385 Bungalow Circle
Hixson, TN 37343
FAX: (865)483-8445
littlejimb@gmail.com
(865)938-7418   TNGA#2105
Byford, Ken   (M1)
58 Quincy Lane
Montevallo, AL 35115
kenabyford@gmail.com
(205)665-5753   SEGR#0406
Bynum, Ronald H   (M1)
121 Sycamore Road
Gurley, AL 35748
ronaldbynum@bellsouth.net
(256)776-9313   SERD#0800
Byrd, James F   (M1)
1158 Cornishville Road
Harrodsburg, KY 40330
jfbyrd@bluezoomwifi.com
(859)734-0534   MICU#3100
Byrd, Jimmy   (M1)
176 E Valley Road
Whitwell, TN 37397
FAX: (615)444-6671
revjimmybyrd@gmail.com
(615)289-3347   SETG#2115

--==<< C >>==--

Cadenbach, Mark   (M1)
91 Elzadah Lane
Salem, AR 72576
cadenbm@nctc.net
(890)955-9250   GRAR#1100
Caicedo, Efrain   (M3)
Aereo 6365
Cali, COLOMBIA, SA
( )   MSCA#8224
Caldwell, Chris   (M3)
829 Chateaugay Road
Knoxville, TN 37923
luke64345@yahoo.com
(865)599-1044   SEET#2200
Calero, Aldrin   (M1)
Cattara 13 3-81
Guacari, COLOMBIA, SA

( )253-0453   MSCA#8212
Camp, Annetta   (M1)
2303 Mill Creek Road
Halls, TN 38040
FAX: (731)285-5792
annetta@cumberlandchurch.com
(731)285-5703   GRWT#9410
Campbell, Coyle   (M1)
186 Old Limestone Road
New Market, AL 35761
(256)379-4392   TNMU#7215
Campbell, Gordon C   (M1)
1469 E Wayland Street
Springfield, MO 65804
gofor12@gmail.com
(417)823-9567   GRMI#4100
Campbell, Thomas D   (M1)
PO Box 343
601 Park Street
Calico Rock, AR 72519
FAX: (870)297-3151
tdcampbellar@gmail.com
(870)297-2319   GRAR#1503
Campos, Eva   (M3)
PO Box 451405
Miami, FL 33245
(786)426-5997   SEGR#0100
Cantey, James M   (M1)
3505 Elmira Drive
Longview, TX 75605
(903)452-6049   MSTR#8111
Caperton, Donald   (M1)
285 Britton Ford Road
Springville, TN 38256
dandjcaperton@vol.com
(731)593-5096   GRWT#9100
Cardona, Nancy   (M3)
Calle 51 #15-32
Dosquebradas, Risaralda
COLOMBIA, SA
nancycardona10@yahoo.com
(576)322-2938   MSAN#8900
Carlock, Jon T   (M1)
248 Cherry Avenue
McKenzie, TN 38201
carlockj@bethel-college.edu
(731)352-0800   GRWT#9133
Carlton, Gary   (M1)
108 Greenbrier Street
Dickson, TN 37055
gwcarlton@yahoo.com
(270)965-4358   TNNA#7300
Carpenter, David   (M1)
909 W Elm Street
Olney, TX 76374
olneycpc@brazosnet.com
(940)564-2339   MSRR#8416
Carr, Jill   (M1)
PO Box 1547
Lebanon, MO 65536
dig.micah.6.8@gmail.com
(417)532-6760   GRMI#4315
Carter, Billy Ray   (M1)
33 Mockingbird Drive
Leitchfield, KY 42754
cartercbc@windstream.net
(270)259-3897   MICU#3203
Carter, Gary   (M1)
8311 County Road 1082
Vinemont, AL 35179
garycarter51@gmail.com
(256)443-8389   SEHO#0202
Carter, James L   (M1)
6155 Hummingbird Lane

Whitesburg, TN 37891
jandjmt@comcast.net
(423)587-8423   SEET#2200
Carter, Patricia   (M1)
2509 Decatur Stratton Road
Decatur, MS 39327
revtree@yahoo.com
(601)604-3813   SEGR#0100
Carver, Gary   (M1)
2810 Cabin Road
Chattanooga, TN 37411
sandgatthecabin@epbfi.com
(423)698-2556   SETG#2100
Cassell, C J   (M2)
825 Aimes Court
Nashville, TN 37221
n4cjc@comcast.net
(615)594-2693   TNNA#7300
Castaneda, Ricardo   (M1)
Calle 65 #98-45 (Interior 174)
Altos de la Macarena-Robledo La
Campina
Medellin, Antioquia, COLOMBIA, SA
rijcah@gmail.com
(574)577-0717   MSAN#8915
Castano, Juan Alexander   (M1)
Calle 127 sur #42-38 Apto 301
Caldas, Antioquia, COLOMBIA, SA
FAX: (574)278-0787
juanalexandercastano@hotmail.com
(574)306-4435   MSAN#8905
Chall-Hutchinson, Deborah   (M2)
190 Ussery Road
Clarksville, TN 37043
challhut@gmail.com
(931)905-1671   TNNA#7300
Chambers, Jason   (M1)
131 E Woods Street
Palestine, AR 72372
jmchambers@memphisseminary.edu
(870)807-1930   GRAR#1103
Chambers, Nicholas   (M1)
11300 Road 101
Union, MS 39365
nachambrs@hotmail.com
(601)697-4470   SEGR#0608
Chancellor, Hilton   (M1)
11905 Preserve Vista
Austin, TX 78738
hiltontex@aol.com
(512)382-1972   MSTR#8100
Chang, Leo   (M1)
819 W Division SE
Springfield, MO 65803
(901)287-9901   GRAR#1100
Chapman, Harry W   (M1)
4908 El Picador Court
Rio Rancho, NM 87124
wrightrev@gmail.com
(505)620-2427   MSDC#8709
Chen, Steven   (M1)
865 Jackson Street
San Francisco, CA 94133
psalm1305@yahoo.com
(415)421-1624   MSDC#8501
Cheung, Luke   (M1)
A-D Flat 3/F 338-340 Castle Peak Road
Cheung Sha Wan
Kowloon HONG KONG
FAX: (852)2706-0114
luke.cheung@cgst.edu
(852)2794-6781   MSHK#8800
Chin, Kwang Sik   (M2)

MINISTERS CONTINUED

1168 Palisade Avenue
Fort Lee, NJ 07024
(201)220-3390 SECE#2400
Cho, Kun Ho (M3)
605-H S Palm
La Habra, CA 90631
pkhch3@gmail.com
(949)241-6167 MSDC#8700
Cho, Sangsook (M1)
7 Falmouth Court
Middletown, CT
lovejcamen@yahoo.com
(860)830-6808 SECE#2143
Cho, Sung Wan (M1)
1603 Coolhurst Avenue
Sherwood, AR 72120
swcho100491@gmail.com
(501)247-5953 GRAR#2135
Choe, Byung-Jae (M1)
876-15 Dokok-1dong
Kangnam-Gu, Seoul, KOREA
(023)463-3939 SEET#2222
Choi, Ezra (M1)
605 Arbor Hollow Circle #2103
Cordova, TN 38018
(901)236-8235 SEET#2200
Choi, Hyoung S (M1)
32132 Huntly Circle
Salisbury, MD 21804
pastor0101@naver.com
(443)880-6776 SETG#2138
Choi, Sean (M1)
7565 Macon Road
Cordova, TN 38016
esloveh2@hotmail.com
(901)826-2993 SEET#2200
Chuquimia, Walter (M5)
18240 S US Highway 301
Wimauma, FL 33598
walter@beth-el.info
(813)399-4050 SEGR#0100
Cinco, Carlos (M1)
611 Cheron Road
Madison, TN 37115
pastorcinco2020@gmail.com
(615)586-1269 TNNA#7314
Cintro, Eddie (M3)
5695 S Franklin
Springfield, MO 65810
eddiecintron7@hotmail.com
(417)894-1480 GRMI#4100
Clark, Amber LaCroix (M1)
80 Bryan Drive
Winchester, TN 37398
revamber@comcast.net
(931)967-2121 TNMU#7249
Clark, J Don (M1)
1601 Lake Ridge Circle
Birmingham, AL 35216
jdsjcl@charter.net
(205)942-4054 SEGR#0100
Clark, Jeff (M1)
327 Haynes Haven Lane
Murfreesboro, TN 37129
jclark7733@aol.com
(615)896-7733 TNMU#7250
Clark, Jonathan (M1)
88 Woodcrest Drive
Winchester, TN 37398
FAX: (931)967-8444
clark3568@bellsouth.net
(931)967-9613 TNMU#7200
Clark, Michael (M1)

80 Bryan Drive
Winchester, TN 37398
michael.clark@winchestercp.org
(931)967-2121 TNMU#7249
Clark, Tom (M1)
2089 Sumach Church Road
Chatsworth, GA 30705
(270)469-5468 TNGA#2124
Clark, Tommy (M1)
124 Roberta Drive
Memphis, TN 37216
fattire77@gmail.com
(615)430-9158 TNCO#7126
Coker, Robert N (M1)
721 Lakeview Drive
Loudon, TN 37774
FAX: (865)458-5360
nickcoker@bellsouth.net
(865)458-8791 SEET#2200
Cole, Dwayne (M1)
6460 Village Parkway
Anchorage, AK 99504
tadpolejr@aol.com
(907)854-5793 TNCO#7100
Coleman, Bobby D (M1)
704 E Webb Street
Mountain View, AR 72560
bobbycoleman@gmail.com
(870)213-5410 GRAR#1514
Coleman, Don L (M1)
85 Orchard Lane
Savannah, TN 38372
(731)925-9710 GRWT#9100
Collins, Paul (M1)
915 Warm Sands Drive SE
Albuquerque, NM 87123
FAX: (505)254-7707
chapp3@comcast.net
(505)294-3842 MSDC#8700
Colvard, Kevin (M1)
20024 Crescent Oaks
San Antonio, TX 78258
FAX: (210)497-8724
rev_kev@satx.rr.com
(205)267-9372 MSTR#8608
Compton, Marcia (M1)
6276 Cascade Circle
Indianapolis, IN 46234
mcomptonma@yahoo.com
(317)209-9798 MINC#5200
Condon, Thomas W, Jr (M1)
6508 Victoria Avenue
N Richland Hills, TX 76180
(817)656-9334 MSRR#8400
Condron, Dudley (M1)
1360 Harbert Avenue
Memphis, TN 38104
dudleywcondron@aol.com
(901)726-1488 GRWT#9100
Contini, John (M1)
4344 Poor Ridge Pike
Lancaster, KY 40444
john@hillsidehritagefarm.com
(859)339-0747 MICU#3103
Cook, Carl (M1)
475 Western Hills Loop
Mountain Home, AR 72653
carlc@suddenlink.net
(870)425-2570 GRAR#1100
Cook, Lisa (M1)
4101 Dalemere Court
Nashville, TN 37207
tgoose@comcast.net

(615)868-4118 TNNA#7300
Corbin, Eric (M1)
816 Bluegrass Lane
Champaign, IL 61822
eric@corbinzone.com
(217)239-9945 GRWT#9100
Corbin, William (M1)
7300 N Lamar Road
Mount Juliet, TN 37122
raven.rest@comcast.net
(615)459-8998 TNNA#7300
Correa, John Jairo (M1)
Calle 2 Norte #16-39
Armenia, Quindio, COLOMBIA, SA
FAX: (576)745-4860
jjcedp07@hotmail.com
(318)285-1209 MSAN#8903
Cottingim, Tom (M1)
353 Atwood Drive
Lexington, KY 40515
FAX: (859)272-4315
t.cottingim@insightbb.com
(859)273-3800 MICU#3100
Coulter, Laurance W (M1)
5226 W William Cannon Drive
Austin, TX 78749
FAX: (512)892-6307
larry@shpc.org
(512)892-3580 MSTR#8604
Cox, Jimmy R (M1)
2250 County Road 156
Anderson, AL 35610
dcox01@msn.com
(256)710-1702 SEHO#0508
Craddock, Barry (M3)
147 Moss Way
Glasgow, KY 42141
( ) MICU#3100
Craig, Aaron (M2)
325 Cherry Avenue
McKenzie, TN 38201
(731)352-6718 SEET#2200
Craig, Peggy Jean (M1)
825 S 13th Street Floor 2
Philadelphia, PA 19147
pjfpeggy@gmail.com
(256)277-1147 SEEC#2400
Craig, Robert A (M1)
1711 Bellevue Avenue Apt D-706
Richmond, VA 23227-5123
robertacraig1954@gmail.com
(573)219-8051 MINC#5200
Craven, Mark (M1)
21 Kingston Stret'
Chattanooga, TN 37414
craven.ma@gmail.com
(423)618-0169 SETG#2100
Crawford, Roger B (M1)
541 Highway 25 N
Carthage, MS 39051
(601)298-1899 SEGR#0100
Crawshaw, Randy (M1)
136 NE 1271 Road
Knob Noster, MO 65336
randy_crawshaw@yahoo.com
(660)563-5149 GRMI#4115
Creamer, Jennifer (M1)
22 Oakhurst Avenue
Ipswich, MA 01938
jencreamer@gmail.com
(831)809-9890 SEET#2200
Crisp, Gregory W (M1)
635 Eden Brook Lane

MINISTERS CONTINUED

Cordova, TN 38018
(901)266-0406 GRWT#9100
Criss, Paul T (M1)
6831 Salem Road
Lakeland, TN 38002
ptcriss@hotmail.com
(901)626-8462 GRWT#9316
Crosby, Ronald (M3)
407 N "A" Street
Calera, OK 74730
( ) MSCH#6100
Croslin, Dennis (M3)
165 Maple Street
Gordonsville, TN .38563
(615)934-2383 TNMU#7246
Cuartas, Joel (M0)
Calle 34 #24A-36
Cali, COLOMBIA, SA
(000)438-2512 MSCA#8211
Cummings, Corey (M1)
1023 W Woodrow Street
Milan, TN 38358
corey@milancp.org
(731)686-1851 GRWT#9108
Cunningham, Matthew Dean (M1)
1646 Brighton-Clopton Road
Brighton, TN 38011
mcunningham0528@comcast.net
(901)475-4252 GRWT#9318

--==<< D >>==--

Dalwig, Roger (M1)
1661 Hickory Lane
Corydon, IN 47112
rcd129@hotmail.com
(812)705-5071 MINC#5200
Daniels, Doy L, Jr (M1)
1095 Crestview Drive
Milan, TN 38358
revdrdoy@gmail.com
(731)686-1851 GRWT#9121
Darland, Chris (M1)
582 Ada Drive
Harrodsburg, KY 40330
(859)734-2254 MICU#3303
Davenport, Donna (M1)
PO Box 234
Wingo, KY 42088
chamberdonna@yahoo.com
(270)376-5488 MICO#3400
Davenport, Mark A (M1)
323 Chimney Rock Drive #1314
Tyler, TX 75703
hoginbama@yahoo.com
(205)427-4941 MSTR#8100
Davenport, Vondal (M1)
97 Main Street
Ratcliff, AR 72951
(479)965-2036 GRAR#1100
Davis, C Timothy (M1)
8880 Childress Road
West Paducah, KY 42086
FAX: (904)994-6003
charles0828@earthlink.net
(850)995-8383 SEGR#0100
Davis, Robert (Toby) (M1)
1211 AR 223 Highway
Pineville, AR 72566
pastortobydavis@gmail.com
(901)826-5755 GRAR#1512
Daza, Edilberto (M1)
Cra 12 #8-47

Cartago, Valle
Colombia, South America
presbicartago@gmail.com
57(314)794-1905 MSAN#8900
Daza, Johan (M1)
8148 Yellow Stone Drive
Cordova, TN 38016
jdaza@cumberland.org
(281)793-3869 MSAN#8900
De Jimenez, Luciria Aguirre (M1)
AA6365
COLOMBIA, SA
pastorluciana50@yahoo.com.co
(300)686-9161 MSCA#8200
De Vries, Raymond (M1)
2080 Stanford Village Drive
Antioch, TN 37013
ray.devries@comcast.net
(615)332-3587 TNNA#7300
De Wees, Jeff (M1)
116 Lancaster Court
Gallatin, TN 37066
pastorjeff@beechcp.com
(931)209-3331 TNNA#7301
Deaton, John (M1)
277 School Lanet
Springfield, PA 19064
deatonjr11@gmail.com
(215)906-7067 SEHO#0500
DeBerry, Jacqueline (M1)
( ) GRWT#9100
DeBerry, Martha (M1)
PO Box 243
McKenzie, TN 38201
1spiritualdirector@earthlink.net
(731)393-5033 GRWT#9100
Deere, Thomas (Tom) (M1)
460 Yukon Drive
Russellville, AR 72802
tdeere@suddenlinkmail.com
(479)498-0318 GRAR#1100
Delashmit, Steve (M1)
2705 Garrett Drive
Bowling Green, KY 42104
FAX: (270)781-2368
(270)796-8822 MICU#3304
Dewhirst, Tim (M1)
3609 Oakbriar Lane
Colleyville, TX 76034
timdew@sbcglobal.net
(817)605-8147 MSRR#8415
Diamond, Cardelia Howell (M1)
1580 Jeff Road
Huntsville, AL 35806
cpclergymama@gmail.com
(256)837-6014 SERD#0814
Diamond, James (M1)
214 Falmouth Drive
Georgetown, KY 40324
jamesdiamond007@twc.comt
(502)642-5020 MICU#3100
Diaz, Esperanza (M1)
Calle 2 Norte #16-19
Armenia, Quindio, COLOMBIA, SA
jjcedp07@hotmail.com
(576)745-0496 MSAN#8903
Diaz, Freddy (M1)
2425 Holly Hall Apt B42
Houston, TX 77054
fredglobeus@yahoo.com
(832)305-2379 MSTR#8606
Diaz, Gloria Villa (M1)
2425 Holly Hall Apt B42

Houston, TX 77054
gloria@newdayinchrist.org
(832)758-5871 MSTR#8100
Diaz, William (M1)
Calle 5 Con Cra 89
Cali, COLOMBIA, SA
nuevaesperanza1983@hotmail.com
( )332-5849 MSCA#8221
Diego, Aida Melendez (M2)
412 SW 87 Place
Miami, FL 33174
revaidamd@yahoo.com
(305)815-1197 SEGR#0100
Dimo, Urelia (M3)
171 Roberta Drive
Memphis, TN 38112
( ) GRWT#9100
Doles, Steve (M1)
7702 Indiana Avenue
Lubbock, TX 79423
steve@cpclubbock.com
(806)787-7551 MSDC#8702
Dougherty, Duane A, Jr (M1)
212 County Road 4705
Troup, TX 75789
revdad.duane@gmail.com
(903)842-474 MSTR#8104
Driskell, James P (M1)
154 Mountain Way
Anderson, AL 35610
FAX: (256)247-3339
patprespax@yahoo.com
(256)648-6758 SEHO#0517
Duke, Michael E (M1)
106 Friar Tuck Drive
Dickson, TN 37055
(615)446-6515 TNNA#7300
Dukes, Britta (M1)
5226 W William Cannon Drive
Austin, TX 78749
FAX: (512)892-6307
britta@shpc.org
(512)892-3580 MSTR#8604
Dumas, Byron (M1)
1775 Theresa Drive
Clarksville, TN 37043
bdumas7346@aol.com
(931)552-8772 TNNA#3302
Duncan, Ronnie (M1)
146 Deseree Broyles Road
Chuckey, TN 37641
ronkduncan@icloud.com
(423)552-0321 SEET#2204
Dyer, Stuart (M1)
3574 Foxfield Trail
Bartlett, TN 38135
(901)388-0612 GRWT#9100

--==<< E >>==--

Earheart-Brown, Daniel J (Jay) (M1)
475 N Highland Street Apt 9L
Memphis, TN 38122
jebrown@memphisseminary.edu
(901)278-0367 TNNA#7300
Earheart-Brown, Paul (M3)
502 E Lamar Alexander Parkway
Box 2519
Maryville, TN 37804
( ) GRWT#9100
Eatherly, John (M1)
1377 Moss Road
Chapel Hill, TN 37034

jrev@united.net
(931)364-2087   TNCO#7134
Eddleman, Keith   (M1)
2787 Stage Park Drive
Memphis, TN 38134
(901)388-9885   GRWT#9100
Edmonds, Wayne   (M1)
112 Dogwood Trail
Eclectic, AL 36024
sweetpea@comlinkinc.net
(334)857-2202   SEGR#0100
Edwards, James Scott   (M3)
226 Jasmine Drive
Alabaster, AL 35007
jedwards53163@bellsouth.net
(205)529-4507   SEGR#0101
Edwards, Joey   (M1)
5279 Ivy Creek Lane
Lakeland, TN 38002
edwardsjoey@bellsouth.net
(901)573-7579   GRWT#9100
English, Don W   (M1)
4311 Guys Court
Bessemer, AL 35022
(205)428-4790   SEGR#0100
Ensminger, Mike   (M2)
188 Grande View Lane
Maylene, AL 35114
me0573@att.com
(205)529-7878   SEGR#0108
Eppard, Andrew   (M1)
1427 W McGee Street
Springfield, MO 65807
reformedminister@yahoo.com
(417)862-6434   GRMI#4314
Espinoza, Virginia   (M1)
PO Box 132
Boswell, OK 74727
vespinoza@choctawnation.com
(580)434-7971   MSCH#6109
Estep, William   (M1)
239 Skyline Drive
Harriman, TN 37748
(865)882-5114   TNMU#7200
Estes, George R   (M1)
7910 Cloverbrook Lane
Germantown, TN 38138
geoestes@gmail.com
(901)755-6673   MSDC#8700
Estes, Sam R, Jr   (M1)
4601 71st Street Apt 234
Lubbock, TX 79424
(806)407-3242   MSDC#8700
Everett, William   (M3)
1906 Cogburn Road
Clarksville, TN 37042
weverett62@hotmail.com
( )   TNNA#7300

--==<< F >>==--

Fackler, David   (M1)
3409 Benton Road
Paducah, KY 42003
woodlawnpastor@live.com
(270)442-7713   MICO#3400
Fahl, D Frederick (Fred)   (M1)
500 3rd Street
Fulton, KY 42041
dffahl@gmail.com
(270)472-1476   MICO#3419
Fancher, Michael E   (M3)
356 Breeding Road

Edmonton, KY 42129
princo1975@live.com
(270)579-3139   MICU#3101
Fell, Ron   (M1)
PO Box 285
Fairfield, IL 62837
r.fell80@gmail.com
(618)638-3744   GRAR#1302
Ferguson, E Blant   (M1)
704 Bear Run
Hiawassee, GA 30546
blantferg@yahoo.com
(706)896-9296   TNNA#7300
Ferguson, Elizabeth   (M1)
PO Box 839
Sewanee, TN 37375
ferguea9@gmail.com
(931)636-8076   TNMU#7200
Ferree, Carole   (M1)
2475 Fallen Timber Road
Campbellsville, KY 42718
ferree047@windstream.net
(270)789-4339   MICU#3100
Ferrell, Timothy W   (M1)
1850 Dunbar Road
Woodlawn, TN 37191
ferrelltw@aol.com
(931)920-2662   TNNA#7310
Ferrol, Ruben   (M1)
13018 E 28th Street
Tulsa, OK 74134
rubeferrol@msn.com
(610)966-7289   MSRR#8400
Ferry, Aaron   (M1)
5360 Summer Rose Boulevard
Knoxville, TN 37918
amferry815@gmail.com
(615)946-3078   TNMU#7200
Fife, Patric   (M1)
73 Jordan Road
Lawrenceburg, TN 38464
pnlfifernak@gmail.com
(931)629-8146   TNCO#7130
Fike, Charles   (M1)
2070 N 1st Street
Milan, TN 38358
(731)686-0224   GRWT#9418
Fisk, James R   (M1)
1 Webb Lane
Bella Vista, AR 72714
jimfisk95@yahoo.com
(479)886-1216   GRAR#1100
Fleming, Christopher   (M1)
133 Minerva Place
Paducah, KY 42001
holyday@vci.net
(615)424-8561   MICO#3415
Flores, Fabian   (M3)
Aereo 6365, Cali Valle
COLOMBIA, SA
( )   MSCA#8222
Fly, William   (M1)
3002 Trowbridge Drive
Paragould, AR 72450
billyfly3@gmail.com
(865)938-6273   SEET#2200
Fong, Cindi   (M3)
1835 Alemany Boulevard
San Francisco, CA 94112
cfong@redeemersf.org
(415)335-8067   MSDC#8700
Fong, Danny   (M1)
1224 Fairfax Avenue

San Francisco, CA 94124
dfong@redeemersf.org
(415)671-2194   MSDC#8512
Fonseca, Roberto   (M1)
Cll 46 A No 4N 25
Colombia, South America
( )446-3311   MSCA#8218
Foreman, Samuel L   (M1)
2811 Laredo Drive
Hattiesburg, MS 39402
slfcpc@yahoo.com
(601)562-1415   SEGR#0100
Forester, Byron   (M1)
2376 Eastwood Place
Memphis, TN 38112
bforester@bellsouth.net
(901)324-1707   GRWT#9207
Fortner, Terry   (M1)
1079 Luzerne Depoy Road
Greenville, KY 42345
terryfortner@att.net
(270)821-6541   MICU#3508
Fortney, Josh   (M1)
765 Windridge Lane
Burleson, TX 76028
jfortney@pathway.church
(214)794-9912   MSRR#8418
Fossey, Donald, II   (M3)
328 Waterloo Road
Cookeville, TN 38506
dfossey@twlakes.net
(931)498-2149   TNMU#7223
Fowler, Emily   (M1)
5225 Maple Avenue Apt 5304
Dallas, TX 75235
emilykaye.fowler@gmail.com
(817)983-3559   MSRR#8400
Fowler, Scott   (M1)
1900 Alex Mill Road
Montevallo, AL 35115
springcreekcp@aol.com
(205)901-8478   SEGR#0113
Franco, Ricardo   (M1)
7 Hancock Street
Melrose, MA 02176
casadefericardo@verizon.net
(781)605-5900   SEET#2200
Franklin, Chris   (M1)
310 Yellow Springs Road
Midway, TN 37809
chrisfranklin104@comcast.net
(423)972-3609   SEET#2208
Franklin, Curtis   (M1)
7620 Cross Mill Road
Paducah, KY 42001
brocurtis@fredonia.biz
(270)545-3481   MICO#3410
Freeman, A Daniel   (M1)
210 Dogwood Drive
Greeneville, TN 37743
(423)638-5925   SEET#2200
Freeman, Jesse L, Jr   (M1)
270 Eastside Road
Burns, TN 37029
mptc@bellsouth.net
(615)202-4594   TNNA#7307
French, Jeff   (M1)
5 Rose Petal Lane
Dawson Springs, KY 42408
brojeff7@bellsouth.net
(270)993-0855   MICO#3400
Freund, Henry O   (M1)
913 Sam Houston Drive

MINISTERS CONTINUED

Dyersburg, TN 38024
freundly@att.net
(731)285-1744 MSDC#8700
Frost, Sherrlyn (M1)
5557 Surrey Lane
Birmingham, AL 35242
FAX: (205)991-5259
sherrlyn@newhopecpc.org
(205)408-0729 SEGR#0104
Fulton, James (M1)
1520 Oak Grove Road
Benton, KY 42025
(270)437-4320 MICO#3400
Fung, David (M1)
(address unknown)
( ) MSDC#8700
Fung, Lawrence (M1)
367 El Dorado Drive
Daly City, CA 94015
revfung@yahoo.com
(415)535-8754 MSDC#8700
Furr, Wayne (M1)
706 E 6th Street
Coal Valley, IL 61240
prespreacher@gmail.com
(309)791-1691 MINC#5200
Furuhata, Kazuhiko (M1)
#310, 9-41-15 Kamitsurumahoncho
Minamiku Sagamihara-shi
Kanagawa-ken
cpc.furuhata@gmail.com
252-0318, JAPAN
(501)430-8885 MSJA#8310

--==<< G >>==--

Gaither, Randy (M1)
No 3 Pacific Street
Belmopan City
BELIZE, CENTRAL AMERICA
rgaither@valuelinx.net
( ) SEGR#0100
Galvis, Alexander (M1)
Calle 76 #87-14
Medellin, Antioquia, COLOMBIA, SA
alexgt7@hotmail.com
(300)778-4354 MSAN#8906
Gam, John (M1)
1235 Sanders Street
Auburn, AL 36830
( ) GRWT#9100
Garcia, Lucas (M1)
875 Scenic Highway
Lawrenceville, GA 30045
(678)698-7971 SETG#2100
Garcia, Maria (Mabe) (M1)
875 Scenic Highway
Lawrenceville, GA 30045
FAX: (678)225-0127
mabega@juno.com
(678)698-7971 SETG#2149
Garcia, Ramon (M1)
2714 Callista Court Apt 104
Naples, FL 34114
revga@hotmail.com
(239)200-5714 SEGR#0100
Gardner, Charles (M1)
PO Box 1035
Elephant Butte, NM 87935
(719)784-7744 MSRR#8400
Gary, Brian (M1)
105 Wilma Avenue
Radcliff, KY 40160
(502)351-6938 MICU#3100

Gaskill, Todd (M1)
430 Haysland Road
Petersburg, TN 37144
tgaskill@pens.com
(931)580-2708 TNCO#7121
Gaskin, Tony (M1)
1414 Saint Joseph Street NW
Cullman, AL 35055
tgaskin46@hotmail.com
(256)338-7893 TNCO#7122
Gates, J B (M1)
PO Box 289
Enfield, IL 62835
rjjbgate@hamiltoncom.net
(618)963-2306 MINC#5104
Gaviria, Mario (M1)
Cra 27 #7-48
Cali, COLOMBIA, SA
pastormariogaviria@hotmail.com
(314)773-2601 MSCA#8201
Gehle, Jeffrey A (M1)
PO Box 182
Burleson, TX 76097
FAX: (817)295-2576
jeff.gehle@pathway.church
(817)295-5832 MSRR#8418
Gentry, Michele (M1)
Urb San Jorge casa 28
Km 8 via a La Tebaida
Armenia, Quindio, COLOMBIA, SA
gentry.andes@yahoo.com
(318)285-1161 MSAN#8900
George, Thomas (M2)
908 N Brown Avenue
Casa Grande, AZ 85222
tgeorge@aerogram.net
(640)447-2676 MSDC#8700
Gerard, Eugene S (M1)
615 N 42nd Street
Paducah, KY 42001
(270)443-2889 MICO#3400
Gillis, Aubrey Thomas (M1)
110 Blue Sky Lane
Alabaster, AL 35007
FAX: (205)664-8323
tomgillis63@hotmail.com
(251)947-1638 SERD#0800
Gillis, Ernest H (M1)
3273 Bruckner Boulevard
Snellville, GA 30078
professorgil64@hotmail.com
(770)982-6587 SEET#2200
Gillock, Ed (M1)
PO Box 157
Savannah, TN 38372
(731)609-6744 GRWT#9100
Giraldo, Andres (M2)
Calle 76 #87-14 Apto 202
Medellin, Antioquia, COLOMBIA, SA
andresgiraldo@une.net.co
(574)422-6669 MSAN#8911
Giraldo, Marcela (M3)
Calle 68 D #40-15
Manizales, Caldas, COLOMBIA, SA
(576)878-5412 MSAN#8900
Giraldo, William (M1)
CLL 62 No 18 11
Cali, COLOMBIA, SA
( )439-5436 MSCA#8200
Giron, Francisco (M1)
(address unknown)
( ) MSDC#8700
Glenn, Linda H (M1)
49 Mason Road

Threeway, TN 38343
lindahglenn@click1.net
(731)618-0192 GRWT#9119
Goehring, Marty (M1)
8600 Academy NE
Albuquerque, NM 87111
FAX: (505)797-8599
mgoehring@heightscpc.org
(505)821-3628 MSDC#8701
Gonzales, Homer (M1)
8924 Armistice NE
Albuquerque, NM 87109
FAX: (505)841-4267
hgabq1985@gmail.com
(505)821-4376 MSDC#8700
Gonzales, Miguel (M1)
200 Bethel Drive
Lenoir City, TN 37772
(865)988-4238 SEET#2320
Gonzalez, Nora (M1)
2515 Blueberry Lane
Pasadena, TX 77052
(832)202-5572 MSTR#8100
Goodloe, Melissa Reid (M1)
225 Macedonia Road
McKenzie, TN 38201
rev.mgoodloe@shilohcp.org
(731)412-9657 GRWT#9131
Goodman, Robert (M1)
2 Kingston Road
Water Valley, KY 42085
rgoodman4gvn@hotmail.com
(580)756-4726 MICO#3401
Goodwill, James L (M1)
7317 Tanbark Way
Raleigh, NC 27615
jim@jimgoodwill.com
(704)526-8729 TNNA#7300
Goodwin, Earl (M1)
1012 Windsor Parkway
Moody, AL 35004
FAX: (205)664-8323
earlgoodwin@yahoo.com
(205)222-1741 SERD#0107
Gough, Ernest E (M1)
8366 Highway 70
Nashville, TN 37221
eegough@bellsouth.net
(615)646-4372 TNNA#7300
Graham, Steve (M1)
804 Sky Blue Drive
Knoxville, TN 37923
eve1ts@hotmail.com
(865)206-0012 SEET#2316
Gray, Drew (M1)
8220 Timberland Drive
West Paducah, KY 42086
drewgray01@gmail.com
(615)332-8360 MICO#3404
Gray, Isaac (M1)
512 Ed Taft Road
Smithville, TN 37166
revgray08@gmail.com
(870)373-4731 TNMU#7243
Gray, Randall (M1)
1230 New Liberty Big Meadow Road
Knob Lick, KY 42154
(270)432-5322 MICU#3128
Green, Harry N (M1)
45 Wood Way
McMinnville, TN 37110
(931)815-9190 TNMU#7200
Green, Larry (M1)

MINISTERS CONTINUED

525 Dearman Street
Smithville, TN 37166
larrylgreen24@aol.com
(615)597-5832   TNMU#7244
Green, Paul   (M1)
5228 Anchorage Avenue
El Paso, TX 79924
(915)751-7960   MSDC#8700
Green, Troy   (M1)
105 Cobb Hollow Lane
Petersburg, TN 37144
thegreens101@att.net
(931)659-6627   TNCO#7135
Greene, Tammy L   (M1)
109 Armitage Drive
Greeneville, TN 37745
tg6386@aol.com
(423)972-5525   SEET#2217
Greenwell, James C   (M1)
7165 Wind Whisper Boulevard
Knoxville, TN 37924
FAX: (865)742-1653
greenwelljc@comcast.net
(865)742-1653   SEET#2200
Griffin, Justin   (M1)
3655 Highway 49 E
Charlotte, TN 37036
jjjjgriff@gmail.com
(615)969-2426   TNNA#7320
Grimsley, Roger   (M1)
215 N Oak Street
Springfield, TN 37172
( )   GRWT#9100
Guarneros, Stephen H   (M1)
506 Clifton Court
Hopkinsville, KY 42240
pastorsteve88@yahoo.com
(270)869-7544   MICO#3400
Guasaquillo, Samuel   (M3)
Aereo 10701, Cali
COLOMBIA, SA
FAX: (408)255-5938
( )   MSCA#8204
Guerrero, Cruzana   (M1)
Calle 83 #74-179
Medellin, Antioguia, COLOMBIA, SA
(574)257-0613   MSAN#8919
Guerrero, Josue   (M1)
Calle 76 #88-65
Medellin, Antioquia, COLOMBIA, SA
josueggutierrez@yahoo.es
(574)412-3504   MSAN#8919
Guerrero, Luz Dary   (M1)
Calle 22 #25-33
Manizales, Caldas, COLOMBIA, SA
clementinajacobo7@hotmail.com
(576)888-4203   MSAN#8900
Guin, Larry   (M1)
125 Glider Loop
Eagleville, TN 37060
lguin43@hotmail.com
(615)668-5236   TNCO#7123
Guthrie, William   (M1)
11130 Frenchmen Loop Apt B
Maumelle, AR 72113
billybarloe@yahoo.com
(501)584-0019   GRAR#1220
Guye, Dean   (M1)
2759 Highway 70 E
Dickson, TN 37055
deanjoy@att.net
(615)446-7687   TNNA#7300

--=≡<< H >>≡=--

Ha, Ting Bong   (M2)
3/F 338-340 Castle Peak Road
Kowloon, HONG KONG
FAX: (852)3020-0365
tingbongha@yahoo.com.hk
(852)2386-6563   MSHK#8803
Hackman-Truhan, Deborah   (M1)
7314 N Miramar Drive
Peoria, IL 61614
cprevdeb@hotmail.com
(931)537-9040   TNMU#7200
Hagelin, Gerald   (M1)
10851 E Old Spanish Trail
Tucson, AZ 85712
azcef@cs.com
(520)275-8110   MSDC#8705
Haire, Shelby O   (M1)
3179 Meeting Creek Road
Eastview, KY 42732
(270)862-3887   MICU#3219
Halford, Angela   (M1)
PO Box 404
Sebastopol, MS 39359
angelahalford1@gmail.com
(501)251-4668   SEGR#0607
Hall, Brad   (M1)
1602 Toll Gate Road SE
Huntsville, AL 35801
(256)533-4845   SERD#0800
Hall, John D   (M1)
109 Oddo Lane SE
Huntsville, AL 35802
johnhall33@comcast.net
(256)880-5129   SERD#0800
Hall, Roy W   (M1)
87 Lee Hall Street
Scottsboro, AL 35769
royhall@scottsboro.org
(256)259-9340   SERD#0809
Hamazaki, Takashi   (M1)
1551-1-202 Inokuchi Nakai-cho
Ashigarakami-gun
Kanagawa-ken
259-0151, JAPAN
gen22-14@qf7.so-net.ne.jp
(046)543-8550   MSJA#8300
Hamblin, James R   (M1)
60 Rolling Meadow Drive
Drummonds, TN 38023
brojim391@gmail.com
(901)840-4747   GRWT#9321
Hamelink, Ronald L   (M1)
5045 Starlite Court
Las Cruces, NM 88012
hamronelink@yahoo.com
(575)640-4341   GRAR#1100
Hames, Anne   (M1)
118 Paris Street
McKenzie, TN 38201
hamesa@bethelu.edu
(731)352-4066   GRWT#9122
Hamilton, Bruce   (M1)
1037 Binns Drive
Monticello, AR 71655
bruce@hamiltonnet.org
(870)224-5007   GRAR#1106
Han, Seung Chon   (M0)
3075 Landington Way
Duluth, GA 30096
kpc0191@gmail.com
(678)469-5015   SETG#2100

Hancock, B J   (M1)
103 W Cowan Street
Cowan, TN 37318
(931)967-8491   TNMU#7200
Hancock, Paul   (M1)
107 Highland Ridge
Hendersonville, TN 37075
pah4331@gmail.com
(615)4269-4331   TNMU#7233
Hannah, Hugh   (M1)
217 Mitchell Road SE
Cleveland, TN 37323
pjhannah23@hotmail.com
(423)473-7852   MSTR#8100
Hansen, Terry   (M1)
16549 Highway 5
Lebanon, MO 65536
(417)533-8106   GRMI#4100
Harbour, Ethan   (M2)
77 Burton Road
Booneville, AR 72927
ethanharbour@gmail.com
(479)849-6329   GRAR#1100
Hardin, Kenny   (M1)
606 Lexington Drive
Glasgow, KY 42141
( )   MICU#3108
Hardisty, Randy   (M1)
4908 Redondo Street
Fort Worth, TX 76180
rhardisty@sbcglobal.net
(817)428-3513   MSRR#8409
Harper, Carlton   (M1)
255 Glenview Cove
Lenoir City, TN 37771
carltonharperone@gmail.com
(865)317-1296   SEET#2200
Harper, Josh   (M1)
227 LaCroix Drive #1
Collierville, TN 38017
jdharperministry@hotmail.com
(615)934-7940   TNMU#7200
Harris, Anthony   (M2)
1604 Parkview Drive
Campbellsville, KY 42718
aharris044@gmail.com
(270)403-1126   MICU#3214
Harris, Edward   (M1)
10000 Wornall Road Apt 2315
Kansas City, MO 64114
ed121@kcrr.com
(816)214-8977   GRMI#4100
Harris, Ernest   (M1)
610 Turtle Creek Drive
Reno, TX 75462
ernie.jeri@yahoo.com
(903)782-9712   MSTR#8100
Harris, Robert   (M1)
619 N 24th Avenue
Humboldt, TN 38343
pastor@humboldtcpc.org
(731)420-6067   GRWT#9116
Harris, Rodney E   (M1)
7420 Conjar Court
Louisville, KY 40214
rodneypat@insightbb.com
(502)368-5501   MICU#3212
Harris, Wendell   (M1)
329 N Louis Tittle Avenue
Mangum, OK 73554
wendellharris@itlnet.net
(580)782-2142   MSRR#8400
Harrison, Richard   (M3)

93 Earl Jones Road
Hodgenville, KY 42748
( )   MICU#3119
Hartman, Gary   (M1)
3001 Hines Valley Road
Lenoir City, TN 37771
g37771@att.net
(865)986-4949   SEET#2200
Hartung, J Thomas   (M1)
2291 Americus Boulevard W Apt 1
Clearwater, FL 33763
revtom6@aol.com
(727)797-2882   SEGR#0100
Harwell, Keith   (M1)
13132 Stinson Street
Milan, TN 38358
(731)613-3780   GRWT#9100
Harwell, Sam   (M1)
23 Lake Hayes Estates Road
Trenton, TN 38382
sambharl@yahoo.com
(731)414-2153   GRWT#9127
Hassell, Samantha   (M2)
510 N Main Street
Sturgis, KY 42459
FAX: (270)333-3118
hassell_samantha@hotmail.com
(270)333-9170   MICO#3400
Hassell, Victor   (M1)
510 N Main Street
Sturgis, KY 42459
FAX: (270)333-3118
hassellvictor@hotmail.com
(270)333-9170   MICO#3625
Hawley, David R   (M1)
127 John Holt Road
Beech Bluff, TN 38313
haw177@aol.com
(731)427-7284   GRWT#9204
Hayes, Brian   (M1)
69 Cactus Drive
Benton, KY 42025
cprevbhayes@gmail.com
(270)210-8165   MICO#3422
Hayes, Drew   (M1)
6322 Labor Lane
LouisAville, KY 40291
dhayes72@gmail.com
(731)796-7076   MICU#3222
Hayes, Jennifer   (M1)
2901 Sandage Avenue Apt 304
Fort Worth, TX 76109
hayesj712@gmail.com
(205)533-1018   TNMU#8400
Hayes, Marcus   (M1)
2901 Sandage Avenue Apt 304
Fort Worth, TX 76109
marcus.hayes@att.net
(270)841-7576   TNMU#8400
Hayes, Sherrad   (M1)
4655 Vintage Lane
Birmingham, AL 35244
sherrad.hayes@gmail.com
(706)773-5201   SEGR#0111
Headley, Daniel   (M3)
9332 Admiral Lowell Place NE
Albuquerque, NM 87111
dheadley7@yahoo.com
(720)724-0961   MSDC#8700
Headrick, Anthony   (M1)
3327 N Eagle Road Ste 110-132
Meridian, ID 83646
chaps2a@yahoo.com

(619)524-8821   SEGR#0100
Headrick, Christopher   (M1)
1913 Vestavia Court Apt B
Vestavia Hills, AL 35216
bravespop@gmail.com
(205)240-0979   SEGR#0100
Headrick, Jerry   (M1)
9950 Old Stage Road
Stockton, AL 36579
willjheadrick@gmail.com
(251)377-9744   SEGR#0100
Heflin, Donna S   (M1)
4144 Meadow Court Drive
Bartlett, TN 38135
rdheflin@bellsouth.net
(901)382-8198   GRWT#9100
Heflin, Robert   (M1)
4144 Meadow Court Drive
Bartlett, TN 38135
rdheflin@bellsouth.net
(901)382-8198   TNCO#7100
Heidel, Jason   (M1)
218 Morningside Drive
Hopkinsville, KY 42240
heidelj@hotmail.com
(270)498-7380   MICO#3400
Heilbron, Luz Maria   (M1)
Cra 12 bis #11-51
Pereira, Risaralda, COLOMBIA, SA
pastorapresbi@hotmail.com
(576)333-9295   MSAN#8916
Hendershot, Charles A   (M1)
122 Tree Shadow
Whitney, TX 76692
(254)694-3852   MSRR#8400
Henson, Kevin R   (M1)
1101 Bear Creek Parkway Ste 3210
Keller, TX 76248
kevin.r.henson@gmail.com
(817)354-1182   MSRR#8419
Heo, Mu Sak   (M1)
170 Applewood Drive #210
Lawrenceville, GA 30046
drhou@hanmail.net
(404)644-6514   SETG#2100
Hernandez, Jhonathan   (M3)
10090 NW 80th Court
Hialeah Gardens, FL 33016
jhoto2006@hotmail.com
(786)508-8578   SEGR#0100
Herring, C E (Ed), Jr   (M1)
969 Campground Circle
Scottsboro, AL 35769
edherring@scottsboro.org
(256)259-2721   SERD#0800
Herston, Terry   (M1)
390 County Road 95
Rogersville, AL 35652
tpaw51@gmail.com
(256)247-3004   SEHO#0513
Hess, Jean   (M1)
2200 E Dartmouth Circle
Englewood, CO 80113
jeanhess@316denver.com
(303)504-0275   MSDC#8710
Hess, Rick   (M1)
2200 E Dartmouth Circle
Englewood, CO 80113
rick@densem.edu
(303)504-0275   MSDC#8710
Hester, Mark S   (M1)
763 Finn Long Road
Friendsville, TN 37737

markshester@att.net
(865)995-1541   SEET#2200
Hill, Jody   (M1)
4030 St Andrew Circle
Corinth, MS 38834
jody.hill34@gmail.com
(662)512-8226   GRWT#9100
Ho, Carmen   (M2)
Tin Yuet Estate
Tin Shui Wai NT, HONG KONG
FAX: (852)2617-0287
ho_carcar@yahoo.com.hk
(852)2617-7872   MSHK#8801
ho_carcar@yahoo.com.hk
Ho, Jesse   (M3)
2/F Welland Plaza
188 Nam Cheong Street
Sam Shui Po
Kowloon, HONG KONG
jessie@taohsien.org.hk
FAX (852)2771-2726
(852)2981-4933   MSHK#8800
Ho, Kelvin   (M2)
11 On Wing Centre, 2/F
Pak She Back Street
Cheung Chau, HONG KONG
kelvinskho@gmail.com
(852)2981-4933   MSHK#8801
Hocker, David   (M3)
309 N Taylor Street
Morgantown, KY 42261
davidhocker@hockerins.com
(270)526-6027   MICU#3311
Hoke, Walter   (M1)
215 Navajo Trail
Georgetown, TX 78633
(512)869-1948   MSTR#8100
Holley, Ann   (M1)
PO Box 345
Lockesburg, AR 71846
ladyrev1115@yahoo.com
(870)289-3421   GRAR#1100
Hollingshed, Lee   (M1)
3612 Harmony Church Grove Road
Dallas, GA 30132
leearmstrong@bellsouth.net
(770)548-0152   SETG#2100
Holmes, Aaron G   (M1)
PO Box 171
Atwood, TN 38220
agholmes@charter.net
(731)662-7595   GRWT#9100
Holt, Billy Jack   (M1)
5039 Highway 37 N
Clarksville, TX 75426
jackdora@windstream.net
(903)428-9909   MSTR#8125
Hom, Patti   (M3)
811 Faxon Avenue
San Francisco, CA 94112
phom@gfccsf.org
(415)486-5998   MSDC#8700
Hong, Soon Gab   (M1)
13600 Doty Avenue Apt 4
Hawthorne, CA 90250
lemuelhong@hotmail.com
(972)446-0350   MSRR#8400
Hood, Charles   (M1)
6535 Bailey Road
Anderson, AL 35610
hooddad11@gmail.com
(256)229-6251   SEHO#0516
Hopkins, Daniel   (M2)

1608 Oak Park Boulevard
Calvert City, KY 42029
danielhopkins2469@yahoo.com
(270)205-1847   MICO#3400
Hopkins, Wayne   (M2)
 1413 E Unity Church Road
 Hardin, KY 42048
 (270)437-4481   MICO#3400
Howe, Francis   (M1)
 129 Manley Street
 McKenzie, TN 38201
 (731)352-5551   GRWT#9100
Howell, Linda   (M1)
 PO Box 80050
 Keller, TX 76244
 lshowell885@yahoo.com
 (601)942-2015   MSRR#8400
Howell-Diamond, Steven   (M1)
 106 Ultimate Court
 Madison, AL 35757
 smdiam@hotmail.com
 (931)636-7336   SERD#0800
Howton, Orvie Ray   (M1)
 4928 Montauk Trail SE
 Owens Cross Road, AL 35763
 orphowton@yahoo.com
 (256)533-9224   SERD#0800
Hoyos, Javier   (M3)
 Calle 34 24A-36
 Cali, COLOMBIA, SA
 ( )445-5556   MSCA#8200
Hubbard, Donald   (M1)
 2128 N Campbell Station Road
 Knoxville, TN 37932
 djhubbard@mindspring.com
 (865)693-0264   SEET#2200
Hubbard, Pratt   (M1)
 1565 Eli Brown Road
 McKenzie, TN 38201
 (731)352-9178   GRWT#9100
Hudson, Barney   (M1)
 10541 Fossil Hill Drive
 Fort Worth, TX 76131
 barneyrev@gmail.com
 (817)851-2960   MSRR#8425
Hudson, Ellen   (M3)
 301 N Royal Oaks Blvd Apt 2614
 Franklin, TN 37067
 ellen.hudson17@icloud.com
 (731)780-1004   GRWT#9100
Hudson, George Cliff   (M1)
 4782 Waverly Court
 Ooltewah, TN 37363
 gchudson3@gmail.com
 (423)238-6333   SETG#2106
Hudson, Jennifer   (M3)
 716 Apache Drive
 Marshall, MO 65340
 (660)631-3893   GRMI#4100
Huey, Sharon   (M1)
 3265 16th Street
 San Francisco, CA 94103
 sharon_huey@yahoo.com
 (415)703-6090   MSDC#8510
Hughes, Charles   (M1)
 114 Gaul Street
 Estill Springs, TN 37330
 cphugs@cafes.net
 (931)649-5189   SERD#0800
Hughes, Douglas   (M1)
 5545 Hocker Road
 Paducah, KY 42001
 milburnchapel@gmail.com

(270)488-2588   MICO#3400
Hughes, Richard W   (M1)
 2954 Bob Wade Lane
 Harvest, AL 35749
 hughesrichard23@gmail.com
 (256)859-3178   SERD#0806
Hullander, Jerry (Butch)   (M1)
 767 Rifle Range Road
 Greeneville, TN 37743
 jerryihs@catt.com
 (706)935-4878   SETG#2107
Hung, Ella Siu Kei   (M1)
 2/F Welland Plaza
 188 Nam Cheong Street
 Sham Shui Po, Kowloon, HONG KONG
 FAX: (852)2771-2726
 ellahung@yahoo.com
 (852)2794-2382   MSHK#8800
Hung, Kevin   (M3)
 28 Hong Yip Street
 Yuen Long NT, HONG KONG
 kevinhk0627@gmail.com
 FAX (852)2639-5620
 (852)2981-4933   MSHK#8800
Hunley, Jearl   (M1)
 2618 Canterbury Road
 Columbus, MS 39705
 jdhunley@cableone.net
 (662)329-1516   SEGR#0100
Hunley, Terry M   (M1)
 48 Charleston Square
 Jackson, TN 38305
 thunley1@charter.net
 (731)660-5685   GRWT#9208
Hunt, Shelley   (M2)
 6035 State Route 506
 Marion, KY 42064
 sheljean@kynet.biz
 (270)704-2189   MICO#3615
Hurley, E C   (M1)
 #2 Killard Road, Killard
 Doonbeg, County Clare
 IRELAND
 hurleyec@gmail.com
 (931)551-6173   TNNA#7300
Hyden, John   (M1)
 6525 Peytonsville Arno Road
 College Grove, TN 37046
 cp1876@hotmail.com
 (615)975-9584   TNCO#7116

--==<< I >>==--

Ikushima, Michinobu   (M1)
 2074 Nakashinden
 Ebina-Shi Kanagawa-Ken
 243-0422 JAPAN
 m.ikushima@tbz.t-com.ne.jp
 (046)232-9888   MSJA#8300
Impastato, Paulino   (M3)
 1547 Mt Zion Church Road
 Marion, KY 42064
 (270)965-9528   MICO#3400
Ingram, Matthew   (M1)
 29 Quincy Lane
 Montevallo, AL 35115
 mbingram80@gmail.com
 (205)914-0829   SEGR#0100
Inoh, Yuki   (M3)
 Tokyo Christian University
 3-301-5 Uchino Inzai-shi, Chiba
 270-1347 JAPAN
 yuki_inoh0615@yahoo.co.jp

(047)646-1141   MSJA#8300
Ishitsuka, Keishi   (M1)
 Nishi Oizumi 6-13-31
 Nerima-ku, Tokyo
 178-0065 JAPAN
 keishi@gmail.com
 (080)5896-1139   MSJA#8313
Ivey, Billy F   (M1)
 409 Rodeo Drive
 Knoxville, TN 37922
 iveybe@tds.net
 (865)966-5946   SEET#2200

--==<< J >>==--

Jacks, Mathew Derek   (M1)
 341 Shadeswood Drive
 Hoover, AL 35226
 pastorderek@homewoodcpc.com
 (205)903-8469   SEGR#0111
Jackson, Lamar   (M1)
 280 Deer Ridge Drive Apt D
 Dayton, TN 37321
 hljaxn@charter.net
 (423)570-9348   SETG#2100
Jackson, Terry   (M1)
 1461 Mount Pleasant Road
 Hernando, MS 38632
 (662)429-9741   GRWT#9100
James, William F   (M1)
 4090 Meadow Field Lane
 Bartlett, TN 38135
 billjames1954@gmail.com
 (615)653-1396   GRWT#9100
Jang, Won Jeon   (M1)
 Lot2-C Teresa Subdivision
 Tabucan Mandurriao
 Iloilo City 5000, Phillippine
 ( )   SEET#2200
Janner, R Tony   (M1)
 104 Northwood Drive
 McKenzie, TN 38201
 FAX: (731)352-3101
 drtonyjanner@yahoo.com
 (731)352-8055   GRWT#9100
Jaramillo, Luciano   (M1)
 6248 SW 14th Street
 West Miami, FL 33144
 ljara@aol.com
 (305)264-1074   SEGR#0310
Jarnagin, Mary L   (M1)
 PO Box 49102
 Austin, TX 78765
 marjar27@yahoo.com
 (512)367-9922   MSTR#8100
Jeffrey, Peter   (M1)
 61 Northwood Drive
 McKenzie, TN 38201
 jeffreyp@bethelu.edu
 (731)352-0792   TNMU#7200
Jeffrey, Sarah Ann   (M1)
 5271 Highway 202 E
 Yellville, AR 72687
 FAX: (870)715-9229
 annjeffrey2001@yahoo.com
 (870)453-7076   GRAR#1100
Jenkins, Henry   (M1)
 PO Box 148
 Magazine, AR 72943
 henryj@magtel.com
 (479)969-8352   GRAR#1401
Jenkins, William E   (M1)
 1836 S Ridge Drive

MINISTERS CONTINUED

Valrico, FL 33594
hopechurch4@aol.com
(813)651-3802   SEGR#0308
Jett, Mace, Jr   (M1)
109 Park Street
Martin, TN 38237
(731)587-0805   GRWT#9117
Jett-Rand, Dana   (M2)
78 Lester Lane
Martin, TN 38237
msdanajett@yahoo.com
(731)587-0805   GRWT#9100
Jimenez, Jacqueline   (M3)
11161 San Ysidro
Socorro, TX 79927
jjimenez2228@gmail.com
(915)234-0887   MSDC#8700
Jimenez, Jorge Enrique   (M2)
Urb Manantiales MzC Casa 6
Armenia, Quindio, COLOMBIA, SA
joenjimu@yahoo.es
(576)749-1166   MSAN#8900
Jobe, J Tommy   (M1)
PO Box 8
Eagleville, TN 37060
cppreacher@united.net
(615)776-7755   TNMU#7240
Johnson, Beverly B   (M1)
801 Riverhill Drive Apt 308
Athens, GA 30606
bevloujohnson@aol.com
(865)977-0405   SEET#2200
Johnson, Daryl   (M1)
425 W Vaughan Street
Bertram, TX 78605
djchurch@earthlink.net
(512)355-2182   MSTR#8605
Johnson, Ken   (M1)
122 Ridge Lane
Clinton, TN 37716
kenjoxav122@bellsouth.net
(865)463-7090   SEET#2314
Johnson, Kris   (M3)
130 Essex Street Box 192B
South Hamilton, MA 01982
kris.johnson2198@gmail.com
(808)741-3370   SEET#2200
Johnson, Lanny   (M1)
120 S Mill Street
Morrison, TN 37357
ljohnson37357@gmail.com
(931)212-1658   TNMU#7200
Johnson, Leslie A   (M1)
11716 Price Drive
Oklahoma City, OK 73170
ljohnson275@cox.net
(405)759-3189   MSRR#6205
Johnson, Roberta Smith   (M1)
397 Ouachita 54
Camden, AR 71701
(870)231-5827   GRAR#1309
Johnson, Rocky L   (M1)
1208 Redwood Drive
Clarksville, TN 37042
jjjjgriff@gmail.com
(423)620-7753   TNNA#9300
Johnson, Thomas C   (M1)
PO Box 566
Helena, AL 35080
revtomjohnson@aol.com
(205)936-1350   SEGR#0100
Johnson, Wesley H   (M1)
6222 Crestmoor Lane

Sachse, TX 75048
wjohnson@transitionconsulting.com
(972)270-6923   MSRR#8412
Jones, Gregory   (M1)
400 Adam Wood Drive Apt D12
Nashville, TN 37211
greg1013@aol.com
(931)249-9512   TNNA#7300
Jones, Harold   (M1)
4123 Wilkesview Drive Apt A
Chattanooga, TN 37416
harold@personalcharacter.com
(478)320-4222   SETG#2100
Jones, Joseph M   (M1)
405 Lakeview Drive
Campbellsville, KY 42718
joepegjones@windstream.net
(   )   MICU#3100
Jones, Michael   (M1)
120 Jennifer Lane
Branson, MO 65616
(417)334-2058   GRAR#1100
Jones, Steve   (M1)
PO Box 368
Burns, TN 37029
stevenejones@bellsouth.net
(615)441-6159   TNNA#7303
Jones, Victor   (M1)
7017 Highway 177 S
Jordan, AR 72519
mommom@centurytel.net
(870)499-5882   GRAR#1100
Jones, C William, Jr   (M1)
109 Lakewood Drive
Lexington, TN 38351
patfreelandjones@yahoo.com
(731)967-7618   GRWT#9209
Justice, Michael   (M1)
250 W 5th Street #B
Russellville, KY 42276
(270)726-6673   MICU#3501

--==<< K >>==--

Kang, Eun Hee   (M3)
147-15 46th Avenue
Flushing, NY 11355
(718)762-0778   SECE#2400
Kang, Jin Koo   (M1)
2310 Hisway
Lawrenceville, GA 30044
agatopia@hanmail.net
(678)462-7526   SETG#2100
Karasawa, Kenta   (M1)
3-15-10 Higashi
Kunitachi-shi, Tokyo
186-0002 JAPAN
FAX: (042)575-5549
smbno6@gmail.com
(042)575-5549   MSJA#8306
Katsuki, Shigeru   (M1)
2-14-16 Higashi-cho
Koganei-shi, Tokyo
184-0011 JAPAN
shigeru.katsuki@nifty.com
(042)231-1279   MSJA#8301
Kays, Michael   (M1)
2505 Canterbury Avenue
Muskogee, OK 74403
msppk@suddenlink.net
(918)577-6255   MSRR#8400
Keller, Abby Cole   (M1)
162 Owen Lane

Greeneville, TN 37745
abbycolekeller@gmail.com
(423)863-6565   SEET#2206
Kelly, Lawrence   (M1)
77 Stonewall Court
Mount Juliet, TN 37122
(615)934-1517   TNCO#7100
Kelly, Patrick L   (M1)
1449 Rainbow Road
Limestone, TN 37681
(423)727-4067   SEET#2200
Kelso, James H   (M1)
131 Lords Way
Dawsonville, GA 30534
elgato@alltel.net
(706)216-7513   SETG#2100
Kennedy, Don   (M3)
5335 Dizzy Dean Road
Booneville, AR 72927
donkennedy@centurytel.net
(479)675-4418   GRAR#1414
Kennedy, Jim   (M2)
613 English Ivy Way
Aberdeen, MD 21001
jpkak@comcast.net
(   )   SETG#2100
Kennemer, Darren   (M1)
8828 Highway 119
Alabaster, AL 35007
dlkennemer@gmail.com
(205)663-3152   SERD#0107
Keown, Gale J   (M1)
1025 Cason Lane
Murfreesboro, TN 37128
galeesther@aol.com
(865)805-5451   SEET#2200
Kerner, Leanne   (M2)
156 State Route 348 W
Symsonia, KY 42082
cooldoll@bellsouth.net
(270)851-9709   TNMU#7200
Kessie, John Paul   (M1)
138 Pony Grass Lane
Bastrop, TX 78628
jplmkessie@verizon.com
(512)585-1617   MSTR#8100
Keung Yung, Amos Chung   (M3)
28 Hong Yip Street
Yuen Long, NT, HONG KONG
FAX: (522)639-5620
amos@xilincpc.org.hk
(522)639-9176   MSHK#8809
Kibler, Taylor   (M3)
1070 W Main Street Apt 1720
Hendersonville, TN 37075
taylorkibler@gmail.com
(615)509-7114   MICO#3400
Killeen, Michael   (M1)
5226 W William Cannon Drive
Austin, TX 78749
FAX: (512)892-6307
mike@shpc.org
(512)892-3580   MSTR#8604
Kim, Byong Sam   (M1)
6290 Dawnridge Court
Paradise, CA 95969
(530)877-4651   MSDC#8700
Kim, Kio Seob   (M1)
27-27 Baysied Lane
Flushing, NY 11358
(718)539-3476   SECE#2400
Kim, Mi Young   (M1)
(IN KOREA)

MINISTERS CONTINUED

( )   SETG#2100
Kim, Min Soo   (M1)
  5350 Taylor Road
  Johns Creek, GA 30022
  samil2110@yahoo.com
  (678)622-2717   SETG#2100
Kim, Yoong S   (M1)
  225 Bayswater Drive
  Suwanee, GA 30024
  yoongkim1934@yahoo.com
  (678)765-7018   SETG#2100
Kim, YoungHo (Steve)   (M1)
  B02 Hyundai I-Space 1608-2
  Burim Dong, Dong An Gu
  AnYang City, Kyunggi Do, S KOREA
  paidion4377@naver.com
  (231)348-8033   MMT
King, Keith   (M2)
  3341 S 137th E Avenue
  Tulsa, OK 74134
  (918)437-5464   MSRR#8400
King, Mark   (M2)
  717 Big Swan Creek Road
  Hampshire, TN 38461
  (931)626-6915   TNCO#7100
Kinnaman, Richard T   (M1)
  2018 Spring Meadow Circle
  Spring Hill, TN 37174
  kinnaman91@att.net
  (615)302-3321   TNCO#7100
Kirkpatrick, Mary Kathryn   (M1)
  401 1/2 Henley-Perry Drive
  Marshall, TX 75670
  mkkirkpatrick@gmail.com
  (903)930-6236   MSTR#8115
Kleinjan, Lori   (M1)
  6516 Farnell Avenue
  Memphis, TN 38134
  lkleinj@prodigy.net
  (901)372-8413   GRWT#9100
Knight, J Geoffrey   (M1)
  2119 Avalon Place
  Houston, TX 77019
  geoff@cphouston.org
  (713)522-7821   MSTR#8606
Knight, Melissa   (M1)
  5730 Haley Road
  Meridian, MS 39305
  revlissa@gmail.com
  (530)632-6472   MSDC#8700
Ko, John Jae   (M1)
  14 Bird Lane
  Hicksville, NY 11801
  spcko@hanmail.net
  (718)762-4348   SECE#2141
Koopman, David L   (M1)
  5606 Brandon Park Drive
  Maryville, TN 37804
  racewthrev@aol.com
  (865)660-2440   SEET#2311
Korb, Leon C   (M1)
  15360 E 350 North Road
  Ridge Farm, IL 61870
  (217)662-8398   MINC#5200
Krueger, Courtney   (M2)
  1505 N Moore Road
  Chattanooga, TN 37411
  ( )   SETG#2104
Kurtz, David   (M1)
  4700 Elkwood Lane
  Arlington, TX 76016
  davidk36@yahoo.com
  (817)683-4783   MSRR#8407

--==<< L >>==--

Labrada, Hector   (M1)
  74 Cumberland Drive
  McMinnville, TN 37110
  ( )   TNMU#7200
Ladd, Sherry   (M1)
  4521 Turkey Creek Road
  Williamsport, TN 38487
  revsherryladd@gmail.com
  (931)682-2263   TNCO#7138
Lain, Judy   (M1)
  1928 Pine Ridge Drive
  Bedford, TX 76021
  judylaine5@gmail.com
  (817)909-6702   MSRR#8400
Lam, Chris   (M3)
  2/F Welland Plaza
  188 Nam Cheong Street
  Shamshuipo, Kowloon, HONG KONG
  chrislam@taohsien.org.hk
  FAX (852)2771-2726
  (852)2981-4933   MSHK#8800
Lam, Dicky   (M3)
  Flat D 2/F
  338-340 Castle Peak Road
  Kowloon, HONG KONG
  lamdicky912@gmail.com
  FAX (852)3020-0365
  (852)2386-6563   MSHK#8800
Lam, Janice   (M2)
  G/F & 1/F 251 Tin Sum Village
  Tai Wai, Shatin NT, HONG KONG
  FAX: (852)2607-2245
  janiceyeung929@gmail.com
  (852)2693-3444   MSHK#8800
Lam, Mercy   (M3)
  28 Hong Yip Street
  Yuen Long NT, HONG KONG
  thlammercy@gmail.com
  FAX (852)2639-5620
  (852)2639-9176   MSHK#8800
Lambert, James   (M1)
  224 Peabody Road
  Meridianville, AL 35759
  (256)828-6850   SERD#0800
Lancaster, David   (M1)
  426 Fugua Road
  Martin, TN 38237
  lancasterd@bethel-college.edu
  (731)588-5895   GRWT#9130
LaPerche, Michael   (M1)
  9317 Moondancer Circle
  Roseville, CA 95747
  pastor-mike@earthlink.net
  (727)859-3998   SEGR#0303
Lathem, W Ray   (M1)
  452 County Road 1462
  Cullman, AL 35055
  lathemray@bellsouth.net
  (256)734-7146   SEGR#0100
Latimer, James M   (M1)
  7621 Richmond
  Memphis, TN 38125
  jimmylatimer@redeemerevangelical.com
  (901)787-7875   GRWT#9100
Lau, Walter   (M1)
  865 Jackson Street
  San Francisco, CA 94133
  FAX: (415)421-1874
  walter@cumberlandsf.org
  (650)583-7878   MSDC#8501
Laurence, Brenda   (M1)

  2823 Nine Mile Road
  Enville, TN 38332
  southernmoma@hotmail.com
  (731)687-2022   GRWT#9100
Lavender, Michael T   (M1)
  308 Main Street
  Martin, TN 38237
  mike_lavender@yahoo.com
  (731)253-7308   GRWT#9117
Lawson, James   (M1)
  1003 W 3rd Street
  Fulton, KY 42041
  (270)472-5272   MICO#3400
Lawson, Jerry L   (M1)
  6039 MS Highway 415
  Ackerman, MS 39735
  lawson@dtcweb.net
  (662)285-8295   SEGR#0707
Lawson, John C   (M2)
  PO Box 645
  Daingerfield, TX 75638
  sharjohn@windstream.net
  (903)645-2183   MSTR#8106
Lawson, Luke   (M1)
  270 N Ridgeland Circle
  Columbus, MS 39705
  luke_lawson03@hotmail.com
  (662)295-9322   SEGR#0706
Layne, Phillip   (M1)
  10699 Griffith Highway
  Whitwell, TN 37397
  44philliplayne@gmail.com
  (423)658-6421   SETG#2110
LeNeave, David   (M1)
  8725 Hamletsburg Road
  Brookport, IL 62910
  mscpchurch_bd@yahoo.com
  (618)564-2437   MICO#5117
Lee, David   (M1)
  3480 Summit Ridge Parkway
  Duluth, GA 30096
  gcjcatl@gmail.com
  (404)641-4359   SETG#2100
Lee, Douglas   (M1)
  3265 16th Street
  San Francisco, CA 94103
  dlee@gfccsf.org
  (415)703-6090   MSDC#8510
Lee, George   (M1)
  314 Kingston Drive
  Florence, AL 35633
  butchleeautos@yahoo.com
  (256)740-0809   SEHO#0514
Lee, Ho-Jin   (M1)
  7565 Macon Road
  Cordova, TN 38018
  hojin.lee70@gmail.com
  (901)754-7070   GRWT#9322
Lee, Sang-Do   (M1)
  1342 Seocho-2dong, Seocho-Gu
  Seoul, KOREA
  (023)474-8405   MMT
Lee, Sarah   (M1)
  ( )   SETG#2100
Lee, Ted Shu Tak   (M1)
  2/F Welland Plaza
  188 Nam Cheong Street
  Sham Shui Po, Kowloon, HONG KONG
  FAX: (852)2771-2726
  tedlee@taohsien.org.hk
  (852)2783-8923   MSHK#8800
Lee, Timothy Daniel   (M1)
  186 Blasingame Drive

MINISTERS CONTINUED

Columbus, MS 39702
pastor@beershebachurch.com
(601)433-3714　　　　SEGR#0702
Lefavor, David　　　　(M1)
414 S Monroe Siding Road
Xenia, OH 45385
david.lefavor@med.va.gov
(813)613-4133　　　　SEGR#0100
Li, Chun Wai　　　　(M2)
1/F Block B
14 Tsat Tsz Mui Road
North Point, Hong Kong
FAX: (852)2564-2898
cwli2000hk@gmail.com
(852)2562-2148　　　　MSHK#8800
Li, Siu Fun　　　　(M3)
Tin Yuet Estate
Tin Shui Wai NT, HONG KONG
FAX: (852)2617-0287
cpyaodao@yahoo.com
(852)2617-7872　　　　MSHK#8800
Liles, Dwight　　　　(M1)
8467 Joy Road
Mount Pleasant, TN 38474
dwightliles@att.net
(931)379-0326　　　　TNCO#7100
Lim, Keum-Taek　　　　(M1)
1342 Seocho-2dong, Seocho-Gu
Seoul, KOREA
limkt114@hanmail.net
(023)474-8405　　　　MMT
Lindsay, John V　　　　(M1)
401 Greenwood Avenue
Marshall, TX 75670
(940)391-1213　　　　MSTR#8113
Linski, David　　　　(M2)
1060 Alpine Way
Indian Springs, AL 35124
pastor@greenschapelcpc.org
(205)240-0943　　　　SEGR#0208
Little, Lee　　　　(M2)
10011 Alexandria NE
Albuquerque, NM 87122
dekal31@hotmail.com
(405)618-7371　　　　MSDC#8700
Little, Russell　　　　(M1)
29 Cotton Row
Medina, TN 38355
russelllittle@bellsouth.net
(731)783-3565　　　　GRWT#9109
Liu, Lai Yuet　　　　(M2)
2/F Fu Tung Shopping Center
Tung Chung
Lantau Island, HONG KONG
FAX: (852)2109-1737
(852)2109-1738　　　　MSHK#8800
Lively, James W　　　　(M1)
906 Lyle Circle
Greeneville, TN 37745
FAX: (423)636-1017
jlively@gcpchurch.org
(423)798-1959　　　　SEET#2206
Lively, Louella　　　　(M1)
c/o Owensboro Care Center
1205 Leitchfield Road
Owensboro, KY 42303
(270)527-3776　　　　MICO#3400
Livingston, Ronald L　　　　(M1)
11314 Maplecrest Drive
Huntsville, AL 35803
hairy404@outlook.com
(　)　　　　SERD#0800
Lockhart, Thomas Richie　　　　(M1)

700 County Road 343
Falkner, MS 38629
nmsdiamonddawgs@yahoo.com
(662)837-7281　　　　GRWT#9214
Lockmiller, Lem Jr　　　　(M1)
PO Box 348
Leesburg, AL 35983
(256)490-3021　　　　SEGR#0403
Lofton, Kathy　　　　(M3)
10636 County Road 1500
Ada, OK 74820
kdnlofton@gmail.com
(580)332-0898　　　　MSRR#8400
Logan, Jason　　　　(M1)
212 Saddlebag Court
Rineyville, KY 40162
jason.b.logan.mil@mail.mil
(502)626-0722　　　　TNMU#7200
Lomax, David　　　　(M3)
1501 Robert Cartwright Drive
Goodlettsville, TN 37072
lomaxdavid53@yahoo.com
(615)753-2493　　　　TNNA#7300
Lombard, Kristi　　　　(M1)
902 Clearview
Krum, TX 76249
pastorkristi@yahoo.com
(940)435-5077　　　　MSRR#8400
Longmire, Ronald L　　　　(M1)
2041 Eckles Drive
Maryville, TN 37804
ronaldlongmire@charter.net
(865)984-1647　　　　SEET#2309
Lopez, Wilson　　　　(M3)
Diag 26M #73A-69
Cali, COLOMBIA, SA
(　)422-3940　　　　MSCA#8225
Lorick, Keith　　　　(M1)
127 Chesapeake Boulevard
Madison, AL 35757
keithlorick@knology.net
(256)325-3865　　　　SERD#0808
Louder, Paula　　　　(M1)
98 Gallant Court
Clarksville, TN 37043
paula@clarksvillecpc.com
(615)804-4809　　　　TNNA#7304
Louder, Stephen L　　　　(M1)
98 Gallant Court
Clarksville, TN 37043
pastorsteve@clarksvillecpc.com
(931)217-0369　　　　TNNA#7304
Love, James R　　　　(M1)
14382 Sonora Hardin Springs Road
Eastview, KY 42732
(502)862-4119　　　　MICU#3100
Lovelace, John G　　　　(M1)
1202 E Cedar Street
New Baden, IL 62265
jlove1234@aol.com
(812)476-5879　　　　MINC#5200
Lowe, Randy　　　　(M1)
222 McDougal Drive
Murray, KY 42071
loweshodle@aol.com
(270)753-8255　　　　MICO#3412
Lubo, Jaime　　　　(M3)
AA 6365
Montebello, COLOMBIA, SA
(　)　　　　MSCA#8223
Lui, Stephen　　　　(M1)
512 16th Avenue
San Francisco, CA 94118

FAX: (415)386-2302
(415)386-2302　　　　MSDC#8700
Lunn, Calvin　　　　(M1)
859 Cranford Hollow Road
Columbia, TN 38401
thelunns@bellsouth.net
(931)381-2397　　　　TNCO#7100
Luo, Tian-en　　　　(M1)
87 Berta Circle
Daly City, CA 94015
FAX: (650)754-9885
tianenyang555@gmail.com
(650)754-9885　　　　MSDC#8700
Luthy, Dusty　　　　(M3)
400 S Friendship Road Apt G
Paducah, KY 42003
dustyluthy@gmail.com
(270)933-2722　　　　MICO#3400

--=<< M >>==--

Ma, Choil　　　　(M1)
300 Ringgold Road Apt 503
Clarksville, TN 37042
choilma@yahoo.com
(931)824-2443　　　　TNNA#7342
Macy, William M　　　　(M1)
1358 Ephesus Church Road
Harned, KY 40144
(270)756-2775　　　　MICU#3218
Madden, Judith Ellen　　　　(M1)
100 SW Brushy Mound
Burleson, TX 76028
jmadden@pathway.church
FAX: (512)258-7325
(817)295-5832　　　　MSRR#8418
Maddux, Cynthia　　　　(M1)
5735 Timber Creek Place Drive Apt 212
Houston, TX 77084
cmaddux1962@gmail.com
(823)343-8867　　　　MSDC#8700
Magliolo, Sam　　　　(M2)
14352 Fairview
Byhalia, MS 38611
samagliolo@fedex.com
(662)838-7720　　　　GRWT#9100
Magrill, J Richard, Jr　　　　(M1)
500 Miller Drive
Marshall, TX 75672
rmmagrill@gmail.com
(901)685-9454　　　　MSTR#8100
Mak, Daphne Suet Chung　　　　(M2)
2/F Welland Plaza
188 Nam Cheong Street
Sham Shui Po, Kowloon, HONG KONG
FAX: (852)2771-2726
daphne@taohsien.org.hk
(852)2783-8923　　　　MSHK#8800
Malinoski, Melissa　　　　(M1)
9087 Fenmore Cove
Cordova, TN 38016
FAX: (423)636-1017
mmalinoski@memphisseminary.edu
(420)620-0089　　　　GRWT#9100
Malinoski, T J　　　　(M1)
9087 Fenmore Cove
Cordova, TN 38016
mlmalinoski@comcast.net
(901)276-4572　　　　SEET#2200
Malone, John W　　　　(M1)
3693 Highway 67 South
Sommerville, AL 35670
(256)778-8237　　　　SEHO#0500

MINISTERS CONTINUED

March, Kevin (M1)
1701 Ray Jo Circle
Chattanooga, TN 37421
kmadm1@aol.com
(423)499-4180 SETG#2100

Mariott, Keith L (M1)
155 Ridgewood Lane
Odenville, AL 35120
kjmariott@windstream.net
(205)903-5251 SEGR#0106

Marquez, Alfonso (M1)
389 Bethel Drive
Lenoir City, TN 37772
amarquez61@bellsouth.net
(865)660-7579 SEET#2320

Marquez, Jose Ignacio (M3)
8976 W Flagler Street
Miami, FL 33174
jimarquez.aviation@gmail.com
( ) SEGR#0100

Marquez, Martha (M1)
389 Bethel Drive
Lenoir City, TN 37772
amarquez61@bellsouth.net
(865)660-7579 SEET#2320

Mars, Stan (M1)
PO Box 274
Mt Pleasant, AR 72561
smars2@liberty.edu
(217)254-5120 GRAR#1100

Marshall, Debbie (M1)
1494 Bucksnort Road
Covington, TN 38019
dsmarshall05@att.net
(901)494-1251 GRWT#9304

Martin, Theresa (M1)
116 Crisman Street
Chattanooga, TN 37415
choochootm@usa.net
(423)903-7260 SETG#2100

Martin, Tom (M1)
116 Crisman Street
Chattanooga, TN 37415
choochootm@usa.net
(423)903-7260 (cell) SETG#2100

Martin, William E, Jr (M1)
741 Chapel Hill Road
Marion, KY 42064
juniormartin@yahoo.com
(870)270-3344 MICO#3620

Martinez, Dagoberto (M1)
Cra 62D #71-113
Bello, Antioqua
COLOMBIA, SA
(574)452-3466 MSAN#8900

Martinez, Rodrigo (M1)
Mz2 Casa 21 Urb Casas De Milan
Dosquebradas, Risaralda
COLOMBIA, SA
oikoinonia@gmail.com
(576)322-2177 MSAN#8900

Martinez, Soledad (M1)
2801 Biway Street
Ft Worth, TX 76114
shirleymartinez1252@gmail.com
(817)812-8247 MSRR#8400

Masuda, Yasuo (M1)
1-11-20 Kokubu
Ichikawa-shi, Chiba-ken
272-0834 JAPAN
FAX: (047)369-7540
fwgc6854@mb.infoweb.ne.jp
(047)369-7540 MSJA#8314

Mata, Elizabeth (M1)
PO Box 1040
San Elizario, TX 79849
hectoryliz@att.net
(915)851-5354 MSDC#8706

Mata, Hector (M1)
PO Box 1040
San Elizario, TX 79849
hectoryliz@att.net
(915)851-5354 MSDC#8706

Mata, Isaac (M1)
PO Box 1040
San Elizario, TX 79849
isaacmata96@yahoo.com
(915)851-5354 MSDC#8706

Mata, Pablo (M1)
230 Flor Blanca
El Paso, TX 79927
pablomata@yahoo.com
(915)319-8407 MSDC#8700

Mathews, Nathaniel (M2)
755 Cherokee Road
New Johnsonville, TN 37134
bro.nate-mathews@hotmail.com
(931)209-6645 TNNA#7300

Matlock, Robert (M1)
156 Dovenshire Drive
Fairfield Glade, TN 38558
revbobm@msn.com
(931)210-0614 TNMU#7200

Matsumoto, Masahiro (M1)
2-14-1 Minami Rinkan
Yamato-shi, Kanagawa-ken
242-0006 JAPAN
matsumoto@koza-church.jp
(046)275-2767 MSJA#8313

Matsuya, Ryuzo (M1)
72-2 Naka Kibogaoka Asahi-ku
Yokohama, Kanagawa-ken
241-0825 JAPAN
matsuya.r@woody.ocn.ne.jp
(045)364-8297 MSJA#8302

Matthews, James N (M1)
241 Morning Star Drive
Huntsville, AL 35811
brojim10@att.net
(256)337-2765 SERD#0800

Mayfield, Randall (M1)
12470 Daisywood Drive
Knoxville, TN 37932
FAX: (865)769-4756
mayfield07@comcast.net
(865)769-4756 SEET#2308

Maynard, Geoffery (M1)
1356 Marcia Road
Memphis, TN 38117
(901)409-5269 GRWT#9100

Mays, Ronald B (M1)
1100 Cindy Lane
Mayfield, KY 42066
rbmays@wk.net
(270)247-0070 MICO#3400

McBeth, David (M1)
109 Gloria Place
Jacksonville, NC 28540
dsj3mcbeth@gmail.com
(910)238-4279 SEET#2200

McCallum, Frank (M1)
PO Box 56
Garfield, KY 40140
mccallum@bbtel.com
(270)580-4796 MICU#3208

McCarty, John (M1)

305 W Martindale Drive
Marshall, TX 75672
mtsjohn@gmail.com
(423)650-8788 MSTR#8100

McCaskey, Charles (M1)
679 Canter Lane
Cookeville, TN 38501
charles@cookevillecpchurch.org
(931)526-4885 TNMU#7200

McClanahan, H Walter (M1)
215 White Bros Road
Humboldt, TN 38343
waltermac2@hughes.net
(731)784-1176 GRWT#9110

McClanahan, Jo Ann (M1)
215 White Bros Road
Humboldt, TN 38343
joannmcclanahan@hughes.net
(731)784-1176 GRWT#9100

McClung, Andy (M1)
919 Dickinson Street
Memphis, TN 38107
scubarev@att.net
(901)606-6615 GRWT#9100

McClung, Tiffany (M1)
919 Dickinson Street
Memphis, TN 38107
tmcclung@memphisseminary.edu
(901)606-6615 GRWT#9100

McConnell, Donald R (M1)
147 Confederacy Circle
Knoxville, TN 37934
donjoyce515@hotmail.com
(865)288-0230 SEET#2200

McCoy, Kenneth L (M1)
1422 Walton Road
Memphis, TN 38117
(901)682-0891 GRWT#9301

McCurley, Don (M1)
4036 McAllister Street
Milan, TN 38358
dcmccurley@hotmail.com
(731)723-3623 GRWT#9106

McDuff, Dwayne (M1)
9770 County Road 5
Florence, AL 35633
fcpdmcduff@comcast.net
FAX: (256)766-0736
(256)764-6354 SEHO#0506

McDuffie, J C (M1)
RR 3 Box 574
Fairfield, IL 62837
mactrapper4@frontier.com
(618)842-5624 MINC#5113

McGee, Charles Randall (M1)
9037 Groveland Drive
Dallas, TX 75218
randallmcgee@sbcglobal.net
(214)328-2488 MSRR#8400

McGill, James A (M1)
433 S Walnut Avenue
Cookeville, TN 38501
jam7235@frontiernet.net
(931)526-6936 TNMU#7234

McGowan, Kriss (M1)
885 Mount Calvary Road
Whitwell, TN 37397
krissmcg658@gmail.com
(423)463-8609 SETG#2119

McGowan, Rhonda (M1)
885 Mount Calvary Road
Whitwell, TN 37379
pastorrhonda@mcgowanministries.com

MINISTERS CONTINUED

(423)619-5679 SETG#2100
McGuire, James D (M1)
220 Southwind Circle #2
Greenville, TN 37745
jmcguire915@comcast.net
(423)638-6380 SEET#2200
McGuire, Timothy (M1)
PO Box 42
Mt Sherman, KY 42764
brotim.cpc@gmail.com
(270)766-9027 MICU#3509
McInnis, Rodney (M1)
6589 Harbor Place
Gadsden, AL 35907
mcinnisrodneyand@bellsouth.net
(256)454-2399 SEGR#0404
McMichael, Jeff (M1)
224 John Drane Lane
Harned, KY 40144
revmcmichael@outlook.com
(270)617-4016 MICU#3207
McMillan, L Ronald (M1)
675 Kimberly Drive
Atoka, TN 38004
mcmillanron@bellsouth.net
(901)837-1101 GRWT#9100
McNeese, Mark (M1)
3306 Greenlawn Parkway
Austin, TX 78757
2mam53@gmail.com
(512)517-1042 MSTR#8100
McNeese, Michael C (M1)
16410 Wesley Evans Road
Prairieville, LA 70769
mcneesemc@cox.net
(520)722-1350 MSDC#8700
McSpadden, Nancy (M1)
120 Roberta Drive
Memphis, TN 38112
revnancy77@gmail.com
(870)612-0067 GRAR#1100
Mearns, Duawn (M1)
15971 State Highway 1 W
Ada, OK 74820
duawn@covenantcpc.org
(580)332-0799 MSRR#6304
Medlin, Kevin (M1)
316 Dandelion Drive
Lebanon, TN 37087
FAX: (615)444-6671
kmedlin12@hotmail.com
(615)444-7453 TNMU#7220
Meeks, Brittany (M1)
710 N Avalon Street
Memphis, TN 38107
bpmeeks@memphisseminary.edu
(901)336-9024 GRWT#9100
Meinzer, Alan (M1)
780 Barren Fork Road
Mt. Pleasant, AR 72561
brotheralan@centurylink.net
(870)612-3936 GRAR#1515
Melson, Glenda (M1)
331 Tickle Weed Road
Swansea, SC 29160
gmelson@fidnet.com
(417)588-2758 GRMI#4100
Melton, Samuel D (M1)
2249 Bucks Pocket Road SE
Oldfort, TN 37362
(423)472-8467 SETG#2100
Merchant, Tom (M1)
18784 Shoreline Way

Fayetteville, AR 72703
merchantt48@gmail.om
(231)557-5435 GRAR#1405
Meredith, Charles (M1)
144 Barbara Circle
Elizabethtown, KY 42701
(270)307-0607 MICU#3210
Merritt, Joyce (M1)
3929 Snail Shell Cave Road
Rockvale, TN 37153
(615)574-3047 TNMU#7200
Messer, James (M1)
3653 Old Madisonville Road
Henderson, KY 42420
jcmess@hotmail.com
(270)827-0711 MINC#5304
Middleton, Bill S (M1)
12826 Union Road
Knoxville, TN 37922
revbill@charter.net
(865)966-1706 SEET#2304
Mikel, Jason (M1)
4630 Mt Sharon Road
Greenbrier, TN 37073
jasonemikel@gmail.com
(615)243-8938 TNCO#7144
Milby, Elizabeth L (M1)
207 Summersville Road
Greensburg, KY 42743
(270)932-5659 MICU#3100
Miller, Carol (M1)
101 Park Avenue
Dickson, TN 37055
lcarolmiller@comcast.net
(615)411-6656 TNNA#7300
Miller, James R (M1)
1214 Whitney Drive
Columbia, TN 38401
rev.james.miller@charter.net
(931)381-3367 TNCO#7101
Mills, David M (M1)
60 Huge Oak Street
Bertram, TX 78605
(512)355-3511 MSTR#8100
Mink, R Allan (M1)
1113 Hidden Glen Court
Burleson, TX 76028
FAX: (817)295-2576
alan.mink@pathway.church
(817)295-5832 MSRR#8418
Minor, Mitzi (M1)
875 S Cox
Memphis, TN 38104
(901)278-6115 GRWT#9100
Minton, Grant (M1)
PO Box 270
Auburn, KY 42206
FAX: (270)271-4603
gminton@logantele.com
(270)542-7991 MICU#3301
Miyai, Takehiko (M1)
A-201 2-2-48 Higashihara Zama-shi
Kanagawa-ken
228-0004 JAPAN
FAX: (046)256-3212
tacke.m@gmail.com
(046)207-6558 MSJA#8304
Miyajima, Atsushi (M2)
Rua Araja
58 Paraiso Sao Joa
48280-000, Bahia, BRAZIL
ariel.atsushi@gmail.com
(5571)3664-1037 MSJA#8313

Montano, Jhony (M1)
Cra 9 No 6 6N 87 Bello Horizonte
Popayan
Colombia, South America
(092)823-8988 MSCA#8227
Montoya, David (M1)
Cra 12 bis #11-69
Pereira, Risaralda, COLOMBIA, SA
FAX: (576)324-4110
adamonva@gmail.com
(576)324-4109 MSAN#8916
Montoya, David (M3)
20900 FM 1093 Apt 11208
Richmond, TX 77407
davinay@hotmail.com
(823)366-6897 MSTR#8100
Montoya, Eduardo (M1)
270 Windsor Drive
Roselle, IL 60172
edmontoya@hotmail.com
(630)980-1577 MINC#5203
Moore, Hillman C (M1)
300 Medical Parkway Ste 2320
Lakeway, TX 78738
hillmancm@att.net
(731)537-9561 MICO#3400
Moore, James R, Sr (M1)
2778 Marguerite Street S
Hokes Bluff, AL 35903
jmoore@microxl.com
(256)494-9030 SEGR#0100
Moore, Kimberly (M2)
1025 Three Island Ford Road
Charlotte, TN 37036
kimberly.a.moore@vanderbilt.edu
(615)545-1595 TNNA#7300
Mora, Wilfredo (M2)
17512 SW 153rd Court
Miami, FL 33187
moraw68@gmail.com
(786)554-1478 SEGR#0100
Morgan, Kenneth P (M1)
5400 Highway 101
Rogersville, AL 35652
FAX: (256)247-1424
kennymorgan330@hotmail.com
(256)247-3890 SEHO#0515
Morgan, Richard (M1)
1468 Williams Cove Road
Winchester, TN 37398
icthuse3@gmail.com
(931)349-4474 TNMU#7214
Morrow, Charles (M1)
5032 Pine Grove Road
Union, MS 39365
morrowp7@yahoo.com
(601)479-0288 SEGR#0100
Mosley, Karen (M1)
PO Box 172154
Memphis, TN 38187
( ) GRWT#9100
Mosley, Steve (M1)
1200 N Arkansas Avenue
Russellville, AR 72801
FAX: (479)880-0071
stevemosley@hotmail.com
(479)968-1061 GRAR#1216
Mullenix, Robert (M1)
1408 Azalee Lane
Chapel Hill, TN 37034
glonix@live.comt
(931)379-3617 TNCO#7133
Munoz, Mardoqueo (M2)

MINISTERS CONTINUED

816 NW 87th Avenue #101
Miami, FL 33172
tonymarda@comcast.net
(305)801-6424   SEGR#0100
Murphree, Hughlen   (M1)
4298 County Road 1719
Holly Pond, AL 35083
hmurph@hiwaay.net
(256)796-5352   SERD#0800
Murray, Joshua   (M1)
3714 Landings Way Drive Apt 305
Tampa, FL 33624
jdm4428@yahoo.com
(870)723-3286   GRAR#0303
Myers, Bill   (M3)
145 G Morgan Road
Laurel, MS 39443
(601)425-1929   SEGR#0100

--==<< N >>==--

Nash, Zachary   (M1)
(on file in General Assembly Office)
(   )   GRWT#9100
Nave, Steve   (M1)
5172 Fall River Road
Leoma, TN 38468
thenaves@wildblue.net
(931)424-0020   TNCO#7131
Navrkal, Amy   (M3)
302 W 3rd Street
Brookport, IL 62910
brinkleydanne2@gmail.com
(618)638-4218   MICO#3400
Ndoro, Wonder   (M1)
111 Roberta Avenue
Memphis, TN 38112
gusungo@yahoo.com
(901)334-5861   GRWT#9100
Nease, Dale   (M1)
500 S 30th Street
Clinton, OK 73601
(580)323-7557   MSRR#6302
Nelson, Charles E   (M1)
209 Classic Court
Springtown, TX 76082
dundeal10@aol.com
(903)641-5466   MSRR#8410
Newcomb, Troy   (M2)
PO Box 858
Salem, KY 42078
newcomb.troy@yahoo.com
(270)210-4902   MICO#3610
Newell, Jennifer   (M1)
2322 Maraco Circle
Chattanooga, TN 37421
newelljennifer3@gmail.com
(423)892-5834   SETG#2108
Nichols, Oscar Lee   (M1)
1035 N County Road 650E
Trilla, IL 62469
(217)234-6551   MINC#5200
Nicholson, Casey   (M1)
1020 Tusculum Boulevard
Greeneville, TN 37745
caseynicholson@mac.com
(423)638-4504   SEET#2200
Nickles, Philip   (M1)
5821 County Road 1114
Vinemont, AL 35179
nickles.phil@yahoo.com
(256)734-9847   SEHO#0206
Niswonger, Richard   (M1)

20941 Highway 16 E
Siloam Springs, AR 72761
rniswonger@cox.net
(479)524-4081   GRAR#1100
Niwa, Yoshimasa   (M1)
15-402 Narakita Danchi
2913 Naramachi Aoba-ku
Yokohama, Kanagawa-ken
227-0036 JAPAN
FAX: (042)725-9909
rsb09335@nifty.com
(045)961-1540   MSJA#8310
Norman, Maury A   (M1)
1750 Shipley Road
Cookeville, TN 38501
maurynorman@yahoo.com
(931)526-1644   TNNA#7229
Norris, Dakota   (M3)
4750 Highway 431 N
Springfield, TN 37172
volsfan2011@gmail.com
(615)681-6346   TNNA#7300
Norris, Freddie   (M1)
330 Lexington Drive
Glasgow, KY 42141
(270)651-7932   MICU#3100
Norton, Kitty   (M1)
251 Westchase Drive
Nashville, TN 37205
kitty.a.norton@vanderbilt.edu
(615)584-1464   TNNA#7300
Norton, Thomas H   (M1)
1049 Lakemont Circle
Winter Park, FL 32792
tomnorton33@gmail.com
(270)505-5218   GRWT#9100
Notley, Sharon   (M1)
16500 S Grey Wolf Apt 5
Odessa, TX 79766
sharon_standrewcp@sbcglobal.net
(432)210-9059   MSDC#8703
Nunn, Donald W   (M1)
203 Bridgers Hill Road
Longview, TX 75604
dwnunn@earthlink.net
(903)297-6074   MSTR#8113
Nye, John   (M1)
210 Crestview Drive
Mount Juliet, TN 37122
(   )   TNMU#7200

--==<< O >>==--

O'Neal Danhof, Claire   (M1)
301 Whispering Hills Street
Hot Springs, AR 71901
acglenn@aol.com
(   )   GRAR#1100
Oh, Taeho   (M1)
42-40 2908th Street #1
Bayside, NY 11361   SETG#2100
Ohi, Keitaro   (M1)
2-14-21 Minami Rinkan
Yamato-shi Kanagawa-ken
242-0006 JAPAN
keitaro_o@hotmail.com
(046)275-9616   MSJA#8303
Okala, Achile   (M2)
5887 Newcombe Court
Arvada, CO 80004
archileok@me.com
(720)820-8511   MSDC#8700
Oliveira, Jose   (M1)

7310 Jasmine Drive
Hanover Park, IL 60133
valdirsoares@yahoo.com
(630)855-0870   MSDC#8700
Oliver, Lisa   (M1)
110 Allen Drive
Hendersonville, TN 37075
lisa.oliver316@gmail.com
(615)319-6466   TNNA#7300
O'Mara, Shelia   (M1)
PO Box 170
Gadsden, TN 38337
chaplainshelia@aol.com
(443)699-2321   MSDC#8700
Ordway, Wendell   (M1)
4775 Calvert City Road
Calvert City, KY 42029
(270)395-7318   MICO#3423
Orozco, Joaquin   (M1)
Cra 3 #7-14
Aguadas, Caldas, COLOMBIA, SA
jeob40@hotmail.com
(576)851-4773   MSAN#8900
Orozeo Ariza, Juan Carlos   (M2)
Aereo 6365
Cali Vale, COLOMBIA, SA
(   )   MSCA#8200
Orr, Melvin   (M1)
806 Washington Street
Newbern, TN 38059
2Orrs.mn@charter.net
(731)627-2445   GRWT#9100
Ortega, Juan   (M3)
COLOMBIA, SA
jortegaus@yahoo.com
(574)323-9305   MSAN#8900
Ortiz, Milton   (M1)
8846 N Cortona Circle
Cordova, TN 38018
mortiz@cumberland.org
(901)486-6679   SEET#2200
Osorio, Fernando   (M3)
Aereo 329
Palmira, COLOMBIA, SA
(   )272-7584   MSCA#8215
Ostander, Shirley   (M1)
210 Glen Park Drive #3
Cordova, TN 38018
(901)827-4830   GRAR#1104
Overton, Janice M   (M1)
3320 Pipeline Road
Birmingham, AL 35243
FAX: (205)968-8105
jan@crestlinechurch.org
(205)281-6819   SEGR#0102
Owen, Rick   (M1)
3305 Wild Oaks Court
Burleson, TX 76028
FAX: (817)295-2576
rowen@pathway.church
(817)295-5832   MSRR#8418

--==<< P >>==--

Page, Rickey   (M1)
736 Rodney Drive
Nashville, TN 37205
FAX: (615)352-2801
rickey.page@wncp.org
(615)353-7850   TNNA#7334
Paredes, Fabio   (M3)
Carerra 7 # 1-76
La Cruztala, Ipiales, COLOMBIA, SA

(092)773-1036   MSCA#8200
Park, Bo-Seong   (M1)
304-28 Sinlim-Dong, Kwanak-Gu
Seoul, KOREA
(002)884-3474   SEET#2200
Park, Jin Soo   (M1)
21155 45th Drive
Bayside, NY 11361
jpkorea@daum.net
(516)558-7298   SECE#2137
Park, Sang Hoon   (M1)
2980 W Melbourne Street
Springfield, MO 65810
hesed-park@hanmail.net
(417)888-0442   GRMI#4100
Park, Si Hoon   (M1)
511 4th Street #B
Palisades Park, NJ 07650
(201)944-7913   SECE#2137
Park, Sung In   (M1)
12320 Alameda Trace Circle #1309
Austin, TX 78727
( )   MSTR#8100
Park, Yang Rae   (M1)
4175 Buford Highway
Duluth, GA 30096
barkmoksa@hanmail.net
(770)912-7710   SETG#2130
Park, Young   (M3)
3340 Bentbill Crossing
Cummings, GA 30041
barkmogun@gmail.com
(404)661-6117   SETG#2100
Parker, Susan   (M1)
655 York Drive
Rogersville, AL 35652
park9301@bellsouth.net
(256)247-3877   SEHO#0500
Parks, Sam   (M1)
10 Lila Way
Cartersville, GA 60120
wsamparks@aol.com
(615)529-2465   TNMU#7200
Parman, David   (M1)
5034 S Monroe School Road
Monroe City, IN 47557
FAX: (812)743-5171
(812)743-2646   MINC#5307
Parish, Johnny   (M1)
114 Savo Bay
Hendersonville, TN 37075
johnnyparish@bellsouth.net
(615)824-5842   TNNA#7329
Parrish, Steven   (M1)
4610 Dunn Avenue
Memphis, TN 38117
sparrish@memphisseminary.edu
(901)743-9545   TNNA#7300
Parsons, Hugh L   (M1)
1526 Welch
Houston, TX 77006
p-h-parsons@comcast.net
(713)522-6126   MSTR#8100
Patterson, James H   (M1)
6705 Ballard Drive #211
Chattanooga, TN 37421
FAX: (423)942-2188
(423)267-8568   SETG#2113
Patterson, Jerry   (M1)
7007 Whitaker Avenue
Van Nuys, CA 91406
(818)994-5828   MSDC#8700
Patton, Malcolm   (M1)

921 Harris Drive
Gallatin, TN 37066
FAX: (615)824-6507
bpatton11@comcast.net
(615)452-5557   TNNA#7300
Patton, Roger, Jr   (M1)
1534 Eden Rose Place
Nolensville, TN 37135
rogerlpatton@att.net
(615)975-5526   TNNA#7333
Payne, Robert (Bob)   (M1)
PO Box 11
Lauderdale, MS 39335
payne.bob.emmet@gmail.com
(205)856-2427   SEGR#0100
Peach, John   (M3)
221 Geronimo Road
Knoxville, TN 37934
peachroot@aol.com
(865)675-5956   SEET#2200
Pedigo, Russell   (M1)
1002 Haney Avenue
El Dorado, AR 71730
russell_pedigo@hotmail.com
(870)862-4689   GRAR#1100
Peery, Terry   (M1)
1431 Spainwood Street
Columbia, TN 38401
coppreacher@gmail.com
(931)381-6871   TNCO#7143
Pejendino, Fhanor   (M1)
Cra 26 #36-40
Tulua, COLOMBIA, SA
(317)654-5750   MSCA#8226
Pejendino, Socorro   (M1)
Cra 26 #36-40
Tulua, COLOMBIA, SA
(317)654-5750   MSCA#8200
Perez, Jose   (M1)
3512 Chesnut Ridge Lane
Birmingham, AL 35216
(205)663-3110   TNMU#7200
Perkins, Ed   (M1)
721 E Paris Avenue
McKenzie, TN 38201
(731)352-2754   GRWT#9100
Perkins, William H   (M1)
PO Box 632
Central City, KY 42330
(270)754-5333   MICU#3100
Peters, David J   (M1)
4010 Sam Bass Road
Round Rock, TX 78681
(512)244-2152   MSTR#8100
Peterson, Lisa   (M1)
7778 Cedar Creek Road
Townsend, TN 37882
petersonli@aol.com
(901)604-0737   SEET#2200
Petty, Linda Lee   (M3)
8601 S Mingo Road Apt 3115
Tulsa, OK 74133
(918)252-4741   MSRR#8400
Peyton, James L   (M1)
1455 County Road 643
Cullman, AL 35055
jakjpeyton@att.net
(256)734-6001   SEHO#0212
Phillips, Kenneth P   (M1)
6419 Town Creek Road East
Lenoir City, TN 37772
(865)986-7344   SEET#2306
Phillips-Burk, Pam   (M1)

3325 Bailey Creek Cove N
Collierville, TN 38017
pam@cumberland.org
(256)684-5247   SERD#0800
Piamba, Juan Carlos   (M3)
Cra 7 #21N-35
Popayan, COLOMBIA, SA
(092)838-5761   MSCA#8200
Pickard, Ronald   (M1)
6292 Golden Drive
Morristown, TN 37814
(423)587-9735   SEET#2200
Pickett, Darrell   (M1)
113 Woods Drive
Glasgow, KY 42141
dpickett@glasgow-ky.com
(270)834-6102   MICU#3107
Pickett, Patricia   (M1)
1460 Cheatham Dam Road
Ashland City, TN 37015
tovahtoo@aol.com
(615)792-4973   TNNA#7319
Pinion, Phillip   (M1)
PO Box 87
Union City, TN 38281
(731)885-9175   GRWT#9432
Pinnell, James (Jim)   (M1)
1525 Parks Well Road
Gleason, TN 38229
revpinnell@hotmail.com
(731)648-5078   GRWT#9111
Pittenger, Ronnie M   (M1)
207 Cowan Street W
Cowan, TN 37318
(615)832-8832   TNMU#7211
Plachte, Richard   (M1)
615 Grover Street
Warrensburg, MO 64093
rap@aerobiz.org
(660)441-4427   GRMI#4315
Polacek, Fred E   (M1)
907 Graham Drive
Old Hickory, TN 37138
revfredp@gmail.com
(615)754-5328   TNNA#7300
Pope, Charles (Buddy)   (M1)
2391 Fairfield Pike
Shelbyville, TN 37160
pope6897@yahoo.com
(931)205-6897   TNCO#7137
Porras, Rene Wilgen   (M3)
Cra 4 bis #10-51
La Virginia, Risaralda
COLOMBIA, SA
renewilgen@hotmail.com
(576)367-9529   MSAN#8900
Potter, Bruce   (M1)
1712 Marion Avenue
South Pittsburg, TN 37380
brucepotter@charter.net
(423)228-4485   SETG#2100
Potts, Danny   (M1)
418 Eddings Street Apt 2
Fulton , KY 42041
(270)355-2264   MICO#3400
Pounds, James D   (M1)
40 Nellie Lane
Savannah, TN 38372
olivetcp@bellsouth.net
(731)925-2685   SEET#0105
Powell, Jeff   (M1)
547B Fawn Drive
Henderson, TN 38340

MINISTERS CONTINUED

jfpowell2003@yahoo.com
(731)608-2040   GRWT#9100
Powell, Omer T   (M1)
11856 Sonora Hardin Springs Road
Eastview, KY 42732
(270)862-4720   MICU#3100
Prenshaw, Rebecca   (M1)
1100 Albermarie Lane
Knoxville, TN 37923
bprenshaw@yahoo.com
(865)531-1954   SEET#2200
Preston, Dennis   (M1)
7447 Knottsville Mount Zion Road
Philpot, KY 42366
dennis.preston@daviess.kyschools.us
(270)925-8144   MICU#3507
Prevost, Abigail   (M1)
4731 Lafayette Road
Hopkinsville, KY 42240
abbyprevost@gmail.com
(731)343-5386   SEHO#0212
Price, Billy   (M1)
196 S McLean Boulevard
Memphis, TN 38104
wmprice@memphisseminary.edu
(901)494-4851   GRWT#2301
Prosser, Forest   (M1)
1157 Mountain Creek Road
Chattanooga, TN 37405
forestprosser@comcast.net
(423)877-4114   SETG#2100
Prosser, Robert   (M1)
1021 Old State Route 76
Henry, TN 38231
(731)243-4467   GRWT#9100
Puckett, Rian   (M3)
55 Ham Street
Batesville, AR 72501
bro.rianpuckett@gmail.com
(731)288-7742   GRAR#1510
Puluc, Paul   (M3)
1421 Greentree Valley Court
Memphis, TN 38119
paul-tuba@hotmail.com
(830)872-6090   GRWT#9100
Purcell, Rick   (M3)
895 Branch Road
Clarksville, TN 37043
rickpurcell@sbcglobal.net
(269)277-7277   TNNA#7338

--==<< Q >>==--

Qualls, Michael   (M1)
5355 June Cove
Horn Lake, MS 38637
mqualls1@yahoo.com
(901)377-0526   GRWT#9100
Quevedo, Mariano   (M3)
289 Golf Club Lane
McMinnville, TN 37110
( )   TNMU#7200
Quinonez, Wilfrido   (M1)
Cra 3 No 36-29, Juan XXIII
BuenaventurValle, COLOMBIA, SA
ipc.divinoredentor@gmail.com
(310)412-1711   MSCA#8206
Quintero, Alexander   (M3)
Carrera 13 #3-81
Guacari, COLOMBIA, SA
( )   MSCA#8212
Quinton, Noah   (M1)
2912 Waller Omer Road

Sturgis, KY 42459
noah.quinton@gmail.com
(270)952-3875   GRWT#9100

--==<< R >>==--

Racines, Jairo   (M1)
CLL 39 No 13-40
Cali, COLOMBIA, SA
(311)385-6546   MSCA#8200
Rackley, Mark   (M1)
3060 Highway 140 NE
Rydal, GA 30171
pastormarkbcpcga@gmail.com
(770)382-3790   SETG#2101
Ragsdale, Donnie   (M1)
915 S Olive Street
Union City, TN 38261
(731)885-0014   GRWT#9424
Ralph, Brian   (M2)
6202 Roxbury Drive #1306
San Antonio, TX 78238
ralphbr1970@gmail.com
(312)315-6915   MSDC#8700
Ramiriz, Araceli   (M3)
235 Vinewood Road Apt DG
McMinnville, TN 37090
( )   TNMU#7200
Ranson, Doris   (M1)
9440 Fenwick Road
Owensboro, KY 42301
dorisranson@bellsouth.net
(270)229-2875   MICU#3100
Ratliff, James L   (M1)
4027 Club View Drive
Memphis, TN 38125
pastorjimfcpc@yahoo.com
(901)758-0125   GRWT#9312
Reece, Lyle   (M1)
8600 Academy NE
Albuquerque, NM 87111
lreece@heightscpc.org
(505)884-2952   MSDC#8701
Reed, Charles   (M1)
10235 Highway 301
Dade City, FL 33525
estchuck12@embarqmail.com
(352)567-7427   SEGR#0311
Reed, Richard   (M2)
236 Madison Street
Dyer, TN 38330
richardcplist@hotmail.com
(731)692-3604   GRWT#9101
Reese, Michael   (M1)
1114 Palmer Road
Lebanon, TN 37090
michaelhreese@bellsouth.net
(615)443-0457   TNMU#7208
Reeves, Donald   (M1)
PO Box 528
Rainsville, AL 35986
reevesd@nacc.edu
(256)228-4057   SERD#801
Reid, Roger   (M1)
1505 Experiment Farm Road
Lewisburg, TN 37091
drrtr@yahoo.com
(931)422-5257   TNCO#7125
Renner, Wallace   (M1)
1648 Griffith Avenue
Owensboro, KY 42303
pwrenner@adelphia.net
(270)685-4359   MICU#3100

Reno, Michael   (M1)
52 Rolla Gardens
Rolla, MO 65401
rollarenomike@gmail.com
(573)578-5321   GRMI#4309
Rice, Keith   (M1)
PO Box 582
Itasca, TX 76055
rsvkeith@yahoo.com
(254)087-2418   MSRR#8400
Rice, Nathan   (M3)
5205 Kelso Lane
Garland, TX 75043
nathanerice@gmail.com
(972)400-0675   MSRR#8400
Rice, Perryn   (M4)
10802 Hayfield Drive
Dallas, TX 75238
perryn@lhpres.org
(931)526-6585   MSRR#8411
Richards, Carroll R   (M1)
210 Allison Drive
Lincoln, IL 62656
FAX: (217)732-7894
dr_cr@comcast.net
(217)732-7894   MINC#5200
Richardson, W Jean   (M1)
7533 Lancashire Boulevard
Powell, TN 37849
jeanandregena@frontier.com
(865)947-3111   SEET#2200
Richter, Justin   (M1)
8600 Academy Road NE
Albuquerque, NM 87111
jrichter@heightscpc.org
(505)363-8738   MSDC#8701
Ricketts, Roger   (M1)
205 Contantz Drive
Canton, MO 63435
( )   MICU#3100
Ridgely, Michael   (M1)
5195 Broad Street S
Trezevant, TN 38258
(731)669-3767   GRWT#9100
Rietz, Allen   (M1)
1239 Hopewell Church Road
Finger, TN 38334
(731)989-7872   GRWT#9100
Rincon, Alfredo   (M1)
12008 Fred Carter
El Paso, TX 79936
yaanaivitaly@yahoo.com
(915)857-1343   MSDC#8704
Rincon, Lyvia   (M1)
12008 Fred Carter
El Paso, TX 79936
yaanaivitaly@yahoo.com
(915)857-1343   MSDC#8706
Rippy, James G   (M1)
442 Trina Street
Gallatin, TN 37066
lgrippy@live.com
(615)681-7086   TNNA#7300
Rivera, Carlos A   (M1)
Calle Dr Jose Maria Vertiz 1410
Departmento 202B, Colonia Portales
Delegacion Benito
Juarez, C.P. 03300 MEXICO
caralrifra@une.net.co
(52)1-55-31058377   MSRR#8400
Rivera, Zenobia   (M1)
Cra 12 #8-47
Cartago, Valle, COLOMBIA, SA

MINISTERS CONTINUED

zenobiadedaza@yahoo.com.mx
(572)214-5060   MSAN#8900
Rochelle, Jimmy   (M3)
   809 Woods Drive
   Columbia, TN 38401
   tnpappy53@yahoo.com
   (931)388-1947   TNCO#7100
Rodden, Linda   (M1)
   363 Cornelison Street
   Lebanon, MO 65536
   linda.rodden@mercy.net
   (417)588-2207   GRMI#4100
Roddy, Lowell G   (M1)
   2583 Hedgerow Lane
   Clarksville, TN 37043
   lgroddy@yahoo.com
   (931)368-1081   TNNA#7300
Rodgers, Howard   (M1)
   336 County Road 1216
   Vinemont, AL 35179
   djbr421@yahoo.com
   (256)739-6296   SEHO#0500
Rodriguez, Jairo Hernan   (M1)
   Cll 42 No 80B 64
   Barrio Versalles
   Cali-Valle, COLOMBIA, SA
   jairo.hrodriguez@hotmail.com
   (572)377-8741   MSCA#8200
Roedder, Unhui Grace   (M1)
   419 S Jonathan Avenue
   Springfield, MO 65802
   kimroedder@hotmail.com
   (417)494-6491   GRMI#4100
Rogers, John   (M2)
   308 Rushing Road
   Paducah, KY 42001
   johnr308@comcast.net
   (270)534-1195   MICO#3400
Rogers, Steve   (M3)
   37 Cool Spring Road
   Trimble, TN 38259
   (731)882-2229   GRWT#9408
Rojas, Antonio Mena   (M1)
   1421 1st Street NW
   Cullman, AL 35055
   antonio.mena.7@facebook.com
   (256)531-8193   SEGR#0100
Rolman, William L, Jr   (M1)
   602 Canyon Drive
   Columbia, TN 38401
   wlrolman@charter.net
   (931)388-2611   TNCO#7100
Romines, Sam   (M1)
   PO Box 127
   Lewisburg, KY 42256
   sam60romines@hotmail.com
   (270)755-4282   MICU#3307
Ros, Ramiro   (M1)
   107 Bracken Lane
   Brandon, FL 33511
   bethel@gte.net
   (813)633-1548   SEGR#0100
Rosales, David   (M3)
   101 N Lowe
   Hobart, OK 73651
   sagradalut@gmail.com
   (580)682-0722   MSRR#8400
Rowlett, Ron   (M1)
   22 Diana Drive
   Savannah, GA 31406
   (912)351-0736   SEGR#0100
Rudolph, Allie D   (M1)
   855 Old Rosebower Church Road

Paducah, KY 42003
rallie307@aol.com
(270)898-4903   MICO#3400
Ruggia, Mario (Bud)   (M1)
   603 Rumsey Street
   Kiowa, KS 67070
   ruggia@aol.com
   (620)825-4076   MSRR#8400
Rush, Kip John   (M1)
   513 Meadowlark Lane
   Brentwood, TN 37027
   pastor@brenthaven.org
   (615)376-4563   TNNA#7331
Rush, Robert D   (M1)
   12935 Quail Park Drive
   Cypress, TX 77429
   robertrush832@gmail.com
   (832)559-1500   MSTR#8100
Russell, Albert   (M2)
   375 Ashton Park Drive
   Millbrook, AL 36054
   chemistry.russell@gmail.com
   (334)290-0399   SEGR#0407
Russell, Olen (Bud)   (M1)
   9595 Wickliffe Road
   Wickliffe, KY 42087
   olen552@aol.com
   (270)562-1096   MICO#3414
Rustenhaven, William, III   (M1)
   PO Box 1303
   Marshall, TX 75671
   FAX: (903)935-3193
   rusty@cumberlandofmarshall.org
   (903)935-6609   MSTR#8115
Rustenhaven, William, Jr   (M1)
   703 W Burleson Street
   Marshall, TX 75670
   rustenhavendolores@yahoo.com
   (903)935-7056   MSTR#8100
Ryan, Jack   (M1)
   8806 Kennesaw Mountain Drive
   Mabelvale, AR 72103
   (501)749-8572   GRAR#1102
Ryoo, Hwa Chang   (M1)
   450 Island Road Unit 146
   Ramsey, NJ 07446   SECE#2400

--==<< S >>==--

Saldana, Manuel (Alex)   (M1)
   536 Telop
   El Paso, TX 79927
   campe13@yahoo.com
   (915)317-9349   MSDC#8706
Salisbury, Rebecca   (M1)
   1033 Twin Oaks Drive
   Murfreesboro, TN 37130
   rebsalisbury@yahoo.com
   (615)410-7801   TNMU#7200
Salyer, Stewart   (M1)
   2211 Foxfire Road
   Clarksville, TN 37040
   stewart.salyer@gmail.com
   (931)980-2829   TNNA#7302
Sanchez, Josefina   (M1)
   7 Hancock Street
   Melrose, MA 02176
   fsfamily64@gmail.com
   (479)970-8654   SEET#2220
Sanchez, Sol Maria   (M1)
   Av Americas 19 N - 18
   Cali Valle
   Colombia, South America

solmarias@starmedia.com
( )   MSCA#8200
Sanders, Thomas R   (M1)
   4201 W Kent Street
   Broken Arrow, OK 74012
   FAX: (918)437-2199
   trsncf@msn.com
   (918)269-0043   MSRR#6201
Sandiford, Holton   (M2)
   4227 E 300th Road
   Casey, IL 62420
   (217)259-3773   MINC#5200
Sansom, Vernon   (M1)
   7810 Shiloh Road
   Midlothian, TX 76065
   vernon@sansom.us
   (972)825-6887   MSRR#8421
Santillano, Ray Paul   (M1)
   1270 Polo Road
   Columbia, SC 29223
   ramon.santillano@us.army.mil
   (915)500-4928   MSTR#8100
Satoh, Iwao   (M1)
   8710 Hickory Falls Lane
   Pewee Valley, KY 40056
   iwaosatoh@gmail.com
   (502)657-9643   MSJA#8300
Schmoyer, Donna Marie   (M1)
   613 Mound Street
   Monongahela, PA 15063
   schmoyerdm@yahoo.com
   (817)266-6572   MSRR#8400
Schott, Fred, Jr   (M1)
   606 Taylor Trail
   Springfield, TN 37172
   (615)384-8572   TNNA#7321
Schultz, Don   (M1)
   708 Gateway Lane
   Tampa, FL 33613
   (813)960-1473   SEGR#0100
Schwarz, Karl   (M1)
   83 W Curtis Street
   Bells, TN 38006
   schw8651@bellsouth.net
   (731)663-3987   GRWT#9430
Scott, Adrian   (M1)
   4101 Willow Way Road
   Fort Worth, TX 76133
   scott.adrian@zoho.com
   (817)205-7760   MSRR#8413
Scott, Jerry   (M1)
   2310 Sentell Drive
   Maryville, TN 37803
   dmjlscott@yahoo.com
   (865)809-2621   SEET#2200
Scott, Linda   (M3)
   960 S Katy Road
   Atoka, OK 74525
   (580)889-2292   MSCH#6100
Scott, Lisa   (M1)
   (On File in General Assembly Office)
   lascott1979@att.net
   (816)332-0604   MINC#5200
Scott, Nathan   (M1)
   960 S Katy Road
   Atoka, OK 74525
   (580)364-6155   MSCH#6102
Scrivener, Carol   (M1)
   746 Willowsprings Boulevard
   Franklin, TN 37064
   csscriv@juno.com
   (731)660-6469   GRWT#9100
Scrudder, Norlan   (M1)

MINISTERS CONTINUED

29688 S 534 Road
Park Hill, OK 74451
ndscrudder@gmail.com
(918)949-1326   MSRR#8400
Searcy, James M   (M1)
1307 Lucy Way
Knoxville, TN 37912
gsearcy@earthlink.net
(817)293-6132   GRWT#9100
Seki, Nobuko   (M1)
2-14-16 Higashi-cho Koganei-Shi
Toyko
184-0011 JAPAN
seki@koza-church.jp
(042)231-1279   MSJA#8300
Seva, Judith   (M3)
7685 Tara Circle Apt 204
Naples, FL 34104
jclthgirl12@gmail.com
(239)269-3917   SEGR#0100
Shanley, Dwight   (M1)
16904 Old Mill Road
Little Rock, AR 72206
dwightshanley@att.net
(501)888-4190   GRAR#1102
Shannon, Randy   (M1)
30282 Highway H
Marshall, MO 65340
pastor_randy_shannon@yahoo.com
(660)886-9545   GRMI#4210
Sharpe, Michael G   (M1)
3423 Summerdale Drive
Bartlett, TN 38133
(901)276-4572   MSRR#8400
Shauf, Steve   (M1)
719 Bellevue Drive
Paducah, KY 42001
theshaufs@hotmail.com
(270)331-5247   MICO#3400
Shauf, Teresa   (M1)
719 Bellevue Drive
Paducah, KY 42001
theshaufs@hotmail.com
(270)331-5217   MICO#3400
Shelton, Robert M   (M1)
7128 Lakehurst Avenue
Dallas, TX 75230
(214)696-3237   MSRR#8400
Shelton, Steven   (M1)
7886 Farmhill Cove
Bartlett, TN 38135
faithcpcpastor@gmail.com
(901)377-0526   GRWT#9308
Shepard, Denny C   (M1)
8514 Newsom Station Road
Nashville, TN 37221
(615)662-1114   TNMU#7209
Shepherd, Sandra   (M1)
525 Summitt Oaks Court
Nashville, TN 37221
woolywagon@gmail.com
(615)772-5358   TNNA#7331
Shin, Kyung I   (M1)
1805 Gallinas Road NE
Rio Rancho, NM 87144
pastorkshin@gmail.com
(505)453-5461   MSDC#8700
Shipley, Howard E   (M1)
3800 Dan Drive
Morristown, TN 37814
hshipley@charter.net
(423)581-1092   SEET#2207
Shirey, John   (M1)

10181 State Route 56 W
Sturgis, KY 42459
amshirey7@ips.com
(270)389-3562   MICO#3400
Shirley, Betty L   (M1)
811 Rotherham Drive
Ballwin, MO 63011
therevbls@prodigy.net
(636)386-3174   MINC#5200
Shoulta, John R   (M1)
1154 Mount Carmel Road
White Plains, KY 42464
johnshoulta@bellsouth.net
(270)676-3563   MICO#3613
Shugert, Rich   (M1)
5208 Bellis Drive
Fort Worth, TX 76244
shugertr@yahoo.com
(817)913-7211   MSRR#8400
Sides, Judy Taylor   (M1)
534 Bethany Circle
Murfreesboro, TN 37128
(615)895-1627   TNMU#7231
Sims, Edward G   (M1)
2161 N Meadow Drive
Clarksville, TN 37043
simseg@aol.com
(931)206-5759   TNNA#7300
Sims, Jacob   (M1)
23716 Alabama Highway 9 N
Piedmont, AL 36272
jacobdsims@gmail.com
(205)907-8273   SEGR#0100
Sisco, Terra   (M1)
811 W Cheyenne Street
Marlow, OK 73055
terrasisco@gmail.com
(618)384-6126   MSRR#6305
Siu, Jonathan Chor K   (M1)
251 Tin Sam Estate
Shatin, HONG KONG
FAX: (852)2607-2245
cpccksiu@yahoo.com.hk
(852)2693-3444   MSHK#8807
Skidmore, Garland   (M1)
2083 US Highway 278 E
Hampton, AR 71744
(870)798-4634   GRAR#1101
Sledge, Jeff   (M1)
241 Long Bow Road
Knoxville, TN 37934
jeffsledge@charter.net
(865)318-5565   SEET#2200
Small, Kevin   (M1)
6492 E 400th Road
Martinsville, IL 62442
revkev61@gmail.com
(618)562-1463   MINC#5211
Smith, Christian   (M1)
2017 Grademere Drive
Cookeville, TN 38501
csmith2490@gmail.com
(931)265-8896   TNMU#7210
Smith, David R   (M1)
PO Box 892
Rosepine, LA 70659
ogreyfox@att.net
(903)297-6074   MSTR#8100
Smith, James A   (M1)
8301 Poplar Pike
Germantown, TN 38138
james1493@att.net
(901)309-1992   MICO#3400

Smith, James   (M3)
222 Southcrest Drive SW
Huntsville, AL 35802
dr.james.smith@netzero.com
(256)655-6541   SERD#0800
Smith, Jerald D   (M1)
2625 Beech Bluff Road
Beech Bluff, TN 38313
jergensmith@aol.com
(731)427-9316   GRWT#9205
Smith, John Adam   (M1)
916 Allen Road
Nashville, TN 37214
john.a.smith.81@gmail.com
(615)545-6486   TNNA#7305
Smith, Kirk   (M1)
813 1st Avenue
Fayetteville, TN 37334
FAX: (931)438-8649
kirks37334@att.net
(931)438-8649   TNCO#7100
Smith, Nicholas   (M2)
101 Cumberland Street
Glasgow, KY 42141
pastornic@gcpchurch.tv
(270)651-3308   MICU#3100
Smith, Robert A   (M1)
PO Box 501
Newbern, TN 38059
ras1957@bellsouth.net
(731)627-3332   GRWT#9417
Smith, Robert H   (M1)
5055 S 76th East Avenue Apt D
Tulsa, OK 74145
rhsmith@sstelco.com
(918)671-5520   MSRR#8400
Smith, Steven   (M3)
100 Valleyview Drive
Leitchfield, KY 42754
( )   MICU#3201
Smith, Timothy   (M1)
214 Jeffrey Drive
Fayetteville, TN 37334
FAX: (931)433-0056
tims38@hotmail.com
(931)438-2820   TNCO#7112
Smyrl, Jerry   (M1)
10617 Hagen NE
Albuquerque, NM 87111
jwsmyrl@hotmail.com
(505)999-8852   MSDC#8701
Snelling, Linda   (M1)
431 Windemere
Ada, OK 74820
lsnelling50@gmail.com
(580)399-0329   MSRR#8400
Snyder, Joel   (M1)
224 Lord Lane
Mountain View, AR 72560
snyder.joel@ymail.com
(870)269-9743   GRAR#1504
So, Lai Yuet   (M3)
2/F Fu Tung Shopping Centre
Tung Chung
Lantau Island NT, HONG KONG
FAX: (852)2109-1737
laiyuet0914@gmail.com
(852)2109-1738   MSHK#8800
So, Patrick   (M1)
2/F Fu Tung Shopping Center
Tung Chung
Lantau Island, HONG KONG
FAX: (852)2109-1737

MINISTERS CONTINUED

cpctwso@uahoo.com.hk
(852)2109-1738   MSHK#8810
Solis, Arcadio   (M1)
    Crr 42 D1 No 55-69
    Guapi, COLOMBIA, SA
    (   )328-5486   MSCA#8200
Solito, Carlos   (M3)
    106 Highway 63
    Calera, AL 35040
    fcg9700@gmail.com
    (205)329-8514   SEGR#0100
Sontowski, Marian   (M1)
    17101 N Western Avenue
    Edmond, OK 73012
    stonegatecpc@gmail.com
    (405)340-7281   MSRR#6307
Sosa, Alexandri   (M1)
    2828 W Kirby Street
    Tampa, FL 33614
    FAX: (813)932-9700
    sosapcus@gmail.com
    (813)960-1473   SEGR#0307
Spence, Thomas R   (M1)
    PO Box 809
    Burns Flat, OK 73624
    tomspence0302@gmail.com
    (580)562-4531   MSRR#6301
Sprenkle, David   (M3)
    5733 Stone Street
    Olive Branch, MS 38654
    dsprenkle@memphisseminary.edu
    (901)604-8707   GRWT#9100
Spurling, Robert T, Jr   (M1)
    305 Wayne Drive
    Hopkinsville, KY 42240
    (865)803-8582   MICO#3611
Steeley, Tim   (M2)
    PO Box 281
    Mt Vernon, MO 65712
    tsteeley@swr5.k12.mo.us
    (417)466-4345   GRMI#4102
Stefan, Gregory   (M1)
    1917 Birchwood Street
    East Pearl, PA 17519
    pastorstefan@att.net
    (931)296-5291   TNNA#7300
Stephens, Blake   (M1)
    2559 Holders Cove Road
    Winchester, TN 37398
    blsteph@edge.net
    (931)939-2628   TNMU#7235
Stephenson, Joseph   (M2)
    PO Box 129
    Bethany, IL 61914
    (217)853-7819   MINC#5200
Stevens, Brittany   (M3
    606 Huntington Parkway
    Nashville, TN 37211
    bstevens5@my.apsu.edu
    (615)719-3362   TNNA#7300
Stone, Paul   (M1)
    3490 State Route 2837
    Clay, KY 42404
    stonepstc@aol.com
    (270)664-6244   MICO#3621
Stovall, Jeff   (M1)
    2829 Trelawny Drive
    Clarksville, TN 37043
    jeffstovall@juno.com
    (931)993-6104   TNNA#7300
Stutler, Tim   (M1)
    1044 Mansker Farm Boulevard
    Hendersonville, TN 37075

tim@goodlettsvillechurch.com
(615)859-5888   TNNA#7328
Suenram, Timothy   (M1)
    117 Saint Andrews Street
    Rockport, TX 78382
    9tdsdt9@gmail.com
    (832)217-6367   MSTR#8100
Sumerlin, Larkin   (M2)
    174 Brookgreen Lane
    Indian Springs, AL 35124
    larkin_sumerlin72@hotmail.com
    (334)357-0007   SEGR#0100
Sumrall, Phil   (M1)
    107 Barnhardt Circle
    Fort Oglethorpe, GA 30742
    phil.sumrall@gmail.com
    (423)903-1938   SETG#2100
Sung, John   (M2)
    26 Old Orchard Road
    Cherry Hill, NJ 08003
    (856)751-0227   SETG#2100
Suttle, Michael   (M1)
    507 Ouachita 18
    Camden, AR 71701
    m_s_suttle@msn.com
    (870)836-0008   GRAR#1100
Suzuki, Atsushi   (M1)
    53-17 Higashi Kibogaoka
    Asahi-ku Yokohama Kanagawa-ken
    241-0826 JAPAN
    asyuwa98@m10.alpha-net.ne.jp
    FAX: (045)362-2603
    (045)362-2603   MSJA#8315
Suzuki, Temote   (M2)
    9-14-15-310 Honcho Kamitsuruma
    Sagamihara-shi, Kanagawa-ken
    228-0818 JAPAN
    temo_suzuki@hotmail.com
    (   )   MSJA#8300
Sweet Brockman, Anna   (M1)
    112 2nd Avenue NW
    Winchester, TN 37398
    amsweet@memphisseminary.edu
    (865)803-8582   SEET#7249
Sweet, Don   (M1)
    3008 Shropshire Boulevard
    Powell, TN 37849
    mariondon77@netscape.com
    (865)938-7435   SEET#2200
Sweet, Thomas   (M1)
    2711 Windemere Lane
    Powell, TN 37849
    tsweet1@comcast.net
    (865)938-0508   SEET#2301
Sweigart, John M   (M1)
    PO Box 876
    Dover, AL 72837
    (479)229-4041   GRAR#1100
Sze, Joseph   (M1)
    Rau Sao Joaquim, 382
    Liberdale, Sao Paulo, SP
    CEP 015068-000, BRAZIL
    pastorsze@yahoo.com
    (   )   MSDC#8700
Sze, Yat Sung   (M3)
    Tin Yuet Estate
    Tin Shui Wai NT, HONG KONG
    yatsungs@yahoo.com.hk
    FAX (852)2617-0287
    (852)2617-7872   MSHK#8800

--==<< T >>==--

Tabor, Don M   (M1)
    9611 Mitchell Place
    Brentwood, TN 37027
    FAX: (615)373-3356
    dontabor@comcast.net
    (615)776-7292   TNNA#7300
Talley, Edward   (M1)
    404 Serenity Circle
    Walland, TN 37886
    (205)854-1886   SEGR#0100
Tam, Wai Sun   (M3)
    Wing B & C
    G/F Ming Wik House
    Kin Ming Es
    Tseung Kwan O, HONG KONG
    tsw428@gmail.com
    FAX (852)2706-0114
    (852)2706-0111   MSHK#8800
Tamai, Yukio   (M1)
    3-17-57 Nakashinden
    Ebina-shi Kanagawa-ken
    243-0422 JAPAN
    yukiotamai@icloud.com
    (046)234-3426   MSJA#8311
Tan, Pek Hua   (M1)
    7 Belhaven Avenue
    Daly City, CA 94015
    ptan27@yahoo.com
    (415)515-0076   MSDC#8700
Tanck, Brian   (M2)
    64 Mercer Street
    Princeton, NJ 08540
    brian.tanck@gmail.com
    (630)730-1577   SEGR#0100
Tanck, Micaiah Thomas   (M1)
    2912 S Broad Street Apt B3
    Scottsboro, AL 35769
    micaiah.thomas@gmail.com
    (205)478-5985   SERD#0809
Tang, Po Kau   (M2)
    G/1F, 251 Tin Sam Village
    Shatin, NT, HONG KONG
    cpc_pokau@yahoo.com.hk
    FAX (852)2607-2245
    (852)2981-4933   MSHK#8800
Terpstra, Tami   (M3)
    10 Rainbow Crest Drive
    Evergreen, CO 80439
    tami.terpstra@yahoo.com
    (303)396-3604   MSDC#8700
Terrell, Elizabeth   (M1)
    2073 Vinton Avenue
    Memphis, TN 38104
    (901)647-2788   GRAR#1100
Thomas, Cassandra   (M1)
    1920 Dancy Street
    Fayetteville, NC 28301
    chcothomas@yahoo.com
    (910)488-4897   MSRR#8400
Thomas, Don F   (M1)
    743 Rain Dance Way
    Cordova, TN 38018
    thomas63981@comcast.net
    (901)412-3695   GRWT#0501
Thomas, Don H   (M1)
    4829 Caldwell Mill Road
    Birmingham, AL 35242
    dhtatn4ybc@cs.com
    (205)742-0785   SEGR#0105
Thomas, Lynn   (M1)
    4833 Caldwell Mill Lane
    Birmingham, AL 35242
    lynndont@gmail.com

MINISTERS CONTINUED

(205)601-5770   SEGR#0100
Thompson, Dee Ann   (M1)
226 W Bellville Street
Marion, KY 42064
deethomp5@hotmail.com
(270)445-0310   MICO#3207
Thompson, Eugene   (M1)
2825 Albatross Road
Del Ray Beach, FL 33444
( )   MICU#3100
Thompson, Tommy   (M1)
9160 Tchulahoma Road
Southaven, MS 38671
(662)393-2552   GRWT#9100
Thompson, W Fay   (M1)
210 Macbeth Lane
Glasgow, KY 42141
(270)646-2218   MICU#3100
Thornton, Jesse   (M1)
1016 S Fly Avenue
Goreville, IL 62939
jessthornton@msn.com
(812)925-6475   MINC#5302
Tobler, Garth   (M1)
136 Boat Landing Road
Oneonta, AL 35121
gatobler@gmail.com
(205)683-0298   SEGR#0100
Todd, Christopher   (M1)
3303 Decker Street
Bartlett, TN 38134
catodd1964@gmail.com
(901)848-9913   GRWT#9320
Todd, Laura   (M1)
3303 Decker Street
Bartlett, TN 38134
littlelaurarose@yahoo.com
(901)496-1443   GRWT#9217
Tolley, Robert (Butch)   (M1)
1445 New Murraytown Road NW
Cleveland, TN 37312
butchtolley@hotmail.com
(423)837-6488   SETG#2100
Tompkins, Wayne   (M1)
548 E Columbia Road 23
Emerson, AR 71740
waynetompkinsministries@yahoo.com
(870)807-2874   GRWT#9221
Topar, Shirley   (M1)
2233 Cambridge Drive SE
Grand Rapids, MI 49506
s_j_topar@yahoo.com
(616)245-0625   MINC#5200
Torres, Rodrigo   (M3)
Aereo 6365
Cali, COLOMBIA, SA
(011)882-8372   MSCA#8205
Townsend, Mary Anna   (M2)
1123 Tyler
Warrensburg, MO 64093
wrenhse1123@gmail.com
(660)909-5966   GRMI#4111
Trapp, Emily   (M3)
4750 Harvest Knoll Cove N
Memphis, TN 38125
(901)756-4738   GRWT#9100
Travieso, Julio   (M1)
15910 Countrybrook Street
Tampa, FL 33624
jutra98@aol.com
(813)963-3727   SEGR#0100
Travis, Kermit   (M1)
3220 Sharon Highway 89

Dresden, TN 38225
(731)364-2315   GRWT#9124
Treadaway, Kenneth A   (M1)
172 Miller County 494
Texarkana, AR 71854
treadaways@ark.net
(870)574-1609   GRAR#1100
Trotter, Wendell   (M1)
1516 Fell Avenue NE
Huntsville, AL 35811
wendelltrotter@knology.net
(256)519-6571   TNCO#7100
Truax, Robert Lee, Jr   (M1)
2989 Champions Drive Apt 204
Lakeland, TN 38002
(901)266-5927   GRWT#9100
Truitt, Robert D   (M1)
1238 Old East Side Road
Burns, TN 37029
FAX: (615)446-7827
rdtjct@aol.com
(615)740-9180   TNNA#7308
Tsui, Jackson   (M2)
258 Carlos D'Assumpcao
Ed Kin Heng Long 4 Andar LMN
MACAU
tsuih@yahoo.com
(853)2882-1702   MSHK#8800
Tsui, Sukie   (M3)
Wing B & C
G/F Ming Wik House
Kin Ming Es
sukiecpc@yahoo.com.hk
FAX (852)2706-0114
(852)2706-0111   MSHK#8800
Tsujimoto, Mark   (M1)
88 S Broadway Unit 3210
Millbrae, CA 94030
mltsuijimoto@gmail.com
(650)697-6901   MSDC#8700
Tubb, Gary Robert   (M1)
103 Forest Drive
Mountain Home, AR 72653
grtubb@yahoo.com
(870)424-0603   GRAR#1505
Tucker, Dave   (M3)
329 Miss Mary Road
Cleburne, TX 76031
digtucker@gmail.com
(817)602-3874   MSRR#8400
Tucker, Greg   (M1)
612A Idlewood Lane
Knoxville, TN 37923
greg.tucker311@outlook.comt
(865)242-4086   SEET#2319
Tucker, James D   (M1)
PO Box 34
Mc Daniels, KY 40152
(270)257-8971   MICU#3100
Tucker, Paul   (M1)
3801 Brush Hill Pike
Nashville, TN 37216
paultucker@gmail.com
(615)430-9158   TNNA#7325
Turner, Andrew   (M3)
3295 Mount Moriah Road
Galatia, IL 62935
turner87029@gmail.com
(618)294-0838   MICO#3400
Turner, Glyn   (M1)
5005 Eagle Drive
Gulfport, MS 39501
glynturner@outlook.com

(585)307-7715   SETG#2100
Turner, O Gene   (M1)
5160 McSpadden Road
Rives, TN 38253
(731)536-0189   GRWT#9100
Turner, Leonard E, Jr   (M1)
12651 Wagon Wheel Circle
Knoxville, TN 37934
pastor@unioncpchurch.com
FAX: (865)675-3787
(865)966-8262   SEET#2315
Turner, Steven W   (M1)
7622 Snider Road
Gilmer, TX 75645
FAX: (903)757-2572
fcpclongview@sbcglobal.net
(903)758-5184   MSTR#8112
Twilla, Kevin   (M3)
287 Owl Circle
Lebanon, TN 37087
( )   TNMU#7200
Tyus, Dwayne   (M1)
901 W Old Hickory Boulevard
Madison, TN 37115
dwayne.tyus@gmail.com
(615)720-2564   TNNA#7332

--==<< U >>==--

Underwood, Jerrell M   (M1)
PO Box 9
Garfield, KY 40140
(270)536-3706   MICU#3100
Ushioda, Kenji   (M1)
2-47-3 Akuwa-higashi Seya-ku
Yokohama, Kanagawa-ken
246-0023 JAPAN
ushioda@jc.ejnet.ne.jp
(046)361-4351   MSJA#8312

--==<< V >>==--

Vacca, Gary   (M1)
2203 Creekwood Drive
Murray, KY 42071
(270)978-0818   MICO#3406
Valdez, Diana   (M1)
Cra 50 D#62-69
Medellin, Antioquia, COLOMBIA, SA
dianamariavaldezduque@gmail.com
(574)263-2154   MSAN#8915
Valencia, Jorge   (M1)
Aereo 4290
Cali, COLOMBIA, SA
( )332-5840   MSCA#8200
Valencia, Nulbel   (M1)
Diag 11D Casa 11 urbGemelas
Dosquebradas
Risaralda, COLOMBIA, SA
(576)330-7704   MSAN#8900
Van Meter, Bill   (M1)
10626 Highway 41
Charleston, AR 72933
revbill46@gmail.com
(479)965-2998   GRAR#1402
Vance, Dennis   (M1)
1320 Valleywood Drive
Paris, TN 38242
rvdvance@hotmail.com
(731)420-4261   GRWT#9428
Vance, Joe
1740 N Friendship Road
Paducah, KY 42001

MINISTERS CONTINUED

( )   MICO#3400
Vanderlaan, D Kevin   (M1)
  17246 Highway K
  Aurora, MO 65605
  pastorkevin2@gmail.com
  (217)620-2723   GRMI#5401
Varilla, Adan Manuel   (M3)
  Calle 48 D E #96A-30
  Medellin, Antioquia
  COLOMBIA, SA   MSAN#8900
Varner, Susan   (M1)
  14709 Glisten Lane
  Little Rock, AR 72223
  smvarner76@yahoo.com
  (901)371-1249   GRAR#1100
Vasquez, Alejandro   (M1)
  Cra 58 #32A-41 Apt 420
  Bello, Antioquia, COLOMBIA, SA
  almaesda@une.net.co
  (574)451-4816   MSAN#8918
Vaughan, Jimmy   (M3)
  1607 E 3rd Street
  Fordyce, AR 71742
  jvaughan103@hotmail.com
  (870)818-1512   GRAR#1100
Vaught, Joseph R   (M1)
  7424 Highland Lick Road
  Lewisburg, KY 42256
  brojoe2@logantele.com
  (270)726-8497   MICU#3100
Velez, Gabriel   (M1)
  CL 8A #16A-26
  Dosquebradas
  Risaralda, COLOMBIA, SA
  (576)330-1168   MSAN#8900
Velez, Gloria Patricia   (M3)
  Cra 4 bis #10-51
  LaVirginia, Risaralda
  COLOMBIA, SA
  renewilgen@hotmail.com
  (576)385-4517   MSAN#8900
Vick, Joe   (M1)
  6064 Old Hickory Boulevard
  Whites Creek, TN 37189
  joervick@gmail.com
  (615)519-5249   TNNA#7300
Vickers, Fran   (M1)
  7225 Old Clinton Pike
  Knoxville, TN 37921
  franv3@comcast.net
  (865)859-0805   SEET#2301

--==<< **W** >>==--

Wada, Ichiro   (M3)
  Tokyo Christian University
  3-301-5 Uchino Inzai-shi, Chiba
  270-1347 JAPAN
  ichirowada@gmail.com
  (047)646-1141   MSJA#8300
Wagner, Hugh   (M1)
  12556 Timberline Drive
  Garfield, AR 72732
  hughawagner@gmail.com
  (479)359-0021   MSRR#8400
Walker, Hobert   (M1)
  PO Box 66
  Rutherford, TN 38369
  rutherfordcpchurch@gmail.com
  (731)665-7236   GRWT#9429
Walker, Michael C   (M1)
  1404 Wilshire Drive
  Odessa, TX 79761

mworator@gmail.com
  (731)643-6730   GRWT#9100
Walkup, Lyon   (M1)
  225 Bertha Owen Road
  Morrison, TN 37357
  dirtroad@blomand.net
  (931)604-3233   TNMU#7207
Walsh, Devin   (M3)
  801 East "M" Street
  Russellville, AR 72801
  (479)890-6716   GRAR#1100
Wan, Sonny   (M1)
  13 Wexford Place
  Aladema, CA 94502
  sonny@cumberlandsf.org
  (415)421-1874   MSDC#8700
Wang, Huiling   (M2)
  5562 S Yank Court
  Littleton, CO 80127
  whuiling88@yahoo.com
  (303)330-3929   MSDC#8700
Ward, Andrew   (M1)
  407 Rose Hill Court
  Goodlettsville, TN 37072
  andrewbward@aol.com
  (615)456-9136   TNNA#7300
Ward, Frank   (M1)
  46 Henderson Cove
  Atoka, TN 38004
  bamaguy68@xipline.com
  (901)837-1972   GRWT#9100
Warren, Christopher   (M1)
  906 Prince Lane
  Murfreesboro, TN 37129
  chris@murfreesborocpc.org
  (615)828-8719   TNMU#7232
Warren, Elizabeth   (M3)
  811 W Wall Street
  Morrilton, AR 72110
  (501)354-4139   GRAR#1100
Warren, Glenn   (M1)
  9735 Crotzer Road
  West Paducah, KY 42086
  gwarren224@gmail.com
  (931)209-5431   MICO#3416
Warren, Gordon   (M1)
  811 Wall Street
  Morrilton, AR 72110
  jogordonwarren@suddenlink.net
  (501)208-1120   GRAR#1219
Warren, Jo   (M1)
  811 Wall Street
  Morrilton, AR 72110
  pastorjo47@ymail.com
  (501)354-4139   GRAR#1211
Warren, Joy   (M1)
  907 W Main Street
  Murfreesboro, TN 37129
  revjoywarren@gmail.com
  (615)828-8719   TNMU#7232
Warren, William   (M1)
  7139 Toro Cove
  Germantown, TN 38138
  FAX: (901)759-3653
  cpcgww@aol.com
  (901)755-8058   GRWT#9310
Washburn, Gloria   (M2)
  PO Box 2484
  Jordan, AR 72519
  grwashburn07@gmail.com
  (870)321-3539   GRAR#1100
Watkins, Robert B   (M1)
  235 Misty Drive

Somerset, KY 42503
  watkr@mac.com
  (319)431-0990   MINC#5200
Watson, April   (M1)
  529 W Bellville
  Marion, KY 42064
  aprilwatson@hotmail.com
  (270)965-2850   MICO#3411
Watson, Dale   (M1)
  1705 Lawnville Road
  Kingston, TN 37763
  revdwatson@comcast.net
  (865)376-2192   SEET#2317
Watson, Johnny E   (M1)
  7 Hickory Lane
  Metropolis, IL 62960
  jewatson01@gmail.com
  (731)414-3065   GRWT#9409
Watson, Jonathan   (M1)
  4017 Claude Drive
  Smyrna, TN 37167
  watsonjonathan@bellsouth.net
  (615)630-9153   TNMU#7239
Watson, Micah   (M3)
  2529 Middle Tennessee Boulevard
  Murfreesboro, TN 37130
  mwatson4289@gmail.com
  (615)692-2742   TNMU#7200
Watt, Eva   (M3)
  258 Carlos D'Assumpcao
  Ed Kin Heng Long 4 Andar LMN
  MACAU
  FAX: (852)2892-1702
  eva6e@hotmail.com
  (853)2892-1702   MSHK#8804
Watts, Glenn David   (M2)
  7400 Willowbend Drive
  Crestwood, KY 40014
  hongkongbrother@hotmail.com
  (502)241-0436   MICU#3100
Wayman, Sam   (M1)
  707 High Hill Creek Road
  LaGrange, TX 78945
  samndonnawayman@gmail.com
  (979)968-3734   MSTR#8100
Weaver, Dennis   (M1)
  1750 Government Road
  Princeton, KY 42245
  dsweaver@memphisseminary.edu
  (731)592-9054   MICO#3626
Webb, Lonnie   (M1)
  500 S 30th Street
  Clinton, OK 73601
  lgwebb.sr@gmail.com
  (970)682-8025   MSRR#8400
Webb, William G   (M1)
  7926 S 78th E Avenue
  Tulsa, OK 74133
  (918)294-9117   MSRR#8400
Welch, Johnie   (M1)
  PO Box 1506
  Dyersburg, TN 38025
  johnniewelch@msn.com
  (731)287-9008   GRWT#9100
Weldon, Mark   (M1)
  1515 Chambliss Drive
  Birmingham, AL 35226
  weldonm@bellsouth.net
  (205)913-3033   SEGR#0100
West, David   (M1)
  2027 Lucille Street
  Lebanon, TN 37087
  (217)732-7568   TNNA#7300

MINISTERS CONTINUED

West, Earl (M1)
246 Maple Avenue
Greensburg, KY 42743
west5010@windstream.net
(207)932-5010 MICU#3116

West, Fred E, Jr (M1)
510 Cedaredge Drive
New Smyrna, FL 32168
jwest616@earthlink.net
(206)409-8321 SEET#2200

Westbrook, James (M1)
1717 Wedgewood Drive
Union City, TN 38261
westbrook731@bellsouth.net
(731)884-0918 GRWT#9100

Weston, Robert E (M1)
11 Summer Bluff
San Antonio, TX 78254
rjaweston@gmail.com
(210)347-0232 MSTR#8100

Whaley, Greg (M2)
4970 Comstock Road
Chapel Hill, TN 37034
grewha@mail.com
(931)364-7637 TNMU#7202

Wheeler, Nathan (M1)
2084 Linden Avenue
Memphis, TN 38104
nathantyac@gmail.com
(901)606-9535 GRWT#9100

Whitaker, Perry Eugene (M1)
235 Sykes Road
Brush Creek, TN 38547
brotherperry@msn.com
(615)631-1844 SERD#0810

White, Diann (M1)
9394 Alex Dickson Cove
Bartlett, TN 38133
diannwhite12@yahoo.com
(901)377-7776 GRWT#9110

White, Mack (M2)
408 W Main Street
Smithville, TN 37166
wnax408@yahoo.com
(615)318-9863 TNMU#7200

Whitworth, Gary W (M1)
1706 Old Hickory Boulevard
Brentwood, TN 37027
(615)915-4180 TNNA#7300

Whray, Richard "Rocky" (M1)
201 8th Avenue SE
Winchester, TN 37398
rocklex1017@att.net
(931)636-4844 TNMU#7228

Wieland, Jack G Jr (M1)
PO Box 116
Napoleon, MO 64074
jgwieland@hotmail.com
(217)823-4331 GRMI#4100

Wiggins, Joe (M1)
2734 US Highway 41A S
Eagleville, TN 37060
jwigginz@aol.com
(615)274-2011 TNCO#7109

Wilkerson, Patrick (M1)
903 Park Crest Court
Mount Juliet, TN 37122
patrickwilkerson3@gmail.com
(865)236-7737 SEET#2301

Wilkinson, Michael (M1)
1174 Tanglewood Street
Memphis, TN 38114
pastormike@kfcpc.comcastbiz.net

(205)533-2001 SEET#2305

Wilkinson, Neal (M2)
1174 Tanglewood Street
Memphis, TN 38114
(615)934-7382 TNNA#7300

Williams, Bobby D (M1)
844 W Highway 22
Union City, TN 38261
(731)885-1710 GRWT#9402

Williams, Cory (M1)
585 Tater Hill Road
Newbern, TN 38059
coromis@hotmail.com
(901)486-5981 GRWT#9410

Williams, Dale (M1)
3156 State Route 2837
Clay, KY 42404
dalewilliams@roadrunner.com
(270)664-2044 MICO#3618

Williams, David J (M1)
20 Acorn Drive
Harrisburg, IL 629463790
(618)252-1851 MICO#3400

Williamson, Dave (M1)
PO Box 67
Dolph, AR 72528
(870)499-7448 GRAR#1513

Wills, Brent (M1)
4607 E Richmond Shop Road
Lebanon, TN 37090
bwills9185@yahoo.com
(615)449-3258 TNMU#7218

Wills, Robin (M3)
4607 E Richmond Shop Road
Lebanon, TN 37090
robinrush24@aol.com
(615-870-4773) TNMU#7200

Wilson, Brenda (M1)
35 Collins Drive
Elizabethtown, KY 42701
susieq2007@windstream.net
(270)249-3835 MICU#3100

Wilson, Craig (M1)
2300 Frayser Boulevard
Memphis, TN 38127
craigwilson2300@yahoo.com
(901)277-4066 GRWT#9306

Wilson, Don (M1)
7300 Calle Montana NE
Albuquerque, NM 87113
don-wilson07@comcast.net
(505)823-2594 MSDC#8700

Wilson, Kevin (M1)
2225 North East Road SE
Cleveland, TN 37311
revkev1000@hotmail.com
(423)284-6397 SETG#2112

Wilson, Thomas (M1)
4543 Lake Vista
Memphis, TN 38128
tomjw217@gmail.com
(901)382-6190 GRWT#9100

Wing So, Patrick Tat (M1)
2/F Fu Tung Shopping Centre
Tung Chung
Lantau Island, HONG KONG
FAX: (852)2109-1737
cpctwso@yahoo.com.hk
(522)109-1738 MSHK#8810

Winn, Don (M1)
375 Cumberland Mountain Circle
Sunbright, TN 37872
dwinn_ky@yahoo.com

(615)478-9910 SEET#2200

Womack, Carey (M1)
114 Doris Street
Camden, TN 38320
camdencppastor@bellsouth.net
(731)220-3900 GRWT#9105

Wong, Bruce (M1)
716 Duncanville Court
Campbell, CA 95008
revbwong@gmail.com
(408)628-1723 MSDC#8700

Wong, Samson (M2)
CPC Yao Dao Primary School
Tin Yuet Estate
Tin Shui Wai, NT, HONG KONG
FAX: (852)2617-0287
wongchishui@yahoo.com.hk
(852)2617-7872 MSHK#8800

Wong, So Li (M1)
2/F Fu Tung Shopping Centre
Tung Chung, Lantau Island
HONG KONG
FAX: (852)2109-1737
soliwong@gmail.com
(852)2109-1738 MSHK#8800

Wong, Yim Ngar (M2)
Wing B&C, G/F, Ming Wik House
Kin Ming Estate
Tseung Kwan O,NT, HONG KONG
FAX: (852)2706-0114
yimngar@yahoo.com.hk
(852)2706-0111 MSHK#8808

Wood, Kevin L (M1)
339 David Street
McKenzie, TN 38201
FAX: (865)588-8581
revkevbuford1972@gmail.com
(865)228-0710 GRWT#9100

Wood, Wayne (M1)
HC 61 Box 600
Calico Rock, AR 72519
FAX: (870)297-3151
bexarwood@centurytel.net
(870)297-2205 GRAR#1100

Woodliff, George (M1)
4405 W Persimmon Street #316A
Fayetteville, AR 72704
mwoodliff@kih.net
(479)410-1933 GRAR#1100

Wright, B J (M1)
301 25th Street
Phenix City, AL 36867
bojobo3@yahoo.com
(334)298-2896 SETG#2100

Wright, John (M3)
( ) TNMU#7200

--==<< **X** >>==--

--==<< **Y** >>==--

Yang, Buhwan (M1)
19 Taylors Run
Tinton Falls, NJ 07712
yangmoksa@gmail.com
(732)458-2203 SECE#2131

Yano, Fumitsuta (M1)
424-4 Kamide, Fjinomiya-shi
Shuizuika-ken JAPAN
(054)454-0313 MSJA#8300

Yarce, Janeth (M1)
3019 W Calavar Road
Phoenix, AZ 85053

janethyarce@yahoo.com
(630)518-0295 MINC#5200
Yarce, Omar (M1)
10925 Neptune Drive
Cooper City, FL 33026
omaryarce@gmail.com
(205)919-9685 SEGR#0100
Yarce, Virginia (M3)
10925 Neptune Drive
Cooper City, FL 33026
ginnyyarce@gmail.com
(954)850-7111 SEGR#0100
Yates, Scott (M1)
8818 New Town Road
Rockvale, TN 37153
scott@scottyates.net
(615)274-3000 TNCO#7141
Yau, Chat Ming (M2)
G/F 251 Tin Sam Village
Shatin, NT, HONG KONG
FAX: (852)2607-2245
summerycm@yahoo.com.hk
(852)2693-3444 MSHK#8800
Yau, Eliza Yuk Lan Chui (M2)
14-16 TsatTsz Mui Road
1/Fl Block B North Point
HONG KONG
FAX: (852)2564-2898
elizaylyau@yahoo.com.hk
(852)2562-2148 MSHK#8805
Yeung, William Kin Keung (M1)
28 Hong Yip Street
Yuen Long, HONG KONG
FAX: (852)263-9562
william@yuonlongchurch.org
(852)2639-9176 MSHK#8809
York, Danny (M1)
5420 State Route 902
Fredonia, KY 42411
nonnieyork@yahoo.com
(270)350-7262 MICO#3413
Youn, Daniel (M1)
6524 Summer Avenue
Memphis, TN 38134
usyoun61@hotmail.com
(901)381-4790 GRWT#9436
Young, Taylor (M1)
2651 Holt Lane
Clarksville, TN 37043
brandontayloryoung@yahoo.com
(615)319-8294 TNNA#7304
Young, Timothy (M3)
8064 Hummingbird Lane
San Diego, CA 92123
tdy223@gmail.com
(415)350-8201 MSDC#8700
Youngman, Betty (M1)
1471 Creekview Court
Fort Worth, TX 76112
bettyy@swbell.net
(817)492-4100 MSRR#8400
Yu, Alexis (M1)
1761 Willow Way
San Bruno, CA 94066
alexis.yu.k@gmail.com
(415)421-1624 MSDC#8501
Yu, Carver Tat Sum (M1)
2/F Welland Plaza
188 Nam Cheong Street
Sham Shui Po, Kowloon, HONG KONG
FAX: (852)2771-2726
carver.yu@cgst.edu
(852)2794-2382 MSHK#8800

Yu, Grace Siu Tim (M1)
2/F Welland Plaza
188 Nam Cheong Street
Sham Shui Po, Kowloon, HONG KONG
FAX: (852)2771-2726
yuleungsiutim@netvigator.com
(852)2783-8923 MSHK#8800
Yu, Pyong San (Sonny) (M1)
139 Silverado Drive
Santa Teresa, NM 88008
pyongsanyu@hotmail.com
(915)329-3451 MSDC#8700
Yu, Wn-yong (M1)
325-1 DongHyen-Dong
Jecheon-city, Choongbuk, KOREA
lifeyu@hanmail.net
(043)652-0540 MMT
Yuen, Amos Pui Chung (M1)
2/F Welland Plaza
188 Nam Cheong Street
Sham Shui Po, Kowloon, HONG KONG
FAX: (852)2771-2726
revyuen@taohsien.org.hk
(852)2783-8923 MSHK#8806
Yuen, Susanna (M2)
28 Hong Yip Street
28 Hong Yip Street
Yuen Long, NT, HONG KONG
FAX: (522)639-5620
susanna@yuenlongcpc.org
(522)639-9176 MSHK#8800
Yung, Karen (M2)
Flat D, 2/F
338-340 Castle Peak Road
Kowloon, HONG KONG
FAX: (852)3020-0365
(852)2386-6563 MSHK#8800

--==<< Z >>==--

Zumbrunnen, Craig (M1)
1210 Country Club Road Apt 3
Santa Teresa, NM 88008
craigzum1@yahoo.com
(580)471-0308 MSRR#8400

ALPHABETICAL INDEX OF CHURCHES

The four letter abbreviation indicates the synod and presbytery of which the congregation
is a member. The four digit number indicates the church number.
(See pages 10-12 for abbreviations of presbyteries.)

316 Fellowship
CO Englewood.................MSDC#8710

--==<<A>>==--

ACTS Korean
TN Memphis....................GRWT#9436
Alabaster
AL Alabaster.....................SERD#0107
Algood
TN Algood.......................TNMU#7201
Allsboro
AL Cherokee....................SEHO#0501
Antioch
AL Reform.......................SEGR#0701
KY Knob Lick...................MICU#3101
LA Quitman.....................MSTR#8101
Antioch Union
TN Union City.................GRWT#9401
Appleton
AR Atkins.........................GRAR#1202
Arkansas Loving
AR Little Rock.................GRAR#2135
Arlington
TN Erin.............................TNNA#7311
Armenia
CO Quindio......................MSAN#8903
Asahi Mission Point
JA 241-0021.......................MSJA#8315
Ash Hill
TN Spring Hill..................TNCO#7101
Atwood
TN Atwood.......................GRWT#9101
Auburn
KY Auburn........................MICU#3301
Austin, First
TX Austin...........................MSTR#8601

--==<<B>>==--

Bald Knob
KY Russellville..................MICU#3302
Baldwin Chapel
AL Cullman.......................SEHO#0202
Banks
TN Smithville....................TNMU#7202
Barren Fork
AR Mount Pleasant...........GRAR#1501
Bartow
GA Rydal............................SETG#2101
Bates Hill
TN McMinnville...............TNMU#7203
Bayou de Chien
KY Water Valley.................MICO#3401
Beaver Creek
TN Knoxville......................SEET#2301
Beech
TN Hendersonville............TNNA#7301
TN Union City..................GRWT#9402
Beech Grove
TN Beechgrove.................TNMU#7204
Beersheba
MS Columbus....................SEGR#0702
Belleview
TN Franklin.......................TNCO#7104

Bells Chapel
TN Dyer............................GRWT#9403
Belvidere
TN Belvidere.....................TNMU#7205
Ben Lomond
AR Ben Lomond...............GRAR#1301
Benton
KY Benton........................MICO#3403
Bertram
TX Bertram.......................MSTR#8605
Betania Mission
CO Cali.............................MSCA#8204
Bethany
IL Bethany........................MINC#5401
Bethel
CO Cali.............................MSCA#8205
KY Center.........................MICU#3102
KY Kevil............................MICO#3404
MO Wentworth.................GRMI#4102
TN Atoka..........................GRWT#9301
TN Clarksville...................TNNA#7302
Bethel #1
KY Harrodsburg................MICU#3103
Bethesda
AR Camden.......................GRAR#1302
TN Fall Branch...................SEET#2201
TN Friendship...................GRWT#9404
Beulah
KY Hartford......................MICU#3501
Big Cove
AL Brownsboro.................SERD#0801
Blues Hill
TN McMinnville...............TNMU#7207
Boiling Springs
TN Portland......................MICU#3303
Bolivar
TN Bolivar........................GRWT#9202
Booneville
AR Booneville...................GRAR#1401
Boonshill
TN Boonshill.....................TNCO#7106
Bowling Green
KY Bowling Green............MICU#3304
Bradford
TN Bradford......................GRWT#9104
Branchville
AL Odenville.....................SEGR#0106
Brenthaven
TN Brentwood...................TNNA#7331
Bridgeport 1st
PA Bridgeport...................MICU#3131
Brier Creek
KY Bremen........................MICU#3503
Brunswick
TN Brunswick...................GRWT#9302
Brush Hill
TN Nashville.....................TNNA#7325
Burns Flat
OK Burns Flat...................MSRR#6301
Burnt Prairie
IL Burnt Prairie................MINC#5102
Byron
AR Calico Rock................GRAR#1508

--==<<C>>==--

Cairo
MS Cedarbluff...................SEGR#0704
Caleb Mission
CO Montebello..................MSCA#8223
Calico Rock
AR Calico Rock................GRAR#1503
Calvary
KY Mayfield......................MICO#3405
TN Clarksville...................TNNA#7342
Camden
AR Camden.......................GRAR#1303
TN Camden......................GRWT#9105
Camp Ground
AR Hampton.....................GRAR#1101
IL Anna............................MICO#5103
TN Decaturville................GRWT#9204
TN Erin.............................TNNA#7312
Campbellsville
KY Campbellsville.............MICU#3104
Campground
IL Greenville.....................MINC#5402
Cane Ridge
TN Cane Ridge..................TNNA#7326
Caneyville
KY Caneyville....................MICU#3201
Cartago
CO Valle............................MSAN#8906
Casa De Fe
MA Malden........................SEET#2220
Casey
IL Casey............................MINC#5201
Casey's Fork
KY Marrowbone...............MICU#3105
Caulksville
AR Ratcliff........................GRAR#1402
Cedar Flat
KY Edmonton...................MICU#3106
Cedar Hill
TN Greeneville...................SEET#2202
Cedar Springs
TN Whitwell......................SETG#2119
Central
CO Cali.............................MSCA#8208
Champ
TN Mulberry.....................TNCO#7108
Chandler
IN Chandler......................MICO#5302
Chapel Hill
TN Chapel Hill..................TNCO#7109
Charleston
TN Cleveland.....................SETG#2102
Charlotte
TN Charlotte.....................TNNA#7303
Chattanooga 1st
TN Chattanooga.................SETG#2104
Cheung Chau
HO Cheung Chau.............MSHK#8801
Chinese
CA San Francisco..............MSDC#8501
Christ
FL Lutz.............................SEGR#0303
IN Indianapolis.................MINC#5305
Christ Church
AL Huntsville....................SERD#0814
Clark's Grove
TN Maryville.....................SEET#2302

ALPHABETICAL INDEX OF CHURCHES CONTINUED

ALPHABETICAL INDEX OF CHURCHES CONTINUED

Georgetown
  IL Georgetown .... MINC#5204
Germantown
  TN Germantown .... GRWT#9310
Getsemani
  CO El Cerrito .... MSCA#8210
Gilead
  IL Simpson .... MICO#5110
Gill's Chapel
  KY Guthrie......................... MICU#3307
Glasgow
  KY Glasgow...................... MICU#3108
Gleason
  TN Gleason .... GRWT#9111
Glencoe
  AL Glencoe .... SEGR#0404
Glory Church of Jesus Christ
  GA Duluth...........................SETG#2144
God's Grace
  MO Greenfield .... GRMI#4104
Good Hope
  KY Campbellsville............. MICU#3109
Good Prospect
  IL Trilla .... MINC#5205
Good Spring
  KY Fredonia...................... MICO#3609
  TN Dukedom.....................GRWT#9112
Goodlettsville
  TN Goodlettsville.............. TNNA#7328
Goosepond
  AL Scottsboro .... SERD#0803
Goshen
  TN Winchester ....TNMU#7214
Grace
  AR Fayetteville .... GRAR#1405
  CA San Francisco.............. MSDC#8510
  MI Lincoln Park .... MINC#5502
Grace Community
  AL Millbrook .... SEGR#0407
Green Hill
  TN Bell Buckle .... TNCO#7118
Green Ridge
  KY Lewisburg................... MICU#3308
Greeneville
  TN Greeneville................... SEET#2206
Greens Chapel
  AL Cleveland .... SEGR#0208
Greensburg
  KY Greensburg .... MICU#3110
Greenville
  KY Greenville .... MICU#3505
Groverton
  MS Morton........................ SEGR#0602
Gum Creek
  TN Winchester ....TNMU#7215
Gum Springs
  AR Searcy .... GRAR#1205
Gurley
  AL Gurley .... SERD#0804

--==<<H>>==--

Halls Creek
  TN Waverly....................... TNNA#7313
Happy Home
  MO Conway...................... GRMI#4306
Harmony
  MO San Antonio .... GRMI#4203
  TN Winchester ....TNMU#7216
Harpeth Lick
  TN College Grove.............. TNCO#7119
Harrodsburg

KY Harrodsburg................. MICU#3111
Heartland
  Lenoir City .... SEET#2306
Heartsong
  KY Louisville.................... MICU#3222
Hector
  AR Hector .... GRAR#1207
Heights
  NM Albuquerque .... MSDC#8701
Helena
  AL Helena .... SEGR#0108
Hendersonville
  TN Hendersonville........... TNNA#7340
Hickory Grove
  AL Moulton....................... SEHO#0507
Hickory Valley
  TN Sparta ....TNMU#7251
Higashi Koganei
  JA 184-0011 .... MSJA#8301
High Point Community
  KY West Somerset .... MICU#3314
Highland
  KY Paducah .... MICO#3414
Hillsboro
  TN Hillsboro ....TNMU#7217
Hohenwald
  TN Hohenwald...................TNCO#7120
Holly Grove
  TN Brighton .... GRWT#9304
Homewood
  AL Homewood...................SEGR#0111
Hope
  AL Huntsville .... SERD#0812
  FL Valrico......................... SEGR#0308
Hope Korean
  NJ Tinton Falls...................SECE#2131
Hopewell
  AL Bessemer .... SEGR#0101
  KY Canmer .... MICU#3112
  KY Salem........................... MICO#3610
  MS Walnut .... GRWT#9207
  MO Lamar.......................... GRMI#4105
  TN Sharon .... GRWT#9115
Hopkinsville
  KY Hopkinsville .... MICU#3611
Horeb-Central
  CO Antioquia ....MSAN#8915
House of Prayer
  AL Decatur......................... SEGR#0214
Houston 1st
  TX Houston.......................MSTR#8606
Howell
  TN Fayetteville ....TNCO#7121
Hubbard
  TX Hubbard .... MSRR#8410
Humboldt
  TN Humboldt .... GRWT#9116
Huntsville 1st
  AL Huntsville .... SERD#0806
Hurricane
  AL Rogersville .... SEHO#0508
Hurricane Hill
  TN Newburn ....GRWT#9413

--==<<I>>==--

Ichikawa Grace Mission Point
  JA 272-0834 .... MSJA#8314
Immanuel
  FL Dade City..................... SEGR#0311
Irvington
  KY Irvington .... MICU#3210

Izumi Mission
  JA 245-0016 .... MSJA#8312

--==<<J>>==--

Jackson 1st
  TN Jackson........................GRWT#9208
Jasper
  TN Jasper ....SETG#2113
Jefferson
  TX Jefferson.......................MSTR#8109
Jenkins
  TN Nolensville...................TNCO#7144
Jerusalem
  TN Murfreesboro ....TNMU#7218
Joywood
  TN Murfreesboro ....TNMU#7250

--==<<K>>==--

Kelly's Chapel
  TN Whitwell ....SETG#2120
Kelso
  TN Kelso ....TNCO#7122
Kenton
  TN Kenton..........................GRWT#9414
Kibougaoka
  JA 241-0825 .... MSJA#8302
Kingdom
  TN Unionville ....TNCO#7123
Knights Chapel
  IN Petersburg .... MINC#5306
Knoxville
  TN Knoxville .... SEET#2305
Korea 1st
  KO South Korea..................SEET#2221
Korean
  MO Springfield .... GRMI#4316
  TN Cordova.......................GRWT#9322
Korean Livingstone
  GA Cumming......................SETG#2130
Kowloon
  HO Kowloon....................MSHK#8803
Koza
  JA 242-0006 .... MSJA#8303
Kunitachi Nozomi
  JA 186-0002 .... MSJA#8306

--==<<L>>==--

La Rosa De Saron
  CO Antioquia ....MSAN#8911
La Virginia
  CO Risaralda.....................MSAN#8913
LaGuardo
  TN Lebanon ....TNMU#7219
Lake Hamilton
  AR Hot Springs................. GRAR#1221
Lake Highlands
  TX Dallas ....MSRR#8411
Lawrenceburg
  TN Lawrenceburg ....TNCO#7124
Lebanon
  TN Jefferson City ....SEET#2207
  TN Lebanon ....TNMU#7220
Lebanon North
  IL Fairfield .... MINC#5113
Lebanon South
  IL Galatia .... MINC#5114
Leitchfield
  KY Leitchfield.................... MICU#3211
Lewisburg

ALPHABETICAL INDEX OF CHURCHES CONTINUED

KY Lewisburg .... MICU#3309
Lewisburg 1st
  TN Lewisburg .... TNCO#7125
Lexington 1st
  TN Lexington .... GRWT#9209
Liberty
  KY Campbellsville .... MICU#3116
  KY Murray .... MICO#3406
  TN Clarksville .... TNNA#7315
  TN McMinnville .... TNMU#7222
Lick Branch
  KY Glasgow .... MICU#3117
Lincoln 1st
  IL Lincoln .... MINC#5405
Lisman
  KY Clay .... MICO#3613
Little Muddy
  KY Morgantown .... MICU#3310
Livingston 1st
  TN Livingston .... TNMU#7223
Lockesburg
  AR Lockesburg .... GRAR#1311
Locust Grove
  OK Locust Grove .... MSRR#6203
  TN Cunningham .... TNNA#7316
Lone Star
  OK Coalgate .... MSCH#6105
Longview 1st
  TX Longview .... MSTR#8112
Loudon
  TN Loudon .... SEET#2307
Louisville 1st
  KY Louisville .... MICU#3212
Louisville Japanese
  KY Pewee Valley .... MICU#3223
Lubbock
  TX Lubbock .... MSDC#8702
LuzD.L.Naciones
  TN McMinnville .... TNMU#7252

--==<<M>>==--

Macau
  MA Andar LMN .... MSHK#8804
Macedonia
  KY Dalton .... MICO#3614
Madison 1st
  TN Madison .... TNNA#7329
Madisonville
  KY Madisonville .... MICO#3615
Magnolia
  KY Magnolia .... MICU#3214
Manchester
  TN Manchester .... TNMU#7224
Manizales
  CO Caldas .... MSAN#8914
Mansfield
  MO Mansfield .... GRMI#4308
Maple Springs
  TN Beech Bluff .... GRWT#9210
Maranatha
  CO Guapi .... MSCA#8220
  TX San Elizario .... MSDC#8706
Margaret Hank
  KY Paducah .... MICO#3415
Mariah
  TN Waverly .... TNNA#7317
Marietta
  AR Charleston .... GRAR#1408
  TN Knoxville .... SEET#2308
Marion 1st
  KY Marion .... MICO#3616

Marlow
  OK Marlow .... MSRR#6305
Mars Hill
  AR Pottsville .... GRAR#1211
Marshall
  MO Marshall .... GRMI#4210
  TX Marshall .... MSTR#8115
Martin
  TN Martin .... GRWT#9117
Maryville 1st
  TN Maryville .... SEET#2309
Mason Hall
  TN Kenton .... GRWT#9415
Mata de Sao Joao
  BR Bahia .... MSJA#8313
Maud
  AL Cherokee .... SEHO#0509
McAdoo
  TN Clarksville .... TNNA#7318
McCains
  TN Columbia .... TNCO#7126
McGee Chapel
  OK Broken Bow .... MSCH#6106
McKenzie
  TN McKenzie .... GRWT#9118
McLeod Chapel
  MS Macon .... SEGR#0708
McMinnville
  TN McMinnville .... TNMU#7225
Medina
  TN Medina .... GRWT#9119
Megumi
  JA 207-0023 .... MSJA#8309
Mercy
  TN Lenoir City .... SEET#2320
Meridian
  TN Greenfield .... GRWT#9120
Meridianville
  AL Meridianville .... SERD#0808
Mesquite
  TX Mesquite .... MSRR#8412
Milan
  TN Milan .... GRWT#9121
Milburn Chapel
  KY West Paducah .... MICO#3416
Mill Creek
  TN Puryear .... GRWT#9122
Mohawk
  TN Mohawk .... SEET#2208
Monroe Chapel
  KY Hardyville .... MICU#3119
Monroe City
  IN Monroe City .... MINC#5307
Monteagle
  TN Monteagle .... TNMU#7227
Morella
  TN Kenton .... GRWT#9416
Morgantown
  KY Morgantown .... MICU#3311
Morning Sun
  TN Cordova .... GRWT#9314
Morningside
  IN Evansville .... MINC#5304
Mt Ararat
  TN Union City .... GRWT#9417
Mt Carmel
  AR London .... GRAR#1212
  KY White Plains .... MICO#3617
  TN Franklin .... TNCO#7127
  TN Huntland .... TNMU#7228
  TN Oliver Springs .... SEET#2310
  TN Somerville .... GRWT#9315

Mt Denson
  TN Springfield .... TNNA#7319
Mt Gilead
  IL Greenville .... MINC#5406
Mt Hebron
  TN Fayetteville .... TNCO#7128
Mt Hermon
  TN Cookeville .... TNMU#7229
Mt Hester
  AL Cherokee .... SEHO#0510
Mt Hope
  TX Joinerville .... MSTR#8117
Mt Joy
  TN Mount Pleasant .... TNCO#7129
Mt Lebanon
  TN Spring Hill .... TNCO#7130
Mt Liberty
  TN Charlotte .... TNNA#7320
Mt Moriah
  KY Summer Shade .... MICU#3120
  TN Pulaski .... TNCO#7131
Mt Nebo
  TN Iron City .... TNCO#7132
Mt Olive
  AR Melbourne .... GRAR#1517
  KY Big Clifty .... MICU#3216
  TN Dyer .... GRWT#9418
Mt Olivet
  IN Washington .... MINC#5308
  KY Bowling Green .... MICU#3312
Mt Pleasant
  AL Muscle Shoals .... SEHO#0511
  KY Caneyville .... MICU#3217
  KY Sullivan .... MICO#3618
  TN Afton .... SEET#2209
  TN Mount Pleasant .... TNCO#7133
Mt Sharon
  TN Greenbrier .... TNNA#7321
Mt Sinai
  TN Nashville .... TNNA#7330
Mt Sterling
  IL Brookport .... MICO#5117
Mt Tabor
  TN Murfreesboro .... TNMU#7230
Mt Vernon
  KY Leitchfield .... MICU#3218
  TN Ramer .... GRWT#9213
  TN Rockvale .... TNMU#7231
Mt View
  TN Dover .... TNNA#7322
Mt Zion
  IL Dongola .... MICO#5118
  KY Glens Fork .... MICU#3121
  KY Philpot .... MICU#3507
  MS Columbus .... SEGR#0709
  MS Falkner .... GRWT#9214
  TX Greenville .... MSRR#8414
Mu Min
  HO Landau Island .... MSHK#8810
Murfreesboro
  TN Murfreesboro .... TNMU#7232

--==<<N>>==--

Naruse
  JA 194-0041 .... MSJA#8305
Neal's Chapel
  KY Glasgow .... MICU#3122
Nebo
  AL Lexington .... SEHO#0512
Needham
  KY Eastview .... MICU#3219

ALPHABETICAL INDEX OF CHURCHES CONTINUED

New Beginning
    TN Memphis .... GRWT#9306
New Bethel
    TN Columbia..................... TNCO#7134
    TN Greeneville.................. SEET#2210
    TN Selmer....................... GRWT#9215
New Bethlehem
    TN Newbern...................... GRWT#9420
New Cypress
    KY Rumsey....................... MICU#3508
New Ebenezer
    TN Troy......................... GRWT#9422
New Hope
    AL Birmingham .... SEGR#0104
    AR Batesville .... GRAR#1510
    IL Yale......................... MINC#5208
    KY Paducah .... MICO#3410
    MO Salem .... GRMI#4309
    TN Lebanon .... TNMU#7233
    TN Madisonville .... SEET#2311
    TN Stewart .... TNNA#7337
    TN Whitwell .... SETG#2115
New Providence
    TN Clarksville.................. TNNA#7305
New Salem
    TN Bethel Springs............. GRWT#9216
    TN Lakeland .... GRWT#9316
    TN Sharon .... GRWT#9124
Newbern
    TN Newbern..................... GRWT#9419
Newberry
    TX Millsap .... MSRR#8415
North Pleasant Grove
    KY Murray .... MICO#3411
North Point
    HO North Point................. MSHK#8805
North Union
    TN Kenton....................... GRWT#9423
Northminster
    TX San Antonio .... MSTR#8610
Nueva Esperanza
    CO Cali .... MSCA#8221
Nueva Jerusalen
    CO Cali .... MSCA#8222
Nueva Vida
    TX Houston...................... MSTR#8612
Nuevo Empezar................... GRWT#9324
    TN Memphis

--==<<O>>==--

Oak Forest
    KY Summersville............... MICU#3123
Oak Grove
    KY Benton .... MICO#3412
    MO Springfield .... GRMI#4310
    TN Henderson .... GRWT#9217
    TN Whitwell .... SETG#2121
    TX Georgetown................. MSTR#8607
Oak Grove Union
    KY Clay .... MICO#3619
Oak Hill
    TN Paris .... GRWT#9125
Oak Ridge
    TN Oak Ridge .... SEET#2313
Oakland
    KY Calvert City .... MICO#3413
    TN Telford....................... SEET#2211
Old Mt Bethel
    AL Rogersville .... SEHO#0513
Old Union
    AR Magazine .... GRAR#1409

Old Zion
    TN Sparta .... TNMU#7234
Olive Branch
    MS Olive Branch .... GRWT#9312
Oliver Springs
    TN Oliver Springs.............. SEET#2314
Oliver's Chapel
    TN Bradford.................... GRWT#9127
Olivet
    TN Savannah.................... GRWT#9220
Olney
    TX Olney........................ MSRR#8416
One Way
    NY Flushing.................... SECE#2137
Orange
    MO Aurora...................... GRMI#4108
Our Good
    MD Salisbury................... SETG#2138
Owens Chapel
    TN Winchester .... TNMU#7235
Owensboro
    KY Owensboro .... MICU#3509
Oxford
    AR Oxford....................... GRAR#1511

--==<<P>>==--

Palestine
    AR Palestine.................... GRAR#1103
    TN Lexington................... GRWT#9221
    TN Newbern..................... GRWT#9424
Panki Bok
    OK Eagletown.................. MSCH#6108
Park Terrace
    AL Sheffield .... SEHO#0514
Parsons 1st
    TN Parsons...................... GRWT#9222
Pathway
    TX Burleson.................... MSRR#8418
Pereira
    CO Risaralda................... MSAN#8916
Petersburg
    TN Petersburg .... TNCO#7135
Philadelphia
    TN Limestone .... SEET#2212
Phillipsburg
    MO Phillipsburg................ GRMI#4311
Piedmont
    AL Piedmont .... SEGR#0406
Pierson
    MO Martinville .... GRMI#4312
Pigeon Roost
    OK Atoka .... MSCH#6109
Pilot Knob
    TN Bulls Gap .... SEET#2213
Pine Bluff 1st
    AR Pine Bluff................... GRAR#1104
Pine Hill
    TN McDonald .... SETG#2117
    TX Winnsboro.................. MSTR#8122
Pine Ridge
    AR Grapevine................... GRAR#1105
Pine Tree
    TX Longview................... MSTR#8113
Pineville
    AR Pineville.................... GRAR#1512
Piney Fork
    KY Marion .... MICO#3620
Pleasant Green
    TN Atwood...................... GRWT#9129
Pleasant Grove
    AR Searcy .... GRAR#1214

    IL Annapolis.................... MINC#5210
    MO Knob Noster.............. GRMI#4109
    TN Moscow..................... GRWT#9317
Pleasant Hill
    AL Bessember.................. SEGR#0710
    KY Owensboro .... MICU#3510
    TN Chuckey.................... SEET#2214
Pleasant Mount
    TN Columbia.................... TNCO#7136
Pleasant Union
    TN Millington .... GRWT#9318
Pleasant Vale
    TN Chuckey .... SEET#2215
Pleasant Valley
    KY Kevil .... MICO#3418
Po Lam
    HO Tseung Kwan O,NT.... MSHK#8808
Point Pleasant
    KY Beaver Dam................ MICU#3313
Popayan
    CO Popayan .... MSCA#8227
Poplar Grove
    KY Sacramento .... MICU#3511
    TN Halls........................ GRWT#9425
Principe De Paz
    CO Cali .... MSCA#8201
Progress
    LA Pleasant Hill............... MSTR#8123
Prospect United
    TN Cleveland .... SETG#2116
Protemus
    TN Troy.......................... GRWT#9426
Providence
    TN Hartsville................... TNMU#7238
Providence 1st
    KY Providence................. MICO#3621

--==<<Q>>==--

--==<<R>>==--

Radcliff
    KY Radcliff .... MICU#3220
Ramer
    TN Ramer........................ GRWT#9223
Red Bank
    TN Chattanooga .... SETG#2105
Redeemer
    CA San Francisco.............. MSDC#8512
Renacer
    CO Cali .... MSCA#8225
Richard City
    TN South Pittsburg.............. SETG#2118
Richland
    TN Lewisburg .... TNCO#7137
Roca De Salvacion
    AL Birmingham .... SEGR#0115
Rock Creek
    OK Honobia .... MSCH#6111
Rock Island
    TN Rock Island .... TNMU#7274
Rockvale
    TN Rockvale .... TNMU#7239
Rocky Glade
    TN Eagleville .... TNMU#7240
Rocky Ridge
    AL Birmingham .... SEGR#0105
Rodney
    AR Jordan....................... GRAR#1513
Roellen
    TN Dyersburg .... GRWT#9428
Rogersville 1st

ALPHABETICAL INDEX OF CHURCHES CONTINUED

AL Rogersville .... SEHO#0517
Rose Creek
    KY Nebo .... MICO#3622
Rose Hill
    AR Monticello...................GRAR#1106
Round Lake
    OK Tupelo........................ MSCH#6112
Round Rock
    TX Round Rock ....MSTR#8611
Rozzell Chapel
    KY Mayfield .... MICO#3419
Russellville
    AR Russellville .... GRAR#1216
Ruth Chapel
    TN Livingston ....TNMU#7241
Rutherford
    TN Rutherford..................GRWT#9429

--==<<S>>==--

Sacramento
    KY Sacramento .... MICU#3512
Sagamino
    JA 228-0004 .... MSJA#8304
Salem
    AR Salem .... GRAR#1514
    KY Greensburg .... MICU#3127
    MS Walnut Grove .... SEGR#0607
    MO Warrensburg............... GRMI#4216
    TN Gadsden .... GRWT#9430
    TN Greeneville.................. SEET#2216
Samaria
    CO Cali .... MSCA#8217
San Lucas
    CO Palmira....................... MSCA#8215
San Marcos
    CO Cali .... MSCA#8218
San Pablo
    CO Guacari .... MSCA#8212
Sandy Springs
    TX Whitesboro.................. MSRR#8420
Santa Fe
    TN Santa Fe ....TNCO#7138
Savannah 1st
    TN Savannah.................... GRWT#9224
Scottsboro
    AL Scottsboro .... SERD#0809
Searcy
    AR Searcy .... GRAR#1218
Selmer Court Avenue
    TN Selmer .... GRWT#9225
Senda de Libertad
    CO South America........... MSAN#8919
Seven Springs
    KY Center .... MICU#3128
Sewanee
    TN Sewanee .... TNMU#7242
Seymour
    MO Seymour..................... GRMI#4313
Sharing
    NY College Point .... SECE#2141
Sharon
    TN Sharon .... GRWT#9130
Shatin
    HO Shatin NT ....MSHK#8807
Shaver
    AR Paris .... GRAR#1413
Shawnee Mound
    MO Chilhowee.................. GRMI#4111
Shell Chapel
    AR Pine Bluff....................GRAR#1108

Shepherd/Hills
    TX Austin.........................MSTR#8604
Sherwood
    AR Sherwood .... GRAR#1220
Shibusawa
    JA 259-1321 .... MSJA#8307
Shiloh
    IL Virginia .... MINC#5409
    KY Campbellsville............. MICU#3129
    MS Corinth....................... GRWT#9226
    TN Greeneville................. SEET#2217
    TN McKenzie.................... GRWT#9131
    TN Palmyra .... TNNA#7338
    TX Clarksville..................MSTR#8125
    TX Midlothian.................. MSRR#8421
Shinar
    IA New London................. MINC#5410
Short Creek
    KY Falls of Rough .... MICU#3221
Sidney
    AR Batesville .... GRAR#1515
Silverdale
    TN Chattanooga ....SETG#2106
Smithville
    TN Smithville...................TNMU#7243
South Pittsburg
    TN South Pittsburg.............SETG#2123
Spring Creek
    AL Montevallo .... SEGR#0113
    MO Dunnegan................... GRMI#4113
Spring Hill
    IL Beecher City .... MINC#5411
Springfield
    AL Rogersville .... SEHO#0515
Springfield 1st
    MO Springfield .... GRMI#4314
St Andrew
    TX Odessa........................MSDC#8703
St John
    TX Arlington .... MSRR#8413
St Luke
    TN Madison .... TNNA#7332
    TX Fort Worth.................. MSRR#8407
St Mark
    TX Fort Worth.................. MSRR#8408
St Timothy
    TX Bedford .... MSRR#8419
Steam Mill
    MS Union......................... SEGR#0608
Stevenson
    AL Stevenson .... SERD#0810
Stonegate
    OK Edmond .... MSRR#6307
Stone Oak
    TX San Antonio ....MSTR#8608
Sturgis
    KY Sturgis......................... MICO#3625
Sudanese
    TN Gallatin .... TNNA#7341
Sugar Grove
    KY Marion .... MICO#3626
Suggs Creek
    TN Mount Juliet ....TNMU#7244
Sulphur Springs
    AR Louann .... GRAR#1315
Sumach
    GA Chatsworth....................SETG#2124
Sumkim Presby
    KO Seoul.......................... SEET#2222A
Swan
    TN Centerville....................TNCO#7140

--==<<T>>==--

Talbott
    TN Talbott .... SEET#2218
Tao Hsien
    HO Kowloon..................... MSHK#8806
Trezevant
    TN Trezevant.................... GRWT#9132
Trimble Camp Ground
    AR Dolph .... GRAR#1504
Trinity
    AR Morrilton .... GRAR#1219
    TX Fort Worth ....MSRR#8409
Trona
    CA Trona.......................... MSDC#8503
Troy
    TN Troy............................ GRWT#9432
Tulua Mission
    CO Tulua.......................... MSCA#8226
Tusculum
    TN Nashville .... TNNA#7333

--==<<U>>==--

Union
    AL Vance.......................... SEGR#0114
    TN Knoxville .... SEET#2315
Union Chapel
    IL Galatia .... MICO#5123
Union City
    TN Union City .... GRWT#9433
Union Grove
    AL Holly Pond .... SERD#0211
    TN Columbia....................TNCO#7141
Union Hill
    AL Anderson .... SEHO#0516
    TN Brush Creek ....TNMU#7246
Union North
    IL Fairfield .... MINC#5124
United
    IL Norris City .... MINC#5119
Unity
    KY Hardin........................ MICO#3422

--==<<V>>==--

Vaughn's Chapel
    KY Calvert City .... MICO#3423
Village
    IL Norris City.................... MICO#5125
Virtue
    TN Knoxville .... SEET#2316

--==<<W>>==--

Walkertown
    TN Afton .... SEET#2222
Walkerville
    AR Magnolia..................... GRAR#1317
Walnut Grove
    AL New Hope .... SERD#0811
    AR Magazine .... GRAR#1414
    TN Burlison.....................GRWT#9320
Warrensburg
    MO Warrensburg............... GRMI#4115
Watertown
    TN Watertown ....TNMU#7247
Waverly
    TN Waverly .... TNNA#7339
Waynesboro

ALPHABETICAL INDEX OF CHURCHES CONTINUED

LOCATION INDEX OF CHURCHES

The four letter abbreviation indicates the synod and presbytery of which the congregation
is a member. The four digit number indicates the church number.
(See pages 10-13 for abbreviations of presbyteries.)

ALABAMA

AL Alabaster
    Alabaster .... SERD#0107
AL Anderson
    Union Hill .... SEHO#0516
AL Bessemer
    Hopewell .... SEGR#0101
    Pleasant Hill .... SEGR#0710
AL Birmingham
    Crestline .... SEGR#0102
    New Hope .... SEGR#0104
    Roca De Salvacion .... SEGR#0115
    Rocky Ridge................... SEGR#0105
AL Brownsboro
    Big Cove .... SERD#0801
AL Cherokee
    Allsboro......................... SEHO#0501
    Maud .... SEHO#0509
    Mt. Hester .... SEHO#0510
AL Cleveland
    Greens Chapel................ SEGR#0208
AL Coker
    Coker............................. SEGR#0705
AL Cullman
    Baldwin Chapel.............. SEHO#0202
    East Point .... SERD#0206
    Faith .... SEHO#0213
    Welti .... SEHO#0212
AL Decatur
    House of Prayer............. SEGR#0214
AL Florence
    Florence 1st................... SEHO#0506
AL Gadsden
    Gadsden......................... SEGR#0402
    Forrest Avenue .... SEGR#0403
AL Glencoe
    Glencoe .... SEGR#0404
AL Gurley
    Gurley .... SERD#0804
AL Helena
    Helena .... SEGR#0108
AL Holly Pond
    Eidson Chapel .... SERD#0207
    Union Grove.................. SERD#0211
AL Homewood
    Homewood.....................SEGR#0111
AL Huntsville
    Christ Church .... SERD#0814
    Hope.............................. SERD#0812
    Huntsville 1st .... SERD#0806
AL Lexington
    Nebo.............................. SEHO#0512
AL Meridianville
    Meridianville................. SERD#0808
AL Millbrook
    Grace Community .... SEGR#0407
AL Montevallo
    Spring Creek .... SEGR#0113
AL Moulton
    Hickory Grove .... SEHO#0507
AL Muscle Shoals
    Mt. Pleasant................... SEHO#0511
AL New Hope
    Walnut Grove .... SERD#0811
AL New Market
    Concord......................... SERD#0802
AL Odenville

    Branchville..................... SEGR#0106
AL Piedmont
    Piedmont .... SEGR#0406
AL Reform
    Antioch.......................... SEGR#0701
AL Rogersville
    Hurricane....................... SEHO#0508
    Old Mt Bethel .... SEHO#0513
    Rogersville 1st .... SEHO#0517
    Springfield..................... SEHO#0515
AL Scottsboro
    Goosepond .... SERD#0803
    Scottsboro .... SERD#0809
AL Sheffield
    Park Terrace .... SEHO#0514
AL Stevenson
    Edgefield .... SERD#0813
    Stevenson .... SERD#0810
AL Vance
    Union............................ SEGR#0114

ARIZONA

AZ Tucson
    Desert Gardens...............MIDC#8705

ARKANSAS

AR Ashdown
    E T Allen .... GRAR#1307
    Fomby .... GRAR#1310
AR Atkins
    Appleton .... GRAR#1202
AR Batesville
    Faith-Hopewell .... GRAR#1502
    New Hope .... GRAR#1510
    Sidney .... GRAR#1515
AR Ben Lomond
    Ben Lomond.................. GRAR#1301
AR Booneville
    Booneville .... GRAR#1401
AR Calico Rock
    Byron............................ GRAR#1508
    Calico Rock................... GRAR#1503
AR Camden
    Bethesda....................... GRAR#1302
    Camden .... GRAR#1303
    Fellowship..................... GRAR#1309
AR Charleston
    Marietta......................... GRAR#1408
AR Dolph
    Trimble Camp Ground .. GRAR#1504
AR Dover
    Dover............................ GRAR#1203
AR Fayetteville
    Grace .... GRAR#1405
AR Fort Smith
    Fort Smith .... GRAR#1406
AR Grapevine
    Pine Ridge.....................GRAR#1105
AR Hampton
    Camp Ground.................GRAR#1101
AR Hector
    Hector........................... GRAR#1207
AR Horatio
    Dilworth .... GRAR#1304
AR Hot Springs
    Lake Hamilton .... GRAR#1221

AR Jordan
    Rodney .... GRAR#1513
AR Little Rock
    Arkansas Loving .... GRAR#2135
    Crossroads.....................GRAR#1102
AR Lockesburg
    Falls Chapel .... GRAR#1308
    Lockesburg...................GRAR#1311
AR London
    Mt Carmel .... GRAR#1212
AR Louann
    Sulphur Springs............. GRAR#1315
AR Magazine
    Old Union...................... GRAR#1409
    Walnut Grove .... GRAR#1414
AR Magnolia
    Walkerville .... GRAR#1317
AR Melbourne
    Mt Olive........................ GRAR#1517
AR Monticello
    Rose Hill ....GRAR#1106
AR Morrilton
    Trinity .... GRAR#1219
AR Mount Pleasant
    Barren Fork .... GRAR#1501
AR Mountain Home
    Fellowship.................... GRAR#1505
AR Oxford
    Oxford...........................GRAR#1511
AR Palestine
    Palestine ....GRAR#1103
AR Paris
    Shaver .... GRAR#1413
AR Pine Bluff
    Pine Bluff 1st................GRAR#1104
    Shell Chapel ....GRAR#1108
AR Pineville
    Pineville .... GRAR#1512
AR Pottsville
    Mars Hill.......................GRAR#1211
AR Ratcliff
    Caulksville .... GRAR#1402
AR Russellville
    Russellville................... GRAR#1216
AR Salem
    Salem............................ GRAR#1514
AR Searcy
    Gum Springs .... GRAR#1205
    Pleasant Grove .... GRAR#1214
    Searcy........................... GRAR#1218
AR Sherwood
    Sherwood .... GRAR#1220

BRAZIL

BR Bahia
    Mata de Sao Joao .... GRAR#8313

CALIFORNIA

CA San Francisco
    Chinese..........................MSDC#8501
    Grace ....MSDC#8510
    Redeemer ....MSDC#8512
CA Trona
    Trona ....MSDC#8503

COLOMBIA

LOCATION INDEX OF CHURCHES CONTINUED

CO Antioquia
    Horeb-Central .... MSAN#8915
    El Rebano..................... MSAN#8905
    La Rosa De Saron .... MSAN#8911
    Senta de Libertad .... MSAN#8919
    Zamora .... MSAN#8918
CO Buenaventura
    Divino Redentor............ MSAN#8206
    Emaus........................... MSCA#8219
CO Caldas
    Manizales .... MSAN#8914
CO Cali
    Betania Mission .... MSAN#8204
    Bethel .... MSCA#8205
    Central .... MSCA#8208
    Filipos .... MSCA#8211
    Nueva Esperanza........... MSCA#8221
    Nueva Jerusalen .... MSCA#8222
    Principe De Paz............. MSCA#8201
    Renacer .... MSCA#8225
    Samaria .... MSCA#8217
    San Marcos................... MSCA#8218
CO El Cerrito
    Getsemani .... MSCA#8210
CO Guacari
    San Pablo .... MSCA#8212
CO Guapi
    Maranatha .... MSCA#8220
CO Montebello
    Caleb Mission .... MSCA#8223
CO Palmira
    San Lucas .... MSCA#8215
CO Popayan
    Popayan........................ MSCA#8227
CO Quindio
    Armenia........................ MSAN#8903
CO Risaralda
    Dosquebradas................ MSAN#8907
    La Virginia .... MSCA#8913
    Pereira .... MSAN#8916
CO Tulua
    Tulua Mission............... MSCA#8226
CO Valle
    Cartago........................ MSAN#8906

COLORADO

CO Englewood
    316 Fellowship............. MSDC#8710

FLORIDA

FL Dade City
    Immanuel .... SEGR#0311
FL Lutz
    Christ............................ SEGR#0303
FL Miami
    El Camino .... SEGR#0310
FL Tampa
    First Hispanic................ SEGR#0307
FL Valrico
    Hope............................. SEGR#0308
FL Wimauma

GEORGIA

GA Chatsworth
    Sumach.......................... SETG#2124
GA Cumming
    Korean Livingstone.......... SETG#2130
GA Duluth

Glory Church of Jesus.....SETG#2144
GA Lawrenceville
    El Redil .... SETG#2149
GA Rydal
    Bartow........................... SETG#2101

HONG KONG

HO Cheung Chau
    Cheung Chau................. MSHK#8801
HO Kowloon
    Kowloon....................... MSHK#8803
    Tao Hsien .... MSHK#8806
HO Landau Island
    Mu Min .... MSHK#8810
HO NT
    Yao Dao .... MSHK#8811
HO North Point
    North Point................... MSHK#8805
HO Shatin NT
    Shatin .... MSHK#8807
HO Tseung Kwan O NT
    Po Lam .... MSHK#8808
HO Yuen Long
    Xi Lin........................... MSHK#8809

ILLINOIS

IL Anna
    Camp Ground................. MICO#5103
IL Annapolis
    Pleasant Grove .... MICO#5210
IL Beecher City
    Spring Hill..................... MINC#5411
IL Bethany
    Bethany .... MINC#5401
IL Brookport
    Mt. Sterling .... MICO#5117
IL Buncombe
    Ebenezer Hall................. MICO#5106
IL Burnt Prairie
    Burnt Prairie................... MINC#5102
IL Casey
    Casey .... MINC#5201
IL Chicago
    Ebenezer........................ MINC#5203
IL Cisne
    Elm River .... MINC#5107
IL Dongola
    Mt Zion .... MICO#5118
IL Fairfield
    Cumberland Chapel .... MINC#5104
    Fairfield........................ MINC#5108
    Lebanon North .... MINC#5113
    Union North .... MINC#5124
IL Farmer City
    Fullerton........................ MINC#5404
IL Galatia
    Lebanon South .... MINC#5114
    Union Chapel .... MICO#5123
IL Georgetown
    Georgetown.................... MINC#5204
IL Greenville
    Campground................... MINC#5402
    Mt. Gilead .... MINC#5406
IL Lincoln
    Lincoln 1st .... MINC#5405
IL Martinsville
    Willow Creek .... MINC#5211
IL Norris City
    United........................... MINC#5119
    Village .... MICO#5125

IL Petersburg
    Petersburg...................... MINC#5408
IL Simpson
    Gilead .... MICO#5110
IL Thompsonville
    Ebenezer....................... MICO#5105
IL Trilla
    Good Prospect................ MINC#5205
IL Virginia
    Shiloh .... MINC#5409
IL Yale
    New Hope .... MINC#5208

INDIANA

IN Chandler
    Chandler........................ MICO#5302
IN Evansville
    Morningside .... MINC#5304
IN Indianapolis
    Christ............................ MINC#5305
IN Monroe City
    Monroe City .... MINC#5307
IN Petersburg
    Knights Chapel................ MINC#5306
IN Washington
    Mt Olivet....................... MINC#5308

IOWA

IA New London
    Shinar .... MINC#5410

JAPAN

JA 184-0011
    Higashi Koganei.............. MSJA#8301
JA 186-0002
    Kunitachi Nozomi........... MSJA#8306
JA 194-0041
    Naruse .... MSJA#8305
JA 207-0023
    Megumi .... MSJA#8309
JA 228-0004
    Sagamino .... MSJA#8304
JA 228-0818
    Den-en Mission .... MSJA#8310
JA 241-0021
    Asahi Mission Point .... MSJA#8315
JA 241-0825
    Kibougaoka.................... MSJA#8302
JA 242-0006
    Koza .... MSJA#8303
JA 243-0422
    Ebina Shion No .... MSJA#8311
JA 245-0016
    Izumi Mission .... MSJA#8312
JA 259-1321
    Sibusawa .... MSJA#8307
JA 272-0834
    Ichikawa Grace Mission . MSJA#8314

KENTUCKY

KY Auburn
    Auburn........................... MICU#3301
    Gasper River .... MICU#3306
KY Beaver Dam
    Point Pleasant................. MICU#3313
KY Benton
    Benton .... MICO#3403
    Oak Grove...................... MICO#3412

KY Big Clifty
   Mt Olive .... MICU#3216
KY Bowling Green
   Bowling Green .... MICU#3304
   Mt Olivet .... MICU#3312
KY Bremen
   Brier Creek .... MICU#3503
   Fairview .... MICU#3504
KY Calvert City
   Oakland .... MICO#3413
   Vaughn's Chapel .... MICO#3423
KY Campbellsville
   Campbellsville .... MICO#3104
   Good Hope .... MICU#3109
   Liberty .... MICU#3116
   Shiloh .... MICU#3129
KY Caneyville
   Caneyville .... MICU#3201
   Mt Pleasant .... MICU#3217
KY Canmer
   Hopewell .... MICU#3112
KY Center
   Bethel .... MICU#3102
   Seven Springs .... MICU#3128
KY Clay
   Lisman .... MICO#3613
   Oak Grove Union .... MICO#3619
KY Dalton
   Macedonia .... MICO#3614
KY Eastview
   Needham .... MICU#3219
KY Edmonton
   Cedar Flat .... MICU#3106
KY Falls of Rough
   Short Creek .... MICU#3221
KY Fredonia
   Fredonia .... MICO#3608
   Good Spring .... MICO#3609
KY Garfield
   Garfield .... MICU#3208
KY Glasgow
   Glasgow .... MICU#3108
   Lick Branch .... MICU#3117
   Neal's Chapel .... MICU#3122
KY Glens Fork
   Mt Zion .... MICU#3121
KY Greensburg
   Greensburg .... MICU#3110
   Salem .... MICU#3127
KY Greenville
   Greenville .... MICU#3505
KY Guthrie
   Gill's Chapel .... MICU#3307
KY Hardin
   Unity .... MICO#3422
KY Hardyville
   Monroe Chapel .... MICU#3119
KY Harned
   Ephesus .... MICU#3205
   Freedom .... MICU#3207
KY Harrodsburg
   Bethel #1 .... MICU#3103
   Harrodsburg .... MICU#3111
KY Hartford
   Beulah .... MICU#3501
KY Hawesville
   Dukes .... MICU#3204
KY Herndon
   Flat Lick .... MICO#3606
KY Hopkinsville
   Hopkinsville .... MICO#3611
KY Horse Cave

Clear Point .... MICU#3107
KY Hudson
   Coyle .... MICU#3203
KY Irvington
   Clifton Mills .... MICU#3202
   Irvington .... MICU#3210
KY Kevil
   Bethel .... MICO#3404
   Pleasant Valley .... MICU#3418
KY Knob Lick
   Antioch .... MICU#3101
   Wisdom .... MICU#3130
KY Leitchfield
   Leitchfield .... MICU#3211
   Mt Vernon .... MICU#3218
KY Lewisburg
   Green Ridge .... MICU#3308
   Lewisburg .... MICU#3309
KY Louisville
   Heartsong .... MICU#3222
   Louisville 1st .... MICU#3212
KY Madisonville
   Madisonville .... MICO#3615
KY Magnolia
   Magnolia .... MICU#3214
KY Marion
   Marion First .... MICO#3616
   Piney Fork .... MICO#3620
   Sugar Grove .... MICO#3626
KY Marrowbone
   Casey's Fork .... MICU#3105
KY Mayfield
   Calvary .... MICO#3405
   Rozzell Chapel .... MICO#3419
KY Morgantown
   Little Muddy .... MICU#3310
   Morgantown .... MICU#3311
KY Murray
   Liberty .... MICO#3406
   North Pleasant Grove ..... MICO#3411
KY Nebo
   Rose Creek .... MICO#3622
KY Owensboro
   Owensboro .... MICU#3509
   Pleasant Hill .... MICU#3510
KY Paducah
   Highland .... MICO#3414
   Margaret Hank .... MICO#3415
   New Hope .... MICO#3410
   Woodlawn .... MICO#3417
KY Pewee Valley
   Louisville Japanese .... MICU#3223
KY Philpot
   Mt Zion .... MICU#3507
KY Providence
   Providence 1st .... MICU#3621
KY Radcliff
   Radcliff .... MICU#3220
KY Rumsey
   New Cypress .... MICU#3508
KY Russellville
   Bald Knob .... MICU#3302
KY Sacramento
   Poplar Grove .... MICU#3511
   Sacramento .... MICU#3512
KY Salem
   Hopewell .... MICO#3610
KY Sturgis
   Sturgis .... MICO#3625
KY Sullivan
   Mt. Pleasant .... MICO#3618
KY Summer Shade

Mt Moriah .... MICU#3120
KY Summersville
   Oak Forest .... MICU#3123
KY Water Valley
   Bayou de Chien .... MICU#3401
KY West Paducah
   Milburn Chapel .... MICU#3416
KY West Somerset
   High Point .... MICU#3314
KY Wheatcroft
   Wheatcroft .... MICO#3627
KY White Plains
   Mt Carmel .... MICO#3617

KOREA

KO Seoul
   Korea 1st .... SEET#2221
   Sumkim Presby .... SEET#2222A

LOUISANA

LA Pleasant Hill
   Progress .... MSTR#8123
LA Quitman
   Antioch .... MSTR#8101

MACAU, PORTUGUESE PROVINCE

MA Andar LMN
   Macau .... MSHK#8804

MASSACHUSETTS

MA Malden
   Casa De Fe .... SEET#2220

MARYLAND

MD Salisbury
   Our Good .... SETG#2138

MICHIGAN

MI Lincoln Park
   Grace .... MINC#5502
MI St Clair Shores
   Faith .... MINC#5501

MISSISSIPPI

MS Ackerman
   Enon .... SEGR#0707
MS Cedarbluff
   Cairo .... SEGR#0704
MS Columbus
   Beersheba .... SEGR#0702
   Columbus .... SEGR#0706
   Mt Zion .... SEGR#0709
MS Corinth
   Shiloh .... GRWT#9226
MS Falkner
   Mt Zion .... GRWT#9214
MS Macon
   McLeod Chapel .... SEGR#0708
MS Morton
   Groverton .... SEGR#0602
MS Olive Branch
   Olive Branch .... GRWT#9312
MS Union
   Erin .... SEGR#0601
   Steam Mill .... SEGR#0608

LOCATION INDEX OF CHURCHES CONTINUED

MS Walnut
   Hopewell ....GRWT#9207
MS Walnut Grove
   Salem............................SEGR#0607

MISSOURI

MO Aurora
   Orange...........................GRMI#4108
MO Chilhowee
   Shawnee Mound.............GRMI#4111
MO Conway
   Happy Home ....GRMI#4306
MO Dunnegan
   Spring Creek ....GRMI#4113
MO Greenfield
   God's Grace ....GRMI#4104
MO Knob Noster
   Pleasant Grove ....GRMI#4109
MO Lamar
   Hopewell ....GRMI#4105
MO Lebanon
   White Oak Pond ....GRMI#4315
MO Mansfield
   Mansfield........................GRMI#4308
MO Marshall
   Marshall ....GRMI#4210
MO Martinville
   Pierson............................GRMI#4312
MO Phillipsburg
   Phillipsburg ....GRMI#4311
MO Salem
   New Hope ....GRMI#4309
MO San Antonio
   Harmony ....GRMI#4203
MO Seymour
   Seymour ....GRMI#4313
MO Springfield
   Korean.............................GRMI#4316
   Oak Grove......................GRMI#4310
   Springfield 1st ....GRMI#4314
MO Warrensburg
   Salem ....GRMI#4216
   Warrensburg ....GRMI#4115
MO Wentworth
   Bethel ....GRMI#4102
MO West Plains
   Elk Creek ....GRMI#4304

NEW JERSEY

NJ Tinton Falls
   Hope Korean ....SECE#2131
NJ Wallington
   Comeback ....SECE#2446

NEW MEXICO

NM Albuquerque
   Heights ....MSDC#8701
NM Rio Rancho
   Westside ....MSDC#8709

NEW YORK

NY College Point
   Sharing............................SECE#2141
NY Flushing
   One Way..........................SECE#2137

OKLAHOMA

OK Ada
   Covenant ....MSRR#6304
OK Atoka
   Pigeon Roost ....MSCH#6109
OK Broken Bow
   McGee Chapel ....MSCH#6106
OK Burns Flat
   Burns Flat......................MSRR#6301
OK Clinton
   Clinton...........................MSRR#6302
OK Coalgate
   Coal Creek ....MSCH#6102
   Lone Star.......................MSCH#6105
OK Eagletown
   Panki Bok ....MSCH#6108
OK Edmond
   Stone Gate ....MSRR#6307
OK Honobia
   Rock Creek...................MSCH#6111
OK Locust Grove
   Locust Grove.................MSRR#6203
OK Marlow
   Marlow..........................MSRR#6305
OK Oklahoma City
   Eastlake ....MSRR#6205
OK Tulsa
   Faith ....MSRR#6201
OK Tupelo
   Round Lake...................MSCH#6112

PENNSYLVANIA

PA Bridgeport
   Bridgeport ....MICU#3131

TENNESSEE

TN Afton
   Fairview ....SEET#2204
   Mt Pleasant.....................SEET#2209
   Walkertown ....SEET#2222
TN Algood
   Algood...........................TNMU#7201
TN Atoka
   Bethel ....GRWT#9301
TN Atwood
   Atwood...........................GRWT#9101
   Pleasant Green ....GRWT#9129
TN Bartlett
   Faith ....GRWT#9308
TN Beech Bluff
   Maple Springs...............GRWT#9210
TN Beechgrove
   Beech Grove...................TNMU#7204
TN Bell Buckle
   Green Hill......................TNCO#7118
TN Belvidere
   Belvidere........................TNMU#7205
TN Bethel Springs
   New Salem......................GRWT#9216
TN Bethpage
   Dry Fork........................TNNA#7309
TN Bolivar
   Bolivar...........................GRWT#9202
TN Boonshill
   Boonshill........................TNCO#7106
TN Bradford
   Bradford ....GRWT#9104
   Oliver's Chapel.............GRWT#9127
TN Brentwood
   Brenthaven ....TNNA#7331
TN Brighton

   Holly Grove ....GRWT#9304
TN Brunswick
   Brunswick ....GRWT#9302
TN Brush Creek
   Union Hill ....TNMU#7246
TN Bulls Gap
   Pilot Knob ....SEET#2213
   Willoughby.....................SEET#2219
TN Burlison
   Walnut Grove ....GRWT#9320
TN Camden
   Camden ....GRWT#9105
TN Cane Ridge
   Cane Ridge....................TNNA#7326
TN Centerville
   Swan...............................TNCO#7140
TN Chapel Hill
   Chapel Hill ....TNCO#7109
TN Charlotte
   Charlotte.........................TNNA#7303
   Mt Liberty ....TNNA#7320
TN Chattanooga
   Chattanooga 1st..............SETG#2104
   Cornerstone CommunityTNNA#2107
   Red Bank........................SETG#2105
   Silverdale ....SETG#2106
TN Chuckey
   Pleasant Hill ....SEET#2214
   Pleasant Vale ....SEET#2215
TN Clarksville
   Bethel ....TNNA#7302
   Calvary...........................TNNA#7342
   Clarksville......................TNNA#7304
   Liberty............................TNNA#7315
   McAdoo ....TNNA#7318
   New Providence.............TNNA#7305
TN Cleveland
   Charleston ....SETG#2102
   Cleveland ....SETG#2108
   Flint Springs...................SETG#2112
   Prospect United..............SETG#2116
TN College Grove
   Harpeth Lick ....TNCO#7119
TN Columbia
   Columbia 1st ....TNCO#7110
   McCains ....TNCO#7126
   New Bethel......................TNCO#7134
   Pleasant Mount...............TNCO#7136
   Union Grove...................TNCO#7141
   West Point ....TNCO#7143
TN Cookeville
   Cookeville 1st ....TNMU#7210
   Dry Valley ....TNMU#7213
   Mt Hermon.....................TNMU#7229
TN Cordova
   Korean.............................GRWT#9322
   Morning Sun ....GRWT#9314
TN Cowan
   Cowan ....TNMU#7211
TN Cunningham
   Locust Grove.................TNNA#7316
TN Decaturville
   Camp Ground................GRWT#9204
TN Dickson
   Dickson ....TNNA#7308
TN Dover
   Mt View..........................TNNA#7322
TN Dresden
   Dresden ....GRWT#9110
TN Dukedom
   Good Springs ....GRWT#9112
TN Dyer

LOCATION INDEX OF CHURCHES CONTINUED

LOCATION INDEX OF CHURCHES CONTINUED

Petersburg.......................TNCO#7135
TN Portland
   Boiling Springs ....TNCO#3303
TN Prospect
   Fiducia..........................TNCO#7113
TN Pulaski
   Mt Moriah ....TNCO#7131
TN Puryear
   Mill Creek ....GRWT#9122
TN Ramer
   Mt Vernon ....GRWT#9213
   Ramer...........................GRWT#9223
TN Rock Island
   Rock Island ....TNMU#7274
TN Rockvale
   Mt Vernon ....TNMU#7231
   Rockvale ....TNMU#7239
TN Rutherford
   Rutherford ....GRWT#9429
TN Santa Fe
   Santa Fe........................TNCO#7138
TN Savannah
   Olivet............................GRWT#9220
   Savannah 1st ....GRWT#9224
TN Selmer
   New Bethel...................GRWT#9215
   Selmer Court Avenue ....GRWT#9225
TN Sewanee
   Sewanee ....TNMU#7242
TN Sharon
   Hopewell......................GRWT#9115
   New Salem ....GRWT#9124
   Sharon ....GRWT#9130
TN Smithville
   Banks............................TNMU#7202
   Smithville.....................TNMU#7243
TN Somerville
   Mt Carmel ....GRWT#9315
TN South Fulton
   Fulton ....GRWT#9412
TN South Pittsburg
   Richard City ....SETG#2118
   South Pittsburg.............SETG#2123
TN Sparta
   Hickory Valley ....SETG#7251
   Old Zion ....TNMU#7234
TN Spring Hill
   Ash Hill ....TNCO#7101
   Mt Lebanon...................TNCO#7130
TN Springfield
   Mt Denson.................... TNNA#7319
TN Stewart
   New Hope .... TNNA#7337
TN Talbott
   Talbott ....SEET#2218
TN Telford
   Oakland..........................SEET#2211
TN Trenton
   Concord.........................GRWT#9106
   Davidson Chapel...........GRWT#9108
TN Trezevant
   Trezevant.......................GRWT#9132
TN Trimble
   Cool Springs............ GCGRWT#9408
   Trimble..........................GRWT#9431
TN Troy
   New Ebenezer ....GRWT#9422
   Protemus ....GRWT#9426
   Troy..............................GRWT#9432
TN Union City
   Antioch Union..............GRWT#9401
   Beech............................GRWT#9402

Mt Ararat ....GRWT#9417
   Union City.....................GRWT#9433
TN Unionville
   Kingdom ....TNCO#7123
TN Watertown
   Commerce.....................TNMU#7209
   Watertown ....TNMU#7247
TN Waverly
   Concord......................... TNNA#7306
   Halls Creek................... TNNA#7313
   Mariah .... TNNA#7317
   Waverly .... TNNA#7339
TN Waynesboro
   Waynesboro...................TNCO#7142
TN Whitwell
   Cedar Springs.................SETG#2119
   Ebenezer.......................SETG#2110
   Kelly's Chapel ....SETG#2120
   New Hope ....SETG#2115
   Oak Grove......................SETG#2121
   Whitwell........................SETG#2122
TN Winchester
   Goshen ....TNMU#7214
   Gum Creek ....TNMU#7215
   Harmony ....TNMU#7216
   Owens Chapel ....TNMU#7235
   Winchester 1st...............TNMU#7249
TN Yorkville
   Yorkville.......................GRWT#9435

TEXAS

TX Arlington
   St John...........................MSRR#8413
TX Austin
   Austin 1st ....MSTR#8601
   Shepherd/Hills...............MSTR#8604
TX Bedford
   St Timothy.................... MSRR#8419
TX Bertram
   Bertram ....MSTR#8605
TX Burleson
   Pathway........................ MSRR#8418
TX Chico
   Zion Valley................... MSRR#8425
TX Clarksville
   Shiloh ....MSTR#8125
TX Daingerfield
   Daingerfield...................MSTR#8106
TX Dallas
   Lake Higlands ....MSRR#8411
TX Denton
   Denton .... MSRR#8404
TX Fort Worth
   St Luke .... MSRR#8407
   St Mark......................... MSRR#8408
   Trinity........................... MSRR#8409
TX Freeport
   Freeport ....MSTR#8103
TX Georgetown
   Oak Grove......................MSTR#8607
TX Greenville
   Mt Zion .... MSRR#8414
TX Houston
   Houston 1st ....MSTR#8606
   Nueva Vida....................MSTR#8612
TX Hubbard
   Hubbard........................ MSRR#8410
TX Jefferson
   Jefferson........................MSTR#8109
TX Joinerville
   Mt Hope ....MSTR#8117
TX Longview

Elmira Chapel ....MSTR#8111
   Longview 1st..................MSTR#8112
   Pine Tree ....MSTR#8113
TX Lubbock
   Lubbock ....MSDC#8702
TX Marshall
   Marshall ....MSTR#8115
TX Mesquite
   Mesquite....................... MSRR#8412
TX Midlothian
   Shiloh .... MSRR#8421
TX Millsap
   Newberry...................... MSRR#8415
TX Odessa
   St Andrew.....................MSDC#8703
TX Olney
   Olney............................ MSRR#8416
TX Round Rock
   Round Rock ....MSTR#8611
TX San Antonio
   Northminster ....MSTR#8610
   Stone Oak......................MSTR#8608
TX San Elizario
   Maranatha ....MSDC#8706
TX Troup
   Concord.........................MSTR#8104
TX Whitesboro
   Sandy Springs .... MSRR#8420
TX Winnsboro
   Pine Hill ....MSTR#8122

Staff	Email	Ext
Cindy Martin	cmartin@cumberland.org	219
Dan Scherf	dscherf@cumberland.org	233
Edith Busbee Old	eold@cumberland.org	228
Elinor Brown	ebrown@cumberland.org	205
Elizabeth Vaughn	evaughn@cumberland.org	226
Jinger Ellis	jellis@cumberland.org	230
Jodi Rush	jrush@cumberland.org	223
Johan Daza	jdaza@cumberland.org	202
Julie Min	jmin@cumberland.org	224
Kathryn Gilbert Craig	kcraig@cumberland.org	206
Lynn Thomas	lynndont@gmail.com	(ext. rings Lynn's cell) 261
Mark Duck	mduck@cumberland.org	204
Mark J. Davis	mdavis@cumberland.org	216
Matthew Gore	mgore@cumberland.org	252
Mike Sharpe	msharpe@cumberland.org	225
Milton Ortiz	mortiz@cumberland.org	234
Missy Rose	mrose@cumberland.org	215
Nathan Wheeler	nwheeler@cumberland.org	218
Neal Wilkinson	nwilkinson@cumberland.org	209
Pam Phillips-Burk	pam@cumberland.org	203
Robert Heflin	rheflin@cumberland.org	207
Shipping/Greg Miller	gkm@cumberland.org	256
Sowgand Sheikholeslami	sowgand@cumberland.org	211
Susan Gore	sgore@cumberland.org	214
T.J. Malinoski	tmalinoski@cumberland.org	232

Our United Outreach

Cliff Hudson   gchudson3@gmail.com   210

Building Lobby:		Conference Rooms:	
8175 Building	227	8175 Building	220
8207 Building	231	8207 Building	208
Fax Numbers:		**Other Offices:**	
8175 Building	901-272-3913	MTS	901-458-8232
8207 Building	901-276-4578	Bethel University	731-352-4000
		Children's Home	940-382-5112
		Historical Foundation	901-276-8602

CUMBERLAND PRESBYTERIAN CHURCH IN AMERICA
Denominational Center
www.cpcoga.org
226 Church Street, NW, Huntsville, AL 35801
(256)536-7481 OR FAX (256)536-7482
administrativedirector@cpcaga.org

Moderator of the General Assembly:
Elder Lewis Leon Cole, Jr., PO Box 335, Warren, MI 48090
(248)770-1540   llcole1951@yahoo.com

Vice-Moderator of the General Assembly:
Reverend Michael Jones, 205 Burwell Road, Harvest, AL 35749
(256)852-8075   mljones30@bellsouth.net

Administrative Director of the Cumberland Presbyterian Church in America:
Reverend Doctor G. Lynne Herring, 3244 Vicksburg SW, Decatur, AL 35603
(256)536-7481(w)   (256)355-7677(h)   administrativedirector@cpca.org   johneherring@aol.com

Stated Clerk of the General Assembly:
Elder Craig A. White, 134 McEntire Lane SW A36, Decatur, AL 35603
(256)565-5751   white8@bellsouth.net

Engrossing Clerk of the General Assembly:
Reverend Lela Fencher, 620 Live Oak Circle, Fairfield, AL 35064, (205)780-4913
(205)789-3913

Church Paper: *THE CUMBERLAND FLAG*
Editor: Reverend Doctor G. Lynne Herring, 3244 Vicksburg SW, Decatur, AL 35603
(256)536-7481(w)   (256)355-7677(h)   administrativedirector@cpcaga.org

SYNODS - PRESBYTERIES - STATED CLERKS

Alabama Synod - Elder Vanessa Midgett, 118 Thunderbird Drive, Harvest, AL 35749
1. Birmingham Presbytery - Rev. Teresa Paige, 228 S Park Road, Birmingham, AL 35211
   (205)706-9057   tcpaige12@yahoo.com
2. Florence Presbytery - Rev. Dr. Nancy Fuqua, 1963 County Road 406, Town Creek, AL 35672
   (256)685-0218   fuq23@bellsouth.net
3. Huntsville Presbytery - Rev. Dr. Theodis Acklin, 3415 Mastin Lake Road, Huntsville, AL 35810
   (256)945-7216
4. South Alabama Presbytery - Elder Minnie McMillan, 54 Riverview Avenue, Selma, AL 36701
   (334)875-9617   mmcmillan@ccal.edu
5. Tennessee Valley Presbytery - Rev. Critis Fletcher, 68 Mattie Street, Russellville, AL 35654
   (256)332-6325   gepolar@bellsouth.net
6. Tuscaloosa Presbytery - Rev. Jacqueline Lang, 904 35th Avenue, Tuscaloosa, AL 35401
   (205)292-1048

Kentucky Synod - Elder Leon Cole, Jr., PO Box 335, Warren, MI 48090
1. Cleveland, Ohio Presbytery - Elder Greg Scruggs, 1117 Mt Vernon Blvd, Cleveland Heights, OH 44112
   (216)645-9584   gsagi57@yahoo.com
2. Ohio Valley Presbytery - Elder Sharon Combs, PO Box 122, Sturgis, KY 42459
   (270)860-4175   scombs1@bellsouth.net
3. Purchase Presbytery - Elder Sherell Sparks, 79 Paraadise Lane, Metropolis, IL 62960
   (618)203-2799   relld2000@yahoo.com

Tennessee Synod - Elder Roy Innman, 190 Latham Loop, Sweetwater, TN 37874
1. Elk River Presbytery - Elder Jacquelyn Cooper, 4705 Indian Summer Drive, Nashville, TN 37207
   (615)440-3010   jmcooper12@comcast.net
2. Hiwassee Presbytery - Elder Stephine Martin, 205 North Point Road, Sweetwater, TN 37874
   (423)486-7633   stephanie.nicole@yahoo.com
3. New Hopewell Presbytery - Rev. Jimmie Dodd, c/o Hopewell CPCA, 4100 Millsfield Highway, Dyersburg, TN 38024
   (731)424-4510   dodd125@gmail.com

Texas Synod - Elder Gladys Brandon, 719 Olive Street, Waco, TX 76704
1. Angelina Presbytery - Elder Tom Jones, 739 County Road 4720, Troup, TX 75789
   (972)285-0642   tjones1239@aol.com
2. Brazos River Presbytery - Elder Joy Wallace, 541 Glen Arbor Drive, Dallas, TX 75241
   (214)415-8734
3. East Texas Presbytery - Rev. Kay Ward Creed, PO Box 1316, Henderson, TX 75653
   (903)657-7169